To my parents, Louis *and* Rose Bernstein,
two pioneers in urban education
before anyone had a kind word to say for it

Preface

What follows is an attempt at a new type of introductory education text, aimed at a new kind of teacher-candidate, and intended for new circumstances in education.

Most of today's education students will work in urban conditions that require a rigorously prepared teacher, better educated and more culturally sophisticated than heretofore. Hence this book, though introductory, is not elementary. It assumes a high level of attainment in the reader and an instructor able to elucidate the debatable, the dubious, and the troublesome.

The unorthodox pervades this text, which simply reflects the times, and a decade of educational changes with more consequences than are currently apparent. With both money and will available, the only visible hazards are those that education has set up for itself in the past: timidity, genteelness, and reluctance to seize power.

This book discusses these hazards and the characteristics in teachers and schools that will be needed for a modern educational system. It considers the interplay between city and country, work and leisure, intelligence and stupidity, white and Negro, teacher and administrator, bureaucracy and public policy, content and method, art and science, America and the rest of the world, because these are some of the interactions that teachers in urbanized America must know about and work within. In doing so, teachers enlarge their domain, and in enlarging their domain, become more than teachers; then teaching becomes instructional engineering—with all that such terminology arouses in the replayed Rousseauism of Paul Goodman and Edgar Friedenberg.

In order to provide a good educational system, we must know how to vote properly, and that in itself is a form of education. Education is vitally affected by politics, and it nests with some dirty bedfellows, angle-seekers, sharpshooters, and downright crooks. Education, therefore, must face the world it exists in, not retreat to a timorous sanctimonious sanctuary. The least we can expect of education is that it know how to operate in this world and how to prepare us for anticipated and still-unanticipated worlds. President Johnson's Great Society, Job Corps, Operation Head Start, and Anti-Poverty programs will inevitably be feeding troughs for district leaders, opportunists, and grafters. Well, nobody said anything about a Saintly Society, and this payoff will undoubtedly be less expensive than was the social goof-off during the years that preceded the Kennedy-Johnson program.

The sociological ambiance of urban education therefore enters into any discussion of American schools, administrators, teachers, teacher-preparation programs, and pupils, which explains why this book may really be two. The first section deals with educational sociology and the second with educational practices. That they are different is certainly apparent and perhaps glaring, but not accidental.

Educational sociology and educational practice are advisably separated for easier discussion and teaching, not because they are so in systematic fact. The gulf between the two seems deep, but is in reality shallow; firm footing is not too far under the surface. In any case, the reader should be prepared for the switch as the author is for outcries that incompatibles have no business being bound within the same covers. Space and time, and matter and energy were so once but now are compatible, commensurable, two faces of the same coin, or however put; perhaps educational sociology and educational practice combined within the covers of the same book are also inescapably wedded within the context and larger considerations of urban education, so that not even a convenience in discussion can any longer keep them apart.

To the student: In an attempt at improved readability, the author has removed to the Appendix most of the corroborative (and sometimes contradictory) data, sources, resources, and technical materials, requiring that you deploy between the text and Appendix as indicated. Things that seem hastily treated and of staccato pace receive amplification in the Appendix, and if you find turning to it an irritant, please understand that the alternative was imbedding the material in the text and slowing you down. This page-turning is your contribution to a less complicated text and, perhaps, a more interesting one.

To the instructor: Let us, for once, assume a candidate superior to teaching, who intends to maintain that margin of superiority, and who is going to teach anyway. You will be seeing more of such candidates from now on. They cannot be prepared like the more complaisant breed that preceded them. They are college trained and require status and better-than-survival salaries. They are becoming militant toward problems and courses of study. They think, they travel, they know they are facing the most difficult educational assignment ever presented to American teachers.

In attempting to meet their levels of maturity and awareness, this book may have over-enthusiastically assumed that they possess more knowledge than their years have permitted them to accumulate. This failing, if it exists, requires you for remedying. Please help out if the book bites off too much for the reader to chew; at least it does not attempt to pre-digest.

A good portion of the book is housed in the Appendix. This reference material is interesting and valuable in its own right and is planned to lure the student to additional reading.

Some things may offend because the text goes over to the attack, less against persons than against characteristics, to cauterize rather than narcotize—not to shock, nor even to stimulate, but to make the educational organism a healthy one.

This book is designed for the teachers who will make that effort.

This endeavor, like others of its kind, inevitably reflects collaboration among colleagues. The ritual of expressing indebtedness is not an empty one, but summarizes chats, arguments, teamwork, strife inside and out of committees, ideas bandied about in the faculty dining room, communication with and visits to adjacent and remote campuses. Of the brains that I have picked, special thanks to Professor Joseph Justman, Chairman of the Department of Education, Brooklyn College; to Dean Walter Mais, Brooklyn College, for easing the author's academic responsibilities, thus making the writing possible; to Harry Gideonse, former President of Brooklyn College, for his support of programs in urban education despite the tired blood in New York education, both city and state; to Dean Joshua Fishman, Ferkauf Graduate School of Education, Yeshiva University, for first giving sympathetic attention to the material that subsequently evolved into Project Beacon, discussed in this book; to Professor Harry Bernstein, Brooklyn College, for many hours of close attention to his brother's ideas; to Dr. James E. Russell, Educational Policies Commission, for collaboration on *Hours on Freedom,* also discussed in this book. They are to be exculpated from the misdemeanors that follow, as are all other colleagues to whom reference is made in the text.

My graduate students at Brooklyn College have contributed term papers, book reviews, and class discussions that I have appropriated without acknowledgment to individuals. It is impossible to do so, but I do acknowledge my indebtedness to their interest, ingenuity, and professionalism. They are no small part of the reputation of the Brooklyn College program in teacher education.

The author's wife, Belle Bernstein, and his daughter, Felice Bernstein, are thanked for their monumental understanding.

A.B.

Contents

xiii)

PART THREE | PROSPECTS

Part One || # The Problem

1

Urban Education and Rural Reclamation

Although cities vary in qualitative tone, in magazines and books read, in toothpastes, breakfast cereals, and cough medicines used, in salaries paid teachers, and in the cost of living index, they are alike in having many people, a body of water, and a prescribed course of study for their children, (1) which changes little from Rome to Milan, New York to Chicago, Philadelphia to San Francisco, London to Liverpool, Madrid to Barcelona. Probably curriculums will become even more standardized in the future. In the United States, with the increase in federal aid and intervention the sameness will increase, as will safe thinking.

Mary McCarthy says, "Those who know Florence a little often compare it to Boston." (2) Such comparisons are tempting as we consider the worldwide urban crisis caused by the influx of new populations in New York, Paris, Moscow, Peking, and El Paso. Formerly the best of the rural population left for the city; now, on the whole, the worst does. Within the last generation, in a historically unprecedented phenomenon, cities have attracted those not good enough for farm life, not those too good for it. (3) Until a century ago, the city pull on rural populations was cultural. Then, with the Industrial Revolution and its work opportunities, the pull became technological. But since 1945, the farm population has been *pushed* cityward by rural technology, not pulled by city technology or cultural advantages, so the least able drain toward the cities precisely when the highly trained are in short supply, in a cityward flow that is unaffected by Iron Curtains, hemispheres, or politics.

Some cities, poorer than others, assume that the inadequacies of these new immigrants are irremediable; in such cities educational programs are minimal. In wealthier cities, paradoxically, where advanced technology sharpens the inadequacy of the newcomers, educational programs are intensified on the assumption that the inadequacies *are* remediable. Thus it seems that optimism or pessimism about people depends on ability to pay for their education, with the result that different cities have different degrees of acceptance or rejection of the new inadequates, different amounts of education available to them, and different employment and training possibilities. (With some exceptions: Wealthy Johannesburg rejects and/or exploits its inadequates. Poor Chihuahua accepts them. Detroit experiments with them.)

Today, when the federal government of the United States legislates equal educational opportunity and municipalities obey lest they lose federal funds, the remediability of inadequacy is legally asserted. We stake federal funds on the probability that education can repair sociological and economic damage.

But if new populations unsettle urban life, old urban populations also contribute to lag. Retail merchants, frozen into accustomed business patterns, fail to adjust to downtown store shopping changes; banks use less initiative and imagination in creating borrowers than in attracting lenders; older ethnic groups such as the Irish, Poles, and Italians fix within their old stereotypes of themselves and ignore new opportunities in occupational mobility. Stagnation can be as unsettling as novelty, and security confused with stability, when small storekeepers impede housing improvement, interest rates for low-income neighborhoods reflect caution rather than enterprise, and labor is more concerned with work contracts and contraction than with goods and their expansion. (4)

Unfortunately, education is not always the anticoagulant it should be in the flow toward improved conditions in the city. On the contrary, it too often contributes to ethnic and group divisiveness—of Englishmen, Irishmen, and West Indians in London and Liverpool; Catholics and Protestants in Liege; and Puerto-Ricans and Negroes in New York. Religion has not made men saintly. For similar reasons education does not infallibly make men human, but merely contributes toward their humanity. We can expect no more.

Dixie, Italian Style

The "economic miracle" in postwar Italy in many ways offers a parallel to our North-South experience. Rocco and his brothers have gone from the *mezzogiorno,* the Italian analogue to America's Appalachia, to Milan and other cities of the industrial North. (5) For his cousins who stay in the South, the *Cassa per il Mezzogiorno* (Fund for the South) is attempting to bring about an economic and social miracle, reversing the long history of tariff protectionism that favored the industrial North and impeded the exportation of southern agricultural products. Today industry forms a growing part of southern Italy's economy, and labor has less reason to emigrate because things are happening at home. Most important, as Carlo Bazan points out, the same labor force that could be trainable in the North is also trainable on its home ground. (6)

In a financial pitch to American investors, the Commercial Office of the Italian Embassy in Washington says:

> By now development in the South has become a remarkably well-balanced process. The service industries, trade and tourism have not stood still. Nor have the people. Their patterns of behavior and their outlook are changing. Motorcycles and automobiles are replacing the horsecart; for better or for worse, television sets are available to almost everyone; chain stores (whose growth, incidentally, has been particularly high in the South), movie houses, and beauty parlors have sprung up where they were unheard of ten years ago. And, more important perhaps, as the former isolation in which millions of southerners once lived falls away, traditional habits and ways of life are also giving way to a new

awareness of the outside world and a willingness to learn and to adapt to new techniques and to new ways of working and living. (7)

The seductive tune played to investors is that "in modern economic conditions it is capital that must be taken to the available labor and not vice versa." But this is so *only if the labor has gotten education and training*. Otherwise, capital is wasted. (8)

Any visitor to Rome on a summer's Sunday evening can see economics made manifest in the scooters and the Fiat *seicentos* and *millecentos* streaming back from Ostia and the sea, passing up-to-the-minute EUR (Esposizione Universale di Roma). This is not just a phase of a country caught in inflation, but the expansion of a nation up to its potential; the heel-to-hip *Autostrada* unifies Italy as neither the Papacy nor Cavour ever did, making Naples and Rome just three hours apart.

Of unfinished business, much remains to be done and done away with. Migrants from the south of Italy avoid training as often as they seek it, because their origins have discouraged initiative. Italy's rural South, wealthy and populous in classic times, has had its possibilities for growth opposed by clerics, absentee landlords, local society, and a peasantry whose self-image is dependent, submissive, and routinized. Again, we may draw parallels with other parts of the world. The Alliance for Progress founders more on Latin-American *latifundistas* than on Castro's communism. (9) Also, the siesta is still common, although air conditioning is making inroads. Most Roman shopgirls would eagerly swap the siesta (air conditioned or un-air conditioned) for a cool working place and a chance to knock off at five.

This brings us to the relationship of comfort to the goals of education, progress and prosperity.

If urbanism, the world over, is concerned with education, it is also concerned with civilized conveniences, amenities, and comforts. Physical man is as much a concern of urbanism as intellectual man. Food within man's gut and air conditioning on his epidermis are the precursors to a cerebral cortex operating with efficiency. The British should have weighed the possibilities of air-conditioning India, but the British have had an unfortunate interlude, between 1914 and the present, in which they saw merit in discomfort. This was the period in which they lost an empire.

England, Comfort, and Harlem

Only education has saved England so far from going over the brink of bankruptcy, to which it has been brought by anachronistic concepts of industrialism. Though England seems to have forgotten how to run a business, it has learned somehow to educate its people.

In Britain a discontented lower class, not fully using its intellectual capacities, not challenged enough, and brighter than the work it does or the life it leads, feels its only way out is a superb education for everybody who can handle it. Alex Campbell says:

> . . . many English parents with correct accents but often modest means are willing to make great sacrifices of their children by placing them during ten formative years of their lives behind the walls of boarding institutions that are not easily distinguishable in their practices and punishments from reformatories for delinquents. The training is rigorous. Tearful tots who are placed in the public school of their implacable parents' choice at the age of eight do not emerge from its discipline until they are 18, at which time they . . . have in many cases ceased to be heterosexual. Their reward is to belong, unchallengeable apparently by anything short of death, to the English upper class. (10)

The eleven-plus examinations have recruited more gifted, the Robbins Report has declared the centrality of the educational effort, and the emerging comprehensive secondary schools and red brick universities have shown that separating the intellectual sheep from the goats implies no diminution in education for either. Ugly ducklings grow up to make better time, when airborne, than swans. (11)

After expending all this effort on the education of its natural-born swans and ducks, however, England often is pained to discover that they can't wait to fly the coop. England's highly publicized "brain drain," especially of scientists, can be explained in large part by the fact that the United States, to which many British scientists and intellectuals migrate, is more comfortable than England. (12) Most of America is comfortable because comfort accompanies power. Wright Miller points out that American Midwest winters are as punishing as Russian winters, but a Minnesotan is far more comfortable than a Muscovite. (13) Until Russians and Britains and Latin Americans are as comfortable as we are, there will be no comfort for us either. Comfort is as important as sex or food, and is as vital to defense as rockets. Indeed, nothing made Hitler so acceptable to the Germans as his restoration of their postwar loss of comfort when he rifled Europe of its tidbits, confections, and slaves to augment German comfort.

Some parts of America, however, are *not* comfortable. Harlem, like China, Russia, and much of England, is unpleasantly uncomfortable. And only by rendering it comfortable can we set the stage for getting it educated. The trouble is that the road to comfort is often blocked by those who are already comfortable and by the very human trait of resistance to change.

Flow and Stasis: People, Capital, Ideas

French agriculture is decentralized. French education is highly centralized. (14) French students riot for a salary because they want to get paid for studying, to the dismay of French farmers and college professors. Yet, as described by Higbee, (14) the French small farmer is no longer the mainstay of a virtuous democracy, but more truly a dependent on it—not the independent freeholder we once had in a young America, but a freeholder become freeloader, salivating for governmental subsidies and handouts. And the French professor, who opposes student campaigns for payment in the *présalaire,* in his turn resists the enlargement of faculty because his own post would thereby become less choice and less distinguished. How similar the French farmer and the French college faculty in their agricultural and educational conservatism!

Thus French educational officialdom, farmers, and labor cannot be counted on to lift French education out of its bureaucratized rut, centralized beyond anything known in America or England. But French commercial needs for technically trained personnel can do so. (14) French industry has overcome French educational retardation almost by itself, thereby sparking student demands not only for the *présalaire* (which are not unreasonable in view of the fellowships, assistantships, and scholarships available in the United States to virtually everybody in graduate studies, and the Russian system of student salaries) but for improvements in education, housing, building, and instruction. The government replies by an extensive expansion program throughout France, because the collegiate enterprise, concentrated around Paris, makes expansion there difficult, but students reject official plans to disperse the collegiate endeavor to the provinces. Who in his right mind would want to leave Paris? Also, is a student as entitled to a salary as a farmer to a subsidy, a manufacturer to a tax rebate, or a newspaper publisher to special mailing rates? We need not be concerned about the French farmer's well-nourished distress, or other cries from a European community settling happily into the greatest prosperity it has ever known, but, rather, about the outcry when students picket to be paid for learning, particularly when the outcry comes from those having long practice with public subsidy, like the French farmer or the Texas oil millionaire.

Everywhere in the world the question arises: Are the new urban populations—Negro, Puerto-Rican, Sicilian, Algerian, Yemenite, Bantu—trainable-redeemable for an automated world? These people have been pushed off the land and toward the city by an agricultural technology (which matches urban automation), that returns redundant farms to nature, restores recreation in the countryside, and creates national parks, places for play and the New Leisure, as well as classrooms-beyond-classrooms that are still undreamed of but urgently require thinking about in programs of urban education. (15)

Resisted by the usually conservative farmer who rejected experimentation, agricultural technology made fortunes for the enterprising minority who embraced it and became agronomists, or absentee landlords of processing, canning, or deep-freeze companies, and did what the individual farmer could not do: raise as much wholesome food as cheaply as possible. Russia, with too many soil-scratchers and not enough agronomists, now knows it must clear away its soil-scratchers who, like weeds, are bad for crops. How fortunate for American and Canadian wheat growers that Russian and Chinese agriculture pursue a will-o'-the-wisp doctrine that allows North Americans to dispose of surplus wheat! Communist agriculture has been kinder to American farm surpluses than soil banks or wheat subsidies! (16)

What is fortunate for wheat growers may be dangerous for the survival of the rest of us. Like gamblers driven by an *idée fixe* that inner purpose, or a system (in this case, Marxism), can beat external probabilities, doctrinaire politics set principle above reality, a terribly dangerous stupidity we can no longer afford if we want human protoplasm to continue. (16) Communists are not ignorant, but affiliation to the doctrinaire makes them so.

Ignorance has other sources. Farm life, like Negro life, makes for ignorance. While farmers remain on the farm, inaccessible to training opportunities, they are ignorant; as long as Negroes live like Negroes, unable to participate in training opportunities, they are also ignorant—so that to be both farmer and Negro makes for ignorance indeed. But get the farmer to an urban center, give him training, and his ignorance vanishes—many of our great scientists are ex-farm boys. Similarly, get a Negro to perceive himself as valuable as any other man, give him the training and skill to back up the belief, and his ignorance vanishes too. Thus county agents and agronomists know that agricultural problems are in large part caused by unsuccessful farmers who do not know which side is up when bread is buttered, though they produce both.

But the countryside that expels the ineffective farmer redeems the technologized urban center. Highet says, "Big cities are both hateful and enticing. Men are often miserable living in them, and yet they cannot leave them." (17) This cityward flow must not obscure for us that urban education seeks classrooms in the country as well as in the city. (15)

Urban man returns to the countryside, though on new terms. Urban life requires nature and urban education requires rural reclamation. Capital formation, capital accumulation, and capital flow are involved. As steel mills, oil wells, computer machinery, and office buildings reflect capital accumulation, so do recreational facilities and the cityward-countryward exchange of people reflect capital flow. Capital, however, flows not for charity but for economic realism, requiring that people flow, and people flow even more reluctantly than capital. They want to stay put, in familiar surroundings, and usually only hardship will drive them to opportunities elsewhere. Similarly, industry is often unwilling to allow its autonomy to become mobile so that command flows reluctantly too, retarding our possibilities. Such stasis in labor, industry, and capital is especially injurious to the most venturesome and continuingly revolutionary society in history, the American. Luckily, we have not had too many examples of stasis, but Appalachia's plight offers one. Harry Caudill, whose *Night Comes to the Cumberlands* (18) illuminated its pall, and who was an original mover in the federal government's Appalachia program, describes white Kentucky miner-mountaineers who could do better elsewhere but remain in Appalachia, which could also do better as a recreational playground.

In this area, white mountain children, like urban Negro children, after testing at average intelligence on school entry, begin sliding, so that their I.Q.'s are below average *after* schooling. Claudia Lewis describes the lives these children lead, Asher describes the tests that test them, and Caudill himself describes the spoils system connected with schools—how graft is as intimately related to schools as to highway construction. (18) Like the courthouse gang, the schoolhouse gang also has its fingers in the public till. Here Caudill's Cumberland country resembles large cities like New York, which also know corruption in school building, school contracts, and school maintenance (19).

Before President Johnson's Appalachia program for workers who preferred partial productive capacity, amid people and circumstances they knew, rather than jobs elsewhere where people and circumstances were unknown, John Walsh and Homer Bigart had described flow and stasis in capital and legislation dealing with Appalachia. (20) Years earlier, when Charles Wilson of General Motors scoffed at unemployed workers because they did not "bird dog" jobs, he was called heartless and unfeeling; but corporate officials are accustomed to moving around without much wrench, because they find the same chain stores, the same national brands, and the same television programs wherever they go. Yet mobility, to the Cumberland people, is painful; and although it is true that this choice is a man's own business, what the choice does to his children, and to the sliding I.Q. of his children, is not. Here society, education, and ethics cannot look on, but must intervene.

The intensity of family feeling that keeps the Kentucky miner-mountaineer home and prevents him from improving his worldly lot elsewhere contrasts with the lack of family feeling that wrecks so many urban Negro homes. Too little people-flow can be as damaging as excessive people-flow.

But what is people-flow? Is it educational development and

ideational growth, or the simple ability to move your body from one place to another? Thus, are roads more important to Appalachia than schools? Or are teachers more important than either roads or new school buildings?

In another example of stasis, the industrial trade association, a potentially powerful but partially used mechanism, alternately fed and starved depending on the whim of its membership, is kept like a ventriloquist's dummy for showcase utterances. Properly used, it could explore new areas, train people, and supply markets now unavailable to its members, thus filling an important need.

Education is a major area in which trade association memberships play an inappropriate role, but which would be a logical outgrowth of organization functions. Consider *The New York Times* dispatch in the appendix on the Gulf Oil contribution to Nigerian education. (21) Any cynical Nigerian would want to know how much Gulf Oil made out of Nigerian resources to be able to return $1 million. Gulf might answer that the Nigerians never got out the oil themselves, making it unearned gravy for people who merely lived on top of it; but a contribution made through a consortium of oil companies or their trade organization might have been sounder corporate good manners and public relations strategy. This course would also more wisely police the honest disposition of the funds to ensure that no Nigerian pockets were lined—thus maintaining the public relations impact, keeping clear of charges of corruption, seeing industry dollars go much further, and doing a job that government cannot do.

Trade organizations can: undertake programs in race relations without fear of boycott; establish grants to educational institutions; concentrate on scholarly research without captious stockholder questions; finance programs for the gifted; deal with minority groups; and become involved with all the aspects of the cityward-countryward flow, with urban education and its costs, from a vantage point unattainable by its individual members.

The freeze in the minds of men, in capital flow, people-flow, authority-flow, and other industrial behavior patterns affects urban education. (22) The constant people-flow in this country, by bus, auto, airplane, and railroad, is encouraging, for to that extent capital flows too. But we could do better. We are losing too many good bets in urban education, in dropouts, unstable family structure, poor teaching, and a bureaucratic narrowness that reflects parallel distortions in business, government, and the professions.

In a period of increasing automation, when even training and skills are no guarantee of employment—think of airline navigators, linotypers, railroad engineers, and stevedores—retraining programs become part of adult education. And adult education must be expanded, because continuing participation in education, over the life span, becomes a man's only surety against loss of morale. The need is especially acute in our metropolises and megalopolises. New York, thereby, has more in common educationally with Milan than with suburban Manhasset. The cities of the world have adult education as a common concern. (23)

Adult education deals with uprooted populations—not the same as rootless populations—with a training that requires mastery not only for production but for leisure, because the man who is at leisure is not the same as the idle man. What differentiates the one from the other is morale, and what gives the man of leisure morale is training. The trained man is not a shiftless one, nor can industrial displacement make him so. Training for leisure therefore is not less important than training for production.

In leisure, unlike idleness, guilt and anxiety are absent. The leisured man has done what he can with himself; if there is work for him, he can do it; if not, he is not inadequate with free time.

We are not yet comfortable with a world where work will be done not by our own muscle, or the muscle of slaves, or by our attentive presence at machinery, but by automated devices that can even make decisions while we are off at a golf course, a bridge game, a garden plot, an art gallery, a concert, or a movie. We are still uneasy about the moral rightness of automated arrangements that allow an abbreviated work week.

But we must adjust to this new morality. If automation's greatest blessing is free time, one of its greatest threats is an anachronistic guilt about free time.

Suburb and Superurb

The suburbs offer no educational sanctuary; the city's educational values and disturbances leak into adjacent suburbs. The educationally deprived live in the suburbs, do the gardening, laundry, cooking, and chauffeuring, and send their children to the suburban school. As metropolises undergo mutual engulfment to become megalopolises, suburbs become buffers where Princeton eases the pain of having to work in Philadelphia, Newark, Trenton, or New York; Wilton holds off New York with one hand and Bridgeport and New Haven with the other. Some cities leak indistinguishably into each other via their suburbs, as with Minneapolis–St. Paul, Baltimore–Washington, El Paso–Juarez, and Fort Worth–Dallas. Where cities cannot couple, they bloat, like Los Angeles over the entire county, San Francisco north to Napa and south to Palo Alto, or Chicago up to Wisconsin and south to Indiana. (24)

In the suburbs we find homeowners serviced by other homeowners or shack renters, but we no longer find the homogeneity of school population that was claimed for the suburbs thirty or forty years ago. And the cries for integrated schooling, teacher organization, and housing—in the suburbs!—match those in central cities.

Therefore the problems of urban education are also to a large extent those of education in the suburbs. Why, indeed, should we expect them to be different? The suburbs do not breed angelic human beings. Their high schools also have retarded readers, truants, behavioral deviates, products of broken homes, and narcotics users. In fact, some inner city high schools are better scholastically and in behavior than certain suburban schools, where drinking, premature pregnancies, and poor performance make teaching as hard as in the presumably "tough" city schools. However the ratio of social problems is lower in the suburbs than in city *public* schools.

The dichotomy of urban-rural education was once possible but becomes trivial as rural education virtually disappears. The urban-suburban dichotomy is breaking down because the poor and deprived live in the suburbs these days too, in order to serve the rich and privileged, generating problems in the suburban schools formerly associated only with city schools. Hence and henceforth in speaking of urban education we will simultaneously be speaking of suburban education too.

2

Family Structure and Education

Family settings define the worst crimes we know—incest, patricide, matricide, and infanticide. The Bible's second misdeed was the murder of a brother. Only the mass murders of war and genocide surpass the crimes caused by family relations. (1)

Books and college courses too often say jolly things about the family hearth, but sometimes home and family life are plain hell, and the chief obstruction to education—not the educational institution, nor the teacher, nor the budget, nor politics, nor educational philosophy. Urban living offers a rich and diverse cultural background in which to raise a family, if the family is stable, but not otherwise. (2) No discussion on urban education can omit discussion on the urban family.

Home influence is overriding. You cannot judge school or teacher without considering the learning readiness of the child; this, in greatest measure, is predetermined by the home. Johnny can't read, while Ivan can, because Americans don't read nearly as much as Russians do, and Johnny's parents are more to blame than Johnny's teachers. Pupil acceptance of the teacher, and pupil rejection (or pupil contempt) of the teacher, depend on the home. Interestingly, pupil rejection of the teacher peaks in high-culture homes and low-culture homes—see Riesman (3)—in one case because the teacher cannot match the parental educational level, and in the other because the parents cannot match the teacher's.

If intra-family matters can be beastly, inter-family ones can be murderous. Whether Hatfield-McCoy feuds, Sicilian vendettas, Hapsburg-Bourbon dynastic wars, or Montague-Capulet bloodletting, families organize the dislike of people for one another. There, the Irishman first learns to dislike the Jew, the Jew the Catholic, the Catholic the Protestant, the rich the proletariat, and the Negro the white—not in the school.

Because disliking one another is more exciting than being educated out of disliking one another, education, an innocent bystander, shares the beating that one side administers to the other, and suffers from large city dissensions even as it pacifies them. Partisanship in the large city is intense and generates the more hate and heat because they are confined. The miracle is that large city education has not suffered more than it has. Somehow, city living encourages a tolerance that coexists with bitter partisanship, so that the very Negro who hates the Harlem ghetto can stand it only because it is located in New York.

Homily on Home and Family— Negro Style

Families agglomerate and cluster, causing neighborhoods, so intra-family beastliness and inter-family murderousness emerge independently and inevitably in Harlem. Crimes of violence are more frequent in Harlem than in the suburbs, and high scholastic endeavor is lower, but look at the types of families involved. According to the Moynihan Report, 70 per cent of the children in Harlem come from unstable homes, and have first-hand experience with unmarried mothers, deserting fathers, "uncles," drunkenness, abandonment, precocious pregnancies, violence, and drug addiction in the very homes where they sleep. But in the remaining 20 to 30 per cent home life is stable and responsible, where the minority-within-a-minority parents desperately seek improvement of neighborhood and school to spare their children community demoralization. The most tragic story in America today is of the stable Negro family in search of a respectable neighborhood in which to live, caught between Negro community disruption and white community rejection, and shouldering the twin burdens of aspiration and discrimination.

Unfortunately for their political wisdom and power, stable Negro families regret white flight when they move in, even though this flight sets the stage for improvement in Negro self-image and social leverage—such white flight means Negro control of the ballot box. (2) Nor can stable Negro family life depend too extensively on enlightened and liberal white allies, because these allies vary in their security and insecurity, and in their aggressiveness and timidity.

Thus the response to the open-enrollment program, even from enlightened and liberal whites, is often unfavorable, which does not mean that the whites are hypocrites or sunshine patriots, as Jencks (4) points out, but that nobody will do your bootstrap lifting for you. Responsible Negro leadership, whether Black Muslim or NAACP, knows that the best-intentioned white liberal help will not substitute for self-help, and that this self-help begins with the stable family and therefrom to a sense of extended family, a virtually indistinguishable equivalent to a sense of tradition. (5)

Open enrollment damages the sense of extended family and is simultaneously a damaging experience for children from low-culture Negro homes. Where open enrollment is a fact, in most northern senior high schools, low-culture Negro children fare poorly. As Havighurst (6) points out, social, class, and cultural stratifications emerge—even in integrated schools—so that the northern senior high school provides a framework for, but no solution to, school integration and is a necessary but not sufficient condition for integration.

Similarly, open enrollment in elementary school paralyzes low-culture Negro children more than white middle-class children. The rate of learning of the low-culture child may pick up, but he fails to reach the learning rate of the high-culture child, inevitably causing a sharp sense of difference and perhaps defeat, resulting in spontaneous separation at recess, at lunch, on the playground, and after school. Contiguity is not integration. (7) The student sitting in reading improvement classes has as much evidence as the student in an honors class that group factors, originating in home, family, and cultural differences, are operating. The liberal, high-culture home cannot reclaim the low-culture home, even where the high-culture home acknowledges a responsibility to do so, nor can high-culture children reshape low-culture children or serve as models for them. Only the school, reflecting society's need for an educated population, can enter into combat with the low-culture home to reclaim the low-culture child and to insulate him against his home, not by involving the high-culture homes nor by educationally deceptive and sometimes meretricious programs like open enrollment, but by invading the privacy of the low-culture home and the time of the child.

Meanwhile, the company of the high-culture, liberal white, rather than the low-culture Negro, is tempting to the minority-within-a-minority Negro family, dimming the sense of *extended* family and causing leadership responsibilities to be abdicated. Negro-white high-culture contacts will be stronger as Negro leadership protects its flanks by political, social, and economic involvements with the low-culture Negro family, the high-culture family's greatest source of strength. Dissociation between the strata of Negro society weakens it both internally and in its inter-race relations, converting leaders into social climbers who turn their backs on the sense of extended family and the group power this generates.

The school and responsible Negro leadership can help counteract the home situations from which uneducated populations breed by extension of the school day, the school week, and the school year, reduction of parent-child contact, amplification of school-child contact, and removal of children from deleterious home and community conditions, so that children go home to sleep, but not for much else. Institutionalization of the child and foster home care, however, are *not* included in this program.

Studies on high school dropouts by Schreiber and others (8) confirm that family values affect educational commitment. Most high school dropouts with superior intelligence leave school because of home indifference, not necessarily financial need, and an attitude that what was good enough for the parent is good enough for the child. Because persuading the child to continue in school is largely fruitless, some conclude that high school is too late and that remedial efforts should begin in kindergarten. (9) Clearly, school improvement should follow family improvement, an almost impossible matter. Minority-within-a-minority Negro families agree an extended family sense will augment their economic,

social, and political leverage, but how can family life that baffles
the schools be included in this extended family sense to build
morale?

For example, when a Negro man cannot get work, nor a
Negro woman gain domestic stability, survival is involved. He may
desert his family. She may live in sexual promiscuity. Desertion
promises to reestablish him as a man, as sexual promiscuity seems
to reestablish her womanhood, where a distorted perspective of
personal integrity permits hysteria to parade as toughness and
apathy as sloth.

The American Negro is not physically apathetic, which is
puzzling because he has every reason to be. Given the opportunity,
nobody works harder. During World War II, and whenever else
employment was offered, Negroes snatched at it. They are far
more energetic than they have cause to be, considering the rewards
they reap from their energy. This perhaps accounts for the dual
roles in which they cast, or are cast, or caste themselves: of lazy
shiftlessness, or of rail-drivin' John Henry energy. The cruelest
libel ever placed against them is laziness, but the libel has Negro
sources as well as white. Any night at Harlem's Apollo Theatre
reveals that the shuffling, indolent Negro is a stereotype that
Negroes recognize and—worse—accept. Stereotypes have survival
value. Negroes accommodate themselves to the different, rapidly-
changing stereotypes pressed down on them from above, because
to get along you have to be agreeable.

Yet, under pressure, stereotypes, toward which Negroes grow
less accommodating, become fragile. Signs of this fragility are
reflected first, in the variety of Negro organizations, expressing
differences among Negroes; second, in the increase in members,
expressing a new political energy among Negroes; and third, in the
growth of leadership, expressing the emergence of executive and
organizing talents.

This organizational proliferation—though partially divisive—
is in the long run desirable. It allows more channels for leadership
to develop; stimulates discussion, strife, and ultimate participation;
and exerts pressure from numerous points on different kinds of
Negroes, generating more activists. Divisiveness is less dangerous
now than quietism or indifference, still a major drawback to Negro
social effectiveness.

Though the Negro has never lacked physical energy, he has

lacked the spiritual energy that comes from hope, systematically drained from him by a southern white society that has kidnaped, debauched, expropriated, murdered, raped, and almost completely wrecked him. After southern white befoulment of the Negroes had evicted them from themselves and from hope, it thrust them into the North, stripped and eroded human beings that urban education had to set aright, to the accompaniment of jeering, "Now that you Northerners have him, you're segregating too, you hypocrites. You're just the same as we are." This lie made a bad conscience easier to live with, because northern *de facto* separation was never the same as southern *de jure* segregation. Precedents for governmental intervention and investment in Negro rehabilitation exist in the reclamation of desert lands, space programs, water desalination, industrial tax rebates, railroad subsidies, farm soil banks, and so on. Negro family life reclamation has just as much right to governmental intervention, to spare parents the guilt, anxiety, and the general rage that drives them to hopelessness, sexual promiscuity, and liquor, and to assure them that their children, at least, are being taken care of. (10)

Unfortunately, the damage has been great and rehabilitation for millions of adult Negroes too late. Strategy will almost certainly counsel investment and involvement with the children rather than with the adults, whose morale is often bankrupt. The Wiltwyck Home, as progressive an institution as we know, reports a doleful tale of recidivism once children return to their neighborhoods. So Negro leadership has its hands full improving the adult Negro's outlook and attitude. Yet a Negro family life reclamation program concentrating on the children may be the best way of radiating effects and beneficially influencing adults, though indirectly. Assurances that government had thrown his children this much of a lifeline would increase the Negro adult's calmness and reduce hysteria and the search for excess. Certainly in many cases we could encourage stability in the home and less need to flee from it, and could begin to make available adult education and retraining.

Substantial numbers of Negro leaders have a good thing going for them and prefer to have conditions remain as they are. Their particular property may be a piece of a numbers running racket, a district leadership, or a church. They are uncertain of their status under social change or with improvement in Negro privilege. They cannot compete in a wider orbit with a higher level of leadership and will balk at any change in the status quo. Because positions of honest leadership are hard for Negroes to come by and because of ignorance among Negroes, it is easier for opportunists to appear.

Where the responsible Negro leader wants to extend his effectiveness, the venal Negro does not. Ellison's *Invisible Man* describes a Negro college president of the latter type, (11) and Frazier's *Black Bourgeoisie* offers sociological parallels. (12) These men do not wish to risk their small, warm places in the sun by overly ambitious aims. They have settled for third best, and until recently may have had some evidence for settling so, but with the evidence changing and with much of the work done and the risks taken, they may become troublesome in their efforts to retain bush-league privileges.

Other temptations await, such as visions of bureaucracy and governmental funds for Negro education, so that when a HAR-YOU appears, with millions of dollars for Negro rehabilitation, its originator is shoved aside in a strong-arm operation that is reminiscent of Al Capone and Prohibition gangsters muscling in on a territory.

One problem Negro leaders face is ideological. Consider: "HARYOU disputes the widely held theory that the limited achievement of Harlem pupils is related to the poor conditions under which they live. Its statistics show 'minimal' correlation between low income, overcrowded housing and broken homes and the achievement of the schools." (13) The school, not the family, is to blame for poor educational performance. But then HARYOU seems to contradict itself:

"So far as HARYOU is concerned, delinquency is the product of the breakdown of family and community culture, brought on by desertion, illegitimacy, neglect." In other words, schools are more delinquent than homes in accounting for educational retardation, but homes are more delinquent than schools in accounting for behavioral deviancy.

Here, Negro leadership, in its hunt for funds, is speaking out of both sides of its mouth, because Negro leadership must be careful about impugning Negro family life, lest it bite the hand that needs it. Negro family life is often a terribly tragic thing from which the emergence of statesmanlike leadership is a miracle, and almost every responsible Negro leader realizes that he is a miracle and that great odds are against his ever having been able to emerge. Furthermore, too much talk about the delinquent Negro family rubs salt in obvious wounds, risks whatever morale exists, can be a convenient out for the circumambient white world, and endangers the flood of federal funds now beginning to come in. For these reasons Negro leadership understandably soft-pedals the nature of much Negro family structure. (14, 17)

In many things, we are what our families are. Thus most Catholics are Catholics because they are born Catholics, most Protestants Protestants, and most Jews Jews; the statistics here seem incontrovertible. Very rarely do people apostasize themselves, so we can conclude that they are what they are because of their surroundings, and not because of rationally ordered belief. Family loyalty determines theological affiliation, and religion is a family matter, patterned by the family and hence pure faith.

And so are our sex patterns and sex habits formed. The patriarchate engenders sexual patterns unlike those of the matriarchate, even to positions during sexual intercourse, according to Robert Graves. (15) If in Negro society in America the father functions differently from the father in white society, we can anticipate sexual consequences. We can expect clash when, in two contiguous societies, one fosters a weak or attenuated father image, and the other a strong one. On the other hand, where deviant individuals have family father images more like those of the contiguous society, for example a white with a weak or attenuated father image, we can anticipate fewer blocks to interracial sex, and similarly with a Negro, whether man or woman, having a strong father image. Strong father image in whites blocks intermarriage, while strong father image in Negroes reduces the barriers, according to Kardiner and Ovesey; (16) this oversimplification requires a closer definition of the "strong" father, who can be a model to be emulated or an enemy to be dreaded, but the Negro father imago is crucial in Negro family structure, where rehabilitation is contingent upon rehabilitation of the Negro father imago. (17)

We know from numerous sources that this rehabilitation depends in greatest measure upon employment possibilities for Negro men, which in turn depends on meaningful training programs for available—not imaginary—job opportunities. Where these meaningful training programs exist, rehabilitation depends on a willingness to enter them and an optimism about future

employment possibilities. Such willingness and optimism ultimately depend on encouragement from Negro women and their
persuasiveness in affecting Negro men. But this is an oversimplification; encouragement and persuasiveness depend on the individual case.

C. Vann Woodward, in his studies of Reconstruction, documents the responsibility of politicians both northern and southern
for the current situation of the Negro. (18) And Negro leaders
additionally accuse the school and white community, whether
reactionary or liberal, but as Pearl Bailey aptly put it, "It takes
two to tango," and politicians, business interests, community
leaders, would never have succeeded as well as they did if so many
Negro fathers had not defaulted on their responsibilities to fight
back. For the absence of militancy and organization the Negro
father bears some responsibility. Indeed, the dreadful conspiracy,
terror, and indifference since 1865 would have foundered, as it so
clearly is foundering now, had Negro husbands and fathers organized as they are beginning to do. (19)

In an immediate consequence, Negro scholastic standards are
at last edging up to white scholastic and collegiate standards, and
more examples occur of high Negro scholastic attainment, with a
start being made toward closing the gap between white and Negro
educational achievement. The background for gains, present and
future, is the Negro father. The Negro mother, no matter how
devoted or how extensive her business talents, cannot do the job
of a respected masculine imago, whether the child is male or
female.

Evidence of masculine imago will come from increase in
Negro voting turnout, an unmistakable measure of Negro purposefulness. The voting booth, like the confession box, washes away
guilt when, in privacy, you come face to face with your duty to
yourself. Voting tabulates this political expression of father image
and masculine imago, which become precise, objective matters on
Election Day. Another indication of an improved Negro father
image can be seen in college entrance. Clarity of perspective now
advises Negro preparation for northern college entrance, rather
than forcing admission into southern collegiate junk heaps.
Greater numbers in academically superior northern colleges, rather
than token admissions to inferior southern ones, offer the better
promise for Negro gains. (20)

In another example, Negro leadership need not publicly

admit that much in Negro family life is too late for repair, as the quietly circulated Moynihan Report indicated, (21) but if the young are to be salvaged and not risked, government intervention and subvention must be concentrated on their behalf specifically, rather than on wholesale family reclamation, with the possibility of greater constructive ultimate impact on families too as a side effect.

The minority-within-a-minority Negro leadership, galled by delinquent minority homes, will know at once if it has succeeded in straightening these out by increase in voting, now that legal impediments no longer exist. Until that time, Negro leadership should concentrate on Negro children.

Every coin has another side, and social stagnation can actually be increased by stable family structure.

In certain trade unions, sons, nephews, and cousins, from generation to generation, are brought into jobs, work their entire lives at the jobs, and give way to successors who are also relatives. Waterfront workers on New York, Liverpool, and Marseilles docks are today in many cases the lineal descendants of grandfathers and great-grandfathers who shaped up at the same docks. In trades as diverse as construction, printing, railroading, and newspaper trucking, family stability leads to occupational immobility, with a relative being brought in as an apprentice, and the membership books jealously closed against outsiders.

A stable family can thereby freeze vocational aspiration or career goals. Many dropouts, despite their abilities, guided by strong father image rather than by available opportunities, reduce their perspectives. The school counsellor's advice counts less than the example of a father who has provided well for his family, who knows the job he has worked at all his life, who sees no reason why his son should not pursue the same vocation and who sincerely feels responsible for that son. The son's values resonate to the father's, and talents that could enrich the possessor and society lie forever untapped. When Schreiber gives evidence that 20 per cent of our dropouts are of superior intelligence, the strong father image is no longer a Freudian pipedream but a national concern. (22)

On the other hand, the mother who temporarily abandons a career until her children have grown may in the act of abandonment strengthen family structure. Families come and families grow, and the abandoned career can thereafter be resumed, with the resulting attenuation of family cares, though not necessarily of family responsibilities. The working mother who has raised a stable family gives an additional image and extended range of occupational possibilities to her children. After children are old enough for school, a woman who returns to a business or professional career is no longer depriving them of the maternal nexus, but may be furnishing evidence of maternal solicitude, broadening the child's career perspectives as the strong father of the intelligent dropout narrows them. Of course, a working mother doesn't have unlimited occupational freedom; a sick child requires her presence and employment conditions must permit her to leave the job until the child is well enough to return to school. Nevertheless, the working mother in a stable family *where children are of school age* beneficially affects family ambitions and horizons, irrespective of family economic level. (23)

Kinsey reports bear on this. That almost half of American college women at the marriage altar are previously deflowered is of less national interest than their career involvements and perspectives during the time they have gained carnal knowledge, which allows them knowledge, concurrently, of the world of business and of the professions. Both kinds can contribute to family stability, rather than family stasis.

Finally, some words on planned parenthood, planned procreation, birth control, or however we nip the bud.

Many geneticists and biologists claim that reduction in lower-class Negro family size and birth rate must precede any improvement in Negro life. We can anticipate imminent government moves in providing contraceptive devices, a diminishing birth rate among lower-class Negroes in the next decade, and improved morale in Negro men and women as a result. If urban education is limited by the characteristics of the urban home, then the urban home will be improved if the lower-class Negro birth rate drops. But won't such birth control information also become available to middle-class adolescents? Will sex adventures among white adolescents become freer than they are now, while lower-class Negro family size drops? Can we have one without the other?

Evidently not. Birth control can mean uncontrolled sex, but it can also mean more composure, better judgment, less hysteria, and therefore sex held in control—we hope. We do not know for certain how birth control materials that we are placing in the hands of Negro women will be treated in the hands of middle-class white girls, but we can reasonably anticipate a proportionate increase in sexual freedom in this group to match a decrease in illegitimacy in Negroes, and a decrease in Negro family instability. The price we pay for regularization of Negro family life is an increase in white middle-class sex freedom—or do you call it promiscuity? Inevitably, in changing the family patterns of Negroes, contraception will simultaneously change the sex patterns of nonmarried whites. (24)

The Conjugation of Latins

Southwest Mexicans, Florida Cubans, and Northeast Puerto-Ricans do not find it easy to retain stable family structure in the United States—not that family structure is particularly stable in lower class society in Mexico City and San Juan as Oscar Lewis describes it. Fidel Castro has released Cubans with strong family ties to join their relatives in America. These immigrants are pre-selected for firm family relationships, and one can predict a rapid acculturation and responsible citizenship for them. Why? Simply because strong family bonds pulled them here, in addition to the Castro push. (25)

We are already hearing of Cubans picking up the pieces, going to school, starting businesses, and making Castro's loss our gain. We are getting the cream of the Cuban crop, people to whom family ties matter. However, unless we provide opportunities for employment and economic security, these family ties can shatter, as they often have with Puerto-Ricans.

In the early fifties, at the beginning of the Puerto-Rican movement to New York, Puerto-Rican women secured employment more readily than did Puerto-Rican men; women in numerous cases were the breadwinners and family instability resulted. In the last few years employment possibilities, at better wages, have opened up for Puerto-Rican men. Social workers report that the Puerto-Ricans have begun to adjust with increasing success to urban living, are radiating out of New York and are forming sizeable colonies in Chicago, Milwaukee, and other cities. Their movement to the mainland has stabilized somewhat as economic opportunities in Puerto Rico have increased, affecting the return flow.

Legislation, rather than prosperity, has caused a drop in Mexican immigration. As one gazes across the Rio Grande from the buildings of Texas Western College in El Paso, one sees the shantytown area of Juarez, the former layover of *braceros* on their way to farm labor opportunities in the Southwest, but El Paso, like Los Angeles and other cities of the Southwest, has a native-born, built-in Mexican population to which many things have happened in the last decade, principally an economic security that permits family stability that permits education to become important. Registration figures at Texas Western College reflect this. A decade back, registration of American-born Mexican students was less than 10 per cent. Currently, registration for these students is almost 60 per cent of total enrollment. Native-born teachers of Mexican ancestry are on the increase in the region's public schools.

But if we are speaking of Latins, we must also consider Italians, a group in which family feeling is strong and as a consequence, neighborhood feeling is equally strong, so that Italian Harlem, Puerto-Rican Harlem, and Negro Harlem tell no story of fraternal feeling of minority groups, but of intense enmity. Minority groups have little friendliness for one another. Italian-speaking Latins do not want to be classed with Spanish-speaking Latins; and Cuban Latins, Puerto-Rican Latins, and Mexican Latins, similarly centrifugal, are wary with one another. (26)

Urban Brotherhood—Like Cain and Abel

San Francisco's Chinatown produces the same kind of school children that Jewish Brooklyn's Midwood section does: studious youngsters, obedient to teachers, and mindful of grades. Does cohesive family feeling among San Francisco's Chinese and Brooklyn's Jews cause this behavior?

But strong family feeling also characterizes Boston Irish, North Bronx Italians, Hamtramck Poles, Cape Cod Portuguese, and Appalachia Scotch-Irish without any comparable school performance. If strong family feeling can coexist with attention to studies and with indifference to studies, it can either mean an absence of relationship or a variety of family values that affect study attitudes in various ways. In any event, this waste of manpower is at an historic watershed, called automation, where family survival will depend on education: We can begin to see that groups once unaffected by educational possibilities are increasingly aware of them and favorably sensitized to them.

Minority groups that improve their levels of education lose habits, patterns, and values that formerly characterized them and separated them. As San Francisco's Chinatown improves its educational level, it integrates more and more into the living patterns of the Bay Area and reaches for living conditions that were only dreamed of a generation ago.

Education dissolves neighborhood antipathies more than religion does. Intermarriage between Italians and Irish is low among the poorly educated and higher among the better educated, though both are Catholic. Similarly, the growth in education through college levels that we anticipate will do more to break down Italian-Irish-Negro-Polish-Mexican antipathies in Chicago, Rochester, and Tucson than all the interfaith and good-will conferences ever called. Indeed, where interfaith meetings work, as with Jews and certain Protestant groups, the high educational level of participants and membership is the major contributing factor.

So we can expect a diminution in minority frictions as minorities extend their education. The melting-pot concept now in disrepute because of cultural pluralism concepts—which sometimes get close to separate-but-equal concepts—never granted a cooling-off of the pot, which was always at melting temperature, but the education that knocks out the dross and then allows a run-off reconstitutes ethnic groups and thereby family relationships in unanticipated ways. Mexican-Americans in Los Angeles are disaffected by Watts Negroes because both groups are of low educational level. The mutual antipathy will remain and nothing will abate it until the educational level of Watts Negroes and Los Angeles Mexican-Americans improves, which in turn requires Job Corps, Head Start, and other Anti-Poverty funds, not as handouts, but as means to keep children learning until they reach maturity. (27)

Even here we can be excessively optimistic. The high level of education among Germans and German Jews cautions us that education without humanity and a sense of mutuality can be brutalizing.

3

Stupidity and Ignorance

Education deals with ever lower levels or ever wider circles of people; lower levels are not the same as wider circles—the very words disclose our feelings about the new populations in the educative process.

Certainly our Negro and Puerto-Rican pupils are not like pupils thirty and forty years ago, especially in the secondary schools. The students in the new English red-brick universities are not the same as students in Oxford and Cambridge. Inevitably, the expansion of education in France, Italy, China, Mexico, and the Soviet Union has brought a new type of student into the school, to some claims that the broadening of education has lowered quality and other claims that students today perform as well as those half a century ago.

Such past versus present comparisons do not eliminate the pressures for educating in the lower levels of human ability and the outer circles of society. Education, like a General Motors product, must be widely merchandised, as Alfred Sloan's memoirs reveal.

Stupidity and Longevity

Yet the lower end of the intellectual range protects its own interests. For some people, it's easier to be stupid because you last longer that way. Though housed in new school buildings, Negro students know that people are indulgent when you sound stupid, so they play-act stupidity because they lose the game but at least live to the end. The shiny new school building reduces neither survival-needs nor play-acting and may only heighten the contrast between home and school, making the school a target for vandals and not necessarily involving it in a departure from stupidity.

The wisdom in stupidity has visceral qualities which compete with cerebral ones. The historical debate on the seat of thought, whether in brain, heart, stomach, or elsewhere—which took a long time to settle because thought is inextricably accompanied by emotion, including the purest, most abstract thought of the mathematician—dealt with the visceral-cerebral competition. Even today, with thought mechanisms geographically localized in the brain, neurological research still faces a brain-mind dichotomy, because thought must travel outside the brain, to the neural switchboards in the reticular formation and thalamus, there picking up emotive concomitants, then returning to the geographical brain, the muscles, or the organs. Thought is always accompanied by emotion, becoming inefficient only when it gathers an unsuitable freight of emotion.

Wisdom is also inevitably emotive, accepting thought when useful and rejecting it when dangerous. For a Negro to consider himself the equal of a white man has been historically risky, and wisdom here counsels caution as to time, place, company, and the thoughts that urge it. These thoughts tempt an intelligent man, but the wisdom of survival suggests that they be put to one side. Thinking can be treacherous.

Nevertheless, a taste of being intelligent, like a good sauce, leaves you hungry for more. When a good teacher cracks the Negro child's play-acting of stupidity, a wide door swings open almost at once—then closes almost as immediately. By stupidity, or mental retardation, or dullness? Or perhaps caution?

The mechanisms of stupidity are like those in disease or fatigue. Stupidity has its own dynamisms. If intelligence is defined as neural, cerebral, and emotive activity of some kind, stupidity may reflect counter-activity in these areas, or else hypo-activity. In some stupidity we have accompanying lower muscular, reactive, and neural activity, but most stupidity reveals reflexes as rapid, coordination as sure, and a neurology as healthy as in the intelligent person. Biochemistry, therefore, offers no hints as to the nature of most stupidity. We must seek further for explanations.

One vague parallel exists in the neurological area of refractory phase phenomena, where nerve transmission is blocked (or the door closed) because of accumulated wastes and ionic imbalance. Possibly, in the stupid child, when attention falters, the door is closed by society, apprehensions, and survival values that must be drained away before the door is opened again. If mental fatigue causes mental toxins, how do you drain these toxins?

Another lies in the different effects of environment, emotion as an aspect of environment, and how expectations and perceptions alter our vision of environment. Darlington points out: "Man propagated crops. . . . But as they improved and multiplied he came to depend on them for survival. Those men who did not improve in their skill were eliminated. *The crops and the stock were now selecting Man . . .* we are engaged in choosing, and being chosen by, environments that fit us in body and mind." (1) [Italics supplied.] As we shall see later, the Negro environment, with respect to emotion, expectations, and perceptions, is changing. A new militance characterizes Negro living—a militance that drains away the fatigue effects of apprehensions and survival fears, allowing the door to be kept open for longer intervals.

The Dynamics of Stupidity

Meanwhile, competent teachers in culturally deprived areas can testify to a frustrating experience that incompetent teachers never have. (2) These competent teachers have seen their presumably stupid pupils show an intermittent sensitivity to a lesson in grammar, mathematics, or history, in which a sudden perspective of possibilities in achievement opened up, in which understanding flowered quickly and withered just as quickly, leaving the baffled teacher wondering what had opened the door and just as quickly closed it. The competent teacher will have fair success in opening the door, but will be unable to keep it open and will helplessly observe the closing, and can only explain it by the usual platitude that interest flagged and could not be sustained.

But the stupidity that closes the door may promise self-defense. Hobbs says:

Contemporary culture often produces a kind of neurosis different from that described by Freud. Contemporary neuroses are frequently characterized not so much by repression and conversion as by an awful awareness and a merciless raw anxiety. The problem of the contemporary neurotic is not lack of insight but lack of a sense of identity, or purpose, or meaning in life. Indeed, in many of the people I work with there seems to be a substantial component of realism in their neurotic condition. Nothing can make a person more anxious, or more guilty, than an unrelentingly clear appreciation of the absurd and desperate condition of man today. (3)

Thus, stupidity can save a sensitive and defenseless human being when his psychic moorings are under attack from birth. Further, Greenacre and Sonntag have evidence of pre-natal effects from anxious mothers. (4) Under oppression you best assure survival by becoming stupid, inhibiting any stirrings of intelligence within you in order to live out your days without danger. Occasionally genetic, stupidity is more often used for survival purposes by timid people, and also by timid rhesus monkeys, timid rats, and timid pigeons, which are selectively bred for intelligence and stupidity, or for aggressiveness and meekness.

But stupidity is also related to the task. According to Tryon, rats bred to be maze-bright may not be as successful in other types of laboratory tasks, becoming emotional or stupid in other contexts. (5) So human intelligence is not a unitary matter, but multifactored, and the mathematics-bright pupil can be creative-stupid, as Getzels shows, and the creative-bright can be science-stupid. (6) Similarly, intelligence varies from situation to situation, so that physicians, attorneys, and businessmen—the presumably bright—do not perform uniformly, sometimes for lack of adequate information, sometimes for reasons of mood, and sometimes for a sudden ineptitude. Supervisors know that teachers in a classroom run students a close second in stupidity and poor judgment, often enough nosing them out and bearing off the palm.

If most stupidity is not the simple absence of intelligence, but a residue of struggle against enemy forces, then we best beat off these forces and increase intelligence by reducing anxieties, fears, and a sense of isolation. By contributing to composure we contribute to competence. As Bayard Rustin says, ". . . demoralization in the Negro community is largely a common-sense response to an objective reality." (7) Hulse adds, "A pretense of stupidity often has survival value for members of a lower caste." (8)

The Stupidity Laboratory

Often we call the stupid "simple minded," but stupidity is not simple, being perhaps more complex than intelligence, as disease is more complex than health. Very likely more factors operate in stupidity than in intelligence, so that stupidity is a more intellectually challenging area of study than intelligence.

The laboratory opportunities for studying stupidity, greatest in a classroom, where stupidity in its pure form reaches lavish development in an enormous number of pupils, are wasted on the classroom teacher, who too typically is affronted by it rather than fascinated by the way it illuminates the human condition as cleverness, talent, and genius never can, promising a breakthrough in behavioral science like the breakthrough in the physical sciences through particle physics and in biology through DNA. As O'Neill says in *Marco Millions:* "Life is so stupid, it is mysterious. . . . What good are wise writings to fight stupidity? One must have stupid writings that men can understand. In order to live even wisdom must be stupid. . . . The stupid man becomes the Perfect Incarnation of Omnipotence." Let's not knock it.

The simple instance, multiplied many times in the school day, of a class opaque to geometry, grammar, or tariff history, is most complex and can throw light on savagery, narcosis, sleep mechanisms, or the homeostasis in stupidity that wants to remain as it is against teacher interposition. As men hotly pursue the inner secrets of the atom, DNA, outer space, and Antarctica, *terra incognita* becomes harder to come by but still appears in the unlikeliest places. So that now economists, political scientists, anthropologists, psychologists, and sociologists are working at the last frontier of all, the interior *terra incognita*—the mind, heart, spirit, and soul of man. But on the periphery of their efforts indolently and ignorantly stands the person most able to pierce this frontier and explore the lands beyond—the classroom teacher, rarely considered an explorer, but a classroom Columbus unaware that he can bring us to a still unachieved understanding of human beings, like the matter of the slow or stupid pupil.

Stupidity, therefore, is a problem for the explorer. As Stefansson has said, (9) the indigenes of the Amazon and Australia didn't know they needed exploring; they were living there. Similarly, teachers are indigenes who don't know they are in *terra incognita.* They are wasting tremendous research opportunities. Our most pressing educational problem is to train teachers who will be classroom explorers of stupidity. In no other way will we ever get the stupid to learn.

The Learning Process and Stupidity

To say that both intelligence and stupidity are related to brain and neural function, or to hereditary and environmental factors, tells us nothing unless we specify how we can manipulate brain, neurology, heredity, and environment. Environment is manipulable, but heredity is too, as Hall and Hirsch show, with rats and mice, fruitflies, and hybrid corn. (10) Brain and neurology are also manipulable with techniques as diverse as hypnotism and biochemistry. Therefore, intelligence and stupidity are similarly modifiable and manipulable, not fixed.

But not the same way. In educating the intelligent we put a sharper edge on the mind; in educating the stupid we reduce the edge's dullness. Sharpening an edge, educationally, is not equivalent to reducing its dullness—educational procedures are different in each case.

Bright children will learn if we remove roadblocks—little more has to be done. The roadblocks may be teachers, home attitudes, or materials, circumstances that can be handled with fair ease. Thereafter we can baffle, mystify, motivate and excite these children to bring their edge to a finer temper. We will learn comparatively little about the educative process in doing so, because, as Ruesch and Bateson point out, (11) the physician learns his business from sick people, not from healthy ones. Thus we discover far more about psychopathology, adjustment, learning theory, criminology, motivation, and punishment-reward systems in the community where I.Q. is depressed, learning limited, teachers inferior, library, museum, and resource facilities minimal, experiences constricted or distorted, and housing bad. These lazarettos show what impedes and encourages art and science more than Periclean Athens or *quattrocento* Florence. Similarly, because college professors deal with the upper levels of intelligence, they think that educating the quick and bright requires a greater intellectual challenge than the slow and dull. The contrary is true. The intellectually impoverished and the culturally expropriated child challenges brain, insight, and curiosity more than the students usually known to college professors. For this reason college professors often confuse the development of intellectual talent with the development of intellectual dandyism, causing the icon-worship we discuss later. Civilizations can no longer afford the luxury of devoting themselves to the talented and remaining indifferent to the remainder of society.

Usually the teacher identifies two problems in stupidity: one is slowness in rate of learning; the second is difficulty in the retention of learned materials. The latter is the far greater problem.

The usual teacher is trained to handle slowness in learning rate and has adequate resources for drill, repetition, and the encouragement of concepts and symbols, many of which are unnecessarily degraded and oversimplified for this consumer. The stupid find great pleasure in the rote of drill and repetition because such busywork exerts a comforting, dulling effect and gives a simulacrum of learning. In concept-formation and symbolic learning the stupid learn the *ad hoc* well enough, having more difficulty in generalizing to other situations. They grasp, although slowly.

But slowness with the new is less frustrating to the teacher than the next day, when stupid children appear washed clean of everything they seemed to learn the previous day. Lack of retention is tremendously unsettling to teacher stability; to go over the same ground again, after all the evidence that the terrain was mastered, leads to teacher cynicism, indifference, futility, and fury.

Not slowness of learning, but difficulty in retention, is the main characteristic of stupidity. The stupid forget.

They cannot separate experiences relevant to learning from inappropriate ones, to control sensations and emotions. Their homes and communities, always in crisis, kick up storms, eddies, and whirlpools that reach the child, who expects tumult as the concomitant to every event, and knows no interior quiet, the instant it leaves the school.

Here the urban stupid and the rural stupid differ. The experiences of the rural stupid are less accompanied by terror, trauma, and crisis. Hunger is quieter. Outlets for aggression, more easily available, do not promise automatic retaliation. The sources of threat are fewer, are more easily grouped and therefore placated. Excess of emotion does not greet every event.

Nevertheless, urban or rural, lower-class society knows apprehension because it is closer to the feral than to the domestic— the source of the next job or the next day's food brings the primitive in again. Difficulty of retention results because school-learned material competes with after-school experiences. The pattering of a rat's paws behind the walls quietly shatters what the teacher told you that day. The blast is noiseless and the fallout is called stupidity. (12)

Forgetting in the period between the departure from school and the return the next day is not caused by the passage of time, but by the interim's competing experiences, events, and reactions during this passage of time; these can either reinforce or contend with school learning. In lower-class society contention with school learning arises from the fear that infuses so many after-school experiences—even play is hysterical and frenetic.

Stupidity means the multi-factors of mind gone askew. Somewhere, somehow there has been a leakage across synapses caused by hyper-emotional states, which may seep into the progress of the bright pupil too, because as Shehan states, "It would be a mistake to proceed to new material before every student in the class has mastered the problem at hand." So the teacher holds back the faster students while he drills the slower ones and waits for complete class consensus on understanding before proceeding. (13) There is something to be said for the theory that the slow student will catch up with current material not by dwelling on it until the whole class masters it, but by pushing ahead to other matters, when the problem may well be resolved simply because it has soaked in while the slow student faces new material.

Tempo here is tricky.

The Sociology of Stupidity

In this last frontier, the internal one, we lack clear notions and definitions of stupidity; just as zero temperature is hard to attain, so is zero intelligence hard to determine. Our weak theoretical structure encourages glibness about our ignorance. For example, we need fixed points for temperature units—like freezing point and boiling point—and also for intelligence measurements, like the ages when children can perform two different tasks, but children, not as fixed as freezing and boiling points, make the units of intelligence loose, even if not quite meaningless. To determine zero intelligence is important for theory and practice and is a constant cry of psychologists, but to discount intelligence tests as worthless because we don't know what we are talking about is to stop work with linear accelerators because we don't know the ultimate constitution of matter. We don't have to know, actually, in order to manipulate, improve, correct, and change—either in electricity, biology, or intelligence. (14) As long as the biochemistry of intelligence and stupidity is unclear, the definitions will remain circular, even while we can differentiate the intelligent from the stupid.

Nevertheless, we do have much to go on, like the variation in human traits, as in height and weight, as well as in intelligence. In the normal curve (or bell-shaped curve, or curve of random distribution, or Gaussian curve), these variations are given graphic form along a *single* continuum (of height, weight, or intelligence). Thus, we can compare Negro and white intelligence along this continuum and get averages (which will usually be lower for the Negro than for the white), maximums, minimums, and distributions.

Here the southern segregationist interrupts to point to the two different averages for Negro and white and to the lack of overlap between the distributions, meaning that we may have two distinct populations. This lack of overlap between the curves of intelligence distribution, says the segregationist, means that whites and Negroes are basically dissimilar in intellectual endowment. Most whites score higher than most Negroes. Only exceptional Negroes score above the average for whites. Similarly, the lower end of white intelligence is at the Negro average.

Proof, says the segregationist, that the Negro is basically dissimilar and inferior. (15)

Not so fast.

The normal curve is also called the curve of random distribution, because it reflects the play of *random* effects which here results in two curves with small overlap (though the overlap is really far larger than the segregationist will admit); but these curves are *not* the outcome of random effects. Indeed, nothing whatever is random about the predictable displacement downward of the Negro intelligence distribution, from what we know of white Southerners, of slavery, of the systematized destruction of Negro fathers, and of the planned, purposeful, non-random aggression of whites against Negroes. Surprisingly, the curve of Negro intelligence has not been displaced further downward in a straightforward (or linear) response to the known and unknown behavioral, neurological, physiological, and sociological characteristics under attack, encouraging us that through these known and unknown dimensions we can influence intelligence and stupidity, ill-defined and poorly measured though they are. Thus, if physiology is affected by rest, diet, and exercise, so is intelligence influenced by emotions, rewards, punishments, enmity, and love, within the limits of the individual's—not the race's—hereditary potential. (16)

The segregationist answer is that the curve is displaced downward by built-in racial inferiority and not by circumstances. If he is right, then this inferiority should have been characteristic of Negro history. But Negro history is not a unitary thing, any more than white history is. Two thousand years ago, when the Greeks, Romans, Persians, and Egyptians had already had long periods of civilization, other white groups in Scandinavia, the Scottish highlands, and interior Russia were at no higher levels than Negro tribes along the Congo. See Tacitus on the German barbarians of this period, when Negro Nubian civilization was at a high level and Negroes had already occupied the throne of Egypt as pharaohs. The Tutankhamen funeral mask in the Cairo Museum is Negro in feature, as is the head of Queen Tiye in the Berlin Staatliche Museum. Egyptian illustrations of the Nubians show elaborately dressed people, who must have known complex weaving and textile techniques. As white history shows uneven regional development, so does Negro history. Whites are made up of Alpines, Armenoids, Celts, Semites, and other breeds. Negroes are not less diverse. Some breeds are more conspicuous in history than others.

But we can over-claim, as this report of a New York meeting notes: " 'Image-raising' must be accomplished without pointing. Examples were cited in which minority segments of the population were embarrassed by being singled out. A caution was also expressed against the 'boomerang' effect of overemphasizing the contribution of a minority group to the extent that it destroys the accuracy of the situation being presented." (17) Nevertheless, when Renaissance painting shows Negroes as court attendants and servants, and a church in Avallon, France, shows a Negro head in its gallery of medieval worthies, we wonder what happened to the descendants of these European Negroes. Obviously they must have merged into the general European population.

Similarly the Jews, two thousand years ago, constituted a considerably larger proportion of the Mediterranean population than they do today. Best estimates are that Jews then numbered 7 million, or not less than one out of ten of the total. But Jews too merged into the general population in the Rhine Valley, Greece, Italy, and Spain, and any contribution they make to history is under another identity. So is Pushkin, whose Negro great-grandfather was a general with Peter the Great, identified as Russian, not octaroon; Dumas *père* as French, not mulatto; and Robert Browning as true-blue-blood-Victorian. Negroes emerge in European history only through their white descendants, and are therefore unidentifiable as Negroes, a perfectly obvious outcome of social, political, and economic pressures. Getting yourself absorbed into the general population is a way of improving your environmental circumstances and allying yourself with social, political, and economic pressures, rather than combating them.

Biochemistry substantiates the simple observation that racial differences exist. But biochemistry also substantiates that racial characteristics interact, with no deleterious consequences in the biochemistry of the descendants. Biochemistry also tells us that we can improve environment without injuring human biochemical processes, and possibly improving them, so that we can arrange for the environment that will reduce stupidity and augment intelligence. The extent to which we arrange environments is a measure of civilization. Civilization means that we build not only roads, structures, agriculture, and industry, but also the quality of humanity, the foremost concern of environmental control and of modern society.

At present, the most efficient lever for improving the quality of humanity is education, though biochemistry also seems to be drawing within target range in the recoverability of human intelligence. (18) Certainly no shortage of problems exists for education or biochemistry, either at the theoretical or the engineering level, but the stage is set for major forward jumps. Because we observe differences in human intelligence, we deduce that human intelligence is alterable and recoverable, and that we can improve operational intelligence by varying the governing conditions.

Not everybody finds this control palatable. The best of people can be appalled. A liberal like Joseph Wood Krutch, who has been skirmishing with behavioral psychologist B. F. Skinner for years, may be as upset as a segregationist, though he quite clearly is not one, with Professor Skinner's attempts to condition, modify, and alter human behavior. Mr. Krutch sees this as meddling interference. Mr. Krutch has no objection to measuring everything in the universe *except* man. The measure of man does not allow the measurement of man, nor tampering with man. (19) Mr. Krutch, for all his soul and perception, is a link between segregationists and those Negro leaders who want to terminate I.Q. measurement in the schools because Negro children are discriminated against by intelligence testing. They undoubtedly are, because the function of any test is to discriminate. Let us see how Negro leadership is abandoning a weapon in abandoning the testing of intelligence.

When Tests Are Tested

The testing movement has made fewer mistakes than its opponents. Tests inadvertently damn some of the elect and inadvertently elect some of the damned, and experienced test makers can even tell you the amount of inadvertent damnation, or error. The opponents of testing cannot do as well. (20) Mass education means mass testing, and mass testing means a certain proportion of inequity which is statistically predictable and contains less inequity than any alternatives.

But evaluation can be a technique to falsify the returns. Hence, for honest assessment, the tests, measurements, and statistics that can be used to cover partisan tracks always require analysis. Negroes can construe testing as an indicator of *the inadequacies of society*. Their enemies can construe test results as evidence of Negro inadequacy, while enemies of testing construe test results as no evidence at all. But test results can testify to social inadequacy, and in any case they offer evidence much too valuable to be thrown away.

A public school system cannot operate without a testing program. The most efficient testing program known, with all its imperfections, is the system of aptitude, achievement, personality, reading, and intelligence tests vital to American school systems, the Armed Forces, and industry—even when testees fake answers, items are badly written, interpretations of results poor, and psychometricians frequently mistaken. But testing systems reduce the risks in personnel selection, in school promotion, in college entrance, and in training programs far more than any other selection procedures that Hoffman, Hildebrand, and Gross can suggest. (20) When a school superintendent feels that tests discriminate against the culturally underprivileged child, and orders their removal by administrative fiat, he surreptitiously opens another door to other tests, as he must. He cannot operate his school system without tests. (21)

These test results understandably trouble the responsible Negro leader, but they are evidence that he is right and that his cause is just. He should use test results to support him, because they do. They are his ally, not his enemy, when they show that intelligence is randomly distributed, *but not within groups in the population,* and that some groups and some families are smarter than others for environmental reasons that are engineered in and engineered out, within the limits of hereditary potential. *Test results, in intelligence, reading, aptitude, and achievement, are evidence that we will never be able to engineer in the racial equality the Negro leader wants until we achieve environmental equivalence on schools, housing, employment opportunities, civil rights, recreational facilities, and public accommodations.*

Testing does not guarantee our success in ultimately engineering in racial intellectual equality. Such evidence comes from other psychological sources, like studies of the effects of interference on retention from Ebbinghaus in 1885 to Benton J. Underwood today; from the neurological studies of Zubek, Welch, and Saunders on sensory deprivation to the vast investigations of animal conditioning. (22) Man is adaptable, trainable, educable, conditionable, and alterable, no matter what his genes—so say all the social sciences, the behavioral sciences, and the arts. If 65 per cent of our characteristics are attributable to heredity and 35 per cent to environment, (23) some qualities of intellect may come from heredity and others from environment; which qualities are most decisive in the classroom and society? Certainly the wise teacher can alter circumstances to reduce stupidity.

Example: if we administer a written test to a slow student and then read a test of comparable difficulty to him, while he listens, he will perform better when the test is read to him, rather than written for him. Here, as in many other areas, we can improve performance and thereby the measurable aspects of intelligence.

To improve such performance, we must first recognize that thinking is a task, and as trying a task as we know of; people will turn to almost any alternative to avoid thought. Thinking comes hard and is a sort of athleticism, easy and pleasant for those who can do it and who have kept in condition, but causing pain, palpitations, breathlessness, nausea, and cramps to those who have not. For these reasons most people avoid thought.

Kant offers another example: "Deficiency in judgment is properly that which is called stupidity; and for such a thing we know no remedy. A dull or narrow-minded person, to whom nothing is wanting but a proper degree of understanding, may be improved by tuition, even so far as to deserve the epithet of *learned*. But as such persons frequently labor under a deficiency in the faculty of judgment, it is not uncommon to find men extremely learned, who in the application of their science betray to a lamentable degree this irremediable want." (24)

Intellect, therefore, should not be confused with intelligence, nor pedantry with brains.

At the other extreme, stupidity, which seems superficially to arise from inner conditions, may more truly be a social matter. An I.Q. of 80 is a fluid, not a fixed, thing, which can be lifted by change in home, diet, community, and way of life.

I.Q. reflects society almost as much as it reflects the individual, and application as much as aptitude, like Shelley's dome of many-colored glass, giving numerous varieties of intelligence. Thought is a mosaic of patterns, ever-shifting, in art, science, industry, athletics, sensuality, abstinence, religion, and war. The varieties of men's activities place a premium now on one quality of thought and now on another. With so many qualities, thought is not readily quantifiable; we cannot tell from scores on the Graduate Record Examination who will go on to a distinguished career as scholar or scientist. (25) Nor can we predict the areas of scholarship, science, or art which will next send out an urgent summons for thought as new problems suddenly emerge. There is more to intelligence than there are ways of measuring it—the nature of intelligence is more complex than our means of measurement. Organized emotiveness, fantasy, and creativity are also aspects of intelligence, as Getzels and Jackson show, and can even contribute to a stupidity score, just as "noise" in an electronics circuit doesn't want to be noise but is made so by engineering definitions; under other conditions it becomes a message. (26)

Similarly, intelligence and stupidity can only be defined by the tasks to be done. We cannot predict what these tasks will be, but if we want intelligence increased and stupidity reduced in dealing with them, responsibilities must be seriously assigned and seriously accepted. We cannot otherwise talk of intelligence or stupidity.

Art opens up new intellectual frontiers, as science does, and as much special intelligence, even of a different kind, is required in a Paul Klee as in a Szilard, though we say some disciplines are more demanding than others. The artist thinks as much as the scientist, though his materials may not be as difficult to deal with.

In another confusion, we blur rapidity of thought with depth of thought. Most school tests put a premium on pace, penalizing slowness, but ruminativeness has its place in things. Psychometricians believe that the slow child is not necessarily stupid; children within the normal range of intelligence, even as low as I.Q. 85, can do everything that the I.Q. 100 can do, but require more time to do it. Hence most of the high school curriculum is within their grasp, including the usual high school mathematics and science, but such pupils need more time to cover the same ground, accounting for the multiple-track system that an educational critic like Bestor proposes. (27)

Nor should wit be mistaken for imagination. Frank Riessman has overly-romanticized Negro life, (28) but he gives ample evidence of the imaginativeness, resources, humor, and perceptiveness of urban Negro youth. The culturally deprived Negro child who scores at I.Q. 85 is not stupid. His I.Q. is equivalent to I.Q. 100 of a middle-class white child. Or consider the instance of a nationally administered intelligence test in which a Negro child in deepest Mississippi scores 90 and the son of a prosperous Massachusetts banker also scores 90. How are we to interpret these scores? Are both children equally bright, because they score the same? Or must we additionally use the background of each child to interpret the scores? Considering the usual educational and cultural background of Negro children in Mississippi, must we not say that the score represents the floor of this child's potential, and that his true intelligence is much higher? And that the Massachusetts boy is a superbly trained moron who is scoring at the very ceiling of his ability because of the cultural and educational advantages of his environment?

So we can say that *most* Negro test scores represent the floor, the bottom, the nadir, the lowest possible estimate of Negro intelligence.

Negro stupidity, like white stupidity, is a fact of nature and therefore can be changed, provided that we are interested in change. Nature wants us to be as intelligent as we possibly can. Stupidity is productive of error, physical attrition, neuropathology, and a harder life than need be. Stupidity generates worse penalties than intelligence ever does and has survival value only when you are under attack, and then is more dissimulation to mitigate threat than anything else. The Negro pupil who adopts the mask of stupidity in order to last longer, when he is no longer under attack, uses anachronistic defenses and is in error at a time when he should be going over to purposefulness. In most northern cities the time is past, almost by a generation, for defense. Conditions no longer advise retreat, nor, conversely, attack or aggressiveness. Instead, they require purpose, training, and the goal-directed militancy that arises from organization, lest over-reaction lead to hysteria and what L. Susan Stebbings called "potted thinking," (29) both by the heretofore stupid and the heretofore intelligent.

Even if stupidity were a genetic matter, we could restructure it as we have restructured the course of rivers, the flow of atoms, and other natural traffic. But stupidity is also a sociological matter, making it further amenable to restructuring. The time has come for a grim determination to lift stupidity from approximately one-third of our population now sitting at one standard deviation below the mean intelligence level. Thinking to some purpose, in Stebbings' phrase, is one way of doing so, but purposefulness may be the truer progenitor to thinking, or more accurately, being purposeful may be another kind of thought.

Let us therefore cerebrate one-third of our population, by means of purposefulness, values, challenge, and work, of which the sum, or product, is militancy toward tasks, the chief aspect of education in the reduction of stupidity and the recovery of intelligence.

The segregationist asks: if races differ in size, pigmentation, kinkiness and color of hair, and blood type factors, can't they differ in intelligence too? Even, for the sake of argument, were it so, we have a more pressing racial problem than comparing the Negro child's capacity with the white child's. And that is getting the Negro child to learn up to his capacity. With all the evidence that Negroes *on the average* do not perform as well on intelligence tests as whites, the more significant evidence is that they are not on the average functioning up to capacity, because of social, economic, and political impediments. I.Q. averages bear this out when deviations from the averages are reported by a statistic called the *variance*. Negro averages are lower than white averages, but Negro *variance* is comparable to white variance. This equivalence in white-Negro variance, rather than differences in average, tells us that Negro performance is not achieving Negro potential.

Furthermore, score spread (or variance) reveals that the southern white, *on the average* inferior to the northern white but with variance as great, is equal in basic endowment, with any dissimilarities traceable to regional, educational, and environmental differences; the southern region depresses Negro and white scores. In the South, therefore, every intelligence test that matches Negro and white compares nonequivalent populations without the same experiences. They are different end products, though similar at birth. (30)

In addition, the "same" region is not the same environment, whether in the South or the North. The Negro and white child in New York have not had equivalent experiences, their neighborhoods are not equivalent, nor their experiences in those neighborhoods. They have therefore never had the same environments.

Remember that intelligence is not a unitary quality, but a composite mosaic of interplay between genes and environment, between the factors of mind within and the factitious, manipulable world without. Good students will perform unevenly. Often the fine mathematics student will not perform as well in social studies or in foreign language, while, conversely, the excellent language student will perform only adequately in science or mathematics, because, very likely, emotive or appreciational differences enter. (26) Bright students will learn what they are required to learn, but not necessarily with an appreciational sense of beauty, elegance, or form—a typical shortcoming of engineering or accounting majors, who become excellent technicians without the slightest creativity or insight.

Intelligence is many things simultaneously, just as a chromosome is, but all these things need nurturing; and the ways of encouragement are complex:

> . . . each in his way is refusing to share the whole pattern, however willing he is to give bits of it. Resistance in the grudging and selective giver turns out to be as important as resistance in the grudging and selective receiver. . . . Once this is recognized, it is possible for us to scrutinize with newly opened eyes each situation in the world where people of a different sex or race, class or culture, seem to fail to accept or to use the opportunities which are offered them, to become "like" the members of another class or race or culture. Many different kinds of failure and refusal become intelligible—of girls to learn physics, of bright-eyed little African children who learn so quickly as small children and turn apathetic and disinterested at puberty, of new immigrants in model housing developments who don't "appreciate" their excellent plumbing, of the contrast between the adjustment of Negro boys and their sisters when both are asked to meet the middle-class standards of a high school in a small Pennsylvania town, of the restlessness and refusal of regular employment by modern Maoris in New Zealand or by American Indian immigrants to the big cities. The situation in which children are taught by individuals whose full status—as men, or members of an excluding race, or nuns, or persons free to travel—they cannot hope to attain makes the goals held up to the pupils seem not to be the wonderful opportunities which they are so often represented to be. So bright girls strangely have no "ambition" and children of discriminated-against minorities turn "dull" at adolescence, not because of intrinsic incapacity, but because the desire to learn is blocked by the knowledge that part of the pattern to which they aspire will be denied them. (31)

Hence, a desegregated, uniform school environment will not necessarily improve Negro performance, but may increase the difference between performance and potential when it cannot compensate for the mother's going to work because the father has no job, nor for the child's noticing that just a subway or bus ride from Harlem the faces are no longer Harlem faces but non-Harlem faces. A child by its hundredth week of life already knows that, and soon after little Negro girls begin preferring white dolls in their play. (32)

As educating the bright is related to political competition between America and the Soviet Union, making the superior mind a concern of politics because it improves our international competitive position, so do programs for the slow offer competitive public relations advantages with the developing Asians, Africans, and Latin-Americans. Let's get some practice at it. We'll be first in the history of the world to have done so. Also, let's get some experience with the education of the underprivileged bright, where again we have very little to go by, aside from Horatio Alger and the experiences of the medieval church.

How Smart Can You Get?

The more we work with the culturally deprived, in order to raise the ceilings available to these children, the more we improve the performance of the culturally privileged. The more we find out about the operating conditions of stupidity, the more we improve the processes of intelligence.

We offer a case study of interaction between cultural deprivation and cultural privilege:

In the summer of 1965 the City University of New York inaugurated the College Discovery and Development Program (CDDP), in which under-achieving junior high school graduates were selected by guidance counselors and teachers and placed in special high school programs to prepare them for 600 *guaranteed* places in the New York City college system, which meant that 600 students who, chances were, would never have gone to college were being prepared to do so through intensive preparation, specially designated teachers, and a scholarship allowance of $5 per week to keep them in books, spending money, sodas, and dating. (33) We need not enter into the results, because it is still too early to tell if these students will do well at college. We are assured that they will do well in high school because they are being paid to do well and if, here and there, some student of unsound mind or unfit personality is continued in the program and in the $5 weekly stipend, this maverick should not reflect too much discredit on the first stage of the program.

We can, however, anticipate some other doubts. Students from the same circumstances as these under-achievers, who have the same potential and are performing up to this potential, are getting neither $5 weekly nor other educational opportunities that the 600 under-achievers are enjoying. In other words, the under-achievers are being rewarded for not having performed, and students who did perform would have profited by being reluctant students. The injustice so clearly visible here is not irremediable nor glaring and requires little dwelling on. The major considera-tion, rather, is what these students will do to the performance of students they will replace on the college rolls, for the 600 seats they occupy will no longer be available to students not in this special program and thereby refused enrollment. One wonders at what point compensatory education becomes over-compensatory.

On the other hand, if the program redeems 600 human souls who otherwise would never have gone to college, then we have clear indication of more college material than ever suspected, that we have too little college space if we really want to root out these college prospects, and that we must track them down to put them on special tracks and have a slot, a seat, and a student's role waiting for them. If we needle our under-achievers into achieve-ment so successfully that they become college-bound, we shall be doing vastly more to create new college facilities than if we had admitted only those who had achieved and had met college entrance requirements. In brief, the culturally deprived are doing more to encourage investment in education than are the culturally privileged—and let the culturally privileged be grateful for this opening up of college entrance bottlenecks.

This extends to the maintenance and improvement of educa-tional standards. In lifting performance on the floor, we lift it at the ceiling too. Every effort we invest in Operation Head Start will gain improvements in Operation Second Chance and CDDP. The broader the base of education the better the quality of education at the top. For thousands of years, from the Greeks to the Romans to the Renaissance to the Enlightenment, concentration on education for an intellectual elite resulted in educational restrictions. Kant played in the same ball park as Plato. Not until the educational base was broadened and new groups were admitted to educational opportunity did intellectual achievement manifest itself in places where intellect had never been before.

4

Militancy and Intelligence

Man is the most aggressive and the most intelligent of the animals. Though intelligence should reduce inappropriate aggression, aggressiveness, instead, dictates the conditions of use of intelligence, not the other way, with aggressiveness the usual framework within which intelligence is exercised. Though war stimulates technology, implying the increased exercise of intelligence, the absence of technology or of intelligence does not inhibit war. Aggressiveness is dominant over intelligence. (1) And, like crimes, aggressiveness can be against persons or against things. (2)

Until Negro militancy (whether violent or non-violent is unimportant) emerged, no basis for judging Negro intelligence existed. Intelligence needs an arena where it can exercise itself: a problem, an intelligence test, a reading assignment, or a maze. Intelligence presupposes goals which, successfully or unsuccessfully approximated, furnish an assessment of intelligence. Militancy generates goals and a groundwork for intelligence.

For the first time in recent Negro history, Negroes are laying out areas where they can exercise intelligence, thereby allowing assessments of their intelligence. Unfortunately, they too often misdirect their fire at people rather than at things, but with more justification since people get in the way of things related to improvement of intelligence. Among these people are Negroes.

Currently, Negroes are not as smart as whites, else they would be heaving whites out of Ole Miss, would own all the real estate in Harlem, and would sit in at least 10 per cent of the seats in the Senate and House. To achieve these goals, they should have fewer babies out of wedlock and drink less alcohol. Instead they should get all the free education offered, vote and go into politics, ferociously boycott white merchants who block equal employment opportunities, and contrive under the law to live anywhere their money lets them. If "people" and "things" are mixed as targets here, Negro intelligence will be sharpened in distinguishing between them. Militancy does that, if used with judgment.

People aren't born intelligent—they live intelligently. True, unintelligent people in affluent societies can maintain life this side of extirpation. But, for living beyond that, observing of intelligent people and then simply imitating them are almost all it takes to become intelligent—but that is very hard. Impediments to imitation—imposed upon the person from outside—are frequent, like getting a good job without training in a white man's world—yet training is available in the large northern cities and free, even to Negro migrants from the South, so training opportunities must be seized to neutralize *that* impediment to imitation. If, after training, closed trade unions and discriminatory hiring are the next impediments to imitation, the stage is set for picketing the trade unions, which allows intelligence to lead from greater strength than moping about a lack of training. (3)

Training deals with things, rather than people, and gives competence with things that later transfers to competence with people, permitting aggressiveness toward things, militancy toward problems, and a legitimate non-masochistic toughness. Best of all, training gives competence and develops courage and genuine confidence, so that the enemy goes on the defensive.

Thus active Negro participation in NAACP or CORE contributes to brighter, alerter learners, more capable of application at hard mental tasks, which places a responsibility on Negro organizational leadership to convert militancy-generated intelligence toward tasks, training, and problems, and away from people, else the possibilities of this new-found intelligence will be frittered away in mere bellicosity. (4) With tasks to do, you become comfortable with the crucial, assured under assault, purposeful under pressure. Fully as important, you realistically differentiate between expectations and aspirations or, put otherwise, between the fantastic and the possible. (5)

These tasks can be mastered in school, or in organized militancy, such as CORE or NAACP, which also has a rich curriculum, requiring typing and stenography; proofreading letters and solicitations for funds; interpreting registration and voting records; speaking to friendly and unfriendly people and groups; researching neighborhood, ethnic, political, and economic configurations; analyzing the mass media, economic indexes, and political trends. Organizational involvement offers a matrix for intellectual development, which, when supplemented by formal schooling, presents an array of tasks that inducts Negro youth into the paths of militance, and encourages a sensitivity to difference between people and things and the aggressiveness appropriate to each, again fostering differentiation between the fantastic and the possible.

Negro children *say* they want to go to college. They aspire, but don't expect to be, airline pilots, teachers, astronauts, or scientists. Organized Negro militancy has punched intermittent holes and made gains unevenly, so that it is easier for a Negro to become a scientist or a college professor than an airline hostess or pilot, or an electrical engineer than an electrician, or a physician than a receptionist in an advertising agency. This is because the opposition to job opportunities has collapsed unsymmetrically, requiring in turn a reappraisal of expectations, aspirations, fantasy, and possibility. The Negro child may have aspirations unaccompanied by expectations, and may be forgiven this indulgence in fantasy, but the Negro leader, if worth his salt, has expectations towards which he strives and drives, while his aspirations follow at a reasonable, realistic distance.

Unfortunately militancy does not always engender such intelligence. Too many Negro leaders confuse aspirations with expectations, militancy with hysteria, aggressiveness against persons with that against things, revivalism with inspiration, and exhortation with the *force majeure* appropriate to time and place. (6) Thus from the sounds they make, Black Muslims do not seem timid or cowardly, nor their programs narcissistic and a rationalization of flight from battle, but they are nowhere near as tough as the non-violent Martin Luther King. Similarly the NAACP and CORE face the white world with varying degrees of accommodation but at least do not confuse tergiversation with a forward direction.

Black Muslimism merely sounds aggressive. It isn't. Nevertheless, Elijah Muhammed has revealed what other Negro leadership has been demure about, that the Negro must set his own house in order, abandoning profligacy, drinking, and narcotics, to prepare himself for responsibility. Curiously, in such road work, the Negro family and community will go into training for citizenship and for departure from Elijah Muhammed, who put them on the road in the first place. Black Muslimism has no future because, as it straightens out the Negro family, it prepares the Negro family for the militancy that develops the intelligence to make other Negro leadership more attractive. Black Muslimism plays an important catalytic part, but an interim one—it prepares Negroes to abandon it. (7)

Right now the American Negro is in the healthiest psychological condition he has ever known because he is more militant than he has ever been. The larger society will welcome this militancy if applied to tasks and skills that improve intelligence and reduce stupidity. The larger society will take its skilled and trained people wherever it can find them, so that social need and not social morality governs, producing the best guarantee for social change.

The growing astuteness in Negro leadership reflects the growth of Negro organizations, the jockeying among leaders, the emergence of professional, paid organizers, and a shift from the conspiratorial toward dispersed general staffs which begin to know —and in the assurance of that knowledge to lead from strength— that an automated America requires the Negro attainment that derives from militance.

Let us examine a parallel. The Jews, like the Swedes, once a ferociously aggressive people and later meek and intimidated, contributed little to culture, art, or science, from 1500 to 1800, as Feuer and Dimont point out. (8, 9) Only after Napoleon did Jews take a conspicuous, almost unduplicated place in the culture of Europe and America. From 1830 on, Jews became tough again; and in Europe no group contributed more or was more associated with political militancy as trade union leaders, anarchists, socialists, bundists, and communists. In this country 20 per cent of Communist Party membership was Jewish, (10) fewer than 3 per cent of American Jews, considering that Communist Party membership never exceeded 100,000 (10) but Jews number over 5 million. Though vastly larger numbers of Jews were led by the timid and careful leaders described by Hannah Arendt (11) and Trevor-Roper, (12) Jews were nevertheless in the original Communist Party leadership in Russia in 1917, in the French and German Socialist Party, and in the American Federation of Labor. (13)

On the right, in the great banking houses of Europe and America, in retailing and manufacturing, in art, music, and literature, Jews exerted influence greatly in excess of their actual numbers. For example, prior to Hitler, 10 per cent of all the Nobel prize winners in science were German Jews. In America and Europe today no group of citizens has contributed more profoundly to decency and democratic living, with little reason to suppose so from their ghetto life earlier in the present century, as Handlin traces it in *Adventure In Freedom:* "One way or another, the Jews were coming to conform to the standards of middle-class life in America. Having acquired respectable employment, they moved off in ever larger numbers to discover respectable housing in the suburbs. On the periphery of the great cities they built comfortable homes and adopted the appropriate symbols of their status. The size of their families shrank as did that of other Americans at this social level." (10)

Jewish achievement was gained by a militancy in executing tasks, militancy against things and problems, as much as against persons. The Helots knew and Spartacus learned that militancy against persons is not enough. You must have resources.

One resource is moral, where you persuade and convince your opponent that he is wrong, by the evidence from religion, ethics, and economics. The greatest resource is mind, where you out-general and out-think the opposition by boycotts; by evidence from psychology, sociology, and anthropology; by pickets; and even by sit-ins where advisable, because ideology without militancy gets you nowhere, just as militancy against people gets you nowhere until it is coupled to militancy against things and problems. As Charles E. Silberman says:

> Negroes must gain a sense of potency if they are to move into the mainstream of American life. And power has to be taken; the nature of power is such that it can never be received as a gift. Hence when businessmen say they're willing to grant some of the Negro demands, "but not if we're

pushed too hard," they're missing the point. Negroes want to achieve their aims by their own efforts, not as a result of white beneficence. Thus, the very militancy and stridency that whites find so upsetting is essential if the Negro is to shuck off his traditional dependency and become truly free and equal, if he is to learn to respect himself, and to be respected by whites. (14)

In this educational warfare between Negro and white, New York lowers admission requirements for Negro and Puerto-Rican students in high schools and colleges, inevitably displacing white students. (15) The Negro leader who seeks this new *numerus clausus* now fights the Jewish leader opposed to it, stating that the Jews got $15 billion from Germany for Jewish dead, and wants similar social restitution, or special privileges, because of the many more Negro millions murdered, enslaved, lynched, raped, and bestialized.

The situations are not quite the same. The Jew could point specifically to German genocide, and got restitution from Germans, but from no one else. Similarly, the Negro cannot blame the Jew, the New Yorker, the Downeaster, or the Minnesotan, for his situation. Their part in the Negro plight is negligible. The Negro can chiefly blame the southern white American as the major contributor to the Negro situation. Indirectly, of course, all Americans have been involved, but to this moment non-Southerners, specifically northern urban whites, are doing more in the way of restitution than Southerners.

To repeat Silberman's words—and Adam Clayton Powell's—Negroes must learn and earn leadership by taking it, not by following it, else any civil rights victories will be followed by new Reconstructions. We've been there before.

Interestingly, segregationists recognize this more easily than liberals do. Much in Negro background has small-town conservative southern, rather than urban northern liberal, origins; and when segregationists say they understand the Negro situation better than Northerners, they are partly correct, because in the formative period of childhood Negroes and whites play together more often in the South than in the North. Such shared childhood experiences leave indelible marks and a community of interests that the northern white liberal, without these experiences, can never conceive of. In maturity, these convert to an antipathy that is as close as you can get to sibling rivalry without having a blood relationship, concurrent with a deep understanding of motive and value that can only exist in those with such common childhood experience. Literature offers numerous illustrations of rich and rewarding Negro-white young boy relationships, from Mark Twain to Faulkner to Baldwin, just as it offers parallel illustrations of the boys grown to manhood and the change to mutual distrust and hatred. (16)

If you are betrayed by a boyhood friend, then betrayal is possible anywhere and you can only ensure against an otherwise guaranteed betrayal by taking your fate into your own hands, and assuming leadership when you should. For this reason, the liberal white should accept leadership only on an interim basis, relinquishing it on demand. Conversion of Negro militancy against persons into militancy against things and problems will never be consummated unless Negro militancy is directed by Negro leadership.

Outside leadership will make mistakes caused by good intentions. The white teacher suspects the Puerto-Rican child's downward glance because the pupil is not looking her square in the eye. But to the Puerto-Rican child this is a deferential sign of respect. Are they rude when they call out, "Hey, Teach'!"? Or is it equivalent to "Maestro!"? Similarly, consider the white teacher's reactions in a Negro junior high school to the postures of the children. What these state is not what the teacher observes. The sidesway in Negro boys that teachers sense as aggressive braggadocio is more a dance than a swagger. Hendrix says that "kinesics," or body-movement, affects the teaching of mathematics, an almost incredible statement, but only to those with little experience in the interchange of mathematics classrooms. (17) How the teacher moves about the classroom and the gestures that accompany what she says are of supreme importance, whether in poetry or in the teaching of geometry, because she is sending messages by body movement, ceaselessly, and these may be misinterpreted just as she may misinterpret the sidesway in a Negro boy's walk.

White leadership must remember these things. It must not misinterpret the Negro's need to lead, nor to replace the white, no matter how liberal, because liberalism has its own patterns of misinterpretation.

Replacing militancy against persons by militancy against

things and problems becomes more possible with industrialization, which brings a greater, though not total, measure of reason and logic into the social relations of men, with always a residue of madness even in the most soundly ordered governments.

The explosion of knowledge causes an explosion of problems, and only an educational explosion can solve these new problems. Shortages of schools and teachers shortchange every section of every society, guaranteeing local and international neurosis and irrationality unless suitable educational investment is brought to bear on the primitiveness in and around us, through the social energy symbolized by money.

These are brave words, but how do you get this militance toward educational problems without a suitable corps of teachers?

5

The Teacher

Teachers are at a low level of prestige compared to physicians, engineers, editors, physicists, or business executives, and most of them lack the qualities needed to educate the new populations in our cities. Teachers are not scholars or leaders; they are not even conspicuous in their communities. The scholar heads for the university, the potential leader for some bureaucracy in the NEA or state educational administration or educational politics; the teacher conspicuous for anything other than conformity has risky community status.

Education has a reversible pecking order, with teachers on the receiving end in educational policy and major educational decisions and on the dispensing end in job security and tenure. In this situation teachers are discharged for communism, atheism, rape, arson, adultery, and smoking, but virtually never because they are poor teachers. Poor classroom performance or other incompetence is never a hire or fire criterion, perhaps because teachers continue in short supply, but more probably because teacher evaluation techniques are loose, making it unhandy and uncomfortable for administrators to prefer charges against incompetents. As society tolerates incompetent ministers, physicians, scientists, plumbers, and politicians, so it accepts bad teachers, the only possible rationale being a hope that children will outgrow the effects of the bad teacher but retain the beneficial effects of the infrequent good teacher.

But accurate measures of teacher performance still evade us. Though we can distinguish the excellent teacher from the mediocre one, how do we measure the distinction? We can easily count the number of children reciting or the hands that go up, but not how the teacher brings the children into the lesson, the class tempo, or the spark in the teacher, all of which are there—but to what extent? We must avoid the meretricious metric, or some new measurement, of which there are many.

Evaluating the Teacher

Perhaps one overlooked indicator of teacher quality is organizational involvement outside of school, rather than classroom performance. When teacher evaluation procedures concentrate on classroom performance, they are unilluminating, since they neglect the teacher outside the classroom and ignore professional contacts and activities. No objective assessment of classroom performance has yet been attained by any of the supervisory tools available because they do not provide assessment of the teacher's professional after-school commitments. For example, teachers resist professional organization either from the right or the left. The clubby National Education Association is better than no teacher organization at all, because teachers have less sense of organization than Hoffa's teamsters, Anastasia's longshoremen, or the American Medical Association. The enormous membership rolls of NEA arise less from teacher willingness to join than from the sophisticated group sense of principals, supervisors, and administrators—perhaps the only case in American organizational history where a superordinate compels a subordinate to become organized. This situation is reflected in the weakness of NEA lobbying activities; for all the NEA's large membership, it swings surprisingly little weight in getting legislation through. Nevertheless, it has exposed teachers to possibilities in organization, thereby partially contributing to any successes its organizational rival, the American Federation of Teachers, is having. (1)

Undoubtedly, superior teachers may have weak or no organizational affiliations and professional commitments going no further than the classroom, but these teachers are rare. Most superior teachers have professional affiliations and work at them, as do would-be bureaucrats, careerists, and apple-polishers on the make, which does not invalidate the opportunities for the infrequent teacher with some capacity for leadership.

The usual teacher is obedient to the hierarchy. She does as she is told, though she has her own ways of covering her tracks and her incapacities when challenges come over the horizon, and here she may show great wisdom in handling administrative pursuit of the new and the fashionably experimental. Administrators often perceive public relations and promotional possibilities in new educational techniques, irrespective of their merit. For example, latching on to urban education is interpreted by school boards as being on the ball, proving that legitimate problems can be an opportunity for getting into the current swim.

The Urban Teacher: What We Have and What We Need

The usual teacher can do a satisfactory, and infrequently a superb, job with the middle-class student, but is disinclined to deal with the lower-class urban pupil. This teacher is apprehensive of these products of sociopathology and certainly has not been trained to teach them. But aside from teacher incapacity and lack of preparation, the contemporary classroom cannot set aright what has been deformed in home, family, neighborhood, and community so long as the social energy symbolized by financial investment is withheld from such classrooms and such children; meanwhile, it's no sin for a teacher to be unhappy with such children. (2)

We have, until recently, been doing passably well with such teachers, having a literate population, a highly productive economy, a responsible citizenry, more automobiles than parking space, more concern with obesity than with starvation, our share of scientists, and an adequate portion of artists. Most of us can read and compute. In some areas where we have done better than any nation in history, we should thank American education and the American teacher. For most of our shortcomings, the American family bears greater culpability than the American teacher, as we said above.

But today our urban Negroes and Puerto Ricans, our rural Appalachian whites, and the other dispossessed, to be educated at all require a tougher, more challengeable, less docile teacher, who has enough drive to withstand the tempting rewards of business or other careers, and who becomes a teacher despite the nine-to-three classroom day, the five-day-week, the forty-week-year, or the routinized life. There are hardly any such. People with these qualities seek a good income and professional growth and career possibilities in which they can help set policies, formulate decisions, and above all capitalize on their leadership potential. (3) They do not see these opportunities in teaching, because they confuse teaching with education. Teaching and education are not synonymous, as we shall discover. Meanwhile, urban education, to get anywhere, must snare this candidate, by persuading him that teaching—that portal to education—offers horizons as wide as business, problems as intricately interesting as science, the status of the professions, and income and financial opportunities that compare favorably with most executive and management emoluments, plus a bonus of virtually no competition for any of these plums. Just a step beyond the classroom are supervisory posts and principalships, another step and we are in the realm of superintendencies, after which appear college appointments, and consultancies at home and abroad in government and industry, with an enormous range of collateral specialties.

These "plums" are not bait to trap the unwary young person and divert him from a more meaningful career; they represent a power vacuum into which the young person with brains and initiative can move, without burying daggers into the shoulders over which he climbs, because the need is great and the competition non-existent. Simultaneously, back in the classroom, another alert, capable young person will get a professional bang out of team teaching, programed techniques, audio-visual aids, closed-circuit television, and the numerous research problems that beg for experimentation. (4) We do not mention love for the young as a quality in these candidates because, as Bettelheim (5) says, love is not enough and must be supplemented by an interest in the young. Nor will interest suffice; it must be supplemented by the personal force and personal needs that make love and interest less a self-indulgence than a means to self-expression.

Such candidates are rare. Our bait is not tempting to the usual teacher, who resents additional responsibilities and seeks no positions of leadership, but rather wants some anonymous rut where thought is organized for him and his classroom day regulated. He flees from initiative and creativity. He wants as much money as he can get for his limited talents, and wants children to teach who are as well ordered as he is.

Chiefly he wants tenure, with the less desirable of its two faces. Tenure can soothe the teacher into a rut, or it can free him from piddling, nibbling financial cares so that he can forge ahead toward new professional horizons. Unfortunately, too many teachers select the rut rather than the thrust forward. Tenure is the teacher's opportunity to stop worrying about job security and start thinking about professional growth. Every teacher should enjoy tenure, but far too many exploit it. They should be penalized—not through tenure practices, but through increment and promotion policies.

A new teacher, idealistically content to remain in the classroom all his life, is prepared in the recently organized fifth year and Master of Arts in Teaching programs, which turn out teachers of fine background and morale for upper- and middle-class children. These programs scrutinize their candidates carefully and prepare them conscientiously, using experienced cooperating teachers in selected settings. (6)

These settings, or training arenas, are excellent for Ivy League graduates preparing to teach in Ivy League-type schools. Most fifth year and M.A.T. programs require above-average college records of their candidates, but unfortunately, candidates so qualified rarely opt for teaching, and until recently Harvard had to recruit intensively and solicit piteously to pick up enough candidates. This reluctance is easing, and the programs, at least at the moment of writing, get more candidates than before, so that the high school in the economically superior community will be less distressed by inferior teachers than it has been.

The fifth-year and M.A.T. programs, designed for the teacher shortage in better communities, have occasionally recruited by glib words, but have been able to deliver actualities, because most graduates, persuaded into teaching, have thereafter found rewarding teaching posts in good communities, at good salaries, with good prospects, teaching "good kids." Few such candidates ever teach in deprived communities, because they are trained for and channeled into the community that can pay. Most teachers, in any case, avoid the poor community even when it pays as well as the wealthy community, as in New York City, where most teachers avoid Harlem.

Teacher Training versus Urban Education

But the problem of teacher recruitment in adequate quantity and quality is matched by the problem of teacher training. On this much has been written, usually in excoriation. (7)

Presumably, the variety of educational, social, and regional backgrounds in teaching candidates dictates a variety of training programs. The candidate from a mediocre southern denominational institution, barely maintaining accreditation, who intends to teach elementary school, and the hand-picked Ivy League graduate in the Harvard M.A.T. program who will teach in Winnetka cannot be identically prepared.

Nor will either type of teacher preparation do for the third type of candidate, so badly needed: the tougher, more challengeable, less docile candidate who usually avoids teaching and its routinized life. When, by some fluke, we lure him into education, how shall we revise our preparation, keeping his quality and scarcity in mind?

Medicine and engineering have curriculums that, reflecting the generally high level of candidates, do not vary too much regionally or quantitatively, despite grand denials by M.I.T. *vis à vis* Caltech, or Columbia's College of Physicians and Surgeons *vis à vis* Western Reserve's medical program. When, as in teaching, the highly able are attracted in smaller proportions than needed, and the least able in greater proportions than desired, giving scarcity of quality and excess of mediocrity, educational preparation cannot be as uniform as medical and engineering preparation. Teaching preparation at its best is rare, and the usual pap is too usual.

But is teaching teachable? Can you teach teachers teaching? Is what's taught learned? Can teaching be taught to the bright student? Can it be taught to the average student? Gilbert Highet will say that teaching is not a science but an art, and therefore cannot be taught, because the teacher is born, not made. (8) If so, can the arts be taught? Well, Beethoven had teachers and so had

Raphael. Beethoven didn't need a teacher to be Beethoven, but he did to learn counterpoint and piano, and Raphael to learn perspective, and how to mix paints, and the chemistry of pigments.

Indeed, virtually all artists and musicians have had formal instruction, the poor ones and the great ones, which made the poor ones less poor and usually—not always—accelerated the development of the great ones. Similarly, few writers, novelists, essayists, poets, playwrights, of any distinction whatever, escaped instruction in literature at school. But as for teacher training, how can the teacher learn to ask questions? Their effectiveness is of paramount importance, whether in a courtroom cross-examination or in a classroom discussion. Thus Hendrix, in discussing the teaching of mathematics, says:

> The teaching of pedagogy has been limited to things that are comparatively trivial and superficial in the past; when it comes to actual teaching, the really important things have been relegated to an intangible called "teacher personality." Now, as we study films and work with them, we can see that many of these things that have been considered unmanageable in the teaching of pedagogy, because they were parts of teacher personality, are really paralinguistic and kinesic. (9)

Hence choreography and body movement, gesture, and voice quality affect the program of educational preparation. Why not? Don't they affect the quality of acting and ballet? One study of family interactions among the poor has shown that the need for symbolic transactions between parent and child is as important as economic transactions. (10) Children can be conscientiously provided for and physically cared for, so that they do not go hungry, but unless the parent knows how to communicate love, the relationship falls apart. Similarly, when children call out answers without being called on, they may feel that they are flattering the teacher and symbolizing their attentiveness; they do not construe such yelling out as disruptive to class management. (11)

The Inter-disciplinary War

This brings us to the battle on educational preparation and education courses.

To begin with, the behavioral sciences emerge when education is democratized and freely available. Education courses then move into their slots, to the dismay of the House of Intellect. Aggressiveness against education attacks the terminology of education, which a classicist like Barzun and a journalist like Fred Hechinger call inflated. Barzun, Hechinger, Rickover, and others of intellectual respectability use simple, straightforward English to show it can be done. Because educational jargon is a weakness in the defense system of the behavioral sciences, critics of education attack it. (12) Educators are usually not angry men, so that when Hechinger pokes away at the trade lingo called "pedagese," they are too much in retreat to attack "journalese." Because educational editors are repetitious and since newspaper columns must be filled day-in and day-out, even if nothing is new, topics recur and are chewed over and over again, making education news columns bottomless pits.

However, aggressiveness against terminology and methodology slyly edges over to the place of education and the behavioral sciences in the academic scheme of things, like department control. Thus aggressiveness against things transmutes into aggressiveness against persons, and simple, straightforward English becomes a vehicle for attack on behavioral scientists in general and professors of education in particular, who, the claims go, have no merit, whose content is pretentious, whose teaching is poor, and whose challenge is inferior. The defense of the behavioral scientists is not appropriate here, but the defense of education professors is, and as in any good defense, an understanding of the aggressor is necessary.

First, the possession of a Ph.D. can mean being either an expert or a scholar; these are not identical. Disputes on desertion of the classroom by the college professor illustrate this difference. (13) The pursuit of research and scholarship, supported by government grant, causes abandonment of the classroom, leaving it in possession of the expert, who knows what is going on but who is not pushing back the so-called "frontiers of knowledge," which are sometimes the backwoods.

Second, the all-university approach to teacher education is undercut by the reluctance of other college departments to play footsie with departments of education for one uncomplicated reason—the other departments do not know beans about elementary, junior high, or senior high classrooms, do not want to find out, and want very much to back away from contamination by the public school system. (14) Theirs is a world of scholarship and research, not education. With some exceptions, the usual college English faculty does not know how to prepare teachers for the high school English class, nor the usual college mathematics faculty how to prepare high school teachers of mathematics. Offer most college faculty members an opportunity to observe actual teaching in the high schools and these faculties will pick up their skirts and run for their lives, preferring to snipe at education faculties from the safety of committee meetings or from the smoky gossip of faculty dining rooms. They claim, "Einstein could not get a license to teach mathematics in the high school system." Of course not, because he would do a terrible job, as would most college professors, if put in any public school whatever.

Third, professors of liberal arts are not artists. Professors of English are rarely poets, novelists, or playwrights; professors of history infect the past with themselves and admit it cannot be otherwise; professors of science repel more students than they attract; professors of classics have been the chief reason why fewer students study Latin and Greek. (15) In brief, most college graduates have not been liberalized by the liberal arts, and professors of education educate no more than other professors do.

Do they educate less? Inevitably. Other reasons will appear later, but the complex amorphousness of education, when teaching and classroom crises have a particularity that demands specific answers, is a major reason.

This disparity between specificity and amorphousness invites aggressiveness from the student of education, too, who resents the absence of short-order recipes and blueprints to classroom crises in college education courses. Nobody resents courses in English literature because they don't make a Milton or a Dickens out of you. Even in professional courses, the young attorney headed for real estate law takes dutiful notes in patent law. But the typical prospective teacher resists education courses sometimes because they are taught as vapidly as liberal arts courses *but more often because they fail to furnish a magic solvent to classroom problems.*

Unfortunately, courses in education are irreplaceable except in preparation for private school or parochial school teaching, where school-home relationships are unlike public school-home relationships. Inferior education courses are better than no education courses at all since, labored though they are, they warn the student that professionalism and an understanding of children are necessary. To liquidate education courses when society legislates education for all is impossible. You cannot operate a state system of society-wide education without education courses. Every country in the Western world that democratically offers educational opportunities to its population has teacher-training courses because it must regularize, or even bureaucratize, the channels between preparation and practice.

But nowhere in the world is teacher training treated with the scorn that it meets in the United States, so that any professional historian interested in the history of education, knowing that this specialization would assign him to the academic leper-colony known as a Department of Education, keeps his interest secret or avocational, to avoid teaching in this Siberia.

Physicians interested in the history of medicine, or attorneys in the history of jurisprudence, are not numerous, and few teachers are interested in the history, philosophy, psychology, or methods of education. But a special dullness attaches to education, arising not from the subject matter but from the people.

Most people in departments of education, whether professors or students, are inferior compared with people in other academic fields—simply because there are so many more of them. (16) According to figures from the Department of Health, Education and Welfare, one-sixth of all doctorates granted in 1963 were in education. They are less able *on the average* (note italics!), but people of high attainment are *as numerous* as in presumably more difficult disciplines, like mathematics or science. The *absolute number* of top-flight teachers is not fewer than the comparable number of top-flight attorneys, physicians, engineers, editors, or advertising executives. The absolute number of top-flight faculty members in college departments of education is similarly diluted. The faculty at much-maligned Teachers College over the past half-century easily has had as many distinguished members as any other Columbia University department, though bloated by so many mediocrities that the *average* is inevitably lower.

As larger numbers are admitted to schools of medicine, engineering, and law, these fields will also witness a drop in *average* quality, even though the *absolute number* of top-flight people remains constant. We shall have no fewer fine physicians, engineers, and attorneys than now, but surrounded by a larger proportion of mediocrities, they will follow in the way pioneered by departments of education, to the accompaniment of sideline noises from liberal articians.

This infusion need not be unsalutary if the mediocrity's role is defined, allowing more physicians to treat the ordinary illness, more engineers to do the routine work, and more attorneys to handle simple cases, just as it has meant more teachers to man classrooms of pupils presenting fewer problems. The addition of mediocrity, the dilution of quality, and the adulteration of the average offer vast new professional opportunities in leadership to the accomplished, top-flight person, allowing him more room to move around, and more lower-echelon people to put to work, thereby augmenting the scope the top-flight person needs if his profession is to remain healthy.

This opportunity for the meritorious person exists most obviously at present in teaching and education, but all the disciplines must face up to the oncoming accretion in numbers, the resulting degradation in average ability, and the reformulation of professional lines of command wherein quality rules the roost, lest social disaster result. Teaching is the prototype. In it we see the leadership vacuum generated by great numbers of mediocrities, and a warning that qualified leadership must be qualified by ability and nothing else, because the vacuum simultaneously spawns timeservers, hacks, and bureaucrats.

Therefore preparation for teaching should not be confused with training for educational leadership, nor should educational leadership be confused with educational bureaucracy. One measure of leadership is willingness to find the hard problem and come to grips with it. The hardest problem in urban education is education of the Negro and other deprived minorities, so the true educational leader will zero in on it—while the bureaucrat will flee it. Thus the preparation of education leaders will reshape education courses accordingly.

Teacher training institutions, like all collegiate institutions, usually are demure, shy, and even in default on their public responsibility to clarify issues and policies. Consider the muteness of the teacher training institutions, public and private, when teachers strike, whether in New York or Utah. The silence is thunderous.

How We Should *Recruit*

In addition to the kind of people entering education, another matter sours the usual education course: the future polluting the present. Some students await teaching with anticipation, others with apprehension, affecting the present course like a pall. The dread in some, and the unrealistic superciliousness in others! In the same class, some are frightened months before they begin teaching, while others have the inflated assurance that comes from ignorance and are lavishly critical of teachers with decades of classroom experience, feeling they could do better without any preparation. Whether intimidated or inflated by overconfidence, both sorts take it out on education courses, which are not too often given by inspired instructors nor too often taken by career-inspired students. Let us turn our backs on these, the majority, and consider the minority whom urban education so badly needs, who anticipate the hard problem with relish and who see in challenge the seed-bed of professional expression. We shall develop for these candidates education courses rich in crisis and climax, because the issues in education, given a competent instructor, are as dramatic as literature, as esthetic as mathematics, and as exciting as art.

How shall we recruit these candidates with go, these oases in the desert, who do not want to be stultified by education courses, who have the quality that urban education requires and can give it the leadership it needs? They must:

First, be dissuaded from other careers. There is more joy, more bounce, and more blast in urban education.

Second, be promised compensation adequate to their ability. They should be able to travel, dress in style, trade in cars with reasonable frequency, buy paintings, records, and books, and maintain their families in comfort and without pinch.

Third, be granted freedom from bureaucracy. W. C. Fields said it before Flannery O'Connor: "A good man is hard to find." But the good man can handle the bureaucrat and turn bureaucracy to his account. That's one of the reasons he is a good man.

Fourth, learn that contacts with children will not reduce them (the teaching candidates) to childishness, a real source of concern to anybody who has observed teachers with years of experience.

Childishness ultimately rubs off on the adult, unless the adult maintains adult contacts and interests.

Fifth, envisage that urban education expands their possibilities and creative opportunities because urban education encompasses the major problems of our times, from non-representational art, to computer design, to urban planning, to labor productivity, to leisure and play.

These candidates will work in our large cities, where modern culture reaches its highest levels of humanity and is balanced by the deepest hate and primitive savagery. Their lives will not be placid, but as demanding as any business executive's and as constructive as any professional man's.

This candidate's career is what he chooses to make it, with Negro, Puerto-Rican, and Appalachian children, but also with politicians, urban planners, corporate heads, and academics. He need never be meek or complaisant and, given a sense of mission, can be as much of a hellraiser as circumstances justify. He will stand up to principals, supervisors, and school boards, because another and better job always beckons. Education has openings for a hundred thousand of him in our major cities, in Africa and Latin America, in government service, or in industrial training. (17)

Unfortunately, and usually, he doesn't know of the prospects in education and, when you spot him, he tells you that he would rather die than teach because he is bright enough to know that teacher needs are not the same as the need for teachers. He wants to be working with tough-minded people, but we can reassure him—teachers are becoming tough-minded in our large cities and, though not as effectively organized as Hoffa's teamsters, are edging that way. Like Negroes, teachers are gaining greater organizational sense, strength, and self-respect. Correspondingly, their need to avoid the crucial diminishes, as a taste of organization leaves them hungry for more in New York, Detroit, Chicago, and Utah. (18)

That organized teacher militancy and organized Negro militancy in our large cities emerge simultaneously is no coincidence. We can go no further unless we educate. Investing mechanisms like GATT, the Alliance for Progress, AID, and the Bank for International Settlements are slowed by educational inadequacy rather than by any shortage of investment opportunities in Africa, Asia, and Latin America. (19) As society once clamored for raw materials, it now clamors for educated personnel, putting teachers astride the bottleneck of the educational flow and making them more decisive a social force than they have ever been. Organized teacher militancy is the consequence.

This setting and these perspectives allow us to recruit with greater effectiveness that candidate of whom urban education is in such need.

6

The Curriculum

Education courses talk ponderously of relating curriculum to community needs, of the distortion of community needs by curriculum, and of their accurate reflection in curriculum. What of these relationships and reflections in the Negro community specifically and the urban community generally?

Where the deserting father is a commonplace, as are narcotics addiction, alcoholism, and gambling, and where sexual irresponsibility begins in early adolescence, will you reflect these in the curriculum? And if not, how realistic and honest a curriculum do you have? How much sense will curriculum make to pupils if dope pushing, drunkenness, and numbers-running are discreetly skirted? You have no choice. You must build these untidy matters into the curriculum, and do so constructively, and not as you do in the middle-class school, else you substitute cream puffs for nutrition, and pedantry supplants programs, as in Sylvia Ashton-Warner's Maori children. (1)

A second unhandy curricular matter is the inner pace of child growth, the readiness for reading at one age level, of socialized play at another, and of ethical values at still another. But the Negro child, in whom these maturational stages are reversed, has social sense its first day in school to know itself Negro, white teachers stronger and more powerful than its parents, and that the white face will love you until your genitals appear and then will flee, because sexual maturation is a declaration of war. How can this be reflected in the curriculum?

Also, in what sequence should we introduce art, science, mathematics, social studies, and language? Although vested interests are represented in this debate, compartmentalization is to be avoided. Mathematics can begin with art, and social studies with mathematics, and so all priorities in the order of presentation should also be avoided, despite the objections of teachers in special methods.

A third item is the articulation and logical development of the subject areas, with progressive complexity and difficulty. But suppose every increase of complexity, difficulty, and profundity draws open a curtain that reveals pointlessness, heartbreak, and rejection, when you find that you are not well received in *Tom Sawyer* or *Huckleberry Finn*, and the hurt is greater because you love the books so, or that cowboys are white, as are all Pilgrim Fathers, signers of the Declaration of Independence, Presidents of the United States, and winners of the West? The repetition of white in all the books, contrasted with the repetition of black all around you, makes you freeze into indifference when the unrelated repetition of the multiplication tables comes your way.

Furthermore, should curriculum build a strong father image in the absence of a father? If many Negroes distrust one another and refuse to depend on one another, something far more deleterious than any mistrust of whites, weak father image sparks the mutual suspicion that enfeebles trust and group action. However, the glorious August 28, 1963, March on Washington was major evidence that Negroes could act together, that the different strata from which NAACP and CORE draw their membership could unite on a common program—just as Jews, formerly split among German, Polish, and Russian Jew, could come together and act jointly. Nevertheless, Negro distrust of Negro continues to be more damaging than distrust of whites, and requires considering in the realistic and honest curriculum.

Murder must also be included in the curriculum, especially the murder conducted under social auspices, the murder arising from machinery. Hand-made murder is familiar enough, but machinery also kills whoever sets himself against it.

Scientists and mathematicians wonder if automated machines

think. Need they, when men think frantically for them? A machine's simply being there causes thinking and action. Therefore, the honest and realistic curriculum must recognize that the machine needs no untrained Negroes. Negroes must make themselves important to the machine; if not, they perish. Thus we can say that murder should be included in the curriculum.

In this murder by machine the first casualties will be those easily picked off, like the uneducated and those whose sense of unimportance shows in reluctance to join with other men, as in Negro-Negro distrust caused by weak father image.

Curriculums encourage strong father images through courses like "Citizenship Education" or "Problems in American Democracy" which work only when reality doesn't contradict curriculum, and it does almost always in Negro society. For the father image to enrich reality and not contradict it, curriculum must first grant the child's evidence that the father is weak. The evidence cannot be ducked. Nevertheless and somehow, the curriculum must restore adequacy to the father. This means that you begin with the facts. One fact is unhappiness, another is inadequacy, and a third is discontent. Their opposites—happiness, adequacy, and content— are in the usual curriculum for the usual child, but where the unusual child becomes more and more the rule in our urban schools, the curriculum must develop unusual materials too. We cannot do so simply by putting Dick and Jane into blackface, or applying burnt cork to American history.

Instead, we must build a curriculum that transforms lack into possession, not only by showing a recognizably dirty neighborhood, but how to change it to a clean one, or why some people prefer it dirty; not only by showing conniving and honest merchants, but how to count change and read package labels; not only by phonics, but how teeth, lips, tongue, and throat make *man* distinguishable from *mad*. We must show how the rote drill of multiplication and spelling makes you more at peace with yourself; how society means conflict, and how force is used and controlled; how democracy is not always a sweet-running, placid flow, but lobbies, pressure groups, filibustering, and people who hate you; how poets and novelists know more about you than you know about yourself; how algebra and geometry don't train your mind but train your imagination, and why they hurt and are hard.

One way of doing this is to let in the world outside the school.

There is no problem about getting individuals and groups (doctors, politicians, food merchants; NAACP, CORE, the Urban League, The New York Times) either to come to the school or to act as hosts to school groups. The reason is simple: they have an axe to grind. The axe may be increased circulation, or votes, or contributions, good will, or customers. Is the school a legitimate place for axe grinding? Or course, provided that all axes get equal time for grinding, if spokesmen for labor and capital, for banks and borrowers, for landlords and tenants, for the left of center and right of center use the curriculum as it should be used: as a forum for debate.

Note that these are dichotomizations, the kind of debatable dichotomizations that form the beginning of the cooperation-competition-leadership trinity that leads to the individualization of instruction, because issues and critical matters arise and the germination of opinions is encouraged (see p. 96).

Such a curriculum is important partly because it helps people think, but more because it helps people to *be,* thus avoiding being murdered by the presence of the machine. (2)

But not all Negro fathers have deserted nor are all weak father images; many participate in organizations, have skills, maintain their homes, and take time with their families. Children from both types of father image will be sitting in the same classroom, which brings us to team learning (as contrasted with team teaching), and the contribution to the curriculum and team learning of the father who has fled because he cannot otherwise retain his masculinity, who was not born inadequate but made so; understanding of the emasculated father restores masculinity to the father and imparts adequacy to the child. Should this be part of the education of the Negro child from the stable home? Does it not reapply the hobbles when devoted and interested Negro parents have removed them? Or does it, rather, remove the hobbles that parents in their misdirected devotion and interest have applied? Curriculum must not debilitate but strengthen. Thus, if the slum child is "tough" in answer to deprivations and if the father, by flight, gains a spurious masculinity, and if toughness restores integrity to the deserted child, then the curriculum must transform such blind aggression and pointless pugnacity to the integrity both child and curriculum seek, and must provide socially sanctioned auspices— the classroom, chiefly—where toughness is examined and transformed by the appropriate use of curricular materials. Indeed, we want toughness in our children, but not cruelty. Rather, we need the voluntaristic toughness developed by competitiveness that leads to cooperation. Curriculum usually deplores competitiveness because of the effect on the loser, which speaks well for our kindness and good intentions, but defeat can lose much sting, with no loss of energy and drive, by imbedding competitiveness in a matrix of cooperation, where one prepares and plans for further conflict and competition. Thereby cooperation and competition, like victory and defeat, become part of stock-taking, resource-seeking, and an improvement process in which the ingredients are understood, tallied, and talked over, so that victory is intensified through the group and defeat diffused over it. Furthermore, the cooperation-competition aspects of team learning must provide for the development of leadership qualities, in the variety of forms that leadership takes.

The experiences of the lower-class child lead to a curriculum as probing, as challenging, and as dynamic as middle-class experiences offer. Similarly, the slow student needs to feel that he is following the same curriculum as other students, that he is reading and studying the same material, and that nothing is being watered down for him—slowed down yes, but not watered down. He wants no alteration in the curriculum for his sake, although he is willing to have the tempo altered. (3)

Merchandising Educational Materials and Techniques

Then how can the teacher prepare materials for the slow student when the professionals have not yet learned to do so? Most teachers are certainly less skilled than textbook writers in materials-preparation, and textbook writers, the evidence shows, are extensively inadequate. Luckily, materials may not be the answer we seek, not even in reading programs, where they are heavily stressed. Instead, we need situations, questions, and contexts for classroom discussion and out-of-class experiences. Materials come later—they are not prior. Our latest hotshot, programed instruction, has fewest materials of all and the least effective ones, despite the noise. (4)

Teachers College is one of the merchandisers in the educational style and fashion industry. Fashions in curriculum, administration, testing, reading, school organization, that have invaded and then retreated from Teachers College, as educational promoter has succeeded educational promoter, are all analogous to the Paris coutourière with a new line each year, whose merchandise must reach all the continents. So Teachers College moves its merchandise in faraway Afghanistan, Nigeria, and Knoxville, and until recently, despite its Metropolitan School Study Council, knew nothing about New York City and less than nothing about Harlem, on the edge of which it sits.

Other educational wholesalers, like the Ford Fund, have talked up team teaching, that active item in pedagogical merchandising which is not without merit: Teachers are no longer alone with children, they have another adult around to talk to, and the perils of slipping into childishness—that great danger when you are alone with children—are reduced. Interestingly, under team teaching disciplinary problems are diminished. One teacher with thirty-five pupils has more trouble than two with seventy or three with a hundred, because each teacher gains authority from the presence of the other, which is why the auditorium on assembly day offers fewer disciplinary headaches than the classroom. Back to back, like a British square, even two teachers in a play yard can fight off vastly superior numbers, in what psychologists call mutual reinforcement, since physical and visual contact with another adult is reassuring.

Incidentally, though team teaching can be a device to overload class size, its greatest danger is the stress on material-presentation rather than on material-absorption. Unless team teaching gets teachers to prepare more conscientiously, it will be worthless. Students, not teachers, must learn and work better as a result of it. (5)

On the other hand, team teachers must learn not to be touchy when observed. Teachers dislike surveillance, no matter how innocuous the onlooker. They submit uneasily to periodical observation by supervisors and administrators because contracts require it, but they show the same uneasiness in demonstration lessons and organized visits when they are observed not by superiors with rating pads in their hands, but by colleagues who are there presumably to learn how they teach their best lessons.

Even more strange is teacher behavior when their inferiors, like student teachers, are sent in to observe. Most student teachers are college seniors. They have no standing in the school except as visitors, yet student teachers are not effusively welcomed in most schools even though they are free manpower to the overworked teacher, who can put them to work on classroom tutoring, on the grading of tests and examinations, on clerical routines, and on classroom teaching itself, thus removing many burdens from the teacher in her day-to-day tasks. Nevertheless most teachers are reluctant to pay the price—this additional manpower is there to observe them teach, and they are reluctant to be observed even by an inferior. Nobody can be lower on the educational totem pole than the student teacher, but even this ineffectual, non-threatening witness is suspected, so that most colleges must offer stipends or free tuition to classroom teachers accepting student observers or student teachers in their classrooms, to reduce the paranoia.

This skittishness of teachers is unique among the professions and arts. A physician on rounds, followed by internes, is deliberately putting himself and his skills on parade so that younger people can learn. Though the apprentice sometimes pays the master, the master, paid or not, does not usually flee opportunities to demonstrate his mastery—but the classroom teacher does.

For team teaching to be successful, two pieces of underbrush must therefore be cleared away: first, the presence of the other teacher must not be needed merely for classroom control; second, the teacher must not fear observation.

Team Learning

However, our concern here is not team teaching, but team learning. If team teaching as described by the Ford Fund has much to recommend it, team learning has far greater possibilities. (6) Much of the remainder of this chapter is devoted to team learning; some preliminary considerations are presented here as scaffolding for the structure we are about to erect.

First, a team is usually organized to compete. It competes most effectively by imposing defeat on an adversary. To assure victory, it must train together, with all the team members cooperating. Competition and cooperation are therefore two characteristics of teamwork and of team learning.

Second, this competition-cooperation matrix requires direction, and hence leadership. Teams usually have captains, those individuals whose superior capacity allows them privileges that other team members do not enjoy; attempts at leadership can cause intra-group competition, just as the attempt at victory causes intergroup competition.

Third, team activity is highly involving and motivating, explaining the tight control the athletic coach has over the team. Even when learning outcomes are puerile, as in the classroom spelling bee, team activity continues to be involving and motivating because *team learning hits at the emotions as well as at the intellect.* Consequences in morale are immediate.

Team learning has within itself the possibilities of digging up the ultimate reason for all learning, the emotive rewards that are too frequently overlooked in the usual, fact-oriented classroom. Whatever their subject matter, materials are never purely rote—whether in spelling or the multiplication table, a historical date, a chemical formula, a theorem, or a declension—but are accompanied by rewards, punishments, an esthetic sense, or an insight. No fact is ever learned, nor is any learning ever rejected, without accompanying emotion.

In team learning, emotion is not merely an accompaniment, but a dominant motif, because competition-cooperation-leadership require the need to achieve victory and avoid defeat, via a baseball, basketball, football, a spelling word, a topic in debate, or a problem. The problem, the unanswered question, is implicit in all group processes, and not less so in team learning. However, unlike a baseball, a basketball, or a football, a problem is not a clear-cut entity readily tossed or kicked around without preliminary formulation.

The formulation is best put in the form of a question, and addressed to the student by himself, after prior clarification by the teacher, who requires intensive training in the techniques of problem setting or question posing. No aspect of the curriculum is more important.

Batting and Fielding Questions in Team Learning

We shall first consider this basic matter and then return to team learning. Our discussion will be chiefly on English, but will have relevance to other curricular areas.

Nothing is harder than asking a good question, as scientists know, and nobody more offhand about it than the usual teacher. Questions can be wise or foolish, like the five wise virgins and the five foolish ones in Matthew 25:1–12, where the wise ones were prepared with the proper materials, but the foolish ones were not. Similarly, wise questions differ from foolish ones in forethought and preparation. Even computers recognize foolish questions, which just heat the equipment. (7)

Though the good question is hard to develop, once developed it is a tremendously effective teaching weapon. Socrates raised questions to elicit statements. Jesus made statements, in his parables, that elicited questions. Both are sound teaching methods because questions are involved. Most teachers talk too much. How rare the teacher who asks rather than says!

Asking assumes an answer, so the teacher should only ask questions that get answered, but the answers need not be in agreement. Indeed, good questions can generate difference in opinions, even contention in opinions. But, as happens so frequently, suppose the student hasn't done his work? How then can he answer, correctly or not?

The word "correctly" implies another kind of question, irrelevant to this discussion, the fact question, which is a legitimate kind of question, but requires little thought in the teacher and a low-level dutifulness in response from the student. What teachers call, technically, the *judgment,* or *thought,* or *pivotal* question is another matter, requiring enormously more preparation in the teacher-interlocutor than in the student-respondent, provided that it is a good question.

To make such questions good, the teacher must have faith in students, knowing that students are less stupid than the teacher thinks they are, and less stupid than they think they are, and that even stupid sudents like to think. A good thought question shows faith in the pupil's willingness to think, whether he is bright or stupid.

Too, a good question is troublesome and not readily answered. The poor teacher seeks answers, any answers, to fill the vacuum, but the wise teacher strolls, and does not rush, toward answers. A good question does not present obvious solutions. If any good, it's hard; and if hard, it requires time and working over and sniffing into and walking around, which make it fun.

Next, the good question has pace and is presented thoughtfully, not hastily, with time given for its consideration, lest it be cheapened and degraded. A top-sergeant type of teacher, in this writer's hearing, asked a class about *The Odyssey,* snap-crackle-pop: "What do we know about Ulysses?" The answer: "It took him ten years to get home." Such inept questions are being put every day about Sydney Carton, Per Hansa, Holden Caulfield, and other figures in narrative fiction. The answer is low-level because the question is, but the question is low-level because it isn't interesting, while risk is and *The Odyssey* deals with risk. Ulysses risked his life to get home. To illustrate further, another interesting issue for questioning and discussion in *The Odyssey* is how the past fits us for the present. If we learn about our parents, their lives, their experiences, does that help us learn about ourselves? Or isn't it any help at all? What of learning about our grandparents? Our great-grandparents? As we go further back into the lives of our remote ancestors, are we crippled and limited by this knowledge, or helped by it? Is this knowledge appropriate or inappropriate to the twentieth century? Do we need this perspective in our lives, or is it hampering when we want to go off to the moon or interstellar space? Will the feelings of Ulysses when he voyaged to the Cimmerian darkness, west of the Hesperides, be like the feelings of our astronauts? Was Ulysses the better or the worse king of Ithaca because he had been to Troy, the Nile, and elsewhere? Will the men who return from interstellar space be fitted or unfitted for life on Earth, because of their experiences?

On Gray's *Elegy Written in a Country Churchyard,* and the lines "Perhaps in this neglected spot is laid/ Some heart once pregnant with celestial fire," a beginning teacher asked for an explanation of the second line and got, "He had heartburn," another addition to the infinite anthology of student howlers, but didn't the inexperienced teacher set the context by a vague question? (8) With the same material, if *pregnant* means "having a baby," does it mean this too? When a woman is having a baby, does she feel heavy and sad, or gay and light? When students answer, as we can anticipate, "It depends," the teacher must pursue the analysis, which in poetry goes deep, and beg for questions that are more rewarding the deeper they go. Of course "It depends," but on what? If a man's heart has such celestial or heavenly fire, what is burning? Something he ate? Or thought? Or felt? Is his heart heavy and sad, or gay and light?

If Robert Frost says in "Stopping By Woods On A Snowy

Evening," "And miles to go before I sleep," and then repeats the same words, is the repetition an accident? If not, why is it there? Would the student read both lines at the same tempo? Would reading the lines at different tempos change the meaning? (8*a*)

Or the teacher—stupid teacher!—asks a pupil to define a noun, and the pupil-parrot answers, "A noun is a name of a person, place, or thing." But what is a name? And what is the naming process? Or the pupil defines, "A verb is an action word." But what is an action? Can a name become an action? Can an action become a name? If so, what are the circumstances? The circumstances are not only all around us, but are also the most fascinating part of grammar. Without curiosity and interest in the classes and in the materials she teaches, no teacher can ask a good question. "A sentence is a complete thought." But what, please, is a thought?

The better teacher will want to know what happened to the babies that Lady, Madam, or Mrs. Macbeth had given suck to, whether they died, disappeared, or why they never appear in the play. Shakespeare mentions them—where are they? Or the teacher may have curiosity and interest about why adolescents are so overwhelmingly servile to the opinions of their friends, and if this relates to their overwhelming hostility to the opinions of adults. Or about the lead sentence in that day's newspaper sports article— what are the nouns, verbs, adjectives, and adverbs in a sentence that the class has never seen before and that does *not* emerge from a workbook?

The teacher must have curiosity and interest about still subtler things when she asks a question and the entire class blurts out the answer in a chorus. Pandemonium and the disappearance of discipline. The teacher did something wrong. What was it? What was operating? How could that kind of question get that kind of result? But notice that the teacher is directing questions at herself, an important preliminary to directing questions at others.

Or, the opposite case, when the teacher asks a question, there is silence; then one hand arises, then another, then a third, eager to answer, but the teacher—wise teacher!—looks around, biding her time, keeping the class in a simmer, while she disregards the handwavers. And she's got the class in the palm of her hand as she's never had it before—why? The teacher must be curious and interested in this manifestation, and why it manifests itself, and the conditions under which it manifests itself.

Some years ago Professor Arthur Jersild (9) recommended the teaching of high school psychology courses. Rather than courses in psychology, we need teachers who sense the emotive values in literature, and the sociopsychological values in the social studies curriculum. Unquestionably, psychological growth ought to be a desideratum in the teaching of the humanities, but this growth will come from psychologically sensitive teachers and not from a psychologically oriented curriculum.

An old, old fable tells of a fleeing man pursued by a giant; to impede the giant's pursuit, the fleeing man throws stones behind him which become mountains, deep valleys, and rivers, which allow him to escape; the fable of Atalanta and the golden apples is a variant. But a more relevant variant is the teacher who, more subconsciously than consciously, perceives herself in flight from a pursuing, remorseless class of pupils. What does the teacher throw at the pursuers? Words, more words, and still more words, to keep a safe distance between her and the class. But suppose the teacher throws questions at the class, rather than words? What a difference in composure this indicates! The teacher who throws questions does not need to flee. That teacher is certain of herself.

Class management and discipline are thereby involved. The beginning teacher, uncertain how to manage a class, should develop the best thought-out thought questions she can and pivot her lesson development and planning on such questions.

For example, in correcting compositions the teacher encounters the sentence fragment, "When I came home." The teacher says, "That's an incomplete sentence because it's an incomplete thought." The pupil disagrees. How can the teacher prove it is? True, the teacher can add to it and complete the sentence. But the teacher can also complete the sentence by shortening it, by hacking off the initial adverb, and then ask students how we can complete things by shortening them, rather than by adding to them. Such questions involve our examining the way our minds work when we think. This isn't easy, but it isn't dull either. It's hard and simultaneously interesting, for stupid pupils too. And if teachers of the stupid disagree, it's because the stupid usually don't get top-flight teachers. So one must be careful about accepting the opinion of the usual teacher of the stupid child, who may not understand us when we say that ultimately the teacher wants the student to ask questions of himself. Thus, in teaching the topic sentence in paragraph construction, the teacher can assign a topic sentence for the pupil to expand, but how much better for the student to learn the techniques of self-questioning and thereby develop the topic sentence into a paragraph by learning how to ask questions of himself. This way he is not only developing topics and paragraphs, but also himself, his mind, and his possibilities.

The experienced teacher will recognize these as motivational techniques, so intimately related to good questioning techniques. But who is being motivated here—pupil or teacher? And can we really speak of pupil motivation without prior teacher motivation, and teachers who ask themselves—and motivate themselves—by these questions: What relevance does this material have to my students? What perceptions in them can be sharpened by it? Why should they be learning about it, or writing about it, or studying it? In brief, we cannot motivate a class without teachers who examine themselves and honestly figure out the appropriateness of materials before passing them along to the pupils for doing.

Good teachers don't expect prefabricated motivations—such as a humorous cartoon, or an anecdote, or a quotation, or some eye-ear-nose-throat device called audio-visual aids—to motivate spontaneously. They're not illegal, but they need supplementing— by questions. These synthesized motivations must be picked to convenient pieces, so they fit into the plans, into the assignment, and are converted from the *table d'hôte* to the *à la carte*. The most basic motivation of all is the good question, and the first person at whom it is directed is the teacher, who asks such things as: "Why should I assign it? Why should students write about it? Why should they learn it at all?"

Questions, when good, encourage division of opinion and disequilibrium. They don't pacify as much as they stimulate, but, in stimulating, they cause answers to emerge, and the emergence of answers exerts a pacifying influence, so that stimulation is followed by pacification—in a living, active, learning class.

Thus, the psychoanalyst doesn't tell, doesn't instruct, doesn't teach—he simply asks and lets the patient talk. And yet, from this relationship, emerges a power in the psychoanalyst as strong as the power of a mother over a child, a terribly dominating power, that—in the mechanism called, technically, *transference*—is almost hypnotic in the obedience, idealism, and worship that the patient begins to have for the analyst. All the analyst does, verbally at least, is ask questions. But they are astute questions, insightful ones, piercing ones—not polite or evasive ones. They cause pain, they unsettle the patient, they put him into disequilibrium.

Such questions cannot be asked in the classroom. They are inappropriate, but the teacher is nonetheless in a semi-transference situation. What pupils feel for parents, they will feel for the teacher. They may like her, loathe her, admire her, despise her—depending on how they feel about their parents. The teacher is (another technical term) a *parent-surrogate,* but not an ancillary parent. We don't require ancillary parents in the classroom, but the teacher cannot avoid being a parent-surrogate, because her students need her, more than they sometimes know. But simultaneously she needs them and their good opinion, more than she is often willing to admit, in another psychoanalytic mechanism called *counter-transference,* so effectively described in the late Robert Lindner's *The Fifty-minute Hour.* (10)

An abiding classroom problem is the student who doesn't do his homework. The teacher must use a question—a wise, thoughtful question—to drop an unsettled residue in the pupil's mind as he leaves the classroom, to stir up a disequilibrium that cannot be reduced to order without taking a peek at least at the homework. The wise teacher is in command of enormous resources to stir up such disequilibrium in the pupil's inner life by means of suspense, conflict, excitement, drama, and understanding. Therefore, teachers should not assign a chapter, or exercises, or problems, but an example of suspense and an instance of conflict, so that if there's a job advertised in today's newspaper or an issue prompting a letter to a congressman, the student learns how best to avoid sounding like a dope to a stranger. How does knowing the form of a business letter allow dissimulating of immaturity? How to be sure a job application is read, or the congressman answers so cordially the reply is a prized possession? And shouldn't classes know that congressmen reply to every letter they get? This further integrates the writing of the business letter with social studies.

Even spelling, though at first glance a matter of pure rote, can be put in a psychological setting, and the teacher can frame questions about who would make the better speller—a professional painter or a professional musician, the man who looks closely or the man who listens closely. Would the pupil learn the troublesome word by writing it over ten times, or spelling it aloud, or taking one really good look at it, staring at it, and then looking away and trying to get an after-image of it—like the after-image you sometimes get on a television tube—by making a picture of it in his mind, rather than a sound of it? Psychology calls these clear visual images *eidetic*. Does the pupil think himself more successful with spelling when he uses the motor approach of writing it ten times, the auricular approach of sounding it out, or the eidetic approach of seeing it? Or is it some combination of all three?

The biggest competition to reading is friends. Thus television is less competition than the need to socialize, so that the school reading assignment best competes by the reading the *teacher* has done. If pupils are to read, the teacher must read, and read alertly —the prerequisite to any reading program the school has. Thus the teacher can compete with the friends and gregariousness available outside the school. Generally, teachers are not interesting people, but dull and stodgy. Even more disturbing is their complacence and smugness about this, as if being interesting and fascinating comprise no part of their job description as teachers. How false they are to learning, which, properly taught, is mind-shaking and soul-shaking! Of course, teachers are not supposed to entertain or amuse, but instruct; they want sobriety in their classes, not giddiness, nor cheap thrills, nor a production for laughs; the classroom is not a fun thing. Nevertheless the classroom does require emotion, artistry, and intellectual challenge, and a good question does challenge.

Also, we want questions that question the questioner, and pupils who ask questions of people, of data, of experts, and of frauds. Questioning communism is so easy, so trite. Questioning democracy is much harder, and less comfortable, but how can pupils become truly loyal unless they do? Pupils ask about the "dead-versus-red" controversy, because they want answers and don't want forever to palter with the interrogative mood, which can become a vain exercise in dialectic and sophistry, when the serious matter of survival is involved. Questions should not be asked for kicks, but because we are on the prowl for answers, if available. Should you live on your knees, or die on your feet? Answers can come from Thoreau, the *Ninth Symphony,* Emily Dickinson, Walt Whitman, and Dostoevsky. If Teller has one opinion and Szilard another, perhaps no answers are possible, just opinions. Therefore, let the teacher be hospitable when students give opinions and not reprimand them for not giving answers.

If most questions are poor, we need not be pessimistic. Most things are—most poetry, most fiction, most painting, most music, and most teachers. So things go.

Experienced teachers will testify to most success in handling classroom misbehavior when they have looked a look of inquiry, without saying anything, because such looks embody questions and not accusations. They have been least successful when they have accused rather than asked with a wordless and soundless look; and they will additionally testify that they have sometimes regressed to the foolishness of saying, rather than asking, and persisted in foolishness when they knew better. But so does everybody.

Nuclear warfare, classroom misbehavior, the first act of *The Glass Menagerie,* sentence diagraming, how to multiply and divide, and why Swedes and Jews eat herring are the soil in which the teacher's questions grow; if most of them are foolish questions, that's not fatal. What will carry the day for the teacher, the pupil, and everybody is the resistance to easy answers and easy statements, and persistence in trying to find out. They'll win if they avoid the easy, glib statement and seek the tough, hard question.

In brief, poetry, philosophy, and psychological research agree here, where they otherwise rarely agree, that students, even slum students, have a well-stocked armamentarium that equips them to face up to thought questions. Something obscures it in the growing up and the developmental process that slum children encounter, but it's there, waiting for the right probe and the right question to bring it to light.

The Play Approach to the Questioning Process

We also know that our best students do well because there is a greater infusion of play in their efforts at learning, or else because they are bright enough to play around with the materials they are learning. In any case, the old sobersides who believes that we must suffer when we learn and who often is in a position to dictate educational policy also confuses play with lightmindedness. It isn't, as Huizinga's *Homo Ludens* proves. Play is a serious matter.

The play approach to study and curriculum is not simple, but more complex than the dull sobriety of most instructional methods, depending heavily on thought-provoking and clash-stimulating questions. The reason is found in Melanie Klein's *Contributions to Psychoanalysis*. (11) Klein, a pioneer in the psychoanalysis of children, develops the thesis that the growing child asks numerous questions of its parents and other adults. Unfortunately, most adults discourage questions. Either the questions are not answered or the child is reproved for asking them, frequently because the questions deal with birth, sex, urination, defecation, and other unsanitary matters. The child soon learns that question-asking is unwise and unrewarding and represses any questions it may have, so that by the time the child enters school it has learned that question-asking pains more than it gains. A major job, then, of the teacher is to reverse this process and to show that question-asking is rewarding, not punishing, in order to revive the repressed experimentation and curiosity that once characterized the child, when its questions like, "Who am I?" "How was I born?" "How do babies come?" "What makes the sun shine?" "What makes feces?" were rebuffed, ignored, or otherwise unanswered.

After entering school, the questions that are asked by the teacher are fact questions that check on the understanding of instruction, so that again questions are associated with possible penalty. Facts are important, penalty is important, and the understanding of instruction is important; but these are derivative from more basic matters, like joy in work, exploration, and the stimulation of far-ranging curiosity. It is the thought question that opens up these more basic areas. We now give some illustrations from the subject matter areas, selected for applicability from grades 6 to 12, where pupils, in team learning, play with work-questions or work with play-questions.*

ART

1. Students take two or three different paints and let them run together on a wet paper, to form a "mingling." The teacher asks: What do you see in your "minglings"? Have you ever looked up at the clouds and watched as they changed from one form to another?—from a face,

---

* These questions represent a sampling of hundreds that my graduate students have collected (or scavenged!) from a variety of sources or else have themselves created independently.

to a bear, to a figure, to a clown, to figures dancing? Which of these are happy? sad?

2. Ravel's *Bolero* is played. Students are told to close their eyes and then are asked: What colors do you see? What kind of movements would you make with your brush? What kinds of shapes do you see moving in the music?

3. The student is given a button, drawing paper, and colored chalks. He pastes the button anywhere on the paper. The teacher then asks: How will you make a drawing using the button? The button can emerge as the wheel of a sports car, a fish eye, or a button on a vest.

4. The teachers says: It is the year 2000. We are in a large space ship hurtling through space. Suddenly lights flash on the control panels. Our ship is in trouble. We must land on a nearby asteroid. We maneuver the ship into a landing position. Slowly, slowly, slowly, we set down. Carefully we open the hatch and climb down. We are in the midst of a weird place, surrounded by weird creatures. What color is the sky? How is the sun shining? What shape are these creatures? What does the landscape look like?

5. Texture rubbings develop awareness and appreciation of textures and materials. With crayons and papers available, the teacher says: Close your eyes. Now run your hand over your desk top. How does it feel? Run your hand over your shoe top. How does it feel? Can we draw the way things feel and can we put these differences on paper?

6. Students take three to five objects out of their pockets or pocketbooks, arrange them on their desks, and then sketch them. The teacher makes independent sketches, showing overlapping, gradation, and foreshortening. The teacher asks: How can drawing help you observe better? Does observation make things more interesting or more boring?

7. Reproductions of Modigliani, Villon, Renoir, etc., are placed in front of the room. The teacher asks: Were the artists trying to paint people or feelings? Can you paint feelings? Can you paint feelings the same way you paint people? Can you take a photograph of feelings? Do you take a photograph of feelings the way you make a painting of feelings?

8. Two students stand on a platform, one at attention, one at ease. The teacher asks: What lines would you draw to show the difference between the two figures? What lines would you draw to show the difference in feelings?

9. The teacher asks: Can you draw a self-portrait without looking at yourself?

HOME ECONOMICS

1. When mothers send their daughters grocery shopping and then become displeased, is it because they are annoyed with the brands bought, or the quality, or the quantity, or overpaying? What must you be careful about in a supermarket? In a smaller store?

2. Tonight you are baby-sitting for a neighbor with a two-year-old son. He is friendly, he is talkative, and he is full of energy. What will your specific responsibilities be? What will the parents' responsibilities be? What can you plan to fulfill your responsibilities tonight?

3. Your neighbor has three children, a seven-year-old boy and two girls, twelve and fifteen. Your neighbor asks you what their responsibilities should be. Draw up a list of responsibilities each child should have and indicate those in which they should share.

4. You expect your next door neighbor for dinner one night, your teacher the next night, and a long lost relative the night after. How would you plan your table arrangements, types of food, and cooking, for the different guests?

5. Upon arriving home from school, you discover your mother has taken ill and must remain in bed for several weeks. If you are the oldest daughter, what new responsibilities will you have to assume? How can you help make your mother as comfortable as possible? How can you keep up your school work and still continue your home duties?

6. Your four-year-old sister is ill and must remain in bed for a week. How can you assist your mother? How can you help keep the child busy? How can the child rest and still be kept from crankiness?

7. Your younger brother or sister is attending school for the first time. The child is apprehensive and shows this in temper tantrums and physical complaints. How can you help alleviate the child's fears and doubts? Do you talk to the child, or do you encourage the child to talk to you?

8. You have been invited on a date by a boy you have been trying to impress. He has left the planning of the evening up to you. What are you going to suggest? How will you prepare for the evening? Should you leave it up to him? How can you tactfully take the lead?

PHYSICAL EDUCATION

1. Working in groups of two, create a sixteen-count dance in which you express and convey through movement the effects on you of the colors white, black, purple, green, and yellow. How will you relate mood to body movement?

2. You and your friend are sitting along the edge of the pool at the deep end. Neither you nor your friend knows how to swim. Along

comes a prankster who playfully throws your friend into the pool. Look around the pool area now and tell me the ways you can assist your friend quickly, even though you don't know how to swim.

3. You are practicing for an important tennis tournament. During practice you see that you are netting your service. Describe why you are netting the ball. Now describe how you can avoid this, mentioning principles concerning motion and muscles.

TYPEWRITING

1. Can you remember when you learned to roller skate? To ride a bike? How did you do it? Can you learn to type the same way?

2. Many of us are afraid of the dark. Blind children are always in the dark. Pretend that you are a blind child—how can learning to type help a blind child? Can a blind child learn to type? How?

3. With a good ball player catching a ball, does he tell his fingers what to do, or do his fingers tell him what to do? What about typing? In typing should your fingers be your masters or your slaves?

4. Why should *not* using your eyes make you a better typist?

ENGLISH

1. Do older people go to as much trouble and danger to make friends as do teenagers? Why do teenagers need a group more than adults do? (Used in connection with *New Boy in Town, Tom Sawyer, Alice Adams, Silas Marner.*)

2. How do modern technology and invention increase or decrease crime? (With *Inchcape Rock, Rififi, The Gold Bug.*)

3. What's the difference between being cared for and being abandoned? Between being spoiled and being loved? (With Robert Frost's *The Runaway* or *Johnny Tremain.*)

4. Do nightmares hurt? Is being hurt worse than being terrified? Is being spanked worse than being scolded? (In discussions of myths of Tantalus, Sisyphus, or Prometheus.)

5. "And Kino drew back his arm and flung the pearl with all his might." Was this action of Kino a victory or a defeat for him? (In discussions of Steinbeck's *The Pearl,* and with parallel forms for the death of Carton in *Tale of Two Cities* and of Per Hansa in *Giants in the Earth.*)

6. Who is responsible for the condition of *The Man with the Hoe*—God, other men, or he himself? (A parallel question can be used with Ahab in *Moby Dick.*)

7. Do people wear black sunglasses to call attention to themselves or to avoid attention? (With *The Minister's Black Veil.*)

8. Was Hester's decision to remain in Boston considerate of her

unborn child, or was she being indifferent to the child's fate? (With *The Scarlet Letter*.)

9. Is it better to be a live coward or a dead hero? To live on your knees or to die on your feet? (With Arthur Miller's *The Crucible* and *Tale of Two Cities*.)

10. What kind of person is more likely to be remembered after death—a cruel one or a good one? (In the discussion between Homer and the manager of the telegraph office on Marcus' death in Saroyan's *The Human Comedy*.)

11. Are we more likely to emulate people we know or people we've heard about? (With *Leiningen Versus the Ants*.)

12. If "the grass is always greener on the other side," does the man who is there agree? (With *Maud Muller* or *The Monkey's Paw*.)

13. If things about which we feel deeply are difficult to convey to others, should we assume that others are unsympathetic or that we are not clear? (The King discussing his problems with Anna in *The King and I*.)

14. If you want children to feel loved and wanted, do you give out praise or duties? (With *Cheaper By the Dozen*.)

15. To attain desires and goals, do you need heedlessness and ambition or obedience and control? (With *Macbeth*.)

16. If dishonesty in another person does not keep you from loving or sacrificing yourself for him (or her), does that prove your love or your foolishness (or nobility)? (With *The Highwayman*.)

17. Does conforming to society's standards make you dependent or independent? (With *Huckleberry Finn*.)

18. If you revenge a wrong, can you relax or should you anticipate vengeance? Do you become more peaceful or more watchful? (With *Moby Dick*.)

SCIENCE

1. How can we see bacteria on the agar plate and not be able to see bacteria in the jar of water?

2. Are we made sicker by the things we see or by the things we don't see?

3. A man pushes against a brick wall for two hours. He is perspiring heavily, he is working hard, but he is not doing any work. How can he be working hard without doing any work?

4. How does an automobile cause and control explosions?

5. How is eugenics different from genetics?

6. How many environments are there in one environment? Does the horse have the same environment as a man, even though he lives in the same place? Is place the same as environment?

MATHEMATICS

1. Why don't we simply say 1? Why do we use such complications as 100/100, 74/74, 31/31, etc.? Do they tell us anything that 1 doesn't?

2. A fly is on the outside of a glass 10 inches high and 12 inches in circumference. If he is 1 inch from the top of the glass and wants to get to a point on the outside 1 inch from the bottom opposite him, how far must he travel if he takes the shortest path?

3. How do the Muller-Lyer illusion and the reversible staircase illusion show the need for geometrical reasoning?

4. When manufacturers make size changes in suits and dresses, how do they depend on the geometrical rules for congruency? How do they change size without changing shape?

5. How does your bicycle embody the rules of geometry?

6. Develop an identity equation that you can use on your friends in playing number-guessing games. How are identity equations different from conditional equations? How many identity equations can you develop?

7. A thief is headed toward the border in a stolen car, has a head start of one hour and is racing along at 50 miles an hour. The state trooper pursues him in an airplane which travels 90 miles an hour. How long will it take the trooper to catch up with the thief? If the border is 120 miles from the starting point, will the trooper catch up in time to make an arrest before the thief crosses the border?

8. A ship sinks 3 miles away from one island and 2 miles away from another island. The islands are 4 miles apart. You are the captain of the salvage vessel. How would you locate the wreck?

MODERN LANGUAGE

1. What do two different forms of address (*tu* and *usted; tu* and *vous; tu, voi, lei,* and *loro*) reveal about Spanish, French, Italian people and how they see their relationships with others?

2. Does the American use of the imperfect and preterit show that we are less or more exact in talking about past time than Spanish speaking people are?

3. Why do I say of the ripe banana *Es amarillo* and of the unripe banana *está verde*?

4. If *ser* is used to express characteristics and *estar* to express conditions, what is the difference between characteristics and conditions?

5. Is knowing something the same as knowing someone?

6. Which "you" would you use if you were speaking to: (*a*) your 25-year-old cousin who has always been a close companion? (*b*) your

25-year-old cousin whom you are meeting for the first time? (*c*) your father? (*d*) your brother-in-law? (*e*) the president of your grade's student council? Would it be more or less difficult to make friends in a Spanish-speaking country than in an English-speaking country?

7. What makes the double negative grammatical in Spanish and ungrammatical in English?

SOCIAL STUDIES

1. What would you do if you were asked by your employer to forfeit vacation time in order to fulfill an immediate order for defense materials? (Class can be turned into a union meeting or labor-management meeting, using sociodrama.)

2. If the Founding Fathers were living today would they be Democrats or Republicans?

3. How do Tschaikovsky's "Overture, 1812," Chopin's "Revolutionary Polonaise," Liszt's "Hungarian Rhapsody," Dvorak's "New World Symphony," Smetana's "Moldau," and Sibelius' "Finlandia" affect internationalism and international feeling? When we didn't play Beethoven during World War I, did that help or hurt national morale? Is international art more important than national morale? Should we admit the Bolshoi Ballet?

4. Did the improvement in women's status improve or worsen the status of men?

5. The place is New York City. The time is 1815. Your father comes home from work and tells the family that it is moving West. How would you feel? What would you think of first? It's 1970. Your father announces that the family is moving to Alaska. Compare your feelings with those of the 1815 child.

6. How could you have avoided the last fight you had without feeling like a sissy? Compare this answer with the causes of the last two world wars.

7. If your boss said, "You're fired," could a union do anything for you that you couldn't do for yourself?

8. Do the common characteristics of all cultures, like architecture, art, religion, economic systems, and the common needs of men cause agreement or disagreement? Why should common needs cause dissension?

9. How many Constitutions are there? Do the plaintiff and the defendant have the same Constitution? Do the segregationist and the integrationist? Do the majority and minority on the Supreme Court?

10. When we dislike people who are different, is it because they are weaker or stronger than we are?

11. Here are some advertisements from leading national magazines. What devices does the advertiser use to encourage you to buy his product? List the things the advertiser knows about you that enables him to use these devices.

Many of these questions will lead to interest in, and involvement with, team discussion. They have high participation possibilities. But gassing away in class as teams, the usual teacher will tell us, is not the same as learning. Learning also involves study, application, memorization, reiteration. How are these grubby matters related to play?

Huizinga tells us that they are, and intimately. The rules of a game are like the laws of algebraic operation. The choreography of a teacher as she walks around a room or sits at her desk, or the pace and tempo with which she illustrates a point, affects classroom climate and therefore the development of the lesson. The degree to which the teacher infuses qualities of rhythm into memorization processes like spelling rules, multiplication tables, or formulas in mathematics and science will influence learning and the patience and willingness with which memorizing is undertaken.

Play releases energy. Just as the thought questions listed above are a means of releasing the repressed questions that the student has sat on ever since parental reproof discouraged inquiry, so other instructional techniques, using play as Huizinga defines and describes it, release inquiry, pursuit, the sense of goal and remove the storehouse of anxiety that too often attends learning.

Play also mobilizes energy, and this mobilization of energy has occupied the attention of numerous psychologists, who have called it "libido" if they were Freudian, "habit strength" if they were Hullian, "schedules of reinforcement" if Skinnerian. Whatever the nomenclature, psychologists need a concept that indicates a pool of energy in the learner, a pool augmented by rewards and diminished by punishments, or vice versa. In brief, in learning and in exploration one expends energy, and often for the mere sake of discovering new energy sources. Non-learning is the absence or misdirection of energy, which can be diverted to savagery, violence, detachment, or narcosis. Everybody, bright or stupid, invests energy, differing only in the efficiency and target of the investment.

The Military Experience with Team Learning

We have attempted to establish the proper use of the question and the value of the play approach as the necessary preliminary to effective team learning, and to team learning we now return only to find that somebody else has been eating our porridge and using our bed, and is also vitally concerned with competition-cooperation-leadership and morale. Our visitor has been the Department of Defense, which asserts that it has been interested in these matters long before the problems of urban education received their current formulations. If so, we should profit by its experiences, or at least examine them.

The building of military morale has been debated since the Persians met the Greeks—see Herodotus—or since the Athenians encountered the Spartans—see Thucydides. Military success depends on team effort. Since World War II and the Korean conflict, military leadership in the United States has been concerned with the ways of building morale. The Korean conflict seemed to show American susceptibility to brainwashing and other morale-diluting devices; a willingness to fight, evidence indicates, is not an individual decision but emerges from a group sense and group identification. Perhaps, therefore, classroom willingness to learn also derives from group identification. Let us see what military experience has been.

In 1949 the Carnegie Corporation granted over $2 million to Teachers College, Columbia University, to support the Citizenship Education Project, for work with school systems throughout the nation in developing units on citizenship education, chiefly for use in social studies and English. No sooner had the Citizenship Education Project set up hundreds of "laboratory experiences" in which students engaged in various community efforts, enterprises, and exertions, than the Korean conflict began and General Eisenhower, then President of Columbia University, suggested to General George Marshall, then Chief of Staff, that the facilities of the Citizenship Education Project were as available to the Department of Defense as to school systems.

During World War II, the Defense Department had itself developed a ten-hour curriculum in citizenship education for all recruits, as part of a larger forty-hour unit called *Information and*

Education, or I&E, but was not happy about the results in either program. Defense personnel were able to identify three areas of difficulty in the ten-hour citizenship education program, for which Teachers College personnel agreed to develop a new approach: (1) instructor level, (2) student level, and (3) place and time.

1. INSTRUCTOR LEVEL. Some instructors were excellent, others were dreadful. Uniform materials were not taught uniformly, so that instructor quality was a variable that needed controlling and reducing. At the same time, the good instructor was to be improved and the poor instructor somehow neutralized.

2. STUDENT LEVEL. Recruits represented all levels of educational attainment, from the barely literate to the Ph.D. Again, uniform materials were on target with some recruits and missed completely with others. Recruit variability was far greater than instructor variability. Could uniform materials be effective with such divergent backgrounds in the recruits?

3. PLACE AND TIME. The uniform materials could be dosed out on bivouac, at four o'clock in the morning, before breakfast, or in a comfortable, air-conditioned auditorium, after lunch, with greater alertness and participation possible in the pre-dawn class than in the modern auditorium, where up-to-date audio-visual aids and drawn shades made a surreptitious post-lunch nap possible.

4. ADDENDUM—THE MILITARY MIND. A fourth variable, which Defense Department personnel did not divulge, and which opposite number Teachers College personnel had to identify by itself, was the differing opinions in the three services—Army, Navy, and Air Force—about I&E and similarly in different military people, some of whom felt such inspirational materials incompatible in a military setting, and a waste of time in preparing for combat; a naive few felt that I&E was working; a third group felt that, working or not, Defense had no choice—this was a citizen's army and you had to prepare citizenship education materials for it.

For several months Defense and Citizenship Education Project personnel worked on the problem and finally developed ten units—one for each of the ten hours that I&E allocated to citizenship education—which were called somewhat grandly, "Hours on Freedom." Each unit tried for uniformity of result from the three variables of instructor level, student level, and place and time, and was therefore deliberately based on the cooperation-competition-leadership values that both Defense and Teachers College personnel agreed were important in building military morale.

Thus, in the Air Force, a group (or "flight," in Air Force terms) of seventy men was broken down into seven committees of ten men each, with each ten-man committee having an equivalent range of ability. This meant that each committee was heterogeneous, and that all the committees were equivalently heterogeneous. In addition, each committee selected its own chairman (and here the leadership factor entered), yielding seven chairmen, or leaders.

Then one of the ten units in the "Hours on Freedom" series was presented. Each unit contained a citizenship problem, in which a crisis situation was described and a decision demanded. Each committee retired to reach a decision, independently. Having done so, each committee had to turn that decision over to its chairman, or leader. The leader, his committee's decision in hand, would then debate the solution and issues with the other chairmen, his committee witnessing but not entering into the debate. Hence in the first stage, in intra-committee discussion, cooperation was the uppermost consideration. Then, when the leader took over as he entered debate with the other leaders, inter-committee competition was the uppermost consideration.

How did it work? *The New York Times* reported (12) that the ten "Hours on Freedom" units were better than anything ever before used in I&E. But they were not successful, though they were superior to most previous citizenship education materials. In part, they were deficient because they could not overcome the variability in instructor, student, and time and place; in part, because resistant recruits wanted out from the armed forces and were cynical about anything originating there; but in greatest part because responsible military thinking has always been split about how *élan,* or morale, can be created in a fighting force, analogous to the split in educational thinking about how morale, or educational aspiration, can be built in a pupil.

Military thinking can be either conservative or liberal, like teacher thinking, because military thinking is not all of a piece. Though all armies indoctrinate for morale purposes, through sermonizing and preaching, or political commissars, or citizenship education programs, most professional military men distinguish between discipline and *élan,* some preferring one and some the other, one group oriented toward victory in battle and the other toward control. Military history sometimes shows a small disciplined force defeating a larger undisciplined one, but also shows large and undisciplined hordes defeating a small and disciplined entity. Similarly, mass education and education for an elite each have their advocates.

Generals are bound to be wrong some of the time, because, in any given war, some will win and some will lose. (13) In the same way, any educational philosophy and therefore any curriculum will have some degree of success and failure. Therefore team learning, like the "Hours on Freedom," is no panacea but merely a considerable step forward, especially with the culturally deprived in our urban schools. It offers the best framework for questions, rather than statements. It allows leadership to emerge and fosters attentiveness in non-leaders. It has really important educational possibilities. Nevertheless, team learning faces the intangible opposition of a spurious sense of order and arrangement, as is sometimes seen in attempts at curricular articulation. Team learning upsets our usual way of doing things.

Team learning does not set homogeneous grouping against heterogeneous grouping, but combines the two for maximum effectiveness. It does not specialize in education for the gifted at the expense of the mass, nor drag the elite to a slower pace to concentrate on the mass, but instead offers the elite more channels for leadership and the mass more stimulation for participation. The history of humanity has always placed these in opposition, a consequence perhaps of limited educational opportunity; but educational opportunities enlarge every day. Quality and quantity education are not mutually exclusive but supplementary, and we can begin to say that we cannot have one without the other. We can no longer have education for the elite unless we have democratically extended education, nor can we extend educational opportunities to the mass unless our elite get every opening, in every direction, that we have come to know of. Otherwise, the social metric which has recently disclosed our losses from segregating our major minorities will also begin to show our losses as the new expansion of knowledge grinds to a halt, or even contracts. It has before.

The face of things which hides inner decay sometimes deceives the military man who equates superior weaponry with *élan,* and the educator who confuses shiny new school buildings with educational gains.

A curriculum which assembles educational materials in terms of cooperation-competition-leadership also educates for militancy toward tasks, modes of attack on questions, and a willingness to scale the heights and assail the problems of the universe, which means that the curriculum must train not only in subject matter but in a will to victory over the enemy, whether the enemy be men or tasks, questions, and problems.

The enemy, however, may have equivalent will. Men may be inimical. Tasks, questions, and problems may be refractory. So, although team learning is based on cooperation-competition-leadership, curriculum must ask how it guarantees immediate goals and remote goals. Great agreement surrounds remote goals and contention the immediate ones, but the immediate ones are the portals to new tasks. Then what additional investments to enhance team learning must we make in materials and educational weaponry?

Content versus Concept in Curriculum

In curriculum construction, the pedant wants learning for learning's sake. In colleges he is against vocationalizing the liberal arts curriculum. In elementary and secondary education he wants the slum child to learn from the world immediately around him, because the child's inferior powers of abstraction require the concrete and useful; the immediate community should furnish the curriculum materials, says the typical Blantock. (14, 15)

Let us define *immediate community.* Is the child's fantasy and dream life part of its immediate community? If so, we mean more than the child's geographical neighborhood. Teachers justifiably do not wish to be psychotherapists, but they do have a responsibility to understand their students. Such understanding is important because subject matter—English, social studies, mathematics, science, foreign language, art, and music—cannot be effectively learned unless it relates to student psychological needs. More bluntly, subject matter would never have arisen nor developed had it not been for these psychological needs, such as:

The need to make more sense of one's self and of others
(English, literature, poetry)

The need to take sides (social studies)

The need to manipulate (science)

The need to daydream (mathematics)

The need for variety (foreign language)

If, historically, subject matter arose from these needs, it
should not be divorced from them in teaching and learning, whatever the curricular area. If advanced courses in physics, chemistry,
cost accounting, and educational psychology have the possibilities
—not always realized!—of broadening perspectives, hence liber-
alizing them, similarly courses in driver education and life adjustment can be humanizing.

Should schools teach people to earn a living? They always
have, from Plato's day to ours. Where's the buck in learning Latin
or Greek? Ask generations of English, French, and German civil
servants and administrative officials. Or in history? Ask social
studies teachers or State Department career men. To recognize the
original vocational reasons in education is not philistinism, nor
inconsistent with the cultural values in education. Only a pedant,
fighting for his amateur status, thinks so. (16)

But pedantry presents another face in Blantock, who would
exclude the cultural and the classics from the slum child's curriculum, though not in the college curriculum; why omission in one
case and inclusion in the other? Because the classics are presumably less relevant to the slum child's needs than to the college
graduate's.

But if *immediate community* goes beyond geographical neighborhood and includes the intimate and personal experiences, fan-
tasies, and dream life of the slum child, then the classics have great
relevance to slum living and slum problems. If the classics and the
humanities are appropriate in the preparation of civil servants,
clubwomen, or Ivy League graduates preparing for their life's
mission on Madison Avenue or in corporate executive offices, their
relevance is not less for a Harlem child who is cold in the winter,
hot in the summer, and uncomfortable the year round. Nor do we
reach way out in left field when we say that man's earliest myths
still have something to say to him. Prometheus the fire-bringer has

great relevance to Harlem's comfort and to any intelligence we want to nurture there, via the proper use of questions: Is fire more important because it makes you comfortable, or because it helps you think? Did Prometheus contribute to comfort or to a reduction in stupidity? Were the gods more incensed because Prometheus made men comfortable or because he gave men control over things, like the ability to digest different foods and to work clay, copper, and iron? On the other hand, can knowledge make you *less* comfortable, as Adam and Eve learned when they were driven from Eden, and the builders of Babel learned when God confused them lest they achieve too much?

Similarly:

Are we interested in Westerns because we believe them? Are stories of the Trojan War, of the gods, and the heroes less believable than Westerns, and why did the ancients find them as interesting as we find Westerns? Can you be interested in the unbelievable? Can a non-believer be more interested in religion than a believer is?

So for the historic long ago, but the geographic far away is also relevant to the slum child and promises similar understanding of his immediate neighborhood. The large and multifarious world is represented in his very bedroom, no matter how barren or crowded, by plaster, metal, paint, wood, nails, copper wire, and steel, from the nation and a good part of the world. How did they get here? By what routes? From which places?

These questions may get some unpleasant and unanticipated answers, always a risk when you juggle with the interrogative. First, our pedant, pouncing on this curriculum, quotes his experience, confusing it with wisdom. Experience, however, is a legitimate weapon in argument; the pedant—as principal, teacher, or supervisor in a slum school—has heard the slum child say: "Prometheus, Homer, and geography! Crap! Junk! None of my business! I don't care what the hell my room is made of!" warning us against too ambitious a curriculum for children of low powers of abstract thought.

However: What's closer to you than your own blood, nails, fingertips, scalp, and skin? What is more immediate? Yet when an experienced—and baffled—biology teacher in a slum school teaches highly immediate blood and cell structure, he gets low response. Meanwhile, the same pupil is immediately involved with the remotest galaxies, whether in the "Captain Video" of a decade and a half ago, or the more recent "Twilight Zone" and "Batman." His own biology is less motivating, and he will find great personal relevance in Draculas and Zombies he will never see and be indifferent about his inner bacterial life and the seething biochemical factory just within his skin, because the immediate often lacks personal relevance, while the remote has it. Unless the immediate, whether biology or anything else in the curriculum, is taught with drama, fantasy, and imagination, it remains remoter than the galactic habitations of *Superman* or *Batman.*

Poor biology teacher in a slum junior high school teaching a unit on reproduction to children experienced in lust, passion, and fornication! The laughter, wise cracks, and raillery must be anticipated—but rebutted, not rebuked. The dirt, the hysteria, and the terror behind them must be understood, so that the biology teacher not only teaches physiology but also the control of physiology.

The curriculum must be restructured around these vague, intangible, impalpable, airy nothings of fantasy life and dream life, to build powers of conceptualization, symbolic appreciation, and abstract thought, and particularly so for the slum child. If the biology curriculum deals with nicotine, alcohol, and narcotics, with no noticeable abatement in transgression, how can the pedant defend his "concrete" and "practical" curriculum, which so often disguises sanctimony, inefficient teaching, and bureaucratic fossilism? Teaching for symbolic understanding and conceptual power covers more ground more quickly and with far greater gains in the pupil than some spuriously "concrete" and "practical" curriculums do, by not merely preaching that these things are dangerous, but by showing why the pupil seeks out these things because of the way he was brought up, the neighborhood he lives in, and how he degrades himself because of loyalty.

For example, "concrete" and "practical" exercises in citizenship education take students out of their classroom seats, send them into the community, and give them first-hand experience—like getting out the vote, organizing school bond appeals, studying community traffic needs, forming lobbying groups, and similar exercises that require actual contact with situations, rather than textbook or verbalized contact, and always safely supervised by teachers. But unfortunately, attractive though these citizenship education programs sound, pupils learn less by doing than by reading. The laboratory experiences usually connected with citizenship education programs allow students to loaf out of school and waste time, except where the laboratory experiences are precursors to symbolic learning and conceptualization. Community experiences that attempt to be "concrete" and "practical," even simple excursions, are chiefly important because they set the stage for symbolic understanding.

How "concrete" and "practical," says the pedant, for slum students to learn more about their slum communities! (17) But they don't want to learn more about their communities—they know far too much about them. They hate their communities, while having a pride of block, or gang, or turf, together with a fear of leaving them. Only reading pulls experiences together to make them meaningful, as teachers have found with hundreds of laboratory experiences and community busywork, like those issuing from the Citizenship Education Project mentioned earlier in this chapter, good as far as they went, but requiring a return to the classroom from the community if learning—as distinguished from exposure—was to be achieved.

The reasons are simple: team experiences, conceptualized by reading, bombard the isolation of individual pupils and allow communication among class members, so that a team sense emerges, that team sense so important for slum children, where centrifugal forces fragment to a greater extent than in middle-class settings. The written word gives coherence and cohesiveness to the laboratory, field, or community experience, which otherwise is diffuse. Team experiences become individualized when coupled with words. A shared social happening thereby becomes a personal acquisition, individually experienced and privately owned.

Too close a view of slum dwelling can drive you mad; if experiencing your community entails that danger, better avoid it— so the slum child senses. Nevertheless, he can handle the danger by knowledge—not merely by observation of the life around him— but by word-work, so that ideas clothed in words come into being.

Earlier in this chapter, we recommended that the curriculum include material on the promiscuous mother, the deserting father, narcotics addiction, alcoholism, and murderousness, because when children misconstrue assaults *against* the body as assaults *by* the body, this misdirected aggression and its targets require clarification in the pupil for better understanding of himself and of those around him. Our "experienced" educational pedant repeats that these children have been taught and are being taught that certain habits are bad—isn't that what we are saying? No. We are not preaching, but inviting imagination about the patterns of aggression. Only so can that poor biology teacher or the citizenship education teacher gain the attention and the learning improvement he seeks.

Now this is not a kindly curriculum, but much like the learning by shock and punishment in Pavlov, Birch, Liddell, and Miller. We have above called it a disequilibrium approach, but its harshness is not thereby reduced. Yet it is gentler than the child's life: Its harshness is directed, and it is honest.

Unfortunately, curriculums are on paper. Because the paper curriculum requires implementation by human beings, an honest, imaginative curriculum requires an honest, imaginative teacher, setting the odds against success. The "experienced" pedant has the clincher when he wants to know where we will find the honest and imaginative teachers our curriculum specifications require, and in numbers enough to matter.

We can only answer by referring the pedant to earlier discussions on recruiting and training and to later ones on related programs involving payment for learning and extension of the school day, week, and year. Through these the divergence between the curriculum on paper and the actuality in the classroom will become narrower. Though this can happen only with an imaginative teacher, we don't need one such teacher for every classroom—one per school is a start, as we shall see later, when we talk about educational leadership, but this one teacher is not smug. He too is in disequilibrium, or dissatisfaction, because things never settle down in a slum community, any more than they do in a hospital, a law court, or scientific laboratory. There are always more things to do and more problems to face. The teacher and the curriculum for whom life is kindly, and curriculum a soothing syrup, have no place in this harshest of environments. When students live with sin and wrong-doing, curriculum must do the professional thing and be there too, just as the physician works with disease and the attorney with disagreement to develop in the student an analytic and *clinical* understanding of the forces within him and the social and physical characteristics of the world around him.

How can we get this clinical attitude to emerge?

The Junior High School—The Test of the Curriculum

We are born twice, and the second time into the social group. *Bar mitzva, rites du passage,* and confirmation ceremonies are virtually universal practices and symbolize this second birth, which, for the teacher, also means a second chance.

The second chance occurs during the onset of adolescence, at exactly the time that the teacher needs the optimistic sense of another time around, another opportunity to set the child aright, because the junior high school years are generally the worst years the teacher has to deal with. They present problems that are not encountered before or after, and these problems are, for the teacher, of greater stress. In comparison with the junior high school student, the child in elementary school is tractable, and the high school pupil organized.

If, therefore, we want to inculcate a clinical sense into our pupils, the severest testing ground for our efforts will be in the junior high school. If our recommendations work there, they should work in the elementary school and in the high school.

But the clinical attitude is a difficult one for the junior high school student to maintain because he is himself entangled with the materials toward which he is supposed to maintain the clinical attitude. The effort involved in keeping materials at an objective arm's-length distance may be far too great for the junior high school student, especially when the materials like alcoholism, profligacy, and self-destructiveness impinge so closely on him.

One major reason is physiological. Children of junior high school age are in the throes of a physiological earthquake. Hair is sprouting in unexpected places, mammaries are busting out all over, genitals are imperiously calling attention to themselves, voices are changing, and growth accelerates. This physiological earthquake has psychological and behavioral correlates. New intellectual and emotional interests arise, but these are also in spasm.

On the other hand, the junior high school child is actively involved in play. Over half a century ago, Karl Buhler's *Arbeit und Rhythmus* contended that play was the precursor to work in most primitive societies, and that play was the matrix from which work emerged. In the development of man and society, play preceded work, and it still infuses our conceptions of work. More recently,

Johan Huizinga (18) has carried this conception into the role of play in art, science, religion, and man's ways of earning his daily bread. Jacques Barzun has given the play concept its latest formulation in his *Science: The Glorious Entertainment.*

Unfortunately, the play concept is not congenial to pedants who manage syllabuses and curriculums. Strict time units are allotted to study units and woe to the teacher who curtails here or extends there the time allotted by the educational bureaucracy to particular study units.

Nevertheless, except for art, music, and physical education, every curriculum area in the junior high school requires the play approach to the soberest study. Sobriety can be reached by play, but sobriety is not joylessness. Joylessness, indeed, is the lazy pedant's way of eluding the complexities of the play approach. For those willing to investigate teaching via the play approach, we have shown how it can be used in all the subject matter divisions in the junior high school. Of course, sanction from worthies like Barzun, Buhler, and Huizinga bows before the earlier words of Plato:

> Then what belongs to calculations and geometries and all the education which is necessary as a prelude to dialectic must be set before them while still young, and not as a scheme of instruction which they must be compelled to learn. . . . Because the free man must not learn anything coupled with slavery. For bodily labours under compulsion do no harm to the body, but no compulsory learning can remain in the soul. . . . No compulsion then, my good friend, in teaching children; train them by a kind of game, and you will be able to see more clearly the natural bent of each. . . . (19)

7

The Bureaucracies
in Urban Education

Now that President Johnson's Great Society legislation has put urban education into the big time, we must assess the bureaucracy that this legislation will spawn.

Harrison Salisbury says, "The real jungle is in the office of the bureaucrats." (1) We intend to be kinder because urban education involves bureaucracy manipulation and changing bad-guy bureaucrats into good-guy bureaucrats.

Consider the politician, whose care and feeding is part of a larger picture of bureaucracy-manipulation, whether ethnic bureaucracy, religious bureaucracy, or legislative bureaucracy. To begin with, manipulation is no sin and politicians are not more sinful than physicians, scientists, and judges, as the following examples will readily illustrate.

The Kefauver Committee related how physicians undertook dubious research for pay by drug and tobacco companies, and Dr. Ray E. Trussell has documented extensive fee-splitting by physicians, unnecessary operations by surgeons, and excessive charges by hospitals. (2)

In another instance of manipulation:

Rand men are "end running" to the Secretary of Defense to sell their positions or realize ambitions for a glamorous

Washington job. . . . Congressmen have been bothered by the effects the nonprofit research organizations are having on industry. . . . private industry has been enriching itself through the taxpayer-financed work of nonprofit corporations. . . . [Representative Chet Holifield] argued in Congress for an amendment to the defense appropriations bill which would protect, for the government, the patents on discoveries made by nonprofit research organizations. . . . Holifield wanted to know "whether the Defense Department is going to continue to give away windfall patent benefits to its contractors which have been paid for by money of American taxpayers." . . . Industry spokesmen frankly admit that new weapons and hardware devised by nonprofit companies like Rand have helped in their non-government business. . . . (3)

See also the inglorious record of the American Society of Biologists, the Mohole controversy, and the regional fights and infighting among physicists for linear accelerators. In other words, scientists are not less self-seeking than physicians and surgeons.

Similarly, suggestions for reform—such as Conant's idea of regional offices of education that cross state boundaries to replace state and local offices—are excellent, but doomed to failure because many bureaucrats would be thrown out of office. (4) A scientist-administrator, however, must learn to manipulate bureaucracy and, hence, politicians; here is how one advocated a program of urban education to politicians:

[Dr. Jerome] Wiesner made two new and noteworthy suggestions: (*i*) federal assistance to special science high schools be operated by city or state authorities, and (*ii*) a major project to expand and upgrade science instruction in Washington D.C. schools.

Both ideas, which were only roughly sketched in the speech, are aimed at helping to overcome deficiencies in background or opportunity which constrict the flow of scientific and technical manpower. Though carefully phrased, probably in deference to congressional, and especially Southern congressional sensitivities, his proposal for the experimental project in the District of Columbia suggests that there are special problems in D.C.—where a large majority of the students are Negroes, many of them disadvantaged, and where school facilities and budget have been inadequate—that make the system an ideal laboratory. . . . An intriguing line in his text reads, "The admission of students would be on the basis of rigorously competitive academic aptitude examinations, with the costs of attendance for those winning admission, but in need of financial assistance, being provided by the school through arrangements with the state and federal government." This implies boarding school arrangements for children coming from rural areas and perhaps from urban slums and hints at a startlingly new type of American high school. . . . Congressional reaction to bills embodying the ideas might well indicate whether or not Congress really believes an emergency in scientific and technical manpower is developing. (5)

Bureaucracy proliferates bureaucracy, like an amoeba sliding around algae and then incorporating the opposition into the happily enlarged but never, God forbid, engorged operation. We must live with bureaucracy, though not love it, because life makes it irreplaceable and things would be worse without it. But we must move it. If educational bureaucracy loves shiny new buildings and abhors prefabricated or remodeled school buildings, we must persuade it of the benefits of prefabricated, readily transportable school buildings (like trailer classrooms) that are indispensable to urban education. If educational bureaucracy adores teaching machines and loathes paperbacks in adequate number, and supports its preferences with statistics on the longevity of the machines, we must thereby learn that statistics exist, even if they are not accurate, and that they must be neutralized or fought by other statistics.

Bureaucracy exists in educationally centralized France and in the decentralized, autonomous districts in America. The non-teaching principal in America and the teaching principal in France both cling to bureaucratic educational structure, so that, whatever the continent, bureaucracy is there, permitting bus transport but disapproving instruction in mobile trailers, although it sanctions libraries in trailers. Bureaucracy responds to pressure; with education anachronistic by decades, and bureaucracy often incapable of directing itself, we must relieve the pressure or apply countervailing pressure, depending on the circumstances.

In fairness, bureaucracy gets more things done than it fails to get done. It strikes off into new directions, making like a pioneer, and sometimes finds itself in a wilderness without any followers, because it houses the experts. For example, government expenditures may directly support steel, oil, electronics, and aviation, but other industries get indirect help, like drug companies brain-picking government scientific research, and advertising agencies brain-picking Census Bureau data and various governmental tabulations of people and populations. Without these aids many business firms would be operating blind. Simultaneously, the data are used less than they might be, as when government experts fail to persuade farmers to try innovations that mean more profits. Similarly, the beneficiaries of government research in instructional techniques are usually not the schools, as was the original intention, but industrial training programs or television commercials.

In urban education a considerable bulk of educational expenditures benefits the architect, the engineer, and the building contractor, rather than the teacher or the supplier of educational materials, because teacher groups and organizations—like the small farmer—are indifferent to the data accumulated by governmental bureaucracy. Teacher groups are hypnotically convinced that school plant is equivalent to education, as Negro parents are hypnotized by the concept of the integrated school or by open enrollment.

The hypnosis originates in the bureaucracies representing teacher organizations or Negro parents. Consider the extended school day, to which the American Federation of Teachers was long opposed. When the ramifications of New York's school integration forced the extension of the school day, teachers worked overtime, were paid for doing so, and were well able to use the additional income. These days the American Federation of Teachers defends the extended school day, having learned that it means additional income for teachers. The bureaucrats operating teacher organizations and Negro organizations show no better sense than other bureaucrats, though their goals may be more laudable.

A Brief History of Western European Educational Bureaucracy

"Standards of excellence" separate the sheep from the goats. For any time or place some education is desirable for sheep and other education for goats. Therefore, excellence—bland as the term is—reflects a conflict situation.

Educational excellence involves us in a struggle against education which lacks excellence, though the struggle can range from violence, to simple avoidance, to a judgment, in a continuum from the death of Socrates to the distaste for progressive education, as Cremin describes it. (6) More than a concept, excellence is a weapon in debate, reflecting social, economic, class, and national divisions; it is a national resource, and so used. German superiority in technical education since the Napoleonic wars has affected European history. Yet excellence, a contributor to power structure and struggle, is not uniformly interpreted in European countries, where dissatisfaction with native patterns coexists with dismay at the achievements of rivals, so that Americans become troubled by what Ivan reads that Johnny doesn't, and Russians are similarly troubled by the independence and creativity that Johnny shows that Ivan doesn't. (7) Russian education causes anxieties in Americans, and American education in Russians. An Englishman will be alarmed by the curtailment of educational opportunities, the scarcity of technological personnel, and the concentration on individual, humanistic values to the detriment of social achievements. Uniformly, educational leaders in diverse countries don't like the educational program in their own countries.

In the United States, these dissatisfactions keep the learner on multi-track education as long as possible, in the belief that a specific excellence is attainable by the stupid child, and another kind by the bright one.

Excellence has always involved taking sides. The Biblical injunction of rod-sparing and child-spoiling was for attainment of excellence against contrary current injunctions, and the last millennium offered numerous instances, even within the bosom of the Church when it was most unified, of Roger Bacon's attacking its deductive system, Dante's attacking its secular inroads, Abelard's mobilizing student opinion like a Williamsburg Chassidic rabbi assembling his followers to attack the prevailing *Misnagdim* theology—so perhaps that when society is as unified or as totalitarian as it can be, dissident definitions of excellence keep leaking in. Whether defined by mass popularity or by a voice in the wilderness, excellence begets an opposing definition of excellence.

When the invention of printing and the emergence of the vernacular tongues coincided with the mercantile needs of explorers, manufacturers, miners, and shippers, excellence converted from the deductive to the empiricism of time and place. Schools, heretofore attached to the houses of nobility and the cathedral schools, set up independently and solicited business from the guildsmen, for whose children reading and arithmetic became the vehicles of excellence. Because the emerging middle class needed men who could read the vernacular and compute business accounts, teachers were recruited who were well trained rather than well educated, and vocationally rather than culturally oriented.

As emerging national states re-channeled piety to loyalty and the Renaissance redirected learning to research, so churchly piety clashed with nationalistic loyalty, humanistic learning, and lay research, but thereafter definitions of excellence split further and humanistic learning clashed with research as well as with nationalistic loyalty and churchly piety. To this day, the monastic and scholastic piety-as-excellence and the contrasting humanistic knowledge-as-excellence have contemporary echoes in citizenship-as-excellence versus culture-as-excellence.

Universal literacy became excellence if you were Lutheran, and anathema if you were not—unless you were contending with Lutherans and needed manpower. So Jesuit education quickly borrowed breadth from Melanchthon's Reformation education to reestablish the narrow authority of Rome. And literacy was no longer a work of the devil but a means of more efficiently indoctrinating the recruits on your side, when the Jesuits saw that literacy, for the Jews a defensive means of survival, could be a weapon in attack.

Technical education began to require the empirical. A surgeon on the battlefield, like Paré, suspected the medicine and anatomy taught at the universities, and the lawyer began to support civil as against canon law. The physician found that he had to learn anatomy from the cadaver, not from Galen's text. The lawyer, especially in England, supplemented reading in the law with the experiences of moot courts, as legal training abandoned the universities for the Inns of Court, with practical training on the actual scene supplementing the bookish. In interesting contrast, the engineer substituted the texts of Agricola and others for the limitations of empirical apprenticeship, so on-the-job training became excellent for lawyers but texts became excellent for engineers.

In the face of university-sanctified texts, the learned societies and academies organized the new empiricism. Beginning in Italy, spreading to France and Germany, and thence to England, these loose assemblies of savants revealed that universities could stifle. As men without affiliation to the university bureaucracy corresponded, met face to face, and fought, they ultimately gained official charters, recognition, and their own bureaucracy.

After 1700, and into the Enlightenment, excellence retained this class-based difference, being variously interpreted as education that prepared you for your station or as education that lifted you above your station. New classes were emerging and excellence wore many faces. Poor boys like Samuel Johnson made their ways in the world as classical scholars and editors, and poor boys like Watt became engineers, while the landowning squirearchy maintained status and power with the rudimentary education it had gained at an Oxford and Cambridge gone into decline. The courtly superficiality that Lord Chesterfield prescribed for Philip Stanhope was opposed to the education that Rousseau prescribed for Emile.

Excellence therefore, like bureaucracy, reflects pecking order, dominance-submission, rivalries and conflict, competition among goals, so that a Watt cannot arise unless something adverse happens to a Stanhope or an Emile.

As Europe became expandingly prosperous in the nineteenth century, class differences became sharper and were reflected in the sharpened consciousness of the kind of education that would advance class interests. Literacy became a many-valenced thing, deemed excellent because it fixed you to your place and enabled you to do a better job at it, as apprentice or blueprint-reading workman, or because it enabled you to transcend your place by studying Marx and Bakunin. Literacy could also be a source of perturbation in society.

The latter half of the twentieth century has seen attempts, for the first time in history, to educate all men—opening the question of the educability of all men—and has lifted the horizons for trained manpower, which has better assurance of security than inherited wealth and power. Knowing is safer than having.

Excellence has further sources. Hunger and thirst drives do not always dominate rats in a maze. The satiated and well-fed rat is also curious. He will sniff at his surroundings, in pure exploration, when he no longer has to eat, drink, or mate. Still more, Hebb's isolation experiments indicate, must man ingest experiences as he ingests food, so that curiosity and exploration needs take over when the crasser needs of food, drink, mating, and sleep are satisfied. (8) So, also, production needs in contemporary society require that more educable people be located and trained in market and product development, lest the processes of research, development, and operation drag to a halt. With educable man, we can transform Gardner's excellent plumber into the sanitary engineer, the tool-and-die man into the mechanical engineer, and the cook into a home economist.

Excellence was, until recently, defined in terms of educable people, but it must now include the stupid too. As we need intelligent people, we need stupid ones. Our need reduces their stupidity, though it does not liquidate it. If the Negro and Puerto-Rican have been in great measure made stupid by bigotry, economic deprivation, and social structure, we can see almost at once where the antibodies to stupidity are. They're not in open enrollment policies which misconstrue propinquity for desegregation, nor in an ability grouping under the same school roof which will segregate far more painfully.

Education is the hardest child labor there is, for the Harlem child and for the Scarsdale child, though excellence for the Negro child cannot be reached by the same route as that for the Scarsdale child. The Scarsdale child has arrived. The Harlem child must begin with a century of unfinished business.

The Bureaucracy of Esthetics

Art, beauty, and their contribution to ethnic and national morale are also in the hands of a bureaucracy, and where they are not, there is little art and less morale.

No other civilized nation in recent years has suffered the collapse after collapse that France has, yet it has survived and regained its place after each Sedan, *Affaire Dreyfus,* Indo-China, and Algeria by a Malraux-morale that builds on French past and French tradition in painting, music, and literature.

Being surrounded by art keeps your spine straight. Art has enabled Italy to keep going as a national entity when it was stripped of all else. The Italian art in the Louvre indicates France's greater strength, the Elgin marbles in London indicate England's power in the Balkans, and the number of Raphaels in the National Gallery in Washington indicates that our ability to buy is greater than Italy's to retain. National morale results. (9)

Negro art, music, and literature engender Negro morale. Negro jazz and African carvings do not carry the intellectual freight of symphonic music, grand opera, or modern art, and no use pretending they do; this folk art represents the first faint stirrings of the search for morale.

The art form chiefly concerned in morale-building is architecture, like Solomon's temple, Venetian *palazzi,* British castles, French *chateaux,* or American skyscrapers. The esthetics of the Negro housing project have been amply belabored, and no repetition is planned here, but if architecture doesn't represent pleasure in things around, it is nothing. (10) Taking pleasure in Harlem, in the noises it makes, the sights it shows, and the lives it leads has been partially demonstrated in Langston Hughes, James Baldwin, Ralph Ellison, and other writers. But architecture creates a larger group morale, one that goes beyond folk art and literature. It is a group undertaking, and the Negro needs a Negro bureaucracy to merchandise it, to guarantee that Negro artists and architects emerge, are recognized, and are followed by other artists and talents, so that rivalries and schools arise and the occasional Hughes, Baldwin, and Ellison are not alone but are surrounded by acolytes and opponents.

To become a market for the Negro artist, Harlem must become a hospitable place to visit so that all who come, Negro and white, are comfortable at 125th Street and Lenox, or at Nostrand Avenue and Fulton Street. Let architecture set the tone in which Negro bureaucracy can take responsibility for Negro tenantry. Pearl Bailey's two-to-tango reminds us that if Harlem absentee landlordism has been avaricious, then Negro tenantry has been slovenly, thus needlessly compounding casual New York garbage removal. Negro bureaucracy has done less about slovenly Negro tenantry than white civic bureaucracy has done about avaricious absentee landlordism. The job requires partnership, that Negro bureaucracy do the appropriate job of handling slovenly Negro tenants while white counterparts do the parallel job of handling avaricious white absentee landlordism in the courts. Nor need Negro bureaucracy feel sensitively tender about the Negro *lumpenproletariat,* which must be allowed to die off because it is no longer remediable. Negro bureaucracy must rather think of the child, especially the child not yet in school, from whom no votes come, who is not on a picket line, nor a dues-paying member, but who is still reclaimable and salvageable. The *lumpenproletariat* is the last of wasted generations and will follow the others. No improvement in housing, education, art, or democratic practices will ever reach it. The young child is another matter and is the only hope of Negro redemption.

Architectural improvement in Harlem and Bedford-Stuyvesant must reflect the needs of these children, so that kindergarten facilities, play facilities, and educational facilities dominate the Harlem and Bedford-Stuyvesant landscape, or at least the back yards, where fences must come down for recreation areas to come up. Weaver describes an experiment here: "The street will be closed off from the rest of Harlem traffic, except for a single service lane. Between the two facing rows of refurbished buildings there will be grass and trees, park benches and play equipment. In basement rooms, tucked a half-flight under the ranks of front steps, there will be day-care centers for the children of working mothers, adult education classes, health clinics, and vocational training programs. In the back yards there will be grass and swings." (11)

Fashionable architecture is of two kinds: new fashionable and old fashionable. The *haut monde* accommodates itself equally well to either. London's Kensington has re-done fashionable Victorian houses that precede this century, as has the Place des Vosges in Paris. New York's Sutton Place and Brooklyn Heights have been similarly rehabilitated, so that a post-Civil War brownstone is as fashionable as a Park Avenue duplex. The recent French film *Cleo 5 to 7* illustrates how Parisian good taste modernizes ancient architectural facilities. If architecture improves morale, a face-lifting of old buildings is as important as new buildings.

The section of New York that is richest in these architectural opportunities is Harlem, especially between 110th and 125th Streets. Negro writers, artists, painters, musicians, and professionals could be the real estate pioneers who recapture the value of the area. Sammy Davis Jr.'s disgust with 127th Street in *Golden Boy* is seriously misplaced, because that very street has as many possibilities as Sutton Place and First Avenue had thirty years ago; it needs the enterprise of the artists now moving into Bowery lofts. Negroes who refrain from pioneering in improving Harlem real estate have no right to complain when the improvers make a profit out of their reluctance.

When fence-free back yards become recreation areas, their use as depositories for garbage diminishes. Here, architecture makes Negro parents, Negro volunteers, and Negro bureaucrats recognize that nothing solidifies power like art and that Negro art will place the Negro bureaucrat in the seats of power as white recognition never will. The Negro back yard in Harlem and Bedford-Stuyvesant is as much the raw material of Negro architecture as Carrara marble was for Italian sculpture, white pine for New England churches, and glass and aluminum for skyscrapers. When Augustus rebuilt Rome, when the Catholic Church sponsored the cathedrals, when the Renaissance merchant-*condottieri* took over in the Italian city-states, when Napoleon rifled Italian art treasures, and when American millionaires like Frick and Mellon purchased *quattrocento* masterpieces, they knew that art is a symbol of power and that the ruler who has made it, or has it made, surrounds himself with its representations current and past.

Negro bureaucracy shows its immaturity by the little it has done for Negro art in America; its political and economic rights have consequently suffered. It doesn't take money to support art. The major sustenance to art comes from appreciation, rather than financial assistance. The Rubenses and the Michelangelos who worked out of expensive ateliers are but one side of the history of art. Others worked for the sheer creativeness in it, in some *vie de Boheme* in Villon's Paris, Rembrandt's Amsterdam, or de Kooning's Greenwich Village. Enough excellent artists exist in Harlem right now for Negro exhibitions and Negro galleries, with loft space available for showing. No political successes will replace the morale and power sense thus generated; only the Negro artist can put this capstone on Negro achievement.

Making Harlem a comfortable place to work and live in, by

beginning with the Harlem back yard rather than with the sidewalk that Jane Jacobs is so fond of (10) or with improvements in what the street looks like, involves the Negro artist and architect. That empty space is available to light, air, and refuse too, but merged back yards mean new recreational facilities and a respected Mediterranean, Caribbean, and subtropical tradition in which building concentrates on the resident rather than on the eye of the passerby, offering within the internal confines the gardens, courtyards, and an elegance that is not the business of anybody walking past but of those dwelling there. Legislation can reward landlords, on a blockwide basis, for such improvements by tax rebates that would encourage the numerous landlords on a single block to enter into joint efforts for the rehabilitation process.

Cultural sources as diverse as the Schomburg Library and the Apollo Theatre, dealing with the Negro past and the Negro present, testify that much more appears in Negro history than most Negroes allow themselves to think about. The Apollo has an excess of "go" to compensate for the lack of it outside, and the statistical scantiness of major artists and art galleries in Negro life can be quickly remedied by showings and publicity. At any time, in Periclean Greece or Renaissance Italy, a dozen or two artists are all that separates a period of artistic richness from one of artistic barrenness. Two or three major Negro artists, plus a dozen mediocrities, are enough for an important art movement, provided that Negro bureaucratic apparatus pushes a bit on the reviewing apparatus in the newspapers and magazines, in order to avoid the harshness that the usual critic mistakes for criticism. In urban planning and urban architecture bad temper substitutes for criticism and more dust is raised than light brought in. See Jane Jacobs, Mumford, and others. (12)

Thus Negro bureaucracy, in providing Negro art with the public relations that German music has gotten for two-and-a-half centuries, need not be concerned with goodness, badness, or numbers, but only with productivity and activity. Here, volume precedes value. Artists must work first; thereafter they can consider how well they are working. Indeed, they get better only after they work. Whether by text or by texture—the two major motifs in modern art—or by program music or by absolute music—the two major motifs in composition—is less important than that the Negro artist start producing. And as artists become rivals of other artists, as Rouault, a Catholic, is of Chagall, a Jew, the existence of schools of art will mean the competition and the participation in polemic that maintains morale. (12)

Such morale leads to intellectual achievement that may, superficially, seem remote from art, like mathematics and the sciences. Projective geometry and the chemistry of paints and pigment were related to Renaissance art, just as the camera was related to the emergence of impressionism, and the microscope reveals forms and figures that affect modern non-representational art. But commercial transactions and the marketplace also become involved, so that Piet Mondrian winds up in modern architecture, product design, package design, and television commercials. Art that is good for business need not be philistinism; esthetics has always invigorated commerce, from the days of the primitive amber trade, to the exchange of textiles and pottery in early civilizations, to the growth of temples and other edifices in market towns, to the emergence of a Sotheby as an international stock market in art merchandishing, with publications like *Réalités* and *Art News* offering the latest quotations, like a stockbroker's market letter, or a racing form sheet.

The late John Fitzgerald Kennedy said he sought the Presidency because "That's where the action is." But there's action as well in *Hamlet,* Emily Dickinson, a Tintoretto, or a Chopin ballade. Politics has action, but so does art, music, literature, science, or philosophy.

This is especially true of ethnic and racial development and artistic growth. Weston La Barre says, "Races are the technique that a polytypical animal has fallen on to multiply its hereditary potential; it is a new way for the varying parts to depend on one another genetically, for the survival of the whole reticulated species." (13) So Negro races may be a scouting party into one possible avenue of adaptation and human, rather than racial, survival. In Negroes, the human race is trying on another possible direction for size. White Southerners might say that the evidence proves that the direction is a poor one, but do we know? The Negro scouting party into the human future may first encounter the mutations ahead in our development. To white racists, Negroes are a remnant of development beyond which whites have already passed, but Negro racists claim that they are the progenitors of a future humanity in which whites will be atavistic.

When Dobzhansky (14) points to the greater social need for

the Negro as society recedes from primitivism, Negroes will bow out from Dobzhansky's misplaced kindness because they do not see themselves as a repository of the primitive, nor do they want to be specialists in it. They've seen whites who can do fine with the assignment. Genetic specialization of the races may mean racial dissimilarity, but not racial inequality. The race horse and the Percheron reflect different genetic pools, which is all right because they don't know the difference, but men do, which instantaneously makes them more alike than unlike. This insight, more than anything else, makes them one species.

Therefore, despite President Kennedy, the action on the bottom of the heap can be as richly rewarding as at the top. And as much action will be found in the Negro artist, artisan, and architect—to make them palpable weapons in Negro development —as in street demonstrations.

Negro artists will be found not in one place but in many, teaching perhaps as substitutes in the high schools, or studying at the Art Student's League, or showing their wares at the Washington Square and Yorkville open air shows. Whether placed in an art gallery that was formerly an empty loft near 125th Street, or offered a commission for a Harlem store-front design, or a backyard landscape in Bedford-Stuyvesant, they are a sure bet to lead the assault on self-hate and spiritual insecurity, and to bring the visitors that mean more business. The Negro bureaucracy's private plans for organized social responsibility must be tied to the artist's inner visions. However, when the Negro bureaucrat participates in Negro art, justifiably, because he has as many stakes therein as the artist, he can freely state what he feels and needs, but cannot demand or prescribe. The Negro bureaucrat must bring to the Negro artist both audience and appreciation, in order to free the qualities the Negro artist can bring to Negro life. As E. M. Forster says in *Howard's End:* "Any human being lies closer to the unseen than any organization." (15)

The Bureaucracy of Deprivation

Until recently within our lifetimes, "enough to go around" meant merely a temporary alleviation of shortage. So men sought one another out to dominate, kill, or otherwise manage to have more to go around. When you did well, the barbarians who did not would soon move in, so, with barely enough, you reduced the claimants. These days enough to go around becomes more incredibly and irrefutably actual. The Kingdom of God begins to resemble the Great Society and nobody in his right mind kicks.

Another major question is no longer theoretical—is it sweeter to have power over things or power over men? With all the newly emerging power men have to command energy, water, food, comfort, travel, ease, art, and beauty, they still want to run for President. If absolute power corrupts absolutely, so absolute weakness corrupts absolutely too, because, weak or powerful, we are corruptible. Nobody would run for President if he weren't corruptible, and we should reject any man who wasn't so tainted— he would be dangerously inhuman and would imperil our survival, but the taint that would allow him to bargain and to dicker and to compromise would arise from the same power-hunger that brought us into peril.

Somehow we require a psychological wrench in the customary machinery of thinking and jockeying, either with leisure time or with working time. We can wreak mischief with either and we will have more of both. Certainly we must avoid guilt about free time and imputation of guilt to others. With working time, the need for fighting and toiling for our bread is so deep in our bones that James's moral equivalents for war must begin with training people to take things easy. We can assure them that we will never run out of problems that are far more important than work, and that these problems can be found in life, art, the universe, theology, science —truly important and significant problems we can now attack without the now superfluous headaches of food, rent, and clothing gnawing at us. (16)

One such problem is bringing the Negro up to his potential and the white up to his, rather than matching the two at their present ambling speeds.

Another is the problem of the Two Constitutions, when, on paper, we have but one; yet the Constitution of the Plaintiff differs from the Constitution of the Defendant, the Constitution of the Supreme Court majority faces the Constitution of the Supreme Court minority. The Two Constitutions are partially reflected in the two-party system and the two avenues along which bureaucracy arises, splits, arrays, and justifies itself. (17) Thereby wings and factions arise in all governments, providing channels by which men come to leadership, which often enough are alternative, or redundant, not necessarily antithetic. Thus who is in power, Republican or Democrat, makes little difference because things get done in much the same way anyhow. No matter how the partisan disputes this and tries to make party differences real, they sometimes are and sometimes aren't. They disappear at the water's edge and the number of times party lines are crossed shows more agreement than the partisan is willing to admit.

The real antitheses lie between partisan and bureaucrat, rather than between partisan and partisan. Most newspapers are partisan. They cannot abide bureaucracy, like the bureaucracy handling the unemployed, the deprived, and their demoralization.

Though skill diminishes demoralization, even if you have no job, the press excoriates the unemployed and the overindulgence of the relief-granting agencies. During the depression, excoriation failed to reduce relief rolls and only increased demoralization, dependence on relief, and illegitimacy. These days most relief recipients have no marketable skills, nor do they seek to gain skills, while people with skills, unless physically incapacitated, try desperately to get off relief. A skill is like an itch. But Miriam Makeba's paraphrase of Descartes, "I itch, therefore I scratch," or in this case, "I have a skill, therefore I must get off relief," is inapplicable to a hard core of untrained, shiftless, demoralized relief recipients, so demoralized that they no longer care, if they ever could.

The recurrent furor in the press about relief recipients obscures understanding that social stability requires a reduction in demoralization, thereby elevating it to desperation, by imparting skills wherever we can. The skilled man, though automated out of a job, more easily retrains himself than the unskilled man.

Thus the skilled linotyper, airlines navigator, or marine engineer automated out of a job is more easily retrained than a younger man without skills—provided that the skilled worker retains his morale, sees social provision for his retraining, and senses no guilt or inadequacy in being out of work. He may be sore, but he is not demoralized.

Elementary skills can also lead out of demoralization, if not toward jobs, because automation and technological complexity increase faster than skill acquisition, at least by more responsible attitudes in matters like birth control and the reduction of illegitimacy. Thus, for the frequently sluttish mother, housekeeping and child care skills, the use of the sewing machine and dressmaking patterns, personal and sex hygiene, and make-up are frequent preliminaries to attitude improvement. For the men, furniture repair, the use of simple power tools, mixing of paint, the simple plumbing of faucets, soldering and wiring hook-ups are the vestibules to the abatement of demoralization and the incursion of self respect.

And, most important, free birth control data and materials, because, as Ingle says, "When schools are desegregated as a result of social pressures or when desegregation is forced without regard for abilities and behavioral standards, then the standards of the school are downgraded; those Negro children who are unable to compete at a high level are placed in special classes, and the school eventually becomes resegregated. . . . The very high birth rate among indolent incompetent Negroes is a threat to the future of this race." (18)

In Harlem, furtively, the department of gynecology of a nearby medical school has begun to distribute thousands of uterine coils to Harlem women, instructing them in the use of this permanently implanted birth control device. We can expect a decrease in Harlem illegitimacy in the next five years, as the distribution increases, but an increase in morale too.

Also, employment must henceforward have wider orbits, so that travel to a new job, perhaps in a new state, compensates for dislocation and the tearing up of roots in the rewards of travel, new faces, new experiences, and no loss of supermarkets, television, or conveniences. Such geographical mobility is less harsh than unemployment and geographical stability. Automation, like the Common Market, will require this mobility, getting acquainted with people and values on the other side of the border—or state line—and bringing training, skills, and education to bear on the problems and situations in a new place.

The educated man has few hesitations about picking up roots and marching on to another geographical situation, or leaping upon a Fulbright across international boundaries, or moving across the continent to another academic post, or finding another corporate attachment in another state. (19) The uneducated and unskilled man has less geographical flexibility. Nobody holds the unskilled back from moving about the country, but they tend to stay in one place, known to them, and there to stagnate. When unskilled Puerto-Ricans come to the major urban centers, or unskilled Negroes leave the South, they are not being enticed but driven—a major difference between the mode of travel of the educated and the unskilled. Nevertheless, the willingness to travel reduces demoralization in both the skilled and the unskilled.

Responsible governmental, industrial, and trade union bureaucracy agree that we must automate and that the concomitant responsibilities to the resulting unemployed cannot be shirked—which means shoring up their income, so that the unemployed do not depress the salary level. Does a large reservoir of unemployed keep labor on its toes, a superb antibody that improves resistance to economic disease? "Joblessness has jumped to 5.9 per cent; it has been over 5 per cent for every month of the past six years. . . . annual business estimates . . . will be glowing this year. The stock market is booming. The voiceless bottom fifth of the population, the underclass, is not doing too well but we on top are doing fine. Prices are stable, profits are high, and there are plenty of unemployed which keeps wages down. We should all remember how lucky we are." (20) Increases in unemployment do not diminish the wages of the *skilled whose services are in demand,* who pick up and go to improve income, as the British "brain drain" to American employment temptations shows. Hence the "open marketplace" is as unthinkable and as delusive in modern society as the divine right of kings. Analogously, the Governor of Alabama calls segregation divinely ordained because separable races are clearly and demonstrably there, as evidence of God's intentions. If so, God must have wanted Negroes to become militant, and must have wanted Birmingham police dogs to bite at Negroes, Birmingham prostitutes to pay off police captains, and Birmingham criminals to bomb Negro churches. The "open marketplace," like the divine right of kings or racial segregation, is a rationale for power plays and nothing more, because if kings are overthrown and interracial sex is pleasing, God must want it that way too.

The universe, like God, is manipulable and not a given datum, because the universe, like God, wants us to do our best with the probabilities we face. People are born Muslim, Jewish, Catholic, or Protestant, most often remaining what they were born, which is why apostasy is infrequent, and why faith and belief are more attributable to mother's milk than to the persuasiveness of theology. Since most popes are born Catholic and most rabbis are born Jewish, statistics would indicate that religion is a family matter, and genealogical rather than theological.

For that reason reformations, religious or otherwise, are a gradual affair, requiring a build-up over centuries of development *in the family*. Thus, the Negro family would not have been moved to militance and the intelligence thereby generated were it not responding to a contemporary image of the universe which says, first, that the universe does move, and second, that it can be moved. Negro families become brighter precisely when automation makes more room for brightness in industrial processes, which is no accident. Negroes are as able as anybody else to let automated devices do their work for them, provided that they produce enough trained people to minister, program, service, and encode the processes these devices work by. Failing this adaptation to industrial evolution, their militancy will become hysteria, which is maladaptive. On the whole, however, Negro militancy is highly adaptive.

But equality does not stop at political, economic, or social equality in training and skills; it goes on to where it hurts, to sexual equality, politely ignored by everybody except Southern segregationists with first-hand experience of the portal to intermarriage, miscegenation. (21) Evidence by the fistful, from the Bible, Othello and Desdemona, Algerian novelists talking of Moorish women, but chiefly from Southern novelists, reveals the biological attractions intensified by racial differences. The Southerner fearing intermarriage because he is so torn by the need to mate with a Negro cannot possibly be differently affected from the Negro, though obviously Negroes have been less active. The Southerner's former "separate but equal" has been replaced by the liberal's "cultural pluralism" and the Negro nationalist's "Negritude." But sex attraction is a hard thing to fight, especially when social equality begins to permit it, just as the growing status of American Jews is revealed in their intermarriage rate, which at 10 per cent exceeds their birth rate, meaning that more Jews are departing from Judaism than are being born into it. (22)

Social, economic, and political eligibility are prior to sexual equality, and *intermarriage is wholesome provided that society is*. Southern literature documents that Southern society is not wholesome, chiefly because Southern white women are too busy sliding into neurosis; so what Negro in his right mind would chase after disease when he is healthy? Ultimately the Negro may want to marry Your Sister, but meanwhile he needs social, political, economic, and educational equality, as the sensible and honest portal to sexual equality and eligibility. Nevertheless, when Your Sister's hand is asked in marriage, we want sister and suitor living in a society in which the relevant measures of eligibility will be Intelligence, Responsibility, Adjustment, Education, Health, and Good Family. In an adaptive, evolutionary society, designed for the survival of human protoplasm, no other measures are relevant to assure that Your Sister will be safe. Indeed, any other measures of eligibility, like race, will make us wonder about the underlying sibling relationships of You and Your Sister in the first place.

Part Two

The Solution

8

The Budget and the Program

The deprived community is best described in terms of crisis, and only partially in terms of poverty, slums, or deprivation. These communities transmit their constant boil and climax to the remotest parts of society, stirring a frenzy and a waste of human resources which is almost as expensive as a defense budget. Urban education costs money.

In urban education, we must refer to genetics, biochemistry, popular music, religion, and working mothers, because it is wide-ranging. The genetic comparisons of blacks and whites are of less moment than efforts to raise the educational level of Negroes to their maximum, because the Negro potential has not even been approximated. Negroes are not learning all they can learn, are not studying as effectively as they can, and are not being educated as well as they can be. Whether genetic or not, does it pay society to improve them? Genetics thereby leads to educational finance. Is the cost of educationally salvaging Negroes disproportionate, like the low-grade ore of iron or vein of coal which can be worked to yield results, but only at excessive expense? Later proposals require that education of Negroes be more expensive than for whites on the elementary school level, equivalent to whites on the high school level, and the same on the college level. To bring

Negro education in the elementary grades up to the level of white education will be expensive because of the contributions to the Negro child's educational disability made by family structure and community. Nevertheless, if a beneficent society consents to the contribution, will society get a return on its investment?

To attain answers, we now examine recent programs that extend the:

1. School day to twelve hours, or virtually double it.
2. School week to seven days, so that weekends are legislated for educational purposes.
3. School year to fifty-two weeks, so that summers become available for educational programs.
4. Beginning of education to three- and four-year-olds where home conditions warrant, as in the Head Start program.
5. Termination of education to the eighteenth year, as in the Job Corps and Anti-Poverty programs.

These programs require the full time of the child, the separation of the child from the home, and enough teaching, educational, social work, administrative, and psychological personnel to operate the program. This requires money, much money, budgeted by the billion, and occasions the question: "Who pays for all this? Can we afford the Great Society?" To answer, we begin with budget, the most refractory matter, and work backward to the least refractory, the time of the child and its family relations.

President Johnson's educational budgets are based on the economics of Myrdal, Schultz, and others, who declare that educational expenditures are capital investments, like investments in plant. (1) The economics of conservatism continue to ask: (a) Where is the investment money to come from? (b) How is it to come from there? But now that President Johnson, with the help of economists like Myrdal and Schultz, has answered the question of from where the money is to come, we must ask about how it will come from there and about the people who will accompany it.

The Expense of Defense

The military boondoggle must seek allies in education, as it already has done in science and business. Military administrators have come far since their hungry pre-World War I days and have since lived well on threats from abroad. If funds are any indication, the largest bureaucracy in America today is the military. (2) Like all bureaucracies, the military is reluctant about yielding its perquisites in staff, privilege, and suzerainty. Originally, the military budget was involved with civilian road-building, bridges, and waterways programs, and from these meager beginnings went on to involvement with science, medicine, and interstellar space. Though until now its rich financial diet has never been involved with urban education, expect a change, because social action by the military has a long history. Without being sanctimonious about war and bloodletting, military history can point to numerous achievements in peace, education, and social expansion. Negroes achieved integration in the Armed Forces before they did in the churches. Since World War II, the military has led education in disestablishing the color bar. Freedom from discrimination is greater in American military life than in American civilian life. So far has the Department of Defense advanced the cause of racial integration, that no young Negro could experience the almost complete integration of defense facilities in the last ten years and return to civilian life unchanged. He could see what the possibilities were. He ate well, slept adequately, and was offered all the training he could absorb. Militarism can be democratizing.

Armies the world over perform vital educational functions. They must have literacy and technical programs, they must have trained personnel, and they must maintain morale, else, in a fate worse than defeat in war, more energetic defense staffs take over, causing the emergence of a Nasser here and the overthrow of a Peron there. To stabilize such unrest, you can increase pay and thereby improve morale, but enlistment terms expire and pay increases no longer serve, and you turn to pensions and other post-service devices. Thus Roman legionnaires were given farmland and we offer Veterans Administration services of various kinds.

On top military levels, a MacArthur, a Gavin, and a LeMay are ushered into important post-service civilian positions. On lower levels, superannuated military personnel gravitate toward other post-service jobs. The talents gained in military operations are not always utilized when they return to civilian life, though a surprising number become teachers on retirement.

For such post-service careers, the United States Armed Forces Institute at Madison, Wisconsin, publishes a series of vocational guides, including such titles as: *Establishing and Oper-*

ating a Beauty Shop, What Is Farming? Managing a Farm, Establishing and Operating a Painting and Decorating Business, Establishing and Operating a Laundry. But it also offers *The Fundamentals of Public School Administration* and works on physical chemistry and Chinese translation. In brief, the Armed Forces are heavily involved in publishing not only vocational and educational guidance, but also materials on remedial reading (*Meet Private Pete*), nuclear physics, and advanced mathematics. (3)

But the military wastes more money than the WPA ever did, and this can be embarrassing. Though an occasional Korea or Vietnam sparks the economy, more stable means for maintaining the military establishment would be desirable. One possibility is retirement perspectives in urban education, in which the pie would be distributed through military channels. Military personnel would be trained and then detached for urban education use, under the aegis of educational authorities. Here is an opportunity for the military to remove itself from its suzerainty over some budgetary and administrative plums, and with grace, in its increasing uncertainty under public questioning about the need for heavy military appropriations. Military leadership has begun to concede budgetary elephantiasis. With more money around than can be used in a purely military sense, the military explains its financial management by assuming that virtually everything makes some military sense.

Mind over Money

Educational funds arise from sheer intention. We are not godlike and cannot decree money as God created the world by simply saying, "Let there be funds," but we are not savages either because intention to create goes a long way in our civilization. We are creating funds all the time. (4) We unquestionably do so in foreign trade. Philip H. Coombs has said:

> Quite rightly they [educators] have insisted that education is not merely an instrument of economic growth, but that it also has other and perhaps even higher aims. Nevertheless, it is this new recognition of the essential linkage between education and economic and social development—between

the growth of people and the growth of a society—that is bringing fresh support today from non-educators for increased investment in education. The World Bank, for example, universally respected for its business acumen, is leading the financial community with its new policy of helping to finance educational development. The Inter-American Development Bank and the US-AID program also have entered the loans-for-education business. The U.N. Special Fund, under Paul Hoffman, is directing a large portion of its "pre-investment" funds into education, convinced that this is the best way the least developed economies can reach the "take-off" point. . . . In a host of situations all over the world, including many developed countries, the major bottleneck to development is the shortage not of money but of educated manpower. . . . The economically advanced nations that join in this effort to help others develop their human resources will surely benefit by the feedback of new ideas into their own somewhat encrusted educational systems. (5)

In contrast, when Arthur Krock speaks of the virtues of the Americans of yesteryear, who did not depend on the government but on "individual work, daring and sacrifice which brought them their rich inheritance, without any of the benefices of government that now makes personal security its ever-expanding goal," in a Goldwater-tinted history of America that never was, he forgets that the American government has given away land by the millions of acres, from the Northwest Ordinance of 1787 onwards, and that the fine, free, upstanding, independent American citizen has been made so by a government that homesteaded him into independence, and compelled him to send his children to school. (5) The American has not worked any harder than the European, but he knew that he was working his own property, or that working it would make it his property. Work, daring, and sacrifice are no special characteristics of the American people. They are also characteristic of Chinese coolies. The difference is in governmental solicitude for its citizens. No government has been more solicitous of its citizens than has the American, and most governments have been far less solicitous. (6) Nothing else accounts for American power today. Solicitude has been directly responsible for American capital formation. Sheer intention has created funds.

As an indirect source of income education itself has much unsuspected fat lurking around that has not been squeezed out of it. Some can undoubtedly be found in school architects, engineering firms, and school building contractors; (7) another source can be in food purchase and school supply contracts; still another in teachers at headquarters when they should be in classes. But the largest reservoir of unsuspected fat is the unexploited time, the hours of day and night in which the school plant is locked tight, remaining unutilized by the community paying the bill.

If education is a resource in capital accumulation, then school plant should be put to work around the clock. School plant lying idle, like machinery lying idle, represents a loss on the investment. However, putting school plant to work around the clock requires additional investment in manpower, like additional teachers and supervisors; most communities resist this. But this additional investment need not be as great as supposed when related to another reservoir of fat, in the relief rolls, and the redeployment of current expenditures that contribute to stagnation, loss of morale, and an inherited place on the welfare rolls from generation to generation. We can reduce the fat in both reservoirs by paying children for doing homework and reading improvement, by paying relief-recipient fathers for gaining skills, by paying mothers for cleaning and maintenance of the activized school plant. Welfare funds thus expended contribute not to apathy but to hope; and many social investigators and social workers, the manpower used for surveillance of welfare eligibility and duplicity, can also be redeployed into a school-centered rehabilitation program.

Unfortunately, many of these "unemployables" are either not trainable or unsuitable for work near children. But the logistics of education, like the hauling of supplies, the cleaning of schoolyards, the maintenance of sanitary facilities, offers places for numerous others in an expanded school day, week, and year program. Aside from the numerous shiftless and unskilled who need not be institutionalized but who cannot fend for themselves and will forever be on relief, many—not most—relief recipients are a financial drain that can be redeployed out of the unemployed and into a financial asset both to themselves and to society. Even on the assumption that not more than one-third of those now on relief are dependable enough for placement in the expanded school program, this means a savings of hundreds of millions of dollars in a city like New York, freed annually to pay the manpower needed to keep the school plant in 'round-the-clock operation, for the sake of 30 per cent of the school's pupil register. With most of the funds thus diverted from other budget lines, from the military or the needy, as here described, no diminution in the services rendered, either to the military bureaucracy or the social work bureaucracy, need be anticipated.

All the above assumes that educational budgeting will not expand. However, it will and must. We make fewer mistakes if we operate on the hypothesis that everything expands, from the universe down, and that, when it stops expanding, it collapses. This is true in economics as it is in astronomy. Expansion is not inflation. Except for rural areas, the usual school plant in the typical suburban and urban area is sufficient to meet its community's requirements in size and dimension, if not in equipment. Too many new and unused school facilities would be inflationary; intensive use of current facilities is expansion. We now consider expansion by extension of existing school facilities.

9

Educational Extenders, Fore and Aft

Under federal government encouragement and financial commitment, we are extending education for the deprived at both ends of the time continuum, not only in high school years for dropouts, but also in pre-school years for dropins, or those three- and four-year-olds in nursery or pre-nursery schools. (1)

Nobody has done more to explore the frontiers in early childhood education than Dr. Martin Deutsch. Though his experimentation is not yet complete, the breakthrough it promises in preparing pre-school children for school and reading readiness has prompted the federal government to invest heavily—or bet heavily —that he is going in the right direction. Dr. Deutsch points out

> . . . it is in the first grade that we usually see the smallest differences between socio-economic or racial groups in intellectual, language and some conceptual measures, and in the later grades that we find the greatest differences in favor of the more socially privileged group. From both teachers' observations and the finding of this increasing gap, it appears that there is a failure in some level of society, and, more specifically, the educational system. Was the school scientifically prepared to receive these children in the first place? And, in addition, were the children perhaps introduced

to the individual demands of the larger culture at too late an age—that is, in first grade?

> . . . children from depressed areas, because of inade-
> quate training and stimulation, may not have developed the
> requisite skills by the time they enter first grade, and the
> assumption that they do possess these skills may thus add to
> the frustrations these children experience on entering
> school. (1)

Dr. Deutsch's experiential enrichment program involves spatial organization, manipulative experiences, and other areas of
deficit. Visual experiences, using pegboards, offer stimuli shaped
like triangles, ellipses, or squares and inserting-withdrawal manip-
ulations involving the rotation, orientation, and sequences of these
shapes, which clearly precede the learning of letters and words.
Alternatively, cards having these different shapes can be presented
in matching games, for similar pre-reading experiences. Dr.
Deutsch also uses "ticket games" in which tickets vary in size,
shape, or color. Similarly he uses Montessori play materials for
quantitative and spatial concepts, and toys of various types in
order to attain experiential depth and breadth not available in the
child's home or neighborhood. Exposure to auditory experiences
and the ability to discriminate among auditory stimuli are also
important in the Deutsch program. For these experientially-
deprived children, mere attendance in pre-kindergarten in itself
offers an enormous range of stimuli-rich opportunities. There is
virtually no comparison between the school and these pupils'
homes in terms of educational preparation.

Thus, simple though they are, classroom tidiness, clothing
closure and opening, and toilet use and hygiene set the stage for
far more complex social relationships and competence; the use of
seating plans imparts not only a sense of order, but a preliminary
talent in map reading and later mapmaking in the way of classroom floor plans; a series of neighborhood photographs recaptures
neighborhood experiences, so that pictures of the fire house, the
police station, the supermarket, the school, the bakery offer exercises in identification. Even television commercials have their use
as effective reading motivators. First name and last name use train
in social maturity. Mass magazines like *Life, Look,* and *The
Saturday Evening Post* offer visual and cutout possibilities—but so

also do wallpaper sample books. The observation of colors in automobile license plates of various states becomes another approach to geography. The prices of groceries can be reported and thereby become training in arithmetic and training in homework assignments. The kinds of brand names in soaps, soups, breads, cereals, milks, and margarines additionally sharpen recognition. Patriotic songs, songs of other countries, various national anthems, and mass recitations like the pledge of allegiance to the flag and other choral readings encourage social behavior on many levels, as do discussions on the best way of taking turns, by running, by pushing, by size, or by alphabetical order. Doll play, like the dressing of dolls in national costumes, and the use of simple tools, offer simultaneous opportunities in a variety of directions—social, manipulative, conceptual, geographic.

Not a bit of this is new to the skilled kindergarten or nursery school teacher, which means that an extensive curriculum exists for the pre-school child, offering the experiential enrichment so necessary for school and reading readiness—provided that we can get the child to the school. What is needed? Merely money. The government investment—or bet—seems amply protected by everything we know of psychology, biology, and good sense. (2)

At the other end of the public school continuum, with the population of dropouts, tens of millions of dollars are beginning to be spent on an experience that originated with the CCC—and paid off handsomely. Vice-President Hubert Humphrey has strongly advocated that we take the lessons of the CCC to heart as highly relevant to the dropout. When the modern CCC transports the adolescent dropout to a work camp hundreds of miles off, it removes him from his neighborhood, but the experience also teaches him mobility. Work skills, learning skills, out-of-door experiences, decent meals and sleeping, play and games, give the dropout what his parents and community were never able to give him.

Note, please, that these skills and experiences which are intended to be ultimately utilizable in urban settings are gained in country settings, which is instructive because it tells us that the countryside, released from agriculture, is available for composure and redemption from the unsettling conditions of modern urbanism. But let us remember that the dropout, returned to his family and neighborhood, can regress unless he can put his skills and experience to use. The probability of his doing so in the place of his origin is low, which indicates that he must be discouraged from returning, that during his stay he must be taught what opportunities exist elsewhere, that the entire country is his, and that he must not be frightened into returning to his home but must begin a new life elsewhere, or run the risks of relapse. He can reduce the risks only by preparing himself to affect his home and neighborhood, a determination that requires strength and allies, so he must also be made aware of the allies available to him once he returns home. This takes political, economic, and citizenship education specifically slanted to the dropout's condition.

Hence we must, with the dropout, always ask ourselves, "What happens afterwards?" The question is similar to that asked at Lexington, Kentucky, with narcotics addicts, who "dry out" successfully as long as they are institutionalized but who slip again once they are released from supportive therapy. No program of reading improvement, skills, and counseling, however rich, can omit this follow-up, which assures continuing contact and mutual responsibility between the dropout and the agency.

So, whether pre-school dropin or post-school dropout, we see education invading the time of the underprivileged child. The movement is inevitable, but not one bit new for the middle-class or upper-class child who has always had his after-school time absorbed by educational plans and purposes, whether by piano lessons, organized games, the presence of a parent, weekends with the family, or summers away at camp.

The After-school Program

Automation is upon us, meaning increased leisure time for the adult. But the mastery of automated processes requires increased time in school. Also, whatever the emotive life at home, the school must teach the patterns of emotive experience to lend greater understanding. For fuller, deeper outcomes in family living, for improved emotive controls, for the exploding boundaries of knowledge, for specialized competence and generalized knowledge, for the survival of society—for all these, time, more time, and still more time must be granted the school day, week, and year, which ultimately gives us improved adult leisure. When, in December

1963, New York's Board of Education opened 233 after-school tutoring centers to "raise the educational potential of pupils in minority group areas" by use of library services, homework clinics, and special help in school subjects, it was invading the time of the underprivileged child as the time of the middle-class and upper-class child had always been. For their services teachers were paid beyond their regular salaries, and college student volunteers were used, but, paid or volunteer, these services were after-school.

These tutoring centers had antecedents in New York's All-Day Neighborhood Schools, which for 1961–62 had an average daily register of 13,000 pupils, and were operating in 12 schools in the city. The student population in New York City, as of October 1961, was 1 million, so that this oldest attempt in New York to serve underprivileged children through after-school programs was insignificant in scope, hazardous in its origins, and survived through a combined miracle of faith and simple nagging. Dr. Adele Franklin, the director, tells of a beginning in a midtown New York settlement house in the depression years, the use of WPA workers, involvement of the Public Education Association, and ultimate reluctant adoption by the Board of Education on a skimpy, partial basis. (3)

Removal of the deprived child from the deprived home is a feature of these schools, as is an extension of the school day, since the children are retained from nine o'clock to five o'clock. Until three o'clock the child experiences the usual school day, but after three an organized recreational, dance, arts-and-crafts, club, and study program takes over. Unfortunately, the child is nevertheless sent home at dinner time to what usually is an unstable home situation, where the mother generally has full-time employment.

For approximately a generation, the All-Day Neighborhood Schools were alone in advocating an extended school day. Then, in 1962, the Graduate School of Education of Yeshiva University developed a teacher preparation program, called *PROJECT BEACON* (capitalized and italicized to sound loud and clear!), which was subsequently elaborated in discussions between Yeshiva University personnel and the Board of Education. Project Beacon envisioned a complete invasion of the time of the culturally deprived child in a twelve-hour school day, a seven-day school week, and a fifty-two-week school year. The precedents existed. For example, the six-day school week is accepted practice in many lands, and if European students up to the graduate level show more progress at comparable ages than do American students, the additional time spent in school may contribute. Also, whenever society feels the need, it makes forays into the time of the child; in the Soviet Union and in the Israeli *kibbutz,* economic need for working mothers results in the *crèche* and the nursery school, allowing utilization of the mother in production and additional family income.

By the summer of 1963, the Board of Education was under heavy attack to do something about the conditions of New York City schools. It was reeling under the charges in the Schinnerer Report, (3a) and accusations from state officialdom and from Negro groups demanding integration. Constrained by budget and shortage of trained personnel, it chose the skimpy piecemeal escape.

Its 1963 after-school tutorial program was designed for voluntary attendance by underprivileged pupils, who would be coached by teachers receiving additional stipends. Many teachers were eager for assignment because it meant supplementary income. Students could come or not, as they pleased or felt the need; in actuality, they were frequently coerced into attendance by teachers who wanted to keep their registers up so that they could keep getting paid, and who, for the same reason, spoke glowingly of the program.

At the moment we know how much is being spent, what the daily register is, how many teachers are involved. We are less certain about pupil-improvement—at least, for those pupils at whom the program was originally aimed, but the program seems to meet a need because average *weekly* attendance in the elementary division is approximately 70,000; in the junior high schools, 24,000; and in the senior high schools, 14,000. Because the programs have a three-day week, *daily* attendance is approximately 33,000. Teachers are paid $12 for a two-hour stint, and the budget in the elementary schools is $1,800,000; in the junior high schools, $785,000; and in the senior high schools, $370,000 annually, or almost $3 million total per year. This sum pays for the services of approximately 1,440 elementary school teachers, 600 junior high school teachers, and 300 senior high school teachers, for an approximate teaching staff of 2,340. The teaching staff is supplemented by a supervisory staff. Each school is assigned a supervisor; and 206 elementary schools, 79 junior high schools, and 60 high schools are participating.

The program, however, seems to be straying from its original blueprint. Less remedial than intended, and becoming more coaching-oriented, the program is ignored by slower students while the brighter ones flock to it. Those who need it most frequent it least and vice versa. We could have expected it, but what has happened is not at all bad—pupils want an extension of the school day. The attendance shows it, and we need not be too concerned about the brightness or slowness of the customers. Our chief concern should be with the bad planning that tries to make a little go a long way.

Our planning for a really expanded school program will be different. The extended school day will retain underprivileged children beyond dinnertime, so that we can provide free suppers as we now provide free school lunches. During this extended school day we will offer recreational, coaching, and study facilities in mathematics, social studies, English, reading, art, and music. Thereafter we will send the children home at eight or nine o'clock, depending on age, for their night's sleep. They will have eaten well, they will have had adequate supervised play time, they will have done their homework, and they will have rested. They are fortified to cope with the promiscuous mothers and putative fathers they will encounter; and society will be fortified with human resources that can in no other way be reclaimed and set to rights.

The after-school program we propose varies by elementary, junior high, and senior high curriculum, and is further compartmentalized by subject matter.

The elementary school child in the after-school program will require opportunity for solitude, so that he can retreat from the group with which he has been through the school day to regroup his resources in order to rejoin the group for the after-school program. The after-lunch resting period is an accepted part of nursery school curriculum, and a similar interim resting period ought to find a place after the regular school day, preferably after a brief game period.

Children are exuberant after a school day and must be allowed to let off steam. Hence a 3:00 to 3:45 period for play and games would appropriately follow the school day, to be followed by a twenty-minute rest, in turn followed by a period in which homework assignments are done, which should take until five o'clock. A supper can then be served, followed by an arts and crafts period for an hour, or alternatively, some TV or radio, followed by games or dance instruction, or special tutoring. This should bring the elementary school child to eight o'clock, when preparations for the return home are in order. Arrangements and scheduling around the above broad plan would be modified as the child grows through the grades.

In the junior high school extended day program, the need for a rest period would be less, provisions for solitude increased, time for assignments increased. But with all these shifts and accommodations to the age of the child, the chief educational fact again would be removal from family and neighborhood. Within this framework, tutorials in specific content areas can become formally integrated within the program, taught by personnel receiving extra pay for this extra duty, or by student teachers as part of their supervised preparation. Competitive team play must form a conspicuously regular part of the program, because girls are almost as involved as boys in team play at this age. Furthermore, this age group must become broadened with visits to museums, newspapers, factories, places of historical significance, and public interest, because a surprising number of these children are ignorant of places beyond a five- or ten-block radius from their homes. One is reminded of Luana in *The Cool World,* already a prostitute in her early teens, and nevertheless a New Yorker who has never seen Coney Island. Thus many Negro children in Brooklyn have never been to Manhattan, nor, indeed, beyond the streets that take them from home to school.

As with elementary school children, the junior high school extended day program provides for free suppers on the school premises, so that the greater geographical mobility possible with children of this age becomes circumscribed by the need to have them at a regular place and at a specified time for the evening meal. They can be sent home at a later hour, which extends the range of program offerings.

The senior high school group, it might be supposed, would be resistant to an extended school day, but after-school programs in athletics, journalism, teams, clubs, and dramatics, are accepted in the high school and are less novel than the extended school day for the younger groups. High school boys and girls have experience in remaining away from home and neighborhood and, with the sense that the school plant is available to them, would have little difficulty in becoming available for a combined study-recreational program.

The above description opens up additional questions. Is the program to be compulsory or voluntary? If voluntary, will it get regular, predictable attendance?

Wherever school plants, settlement houses, or social agencies hospitably extend *meaningful* services to the community, these services are used. We therefore need have no concern about the extent of voluntary use of the program. Rather a contrary situation is to be dreaded, that we may be unable to secure the right personnel in sufficient numbers to staff the program. Can we locate enough capable physical training instructors, teachers of dance and art, remedial reading teachers, instructors in mathematics, and teachers of science to service the numbers of children who voluntarily participate in the program?

Retired army personnel, college students seeking part-time work, regularly appointed teachers often "moonlighting" in other jobs in order to augment income are there. Ultimately, however, we will have to train more teachers than we are now doing.

Another question arises: if the extended school day frees mothers for employment, does it not also free them for more licentiousness? Surely, but far less than unemployment and relief rolls do because we have now no excuse for maintaining physically able mothers on welfare rolls unless we admit we have no work for them. But if we grant tax allowances and rebates to slum landlords for cleaning up their properties, we can also pay these mothers to clean public buildings, maintain their neighborhoods in less filthy conditions, act as adjunct janitors on their floors, and in one way or another earn their keep in the new time they have been granted. Our hospitals alone could find work for thousands of untrained mothers in cleaning, kitchen help, and nursing assistantships. Further, the new free time offers opportunities for such training to be given, and for the insistence that such training be taken, lest relief funds be withheld. The mother no longer has the child to excuse her in her aimlessness. We may find that heretofore unutilized mother-daughter classes in reducing and beauty care, father-son classes in volleyball and basketball, and family recreation clubs with picnics and outings will at last be patronized, thus improving the community relations of the school that will now remain open twenty-four hours a day, to keep a light burning through the night, even if nobody walks in. (4) Saloon, bistro, and nightclub owners run their businesses that way. They have more insight, apparently, than school administrators.

The Weekend Program

Unfortunately, the gains of an extended school day can be lost in home and neighborhood over the weekend, so Saturdays and Sundays become traps unless we spring the traps and their captives too by plans and programs for otherwise weakened weekends. Means exist for doing so even in the dead of winter in the countryside surrounding metropolis and megalopolis that is never more than a few hours away. Children can reach the countryside before nightfall when school closes at three o'clock on Friday, to begin, depending on grade, a weekend program of supreme educational value. The value is enhanced partially because they are away from family and neighborhood, but also because study programs will be subordinated to recreation in attractive areas. The real estate is available, and buses and roads make transportation simple.

Let us be warned against that noble word *community* and the sociological fakery committed in its name. What a bottomless sink when from Brooklyn to San Francisco money is spent to keep children where they are! How inefficiently will these funds be spent simply because they will be spent in the community! How efficiently they would be spent were the youth they are to service withdrawn from the community and placed in another setting! (5)

In a city like New York, tens of thousands of children would participate. Many of these children will not come from culturally deprived homes, nor can these be turned away. The hebdomadal, mass exodus constitutes an enormous, but soluble, logistical problem. Under analysis, it is not appalling.

First, housing. Fireproof quarters are essential and are available in prefabricated structures which offer every comfort, in addition to safety, and are inexpensive to erect and maintain. Such structures now exist and are being produced both in this country and in Europe. Indeed, a subsidiary of the French Schneider-

Creusot vows to erect steel prefabricated school and housing structures in this country under the costs of domestic manufacturers. The Ford Foundation's Educational Facilities group has described the characteristics of such structures in a number of readily available materials.

Second, staff. Regular teachers, college students, student teachers, bus drivers, kitchen help, physicians and nurses, retired military personnel, parent volunteers, religious leaders, and nature counsellors can be recruited in adequate number, not only from among city dwellers, but also in the country areas to which the children are sent.

Third, inceptions. We cannot sprint into this program, but must begin with a couple each of elementary schools, junior highs, and high schools, testing our progress as we go and extending the program by stages. Thus in New York we begin with one school in Harlem, another in Bedford-Stuyvesant, and a third in Morrisania, broadening school coverage year by year, having a desperate time as we fight off the clamorous applicants. But we shall at least be on our way and learning our business.

Finally, the tryout area can be in the city as well as the country. We cannot omit the city's weekend resources in museums, theaters, play areas, and parks. Weekend programs must involve city experiences, even as we go forward with the countryside program, thereby gaining experience in our logistical, recruiting, and curriculum problems. Federal legislation now operationally affecting marginal farm areas can regularize currently directionless government expenditures, and funds now being expended without purpose can gain meaning and return.

Unlike the grade separation by elementary, junior high, and senior high school, the weekend program permits mixed housing by grade, though not by sex, so that in the same quarters we will find children of all ages. This heterogeneous age grouping permits certain economies but also has educational value, involving responsibility for the younger by the older. Then high school juniors and seniors can be delegated counsellor-in-training responsibilities in certain games and activities, and be paid suitably for assumption of these responsibilities. In addition, this heterogeneous grouping permits a program of nature study, hiking, sports, games, athletics, and arts and crafts that can be separately and flexibly planned for each level. Thus appropriate movies can be shown to the elementary school group, but not to the older groups; and games and physical activities, though adjusted to this younger group, can be conveniently supervised and coached by the high school juniors and seniors. The junior high school group can concentrate on hiking, camping, and nature study, all integrated with school study in biology or general science. The senior high school group can have its core activities centered in construction and building projects, training in the use of tools, overnight excursions to places of interest, and such appropriate studies as astronomy and geology. (6)

The Summer Program

Teachers "moonlight" as owners of or counsellors in summer camps. College students work in summer camps. Parents on the upper and lower end of the economic ladder have experience in shipping their children off for varying periods and getting them back some weeks later none the worse and the parents much improved.

Summer camps vary from the settlement house camps to music camps, riding camps, sailing camps, work camps, and camps for aspiring physicists. They are widely adaptable to interests, income, ethnic affiliation and religious cuisine, sports preferences, and geography.

Cities in the summer are very tolerable places for adults who have jobs to go to and weekends to plan for, but cities in the summer are a veritable hell for children. "New York is a summer festival" for grownups only, because the better restaurants are less crowded, air conditioning allows you to keep the windows closed, the insects out, and let in only air that has been properly filtered into fitness for breathing. Grownups can make themselves comfortable in most American cities even in the hottest summers. What exacerbates summer living in American cities more than temperature or humidity is the presence of children who, themselves troubled by urban heat, communicate this distress to their elders, whose irritation with urban life thereupon increases. No greater boon—aside from air conditioning—befalls the American urban parent than the ability to ship a child out of the city for the summer.

Charity camps, Boy Scout, and Girl Scout camps make this possible for many poor children, usually for a two-week fraction of the summer, but we have enough countryside available for all urban children for an entire summer, and the countryside need not be contiguous to the city.

Though large institutions like the Boy Scouts have their fingers in it, summer camping is often a small business, involving a petty entrepreneur, like the mom-and-pop retail grocery store before the supermarkets moved in. Such camp owners could object to a municipality as rival endeavor, though their facilities do not provide for the culturally deprived. On the other hand, a marginal camp owner would be interested in using his experience and training, if suitably paid, or in the leasing of his facilities to a city, liberating its deprived children from family and neighborhood.

Experience, indeed, is available here, where we have comparatively little in the extended day, or weekend, for all kinds of children, in all kinds of terrain, from the seashore to the mountains. We know that the summer camping experience is eagerly anticipated by most children, a treasured memory when past, and an oasis in the horror of city living, a horror especially acute during the summer, when heat deepens fury and riots occur because tempers are shortest then. To remove the deprived child from the city for an entire summer becomes an urgent necessity, if we are to keep his sanity. And the sanity of his parents too.

Until we air-condition Harlem, it will riot because it's too hot to sleep. The least we can do is get the child out of it. Riots are cheaper than setting up new power facilities to air-condition a slum, and children are cheaper than riots. Air conditioning and summer camps cost more than Harlem can afford, and more than the municipality claims it can afford, but can both take the price of a riot any better?

New York City's educational budget is now approximately $1 billion, and a summer camping program might increase that figure—at most—by 20 per cent, but a two-month span gives us enough time to give the child's education some decided forward thrusts. If we specialize, the summer offers opportunity for a diagnosis of the particular child's learning disability and concentration on it. Thus, for many children a program in reading improvement will constitute an entire summer's school program, and they will emerge with more gains in reading than they can attain during the regular school year. Similarly, other children will attack weaknesses in mathematics and science. Children without weaknesses have the time for advanced work in language, English, reading, mathematics, or science, so that the summer allows children to get along snappily in their studies, *which means corresponding economies in regular school operations,* whether through acceleration or enrichment.

Acceleration masquerades under the names of "rapid advance," or "special progress," or "advanced placement," and allows children to trot along more rapidly in their school work. (7) It is favored by many school officials because it gets children out of school at an earlier age and saves money. The summer camping experience allows for such acceleration and hence for savings in the total educational budget. At the same time, enrichment procedures are available through remedial and make-up work for the slower student, and coaching and tutoring for the brighter one. Money may therefore be a deterrent to air-conditioning Harlem, but not to providing summer-long camping experiences for Harlem children. For example, the high school student taking one major subject for four summers has saved himself one term in high school and the school system the expense of keeping him in school for that time. The savings are even greater for the elementary school child spending eight years in summer camp.

Aside from the comparative merits of acceleration and enrichment, the summer camp lends objectivity to home and neighborhood ties and substitutes values more socially desirable than those the child has left behind in the city. Without setting child against parent, we can build habits of personal cleanliness, social responsibility, group feeling, and citizenship that can be further reinforced in the school's extended day and week after the return home. When Jeremiah bought the lands of Hanameel (Jeremiah 32 : 6–44), because the country was safer than the city, he also forsook the city's evildoers (Jeremiah 16 : 2–8), because they weren't safe to fool around with. The bosom of nature can offer nourishment not available to the city dweller, and in the right doses can make him see city dwelling in a clearer light. We want our deprived children to see some of their homes and all their neighborhoods in this clearer light. We have earlier said some unpleasant things about the brutalizing effects of country living and the peasant mind that unrelieved farming develops. We qualify these unpleasant things by granting the civilizing and pacifying effects of a touch of earth to city people. The country, if you don't have to work it, offers space to play, learn, and slow down in. Also, under this program, it spares children their homes, a most important use for government lands and park areas.

With less acreage these days producing more agricultural product, we have the greatest opportunity since we were neolithic to use abandoned farm lands for pure recreation. The federal government has paid out billions for farmers to avoid being farmers, to stop raising crops, and to return farm lands to nature, to conservation uses, and to public recreational facilities. Weekend programs and summer camping programs for low-culture children, allowing urban schools to remove these children from home, community, and city, with all that this promises for the improvement of skills and attitudes, *at a reasonable level of public expenditure,* in programs that are financially practicable and indeed economical, put the ultimate capstone on these federal plans for rural development. (8) No innovation for the wealthy child, who is routed to boarding school, preparatory school, summer camp, and is surrounded by educational auspices, the lengthened school day, week, and year is also good for slum children.

We thereby extend the number of college graduates a decade hence, and we spare these children drunkenness, sexual promiscuity, and crowded bedrooms, so incompatible with work, homework assignments, privacy, healthy involvements, and planned living.

We want them in college. We want them doing assignments. The curriculum is too crowded to be completed on school time, within the usual school day. The program permits homework assignments to be given and done, thus gaining us more college graduates, more technically trained people, and a more emotionally composed society, and allowing us to nullify the emotional disruption of an "uncle" or a mother sleeping around. The program would within half a decade transform the morale of slum dwellers—children and parents—raising to productive citizenship the one-tenth of our population that now costs more than it contributes.

And much of the program is possible out of current funds, if these are judiciously expended.

A moral impediment appears. If the state displaces the family in the nurture of the child, is not the home's sanctity invaded? Yes, if the home has the sanctity generated by responsible parents; but suppose parents do not sense this responsibility, certainly not in any identifiable manner? Then the moral objection is not real because the state displaces a vacuum, not an actuality, with every moral—and certainly legal—right to do so. Where social entities break down, in farming, railroads, labor, industry, the government moves in, filling power vacuums and wiping intolerable situations out of existence, provided that there are enough votes in it. Even the conservative *Wall Street Journal,* opposed to such governmental interventions and subventions, enjoys postal rates that reflect government intervention, for which other users must pay. We need only compare newspaper postal rates with first class mailing rates over the past thirty years. The government moves, or doesn't move, depending on the pressures put on it.

The government has begun to move on behalf of these virtually homeless children. It has already traveled a distance that would have been thought incredible when Eisenhower left the White House. Until recently, the moral pressure for government intervention was inconsequential compared to political, economic, and sectional pressures for governmental aloofness. The government has tacitly agreed that some homes and families are without any sanctity we are bound to respect and that mitigating the murderous effects of such homes and family living is a moral blessing. When the promise of useful involvement in society is curtailed because homes are educationally and culturally handicapped, the moral thing to do is to restore the stability that has fled.

But are we not institutionalizing children, as in a Soviet *crèche* or an Israeli *kibbutz?* The cases are not parallel. Our slum children, particularly our Negro children, come from a setting where the prevailing social atomosphere is not sheltering, whatever the individual family effort may be. *Crèche* or *kibbutz* children are not blasted children, though they may have other personality shortcomings. (9) They contribute, they are responsible, and they lead fully participating lives. Too many Negro children are blasted. Though a sheltering, loving home is superior to government intervention, government intervention is superior to the rootless, immoral home. We can lead these children to fully participating lives by first leading them forth from unsuitable homes. In addition, governmental intervention can improve the rootless Negro home by lifting the guilt and anxiety now there. Remove these and you've made room for the sanctity of the home.

Nothing in morals or ethics can legitimately object to the extended school day, week, and year. Financing is not beyond reach. What chiefly hinders us is stereotyped political thinking. We now deal with one important stereotype.

10

Money Incentives for the Learner

Payment to Pupils

Educational budgets are heavy because we expect to pay the teacher, the principal, the supervisor, the administrator, the social worker, the attendance officer, the school nurse, the school doctor, the school clerk, the school janitor, and the remaining paraphernalia of educational bureaucracy—but never the pupil.

Why?

The Russians have done some thinking about this stereotype, which is why they may be graduating more engineers than we do. Just as Russians pay their students, Professor B. F. Skinner "pays" his rats and pigeons for learning. (1) Similarly, Professor Irving Lorge's experiments in the Depression, with token payments to WPA subjects, proved that people learn when paid, and will not learn when it pays them not to learn, which is why people do not learn up to capacity. (2) In our graduate schools, assistantships, fellowships, scholarships, and post-doctoral grants, we pay people for learning.

If we pay the teacher to teach, should we not pay the pupil to learn? Or, better yet, pay only when he does learn?

Is this bribery?

Perhaps one of the great troubles of American education is too much socialism and not enough capitalism. Some healthy capitalism would allow us to pay students in proportion to their achievements; we grade them that way. If a Negro boy or girl wanted some spending money, it could be earned by turning in appropriate grades, doing the requisite assignments, and passing suitable examinations. We use the incentives of private enterprise with everybody except the pupils.

"You're bribing them to learn!" the pseudo-moralist objects. Then scholarships, fellowships, and assistantships are also a species of bribery. At what point does bribery become reward? When does a gift become subornation? Like Skinner's pigeons, Lorge's WPA subjects, and the monkey coin-slot experiments, children rewarded are not children bribed or degraded, but children improved.

Punishment and reward, like reproof and praise, are motivational devices, but may not be similarly so with good students and poor ones. Punishment and reproof are the generally prevailing practice, even with the better student, as a means of goading him to greater effort, but then he has the ability to visualize the long-deferred goals of praise and reward as the slower student cannot. This hints that the slower student must be given more frequent, and smaller, rewards as he proceeds, but the rewards must be clearly visible and immediate to reinforce the next stage, or passage, of learning. Hence a terminal Regents scholarship of hundreds of dollars may have less reality than the two or three dollars a week you have just earned for completing your algebra and social studies and French assignments perfectly. (3)

Furthermore, we have here a guarantee as tight as we can get that curriculums will work in deprived neighborhoods without being watered down, that we can retain standards and values, and that we can hold the culturally deprived child to these standards and values without adulteration.

In addition, we have a means of self-policing by the individual pupil who is in the running for the two, three, or four dollars a week that performing well gains him, which, in turn, sets the stage for a new effectiveness in team teaching and the far larger class size that effective team teaching permits, and the consequent economies that we can plow back into improved schooling. But team teaching, as we said before, is the precursor to the emergence of cooperation-competition-leadership, team learning, and the sense of group responsibility that is the best investment democracy can make.

The same voice that cried out "Bribery!" now says, "You're encouraging cheating! Your 'team learning' is only an opportunity for them to copy from one another!" Unquestionably, if the teacher's assignments and tests allow this. Then the teacher is cheating, not the student.

In brief, Negro educational achievements could be radically improved if we paid Negro pupils for studying, varying payment in direct proportion to work done and grades received. We could increase Negro intellectuality within a year, and not only teach the Negro child that it pays him to learn, but that there is a future for him in his education, and that people care. Not finances, but loyalty to stereotypes makes people think otherwise.

The symbol structure of dispossessed groups requires basic reordering. Payment for learning disssolves the self-doubts and self-misgivings in these children.

Direct payment to the learner streamlines the educational budget. We should need fewer attendance officers and babysitters masquerading as teachers—those heretofore indispensable middle-men in the educational process—but more library and study space. Economy-size, or large assembly classes, and team teaching make greater sense, as we break our stereotype. We increase self-reliance and inner responsibility, we involve parents and the home as never before, because money has entered the picture—solid, tangible, palpable, hard cash—to reorder the child's symbol system. We can remove the teacher from the classroom, substitute a teaching program, and be sure of attentiveness. With hundreds of children in a large assembly hall, we can darken the lights, show a closed-circuit television program, and know they will neither fall asleep or horse around. So many audio-visual lessons take place figuratively and literally in the dark!

Our questioner asks: "The child's father is a drunkard and the mother a narcotics addict. How do you know if the money the child earns by learning doesn't go to pay for alcohol or her-oin?" (4) We can improve on the question. The child himself may be using wine or marijuana. Funds can be misappropriated and we would be callow to think otherwise, but we can make all sorts of preparations, as long as our eyes are open and our perspectives clear. All the evidence is that payment for learning will straighten out values more often than it distorts them. Not *always;* but *more often* nevertheless.

Research will come into the picture as we try to determine

how much to pay pupils, the suitable incentives, and the gradient of a sliding pay scale. Will pay rates be the same for mathematics, English, social studies, and modern language, as for home economics, art, and music? Will we pay the same for major subjects as for minor subjects? These pay schedules need not be too difficult to set. Part of the Lorge WPA study seemed to find that increase in stipend did not increase learning rate, meaning that a minimum salary will encourage a child to learn almost as much as if we doubled or tripled his salary. With Skinner's rats and pigeons, on the other hand, output is increased by suitable increase in reward. Which result applies to our program? Only research can determine this.

Pupil-payment-for-learning allows us educational scope we have never had before. We can at last attract those teacher prospects who would rather be dead than in an education course. We can finally recruit for quality, because we can enlarge class size, give executive responsibility to teacher-leaders, impose standards on the learner, and police those standards. We can reward with greater effect and punish realistically, since money combines the material and the symbolic. We will reduce defeatism in Negro children now learning poorly, and will more successfully bribe those children now learning well, but without subvention, to raise their sights because even our best students—at Winnetka, the Bronx High School of Science, and elsewhere—are not doing as well as students in England, France, Germany, or Russia. Our best and our poorest are giving us diluted performance. Not until the doctoral level do our students perform equivalently with European graduate students—precisely when we offer subventions on a grand scale! We can without difficulty gear subventions to home need, as well as to performance, because both are legitimate measuring sticks. We have had much experience in doing so, as in the New York State Regents scholarships.

As militance and non-violence are not mutually exclusive, neither are delinquency and intelligence, say the Gluecks, (5) which is why the Mafia can handle international transactions. But pupil-payment-for-learning can help make them mutually exclusive, can disrupt undesirable behavior, and can generate a sense of participating citizenship, because shock and punishment will become associated with non-payment for non-learning, and we will thereby generate a sense of sin, rather than of bribery, and we have the non-learner over the porkbarrel as never before because money—not we—has convinced him that he is a wrongdoer.

Ultimately, thereby, we develop a love for learning. In impoverished European Jewish communities, the Jew who learned, rather than earned, was greatly esteemed. If his wife worked to maintain the family, his psychological integrity was not blasted—unlike the unemployed Negro who depends on his wife for maintenance—because learning was reason enough to maintain the man, or, in our terms, to pay him. The learned Jew was often dependent, timid, introverted, and withdrawn, but not fragmented, and in complete harmony with the community. He too was being paid for learning.

Payment in Adult Education and Adult Retraining

We shift scenes, from classroom to industrial setting, to describe a teacher-executive called a *training director,* who contributes to policy and decision in large business and industry. (6) To increase profits, he:

1. Develops programs in sales training, so that sales personnel can handle customers, persuade them, please them, and secure orders

2. Organizes engineering seminars for technical personnel on new products, new techniques, the improvement of old ones, reports of defects, discussions of quality control and materials, and the technical achievements of competing firms

3. Plans programs on executive development to reduce jockeying in upper-level echelons or to sharpen executive perspectives, by using resources as diverse as psychoanalysis, reading speed courses, interviewing techniques, or group dynamics, to ensure an executive team that operates smoothly even in high gear

4. Develops resources for consumer, stockholder, and community relations, working with public relations and advertising personnel, to show the advantages of buying from, investing in, or working for the company

5. Is involved in personnel relations, the communications of

management to line-and-staff and the resulting feedback in worker suggestions, incentive plans, trade union conflict and cooperation, complaints and unrest, and productive efficiency based on time-and-motion studies

6. Deals with community programs of urban education, vocational and technical education, and retraining

7. Uses the techniques of lecture, recitation, performance, blackboards, audio-visual aids, teaching machines, team teaching, textbooks, and grades

8. Occupies an important position in the business hierarchy —although a teacher—because he pays for learning improvement

In contrasting the training director and the teacher in morale, function, curriculum, company image, and self-image, we see why the teacher-in-classroom is one breed of cat, whereas the teacher-in-industry is another, partially because payment for learning is accepted practice in business; what else accounts for the training director's contribution and status? He exists in England, the Scandinavian countries, Italy, Germany, and the Soviet Union— wherever large industrial complexes are made possible by the promise to pay for learning, so making it possible to rise to a better job.

Not always. Some people are not persuaded by the promise or the evidence put before them, which reduces competition for those who are persuaded. Similarly, if learning-for-pay will not work with everybody in Harlem schools, that is not important as long as it works in significantly more cases than the present educational program, and at reasonable cost.

Management groups like the American Management Association, the Committee for Economic Development, and the National Industrial Conference Board are involved in training programs, assessing old ones and experimenting with new ones in the search for greater profits and efficiency. Placed in middle or top management, the training director promises people from all levels of the industrial hierarchy more money and advancement if they do well in his training programs—and this learning-for-pay promise usually delivers.

Just as, usually, delivery is deferred because others are seeking job mobility also, so some tolerance for delayed reward is required. Anticipation of ultimate gain, however, cannot be too attenuated. Delayed reward builds on immediate reward. Skinner's hard-working pigeons achieve enormous productive output, but only after easy work gains results; thereafter they are taught that hard work will too, so they work hard. Negroes work hard, but the bigger picture is getting them to train hard and learn hard for a deferred benefit. Negro children must be taught anticipation, that learning hard gets results. Payment-for-learning does this, not by bribery but by setting distorted symbolic values aright at last. After all, the child's teacher takes in-service courses for salary increments and promotions. There's money in it.

Curricular Psychology

We are about to coin a new title for an old thing, a forgivable matter when old things regain a former importance as new light is cast on them. For some time the nit-picking discipline known as "the psychology of the school subjects" was scorned by educators because spelling, arithmetic, handwriting, geography, history, and the other school subjects were each assigned their own special pedagogic, placed in a compartment, and specially taught in a special methods course. The number of such courses bloomed like a jungle growth. (1) Some special subjects, like reading, emerged from this slough because concentrated research was done in the area, and meaningful strategies developed for teaching.

But research has revised approaches to other curriculum areas, reviving the feeling that the school subjects cannot be similarly motivated, reviewed, drilled, conceptualized, taught, and learned. Thus one cannot teach grammar as one teaches poetry, though they have language as a common prowling ground; grammar has more in common with mathematics instruction than with literary judgments, and poetry has more in common with mathematical imagination than with the prosaics of usage. If so, much is lost by ignoring instructional differences, especially when we cannot teach high-level pupils as we do low-level pupils, deprived pupils as we do privileged ones, nor badly behaved pupils as we do well-behaved ones. We have pushed further into the nature of mathematics, linguistics, foreign language, science, and social studies than the early psychology of the school subjects ever did, and we are constrained to reevaluate this psychology in the light of curriculum developments; today, this study can be called curricular psychology.

Thus faculty psychology, out of date for more than half a century, was re-styled into modern factor analysis and the psychology of mental factors, given a mathematical rationale, and is now modish again. Curricular psychology is a reexamination of the old psychology of the school subjects. It has arisen because of what the English teacher has subsequently learned about linguistics, the mathematics teacher about mathematical manipulation versus mathematical exploration, the social studies teacher about the social and behavioral sciences, the chemistry teacher about chemical bond theory, and the foreign language teacher about the audio-lingual approach. And then the teaching machine and programed instruction!

We are also preparing new kinds of pupils, and we are being given much more money than ever before to prepare them. Specifically, then, let us examine curricular psychology as it relates to subject matter divisions.

The Teaching of Reading

We have described conditions for learning, but now we must consider the materials to be learned.

At the vestibule to all learning is reading. Where experiences have been meager, reading furnishes substitute experiences. On the other hand, without experiences during the pre-school years, the child has difficulty with the symbolic and the conceptual that reading demands. Hence experience and readiness for reading interact.

The "poor" reader is not the same as the "retarded" reader. The retarded reader is below his own potential. He is more intelligent than his reading score indicates, and the gap between reading score and intelligence measures his retardation. He is generally remediable. The poor reader has low intelligence, may be reading up to that low intelligence level, and that level is a measure of the odds against his ever improving. (2)

Though reading improvement materials exist in great quantity, reading problems persist, nor has the quantity of materials diminished the incidence of problems. Perhaps the reading materials now available are not suitable; perhaps these materials do not interact effectively with experiential deprivation; perhaps no reading materials can remediate family, community, physiological, and psychological contributions to reading deficit; perhaps reading improvement depends on teaching and presentation, rather than on materials, because the best of materials will be ineffective with a poor teacher. Hence our discussion must consider what goes wrong with reading materials, must investigate new approaches to materials that cancel teacher ineffectiveness, and must describe the ways of maximum leverage in the planning, policy, and assessment of reading programs.

We shall find that pupil age affects reading performance and reading disability. The teacher trained in reading improvement techniques for the elementary grades cannot transfer this expertise to the junior and senior high school; new reading problems emerge in adolescence. Though reading problems in junior and senior high school stem from reading problems in elementary school, they add some crucial ones of their own.

Unlike the poor reader in the elementary school, for whom reading consultants and remedial reading specialists exist, the poor reader in junior and senior high school is assigned to a reading improvement class typically presided over by an English teacher without special training in reading improvement techniques, and without sensitivity to other varieties of reading problems in social studies, in mathematics, or in science, because the departmentalized secondary school curriculum restricts opportunities to gain this awareness. The subject matter boundaries are impermeable because teachers are ignorant of the different reading problems in the different disciplines, and thus lack the techniques that will allow reading materials to pass across these boundaries.

To discuss reading instruction in the elementary schools would be repetitive, since a vast variety of approaches have been considered in terms of reading readiness, new alphabets, and other devices. (3) Instead, we shall concentrate on the comparatively unexplored area of reading improvement in the junior and senior high school because the unique problems of urban education emerge on these levels with special sharpness.

Most reading materials now in use, enthusiastically merchandised though they are by publishers, are not successful in the classroom. The reading teacher needs a skeptical awareness of the shortcomings and advantages of reading materials, else the quality of the teacher will surely be low, which is only saying that teachers should have some sophistication, and their preparation should too. This preparation should furthermore consider the accounting, the evaluating, and the assessing of reading materials, their usefulness and inadequacy, and how the reading program of a school and a school district should be managed.

Even further, the inadequacy of materials must be analyzed in terms of pupil reaction, which in turn leads us to the interest levels and the interest involvements of junior high and senior high school pupils, which, unfortunately, are not always aseptic, nor admissible to the light of day. Reading programs often fail because of pupil reluctance to give up these interest involvements, and because of teacher bashfulness about exploring them. The reading program must be sophisticated enough to anticipate both teacher-shyness and pupil-interests, knowing what the reasons are. (4)

This teacher's preparation should scrutinize administrative and supervisory preferences in reading materials. Anthology adoption, the book purchase rationale, and the modes of materials acquisition reflect publisher pressures only in part—they also reflect a concern for public relations, and what Mrs. Grundy, that well-known taxpayer, will have to say, while educational possibilities follow at a respectful distance behind these primary criteria.

Nevertheless, far more strategic are the personal, human, and technical qualifications in the reading teacher, and the facilities by which teachers can gain these qualities. For example, the secondary school teacher is a subject matter quasi-specialist and views reading disability from a particular subject matter perspective. Hence, the science teacher, the mathematics teacher, the English teacher, and the social studies teacher do not perceive reading disability the same way. One places great value on speed and appreciation, another on comprehension and retention, a third on analysis and evaluation. Though these qualities are not mutually exclusive, interest in a novel does not transfer to the conceptualization of Ohm's law, or the formula for the solution of a quadratic equation. The psychological stresses set up by the extended "soak-in" time needed for the meditation in mathematical reading are not the same as the suspense and stresses set up by seeing how a short story by Poe will end.

Most important of all in the preparation of the reading teacher is flexibility toward heretofore unexplored areas of reading materials, like the world of Broadway show music, a brand new area untrammeled by preconceptions and pedantry. Or see how the classified telephone directory can give exercise in dictionary skills, bestowing the same skills but in a context far more immediate, or how advertising copy and television commercials, newspaper head-lines and captions, mottoes, phonetics, speech analysis, and tape recorders offer a highly unorthodox reading program which re-mains unexplored because teachers are great believers in the orthodox and the well-explored.

Words and Lyricism

Some years ago, the author of this book was attending an international meeting in Stockholm. One evening he turned on his hotel radio and at once found himself bathed in American popular music, by Sinatra, Presley, Lombardo, Goodman, Monk, Sarah Vaughan, and others. The author, in later discussions with Swed-ish school officials, learned that English was compulsory in Swed-ish schools and that the same students who listened to American music with such avidity were simultaneously reluctant to learn English—either the American English or the British English that Swedes teach—and that Swedish schools do not incorporate into the language curriculum the motivational values of American show music, like the lyrics that accompany the music. The visitor discussed this possibility with his hosts, illustrating by "I'm in Love with a Wonderful Guy," from *South Pacific,* in which appear vocabulary words like *protestations, faith, naive, fearlessly, nor-mal, blueberry, conventional, dither, trite, cliché, bromidic*— words which are as difficult as those in most high school vocabu-lary lists. The hosts wanted to know if this resource was used in American reading programs, and the visitor hastily backed out of Sweden, leaving the matter unresolved, and was thereafter careful not to open the matter in France, Italy, and elsewhere, always finding that American show music is enormously popular with the twelve-to-eighteen-year-old groups, but not used in teaching English as a second language.

He remembered what Plato had said about the mind-opening possibilities of music in Book IV of *The Republic:* ". . . for the methods of music cannot be stirred up without great upheavals of social custom and law . . ." because of the drives—martial, peaceful, tranquilizing, stirring—in music, as well as some nastier, sexier aspects of music that Abel Green has mentioned: "In the past such material was common enough but restricted to special places and out-and-out barrelhouses. Today 'leer-ics' are offered as standard popular music for general consumption by teenagers. Our teenagers are already setting something of a record in delinquency without this raw musical idiom to smell up the environment even more." (5)

And: "The study of the Mishna was also accompanied by a chanting of its chapters; a famous remark of Rabbi Jochanan . . . was: 'He who reads the Scriptures without melody and the Mishna without song, of him it can be said . . . : "the laws I did give them are not good." ' " (6)

The visitor returned home, noting that in the American secondary school students customarily reassemble at the end of the school day in a nearby ice cream parlor or pizza palace and there busily push coins into juke boxes, to the annoyance of any passing English teachers who recognize the coin-pushers from remedial reading classes. The students are listening to an inconsequential song with lyrics that would scarcely challenge a third grade reader. But an adjoining record in the juke box is "The Girl That I Marry," from *Annie Get Your Gun,* in which appear *nursery, satin, cologne, gardenia,* and the formants /ur/, /er/, /at/, and /ia/, allowing us to create sound families, new words, additional vocabulary, practice sentences, and thereby both recognition and recall vocabularies.

In addition, sex being what it is in adolescence, we can capitalize on songs that have specialized sex-linked appeal, thus:

Boys' Selections	**Girls' Selections**
"Ballad of the Gun" (*Destry Rides Again*)	"People Will Say We're in Love" (*Oklahoma!*)
"Some Enchanted Evening" (*South Pacific*)	"I Feel Pretty" (*West Side Story*)

"Younger Than Springtime" (*South Pacific*)

"Oh, What a Beautiful Morning" (*Oklahoma!*)

"Surrey with the Fringe on Top" (*Oklahoma!*)

"Something's Coming" (*West Side Story*)

"Maria" (*West Side Story*)

"You've Got To Be Taught" (*South Pacific*)

"You've Got To Have Heart" (*Damn Yankees*)

"Fair Warning" (*Destry Rides Again*)

"I'm Gonna Wash That Man Right Outta My Hair" (*South Pacific*)

"I'm in Love with a Wonderful Guy" (*South Pacific*)

"Shall We Dance?" (*The King and I*)

Even in this limited representation of show songs appear such vocabulary words as *genius, overdue, autograph, consistent, link, gossip, gist, bouquet, glow, suspect, fickle, earthly, roving, embers, goads, beckoning, reckoning, beam, petal, enchanted, perchance, invade, charming, attractive, entrancing, committee, organize, haze, maverick, fringe, flutter, upholstery, blur, embrace, restless.*

Learning a vocabulary is not enough. We must also get retention. This requires practice in phonics, leading in turn to the acquisition of additional vocabulary. For example, from one song only, we can expand as follows, using "Oh, What a Beautiful Morning":

/ight/	/aze/	/ant/	/ee/	
bright	haze	elephant	breeze	queer
light	amaze	elegant	weeping	deer
might	blaze	chant	sleeping	tree
night	craze	slant	seeking	feeling
blight	daze	assistant	weekend	needle
			eerie	

/tt/	/us/	/ss/	/ing/	/ld/
cattle	music	mess	going	scold
rattle	busy	kiss	morning	child
settle	fuse	hiss	feeling	mild
kitten	rusty	crass	ingrown	mildew
muttering	dusty	brass	linger	colder

fattening	custard	assistant	cheating	shoulder
mitt	bustle	lassitude	fringe	should
	business	sunglasses	harbinger	could

/oo/			/ea/	
look	stoop	leader	dean	deal
mistook	troop	scream	death	earn
stood	understood	tread	deaf	earthquake
brood	boon	bread	each	easel
hood	boom	thread	eagle	breakfast
boot	look	eating	eager	
room	moose			

/ph/		/ng/	/nd/	
phase	telegraph	longer	standing	handkerchief
telephone	pharmacy	stronger	ending	branding iron
sophomore	phlegm	hunger	lend	Newfoundland
phonics	phrase	anger	blindncss	mandate
photograph	biography	lunge	Indian	window
		engulf		

Thereafter, and still expanding the possibilities in the one show song "Oh, What a Beautiful Morning," we can develop that joy of the orthodox, non-exploring teacher, vocabulary exercises and tests, thus:

Directions: Choose the word that is closest in meaning to the underlined word. Circle the word or words that are similar.

1. *ditty*   glove—happiness—song—drama
2. *blight*   disease—fright—blink—house
3. *lunge*   midday meal—sudden jump—new car—hope
4. *engulf*   hole—swallow up—circle—rifle
5. *phrase*   house—blanket—people—group of words
6. *mandate*   table—meat—order—company
7. *pharmacy*   farm—butcher store—supermarket—drug store
8. *harbinger*   forerunner—victory—brace—singer
9. *moose*   large box—large animal—rope—two mice
10. *muttering*   jumping rope—crossing the street—talking low

By breaking stereotypes and encrusted thinking, new sources of reading materials, unorthodox though they are, can be brought into the classroom and can be used in drills, exercises, recitation, and vocabulary acquisition, which should be comforting to the non-pioneering teacher who is in despair because the usual materials don't work. In addition, this teacher should compare the word list above with the usual word list in the ordinary, orthodox vocabulary list, because *it is even more difficult!*

If Broadway show music offers a new world of important materials to the reading teacher, how can the teacher put these new materials to use? The method is simple:

1. The teacher distributes mimeographed copies of the lyrics to each member of the class.
2. The song is played.
3. The vocabulary is taught.
4. The students learn the song and learn to sing it.
5. The formants (/ur/, /er/, /at/, /ia/, etc.) are isolated and presented.
6. New word lists containing the formants are taught, illustrated by sentence use, and the class is quizzed on mastery.
7. The students become bored.
8. The teacher proceeds to another song, repeating the above steps.

The Noise Factory Within and the Printed Page Without

Another source of materials is less unorthodox, is lying around under the noses of reading teachers, is a far more meaningful aspect of the phonics versus whole-word controversy which has embroiled reading experts in recent years, and is certainly more relevant to the reading problems in junior and senior high school.

Consider the usual junior high school poor reader. Speak to him at your normal rate of speed. He'll understand you, and then reply at a normal rate of speed. In other words, he listens and speaks with a normal intake and output of sound and speech. But if his intake and output of speech sounds is of absolutely normal rate, why does he have difficulty with the *written* word? Chiefly because he doesn't symbolize the written pattern into the sound of speech as you do, so we must bridge the gap between the symbolic and speech. In doing so, we are encountering what the teacher of the deaf child does, and can perhaps borrow some of this teacher's techniques, such as the hand mirror which is given the deaf child so that he can watch his mouth as he utters certain sounds, to see as well as to establish the relationship between tongue-teeth-lips-palate-breath and the sounds which should be coming out.

In giving a hand mirror to our slow readers, we are teaching them how to keep an eye on themselves as they go about making noises, like what happens to tongue-teeth-lips-palate-breath in a sentence like "The mad man made most of the mast." How do we rearrange t-t-l-p-b in producing *mad* as differentiated from *man? most* from *mast? like* from *lake? fault* from *vault?* Numerous other exercises exist in speech texts which allow the slow reader to do some inner investigation of the deployment of his own personal t-t-l-p-b and how this relates to formants, morphemes, and phonemes. (7)

Indeed, Russian psychologists report that much of the success in Russian reading programs can be attributed to the Russian educational practice of teaching speech before teaching reading, because increased self-awareness of the manufacture of oral utterance is a necessary preliminary to reading readiness. A child who understands how the *th* of *with* is different from *th* of *thought* has been introduced to a complexity within himself and a sense of noise-making that gives the retarded reader some sophistication about the way he makes sounds come out of his mouth, in another aspect of experience-enrichment.

Phonics, as usually defined, does not offer this sophistication. The poor reader in junior and senior high school has usually been exposed to phonics and can, in greater or lesser degree, utter the sounds represented on the printed page, though awkwardly. His familiarity with phonics is proved by his reading on the third or fourth grade level.

But phonics is not phonetics, which deals with the conceptualization of self-made sounds, the configurations of tongue-teeth-lips-palate-breath, and the noise factory within you that you have never stopped to think about. Phonetics, according to Russian educators, comes first, because the poor reader is even less familiar with his own noise factory than with the patterns on paper that he laboriously sounds out. We have greater assurance that the externalized phonics on paper will work if we first devote some analysis to the internalized phonetics mechanisms within us.

Whatever the mix, phonetics-phonics is only the precursor to explorations in the symbolic.

The Proverbial in Contention

Materials like proverbs and figurative language are known and used by the orthodox teacher, but chiefly as springboards to sermonizing, rather than as targets for analysis. Mottoes and proverbs are handed down to us, and should also be manhandled by us, not merely accepted. To compare, contrast, and otherwise juggle apothegms and aphorisms may partially encourage iconoclasm, but will also encourage symbolic processes.

In the examples below, some vocabulary is held constant while other vocabulary is varied, so that in this sample of proverbs dealing with *love* the word held constant is explained and defined in a variety of conditions. Thus from H. L. Mencken's *A New Dictionary of Quotations:* (8)

1. Love and hatred are natural exaggerators. (Hebrew)
2. He who finds love finds nothing. (Spanish)
3. It is easy for them who have never loved to sneer at love. (Welsh)
4. The greatest love is a mother's; then comes a dog's; then comes a sweetheart's. (Polish)
5. Love cannot be commanded. (Latin)

Contrasting quotations by the dozens can be added to the above list, to enlarge and ventilate symbolic understanding. More ambitiously, students can be required to furnish stories, instances, and illustrations arising from other proverbs. Much here is dependent on the ability of the teacher; unfortunately, teacher ability is a risky thing to hang a reading program on, which is why proverb-collocation, where teacher judgment is minimal, spares us this risk when we ask pupils if proverb-pairs agree or disagree:

1. Absence makes the heart grow fonder. (American)
   The cure for love is absence. (Spanish)
2. When a man is alone, he is safe. (Arabian)
   He who eats alone chokes alone. (Arabian)
3. A mule always boasts that its ancestors were horses. (German)
   They brag most of their ancestors who are unworthy of them. (Danish)

4. Every eel hopes to become a whale. (German)
   Where ambition ends, happiness begins. (Hungarian)

With the competent and well-trained teacher, these can be punch lines as well as springboards, meaning that students can use them to end a story as well as begin it, or else the teacher can present incomplete stories to the slow reader for him to judge which of the two matched proverbs best ends it.

We are well beyond phonics-phonetics now and into the realm of the conceptual-symbolic, as in new comparisons, in this case with the literal and the figurative:

1. They held the money tightly *in the palms of their hands.*
   The Beatles held the audience *in the palms of their hands.*
2. She aimed at his back, but the snowball *went to his head.*
   The teacher's praise *went to his head.*
3. Jimmy *fell flat* on the ground.
   Jimmy's joke *fell flat.*

The Teaching of English

Nowhere does pedantry obstruct instruction as in English, whether originating with mandarins in college faculties or vulgarians in school faculties. The mandarin-pedant is doubtful that literature affects life, or that he is involved in having literature affect life. The vulgarian-pedant is certain that literature must affect life because it is so good for you. Neither will allow the living to affect literature. (9)

For example, college mandarins will publish and dispute about *Hamlet* with medieval and sometimes interesting scholarship, because *Hamlet* is important to them and because a man called Shakespeare, who wrote plays, earned a good living from them, and died is also important to them. They are astride a privileged conduit-funnel with the deceased at one end and we the living at the other, affording them income and professional status. The dead man was up to his ears in show business because there was a buck in it, as there is in him and has been for hundreds of years, and especially every centenary for writers of notes, both prefatory and foot, editors, theatrical producers, actors, and mandarin-pedants.

In comparison, the vulgarian-pedant pushes Shakespeare and Robert Frost because they are in books, and the syllabus includes the books, and the class must cover the syllabus, and all this adds up to graduation, and graduation is cultural.

As a consequence, English instruction loses vitality and contact with the impulse that creates literature. Just as the novelist, poet, or playwright looks to some aspect of life—however we define that elegant four-letter word—we must use the literary work to lead the pupil to the life he knows, to considerations that too often escape him. Indeed, the chief merit of literature is its ability to illuminate the dark places in *us,* and not Hardy as pessimist, or the architecture of the Elizabethan stage, or the life of George Eliot. We have time for these after we have set *The Return of the Native, Macbeth,* and *Silas Marner* in a context of actuality, a backbreaking enough job.

The private life of the student is relevant to literary appreciation, which begins with his readiness in terms of age, experience, interests, and aptitudes. To sharpen this readiness, the teacher must assume that appreciation of the literary work depends on the nature of the reader. Books, plays, and poems are written for restricted or extensive audiences, but the sense of audience is inevitable, whether the author is an Ibsen writing in a public cafe or a Proust in a hermetically sealed bedroom.

In this audience each man creates his own Rorschach. It cannot be otherwise, nor should it be. If a Harlem boy sees Bernardo, Francisco, and Marcellus (*Hamlet* I, 1) as a precision drill team, no harm has been done to Shakespeare. We should do much to guarantee tears when he sees Ophelia mad, and sadness when the play ends, else he just won't get it if the vulgarian-pedant denies his right to be an audience and substitutes a lecture for a show. Literature must enlarge student experiences.

Mandarin-pedants feel otherwise. Here is an example: "Re-creation demands that a reader move *into* the work, not away from it, that he refrain from making judgments on the rightness or wrongness of the conduct represented in the work, or from offering other alternatives to the behavior portrayed, or from discussing its social effects in the everyday world he lives in." (10)

This is pure icon-worship. Similar icon-worship occurs in mathematics, where computation is mistaken for fantasy, and in science, where cook-bookery is mistaken for scientific method.

Churches are proper places for icon-worship; literature is not. Stripping away all literary icon-worship is required for the emergence of literary appreciation and particularly so with the culturally deprived. These pupils' primary need is deeper insight into themselves and into what is around them. So literary structure, the modulations of language, the understanding of characters, the patterns of villainy, the wellsprings of virtue become blinding searchlights focused on the people they know, the events they have experienced, and the lives they lead. With the culturally deprived child literature should first mean illumination, not a series of highly recommended effigies processed for the market by mandarin-pedants and retailed by vulgarian-pedants.

The ways of feedback to gain insight are numerous and subtle. The teacher may take much trouble responding to a composition that the student has written, will return the conscientiously corrected composition to the student, only to see the student crumple it and throw it away, in disgust with his performance. Then let the teacher give the student a folder, have him straighten out the crumpled paper and place it in the folder. The next composition will be more thoughtfully prepared.

If "curricular psychology" is a new name for old-hat "psychology of the school subjects," and "factor analysis" a mathematical facelift for "faculty psychology," then "linguistics" is a restyling of "grammar." Grammar, if you hadn't heard, is dead for a number of reasons: It didn't improve written expression; it didn't teach pupils better speech, it had no resemblance to actual language; diagraming was a senseless exercise; the predominating rules had been thoughtlessly borrowed from Latin, with no appropriateness to English.

Its avatar, "linguistics," has in its brief existence already split into a half-dozen schools, each with its own explanation of linguistic events, and with some explanations more complex than the events they explain. (11) Thus sentence diagraming is required to make the explanation visual and comprehensible, but we don't call it diagraming any longer; rather, as in Chomsky's "transformational grammar," (12) we use such aliases as "strings" or "immediate constituent analysis." But the great blessing of all the schools of linguistics is their honest attempt to analyze the complexities of English. This sense of complexity, of the absence of easy answers, of the stupidity of glib definitions stimulates classroom possibilities for both bright and slow because the new grammar does something that the old grammar didn't. It takes the lids off our minds as they work. Hence everything we say, not merely properly balanced sentences or well-formed prose, becomes available for grammar study. Grunts, snorts, exclamations, inflections, tones of voice that change meaning, fragments, ambiguities, and today's newspaper can be analyzed into shape and orderliness.

What an enormous benefit to the culturally deprived child who is thereby given significant clues to the turbulence around him! Indeed, and the author can testify to this from personal observation, the well-taught grammar lesson—all right, call it linguistics—is almost a group psychotherapeutic session. Negro children in Bedford-Stuyvesant will leave a well-taught grammar-linguistics lesson with an air of composure, competence, and well-being that indicates that a sort of spiritual laundering has occurred. Unfortunately, probably only a dozen English teachers in this entire district of tens of thousands of children can teach this way. If so, we are faced with a major problem. Our linguistics-grammar knowledge is far ahead of our teachers and of our teacher-training programs.

The teaching of English may not be cultural imperialism or cultural colonialism, but it certainly is cultural penetration, and it is unavoidable. When the Agency for International Development opens a teaching center at the American University of Beirut for English as a second language, it brings the resources, the literature, the research, and the information written in English to bear on the problems in the Middle East. When the NDEA Reading Institute in El Paso makes a special effort on behalf of teachers of Spanish-speaking children in the Southwest, it brings the same considerations to bear on the problems there as in Puerto-Rican Harlem. (13)

The Teaching of Mathematics

If mathematics is hard, what makes it so? Why do pupils have difficulty with mathematics? Leaping 25 feet, or running 100 yards in ten seconds, or lifting 200 pounds over your head is hard, but training allows men to approach these goals, even though they may never achieve them. Both the man who achieves and the man who doesn't have an equivalent sense of fitness and tone. A middle-aged man in condition has as much sense of physical well-being as any professional athlete.

Mathematics instruction should offer an analogous sense of intellectual well-being and intellectual competence. What is chiefly wrong with mathematics instruction is not its old-fashioned curriculum, but its old-fashioned instruction. The New Mathematics is meaningless when instructors are still rushed by the administrative compulsion to cover the syllabus; unharried mathematics achieves a pupil sense of intellectual well-being and competence either with New Mathematics or with Euclid. All our brave talk about curriculum changes is meaningless without a teacher who is not in a hurry, who allows meditation, and who permits the mathematics class to be an occasion for fantasy, working at problems until the answer arrives, bearing a concept with it. (14)

The mathematics problem must be toyed with and played with, rather than worked at, so we need a mathematics teacher who sees a mathematics problem as a recreation, rather than a task. But mathematical skills are needed for the solution of the recreations and the tasks, and are a simple function of drill, like the multiplication tables. The satisfactions that mathematics offers combine intellect and emotion, in a context of relaxation, that require the learner to reduce his pace, to take it easy at an *andante* amble rather than a *presto* gallop. Even those mathematicians who have been able to swallow an entire world of mathematical concepts at one gulp, like Von Neumann and Gauss, have preferred to savor concepts, releasing them to digestion with reluctance.

Then what of the nastiness of drill and rote, which are so much like the repetitiveness of prayer? Herrigel describes how Zen Buddhism helps the archer, the swordsman, and the wrestler become a better combatant, as nations go to war feeling that God, Christ, or Yahweh is on their side. (15) Briefly, as in bowmanship or getting on the green in fewer strokes, in Zen Buddhism you concentrate on yourself rather than on your opponent, thereby reducing panic. But Zen concentration-exercises require practice and repetition, and there we are again, whether in golf, murder by archery-swordsmanship-karate, or in mathematics. Practice reduces anxiety, and if we choose to call it rote, so much the worse for us.

A recurring word among mathematicians is *elegance*. They fondly give the word a meaning akin to *style* or *artistry,* like Hemingway's definition of beauty as "grace under pressure," or Berlioz' description of the balance in orchestral instrumentation, or old time sports writers describing Nap Lajoie's lope after a fly ball.

Added to tempo and elegance is faith either that an answer is somewhere around or that an answer is impossible. In either case, as the mathematician sees it, "everything works out"—with a faith in attaining goals by asking relevant questions and raising appropriate problems.

Curricular psychology must recognize how pace and faith enter into the esthetics and emotiveness of mathematics—and how the soothing aspects of drill and repetition contribute to the savor, else mathematics becomes a police action. Successful mathematics teaching allows rumination, meditation, and soak-in time, in addition to repetition and drill, all of which lead to the elegance that is the essence of mathematics.

In mathematics the subject matter is public but the mode of study is particularly and uniquely private, indeed especially introspective, and needing work, repetition, and drill. Teachers think drill loses them customers. On the contrary, drill serves a useful psychological purpose. When Freud described the repetition compulsion, he showed how it drove away anxieties. Repetition, as in prayer or ritual, serves the same purpose, and drill's comforting effects are similarly repetitive, provided that the teacher does not become a drill-master. Drill under a drill-master is bad business; but drill, repetition, and memorization under a teacher who is pounding out the beat is salutary.

One of the weaknesses of the New Mathematics is its comparative lack of concern about the difference between drill-master and the teacher who can pound out the beat. The New Mathematics has aroused much resentment in mathematics teachers, who had to repress their resentment because the New Mathematics had the professional imprimatur of mathematicians and therefore the ring of authority, so they knuckled under. But many mathematics teachers, for the first time in their lives, heard themselves repeating one of the oldest platitudes in progressive education, that they were teaching children and not subject matter, showing how curricular psychology can make some strange bedfellows.

The Cambridge Conference on School Mathematics says: "The building of confidence in one's own analytical powers is another major goal of mathematics education." (16) Very true— but how does the teacher, not the material, build this confidence? And how do you do so with a boy far more concerned with his haircut, or with a girl more concerned with her makeup? And how can the gang spirit lead to differential equations? The first thing the teacher must do is live with the haircut and the makeup—even before we talk of elegance, artistry, or drill—because then the adolescent will more readily accept mathematics and be less likely to fight it. In saying so we subscribe to other statements made by the Cambridge Conference:

> Obviously the task of leadership in a Socratic inquiry is harder, as a matter of pedagogic technique, than the task of teaching by drill. It also requires a much deeper mastery, in a purely mathematical sense, of the subject matter. It requires that the teacher recognize, as quickly as possible, the validity of unexpected responses. It requires also that the teacher be able to tell when a response which is not correct as stated nevertheless includes a valid idea, so that the discussion can then be guided in the direction of the valid idea. Such work requires far deeper understanding than lecturing does. Without deep understanding, the only responses whose validity the teacher can recognize are the responses given in "the book." . . . The only way that we can see to eliminate such behavior in well-intentioned teachers is to alleviate the purely intellectual incomprehension which forces them into it. (16)

Elsewhere, the conference says:

> The student should never, for fear of being wrong, hesitate to state the results of his best efforts. Wrong statements are not to be embarrassingly rejected, as is the common practice. Worse, correct statements that the teacher did not want are often rejected. Half-formed ideas should be used as stepping stones to true or more relevant statements. (16)

True, but it leaves much unsaid about the characteristics of the mathematics teacher. How many teachers agree with the report that problems are more important than answers?

Both the practitioner of applied mathematics and the creator of pure mathematics spend much of their time and effort on "here's a situation, explore it," not only on "here's a problem, solve it" or "here's a theorem, prove it." It is good to admit this to the students and to let them work on mathematics in this manner themselves. (16)

However, the usual mathematics teacher in the schools has been attacked often enough for inadequacy, and the time has come to redirect the attack to the administrator who rates his teacher by student performance on standardized tests, by college admission requirements, and by parental concern. The very colleges granting released time to mathematics professors to work on curriculum improvements like the Cambridge Conference are simultaneously stamping out admission acceptances to students drilled by teachers chivvied by administrators anxious lest the school's record of college admissions offend the taxpayer. (17)

One cannot divorce reform and improvement in the mathematics curriculum from college admissions. If these engendered fewer tensions in parents and administrators, some of the heat would be taken off teachers. Until then, teachers will teach for students to pass tests, not for rumination, meditation, or elegance. All the prescriptions for teacher preparation will be nullified by rigid college admissions policies and intense competition for college admissions.

Robert J. Schaefer has eloquently said:

Teaching young people to give back desired responses to particular intellectual questions—which is wholly within our knowledge and our power—is only to provide the crudest introduction to the life of the mind. The ability to reiterate the multiplication table or to solve a quadratic equation, as every teacher knows, is hardly sufficient evidence that a student appreciates the elegance and order of mathematical relationships. (18)

Aside from some doubt that every teacher knows this, the statement is in agreement with what most good mathematicians also know.

Ergo, textbooks should be forbidden in the classroom if they interfere with rumination, meditation, and soak-in time. For the beginning student in algebra and geometry, the textbook is far too formidable. It gets in the way of discussion, of the use of fingers, chalk, blackboard, pencil, and paper to build up to elegance and the primary sense of how pretty everything is in mathematics. For an appreciation of this prettiness in mathematics, the student must turn to the teacher, not to the textbook, and the teacher must talk, explain, give assignments, and illustrate from his own know-how— not until weeks have gone by and the student has been ensnared by this prettiness should the teacher call upon the textbook.

Mathematics is hard because rumination, meditation, and soak-in time may make us impatient. If we learn to reduce restlessness in ourselves, so that rumination and meditation come easier, then mathematics will come easier too. But impatience is hard to reduce when you begin the school day with a time clock and end it with one. For over two generations the time clock has wrecked teacher morale and any possibilities for rumination and meditation, so that nobody any longer has any soak-in leisure on school time. As long as this is so, any change in the mathematics curriculum is a farce. Even Beberman is backing away from the Beberman program, (19) but his curriculum modifications mean little as long as teachers must pace themselves against a time clock so that a syllabus can be covered, and the curriculum can be run—as if mathematics were a race track!

Just as the mathematics class must be sealed against textbooks and time clocks, it must be permeable to: pencils and erasers; tape measures and rulers; protractors; pennies for tossing and dice for rolling to develop the normal distribution and the binomial theorem; graph paper; string to measure lengths; abacuses; plumb lines; school-made theodolites; shapes of cubes, pyramids, cylinders, cones, spheres, squares; clay and silly putty to shape pyramids and cones; and knives to cut the clay to illustrate conic sections. The teacher can therewith, without textbooks, demonstrate, prove, and above all chat about the area of desk tops, the cubic measurement of the classroom, the height of the building across the street, the alternate interior angles of fire escapes. He can show how a see-saw is like an equation, and how sing-song helps you memorize the multiplication table and thereby makes long division easier, and how formulas wrap up everything the students have been doing with the materials. Thus the minutes and seconds on the face of a wristwatch become portals to arcs, chords, and the 360 degrees of a circle; and the nickel, dime, quarter, and fifty-cent piece become vestibules to the decimal system.

You cannot think mathematics without being relaxed and thrusting all sense of hurry aside. The pupil must be freed of all *concern* about the outside world, but not of his *curiosity* about the outside world. A Negro pupil crammed with anxieties that show as misbehavior cannot learn mathematics, not until he is decelerated and serene. But if this happens, mathematics will flourish in him in a positively accelerated curve with no asymptote anywhere in sight.

The Teaching of Social Studies

Excitement cannot be kept out of any discussion on urban education. Enmity and love, attraction and revulsion, attacks and retreats, clash between town and country, the privileged and the deprived, the ignorant and the educated, lids sat on as long as possible and lids blown off—all mix with the sobriety of cerebration, careful planning, and the production possibilities of an automated age. This brings together the bloodlessly intellectual and the bloodily emotional in a melding of politics, civics, economics, and history that constitutes social studies. Social studies is dramatic, which makes it interesting to write and read on, and to do something about. (20)

Social studies should attempt objectivity, but not remoteness. Human transactions, like chemical reactions, sometimes require heat, and we do well to avoid pedantic coolness if our students are to encounter the full possibilities of their times. The encounter requires mutations in our accustomed thoughts and feelings, so that we look at people and their needs as we never have before, the better to manipulate them, or, euphemistically, to plan for them.

More than conservatives are willing to admit, we have been a planning society. Land grabs by American railroads, power grabs by American labor, community forecasting by utilities companies are executed sometimes in the spirit of avarice, sometimes in generosity, sometimes in jockeying for self-advantage, and sometimes in planning for the nation's good. Now we must plan as never before, because we face outer space, inner chaos, unlimited food and power, and new populations who must be trained for the complexities of civilized and urban living. Cities have always been educational and sociological headaches. From the time of Sodom and Gomorrah, country folk have always looked with suspicion on the urban condition. The urban rabble of classical Rome or Blake's London manifest little difference from our own urban squalor in Harlem.

As we have said, social studies deals with the unsocial, the anti-social, the asocial, and the non-social—in other words, social studies deals with the combative. In tariff history, we talk of the jockeying of competing interests. In civics we talk of institutionalized rivalries. In history we talk of warring dynasties. In economics we talk of strikes, lockouts, and contention for markets. Strife, rather than the socialization of strife or the pacification of strife, is the heart of social studies. This should make it highly motivating were it not that social studies is taught by teachers, the least combative of our social groups, who use a syllabus which seeks to flatten out the contentious in human affairs; we wind up with the humanitarian Edward Steichen *Family of Man* approach.

Nevertheless, social studies, presented through questions and problems, is unendingly interesting. For example:

1. How did local places get their names? Lenox Avenue? Fulton Street? Nostrand Avenue? Lexington Avenue? Triboro Bridge? Samuel Gompers High School? Gouverneur Morris High School? Evander Childs High School? Erasmus Hall High School?

2. If your home were to burn down, and if you had insurance, what would you do? Where would you turn for help if you had no insurance? What problems would you face without insurance? How would you deal with them?

3. (In discussing the Industrial Revolution) Why is it possible to purchase a coat, a hat, shoes, and clothing that will fit you when the storekeeper never saw you before?

4. (On geography) What would you do if it rained three or four months in the year? A possible answer: "I'd let it rain." The resourceful teacher replies: "But how would your life be affected?" And an extension: How would life in our city be affected?

5. (On the Westward movement and immigration) You are living in New York State in 1760—why would you want to move West? You are living in Europe in 1890—why would you want to come to America? In Europe in 1920? In 1960?

6. Compare the Missouri Compromise and the feeling of the

South when Alaska and Hawaii were recently admitted to statehood. What are the differences and similarities?

7. Compare the Articles of Confederation of 1787 with the UN charter.

8. Compare the Northwest Ordinance with present neo-colonial policies in Africa.

9. Compare the functions of the federal government in the Louisiana Purchase and federal aid to education today.

10. In comparing the Monroe Doctrine to SEATO, how has American foreign policy changed?

11. "New Words in the News" are selected, defined, studied for etymology, and incorporated in a vocabulary list.

12. Students write anonymous letters to Dear Abby or some other newspaper columnist. The teacher collects these anonymous letters and redistributes them to the class. The students then write *signed* answers, pretending to be the columnists, and the answers are discussed.

We have discussed the telephone yellow pages as a suitable and logical substitute for the dictionary in teaching dictionary skills, but it also offers social studies information on services, stores, transportation, and the identities of bus, airline, and railroad companies. Similarly, transportation agencies have timetables, which can be studied for geography. The study of road maps leads into the teaching of latitude and longitude by means of the layout of avenues and streets, thereby introducing the pupil to Cartesian coordinates. The newspaper's radio and TV programs show that the newspaper knows days ahead what programs you'll be seeing on the split-second days later, hinting how society can plan for sequence and order when it wants to. Automobile road maps of Pennsylvania can teach us about Valley Forge and Gettysburg, and a Negro pupil from Bedford-Stuyvesant can quickly see with a Long Island map where it was in Brooklyn that Washington retreated from, and the streets too.

But these are preliminary exercises and sideshows to the main intent where philosophies and creeds are at war.

We are about to open areas for discussion that may be rejected by many educators as unsuitable for the young, despite the evidence from Richard Hughes' *High Wind in Jamaica,* Miller's *The Cool World,* and Golding's *Lord of the Flies* that the bloodthirstiness of the young is even less trammeled by responsibility for others than the bloodthirstiness of adults. We accept this limitation on the curriculum, though not convinced that the stomachs of the adolescents are so easily turned queasy by our suggested social studies syllabus. But we will not budge in our conviction that teachers should be familiar with the considerations that follow.

The social studies curriculum deals with the division of labor in modern society, but modern society has no such specialization in its religious worship. Modern worship is usually monotheistic, but modern production, with its specialization and division of labor, would seem to require polytheism. Among religions, even Catholicism denies any bent toward polytheism in its Trinity and catalog of saints. Nevertheless, polytheism provides specialist gods for an age of specialization more appropriately than monotheism.

Of course, the specialist gods will have to be updated, but less than the social studies teacher might suppose. Zeus on Olympus or Wotan on Valhalla can be rehoused in dialectical materialism, or input-output, or free enterprise, his thunderbolts replaced by electronic circuitry, and images of him set up for the convenience of worshippers in local banks and stockbrokers' offices.

The social studies teacher cannot risk his job by teaching or recommending polytheism. (21) But he doesn't stick his neck out by discussing economics model-making, how model-creators worship their creations, and how economic man makes models in his own image.

The social studies teacher should point to the room for everybody, and the parking space, in the galaxy, beginning with the Moon and with Mars. But we ought not expect too much. The discovery of America offered no outlet to reduce the rivalries of emerging nationalism; rather, it sharpened them. Similarly, space exploration guarantees no reduction in American-Soviet rivalries. Life on Mars will not reduce terrestrial ambitions, and even with Mars barren it would be fought over as much as the Sahara, the Arctic, or the Himalayas—places where for a long time most men thought you couldn't get a dime. You just can't ever tell about real estate. The Sahara yields oil and Siberia contributes heavily to Soviet economy.

Life on Mars or not, its exploitation possibilities problematical or not, its capacities for throwing a blinding light on human psychology are beyond debate because, even before we get there, Mars is offering us insights into man and kicking off results and data right now.

For example, how will you communicate with Martians? First, are they living? Second, are they sentient? Third, are they intelligent? Fourth, if intelligent, are they sane? Problems in communicating with schizophrenics, and the development of language and speech in young children are very similar. Similarly, sentience and intelligence are different; on Mars they may cause our behavior to be vegetarian or carnivorous. If we encounter intelligent, environment-affecting life on Mars, ought we not to taste it? Or will that be cannibalism? But, if we find intelligent, but non-environment-affecting life on Mars—something like a cow—ought we not to incorporate it in our diet? Ultimately, we cannot truly explore Mars without trying it on the tongue, as we have done on Earth for aeons, thereby learning about alcohol, salt, sugar, alkalis, poisons, chemistry, physics, and science.

Thus we have long known villainy and nightmare and must now look to the stars for further illumination, not to read by but to figure ourselves out by, and why our Iagos, Scarpias, and Hitlers have affected the human condition more than Socrates, Jesus, or Hillel. We know little about villainy, though nothing affects us more seriously. Similarly, a peaceful and rational man behaves reasonably and logically, goes to bed, turns off the light, and creates himself foul nightmares. (22) Outer space will give us many answers to the irrationality of villainy and nightmares within us.

For instance, imagine some Iago in an outward-bound space rocket. Iago, on Earth, never diminished his villainy or altered his other experiences simply because he knew he could not live forever. But as Iago-astronaut breaks the intactness of gravity, he must substitute for gravity or else fall to pieces, meaning that mechanisms in the capsule must maintain gravity and thereby his intactness. This takes a lot of work. Does the work confirm him in his villainy or does he begin to feel villainy not worth the effort? Does he become more saintly or more the sinner?

With evidence beginning to come in that space travel induces manic states, we may soon find that our best astronauts are our hebephrenics.

Social Studies and Social Instruction

The social studies teacher looks thoughtful and somebody says to him, "So you're going to have an *idea!*" as if in imitation of "So you're going to have a *baby!*"

But some thoughts and ideas in social studies had best never see the light of day, especially when they deal with religion and sex. Obviously, unusual ideas only occur to those to whom ideas are a usual thing. Furthermore, unusual ideas are usually misunderstood, which doesn't mean that the misunderstood is equivalent to the unusual. The usual can also be misunderstood; depend on most people to do so. The enormous risks of misunderstanding put the social studies teacher in the position of knowing far more than he can teach, particularly in the areas of religion and sex.

When Nathan Glazer warns Negroes that Jews will never accept any *numerus clausus* in education because their present status in society reflects assiduity, application, and hard work, he forgets that intermarriage contributed to Jewish status. (23) In the first decades of this century, aspiring Jewish teachers found that the Irish Catholics who had preceded them had in great measure evicted Protestants from the educational power structure. Dozens of young Jewish teachers apostasized themselves and married Irish Catholic girls. It helped in political and professional connections, leading to principalships and superintendencies. Marriage to Italian girls was rarer, because Italians were not as likely to be in seats of power. However, as Jews gained political power, apostasy dropped and, in fact, became a hindrance to upward mobility. Like church systems and military systems, school systems are a means to mobility; but Jews have sometimes been out, trying to get in, and when in have tried to keep others out, as when Nehemiah and Ezra restored the Jerusalem wall and forbade intermarriage with non-Jews. To Nehemiah, the protective wall took precedence over the proselytizing Temple, because he scorned Solomon, the king who built temples rather than walls and who married gentile women.

Cities offer economic pathways and political pathways that affect marriage pathways. The imminent increase in Negro-white intermarriage will reflect new economic possibilities available to Negroes. Can the social studies teacher mention this? Not readily. Nevertheless, he must keep it in mind, although discreetly.

For example, we know that there has been little Negro-Jewish intermarriage or offspring, legal or illegal. Most Negroes do not have Jewish surnames because Jews were rare in ante-bellum America, except in Charleston, and still rarer were Jewish slave owners. The social studies teacher cannot tactfully mention this to a class of Negro children, but he can teach his class much by discussing the surnames in the class, how many of them are Anglo-Saxon, how many refer to occupation, how many to places, and how many to traits. Incidentally, he is entering the first phases of grammar instruction because he is talking about proper nouns. Similarly, he can discuss how local places got their names, and carry forward a study of local history, showing how people have names, as do places, and things. In doing so, the social studies teacher is not telling all he knows about how Negro children got their surnames.

If the social studies teacher told all he knew, he would drive his pupils to apathy and despair. Can he tell his class that the chief reason men cannot control their affairs is because of other men? And that nations cannot control their affairs because of other nations? And that instability in men and nations is virtually guaranteed for the future because of man's nature? Hardy in *The Dynasts* and Tolstoy in *War and Peace* discussed the utter unmanageability of the Napoleonic wars, how the loose ends far exceeded the controllable strands, and how the men at the top had no idea of what was doing anywhere else. Men are helpless to control events because men are in a bind when it comes to men. Men should know this. Children shouldn't.

Nor should they be told the difference between military posture and military posturing, because military men themselves do not always know the difference. The personalities of the young are not organized enough and hence not firm enough to withstand the knowledge that our leaders do not know half the answers they should to make competent judgments. Political leaders and newspaper editorials must sound as if they know the answers, when they know nothing of the sort, and presidents and premiers are as helpless as an oyster in the tentacles of an octopus. They persuade us that they are free agents, but a social studies teacher should have a personality organized enough and firm enough to know that the leaders are clearly oysters, even as the teacher withholds this knowledge from unprepared pupils.

Such posturing occurs in moon shots, Mars shots, and underground nuclear explosions, like the posturing in Chinese wars described by Ernest Brahmah in *Kai Lung,* where marching, firecrackering, and oratory ritualized and reduced blood-letting without reducing bellicosity or cruelty, like our bloodless nuclear explosions which hurt nothing except the air we breathe, which smells just the same. This dreadful message is for adults only, and not for children unaccompanied by parents.

Exactly a year before Paul Revere's ride, Edmund Burke, speaking in the House of Commons on tea taxation in the American colonies, said: "They tell you, Sir, that your dignity is tied to it. I do not know how it happens, but this dignity of yours is a terrible incumbrance to you; for it has of late been ever at war with your interest, your equity, and every idea of your policy."

Some years later, editorials, presidents, and premiers, relate nuclear testing and also the Congo and Viet Nam to national dignity, but not necessarily to national interest. We are in a bad way when we confuse national dignity with national interest. This confusion cost England the Middle East, as Koestler points out in *Arrival and Departure*. (24)

How can the social studies teacher draw open the curtain on this nightmare without disrupting the defenses of the young? Can he begin with the individual's confusion of personal dignity and personal interest? It certainly would be less damaging to do so.

For the same reason, premature sex experiences can also be disrupting, and not as integrating as our Paul Goodmans assert. If sex is an accepted lure in international affairs, Profumo scandals, the CIA, military installations, gold flow, armaments, nuclear research, germ warfare, and water desalting, then little boys and girls should not be playing around where Allen Dulles and effective espionage are lighting more matches than we can safely afford. (25) The social studies teacher can reduce pandemic sex to an absurdity, to greater simplicity, or to non-existence, as he presents history. Much in society hinges on homosexual activities. The social studies teacher should know the homosexual's rationalizations: if romantic love is possible with the opposite sex, then why not with members of the same sex? The onanist can similarly rationalize a passion for milk bottle openings, fence knotholes, or his own right hand, that always available port in a storm; similarly, necrophilists with corpses, shepherds with sheep, and Pasiphae with a bull. Robinson Jeffers in *Roan Stallion* and Havelock Ellis in *Studies in Psychology of Sex* offer additional techniques, and classical Greece and Renaissance Italy back up—so to speak, that is—the historical validation of homosexual claims for acceptance in contemporary society. Society cannot do so because homosexuality has always been the blackest sin in a society which cannot face how much of it is rotten; how often its underworld is related to government, how many police take graft, how frequently politicians are venal. Should the social studies teacher know all this? Without doubt. Should he teach it? Only insofar as the young do not crack up under the knowledge. The child is important because stability is built around it, and all the institutions of society derive their strength from it. We cannot let it know too much too soon, but it must be given the knowledge that gives it the power to handle further knowledge.

Thus, under the surface of foreign relations are personal needs. Viet Nam, the Middle East, and our entanglements elsewhere defend the involvements of our large corporations only in part. Of course, these entanglements maintain a flow of oil which we really do not need, but their chief importance is to maintain political appointees in their jobs. Feeding Egypt despite its insults and supporting Indonesia to survival despite its varying orientations keeps State Department employees in work and in striped pants. The striped pants market, as well as Indonesian rubber, Arabian oil, Vietnamese tungsten, or Egyptian cotton, occasions much of our foreign policy.

Can we impose these facts of sexual and international relations on our children, and thereby put an intolerable strain on them? By what right, when society can only exist by brushing other disquieting things under the rug, from incest urges to the differences in justice for the rich and the poor? Without ego strength, as vital for the group as for the individual, society represses awareness of these irritants. Only a very strong society, its organized activities based not on legislation but on the responsible citizenship and individual ego strength of its people, could face such corruption and live with it. Lacking such individual citizens, society has no alternative but repression, whether of permissiveness with homosexuality, or acceptance of the prevalence of graft, or the need to keep State Department employees in striped pants. The social studies teacher should guide himself accordingly.

Is this, then, hypocrisy? Not according to Montaigne:

> . . . all peculiar and out-of-the-way fashions proceed rather from folly or ambitious affectation, than from true reason; and that the wise man should, in respect of his inward thoughts and opinions, withdraw his mind from the common

crowd, and keep it at liberty and with power to judge freely of things; but, in respect of his exterior, that he should wholly follow accepted forms and fashions. Society in general has no business with our thoughts, but as for the rest, such as our actions, our labours, our fortunes, and our own lives, they should be given over entirely to its service, and to common opinions: as the great and good Socrates refused to save his life by disobedience to the magistracy, and a very unjust and very iniquitous magistracy at that. (26)

Typically, we do not agree with Montaigne, since in comparison to your own life everybody else's life is unimportant. The history of torture, mass exterminations, Thirty Years Wars, Albigensian Crusades, and Mohammedan jehads gives evidence that we are willing to kill millions of others to maintain our own lives, nor are we appalled by the oceans of blood we shed for our own few quarts. The paranoid is not far off base in suspecting his fellow man. (27)

Suppose, in a farfetched illustration, that next week experiments in extrasensory perception, psychokinesis, and telepathy prove their practicability, that techniques have been found for putting these into the hands of everybody, for everyone's use. What would A. T. & T, Bell Telephone, and Western Electric do? How would they salvage their investments of billions of dollars? What government intervention would they seek? (28)

Then, is the bad press gotten by these ESP experimenters being surreptitiously managed by these companies? What incredible paranoia! But the "incredible" and the difficult-to-accept are not the same. ESP and telepathy are difficult to accept and it is incredible that A. T. & T. secretly plots the ridicule of ESP to defend telephony against telepathy. But one never knows, because the verified historical plotting of man against man is equally incredible. Dreyfus and Van der Lubbe were framed with unbelievable finish and expertness. British espionage tricked out a dead body and set it afloat to snare Germans, and the CIA, with loving surreptitious care, manufactures rumors that start and stop international activity. A thousand years of European history hinged on the faked Donation of Constantine.

All this is material for the social studies teacher. Need he present it? No. Need he know it? Yes. But if he need not present it, then why need he know it? Because that's where depth and enrichment come in and that's what they mean—the administration of adequate dosage. To throw all this at students is cruelest pedantry, but to use it for dimension and perspective in social studies brings the strength to the pupil that he will need to increase his level of tolerance for the unpalatability of too terribly much of human history and society. It's like learning how to smoke or drink. You vomit at first but thereafter it's fun.

The Teaching of Modern Languages

Read it or speak it? You can't have it both ways, unless you're a specialist. Teachers of modern language are under pressure to adopt the modish audio-lingual techniques of World War II and adapted by Nelson Brooks for school use. The flaw in Brooks's audio-lingual approach is in thinking that your accent is of any importance, and that if you sound like a native you can speak like a native. (29)

The fact is, as Aubrey Menen points out, (30) that you'll never succeed in sounding like a native, nor should you even try. Furthermore, we have far more opportunity to read foreign languages than to speak them. Foreign newspapers arrive overnight in New York, and the rewards of foreign language learning are in reading *Le Monde* or *Il Messagero* the next day, or not much after a subscriber in the provinces gets them. If you cannot be in France or in Italy, you can read *L'Express* or *Epoca* to see what's been doing that week. The American, unless he resides abroad, will do far better in getting a feel of foreign life and activity by a reading grasp of the language than by conversational glibness with a handful of phrases.

Indeed, the French accent of Paris is not that of Marseilles, nor the Italian accent of Naples that of Milan, just as the English accent of New York is not that of Houston. Any attempt to homogenize accent by teaching the French of Paris, or the English of Oxford, shortchanges the American student. He will do far better by unabashedly sounding like an American, provided that his grasp of vocabulary and idiom is as facile as only a solid program of reading and grammar can make it. The foreign speaker sounds least foreign and most attractive when his foreignness comes through simultaneously with a familiarity with the structure and forms of the second language.

An awareness of foreign thinking is more important to Americans than it has ever been. Our students must learn to read foreign newspapers, magazines, and books because we must learn to listen to Europeans and Latin Americans, rather than leaving them amazed at our parrot-like ability to mimic the sounds they make. Indeed, the ability to mimic the sounds can vitiate our ability to sound like Americans, though we should make every reasonable effort to have our French, Spanish, Italian, or German as painless as possible to the native ear.

If the goal in foreign language instruction is mastery, then we must count the sacrifices we must make to gain that mastery. A four-year course in high school French will not confer mastery. An additional two years is required before the beginnings of competence are attained. Only at this point can conversational fluency really arise. Speaking a language requires as much drill and repetition as reading it does. To have the right sound come out requires as much rote as memorizing the declension.

Can we ever learn to speak a foreign language like a native? As Aubrey Menen says, any such aspiration is ridiculous:

> I do not mean to be modest. I have worked ten years at learning the language and I have not done so badly. I have lived in the language for long periods, speaking no other. And if I may be forgiven the observation (since we are dealing with a Latin race), I have even conducted a stormy romance in that elaborately subtle and emotional tongue; what is more, I got away with it. I was very proud of this feat until, much later, I learned that my success had been partly due to my comic mistakes in speaking.

Clearly, foreign language instruction must begin with the assumption that the pupil will *never* learn to speak the language like a native. Nevertheless, he must make every effort to do so—but only while learning its literature, its culture, its newspapers, its magazines, its songs, and its cartoons, but not before. These are far more important than mimicry.

The American must learn how foreigners think because their modes of thought have all the power and validity of ours, because they are more contiguous to us than they have ever been, and because this knowledge enriches American life on this side of the Atlantic and Pacific.

One major virtue of the audio-lingual approach is its attempt at actuality, unlike the frozen, remote approach of traditional language instruction which depends so heavily on the textbook. *Epoca* in Italian and *Paris Match* in French are but two foreign language picture magazines that resemble *Life* and *Look* in format. Every school library should subscribe to such magazines, to give this sense of actuality to foreign language instruction.

Similarly, travel agencies and tourist offices offer a wide variety of posters and other free materials. The alert language teacher can bring actuality into the classroom by an Yves Montand or Sergio Franchi song. Foreign lands are not so foreign, and are indeed close by, when the teacher posts the menu of a French or Italian restaurant not too far from the school, and adds new culinary terms and kitchen operations to the vocabulary list.

Unfortunately, nothing is so quickly forgotten as a foreign language not used. If native speakers get rusty in their native tongues after years away, how readily will pupils forget their smattering! Almost immediately, and the foreign language teacher must keep this ready lapse into oblivion in mind by making it hurt to lose touch with what has been so painfully acquired. Thus the student must be reminded that there is just as much going on in the *Tour de France* or in Italian soccer as in baseball, that French restaurants are the most exciting restaurants in the world, that Italians are peppier than we, the Norse better skiers, the Swiss streets are cleaner, and that Europeans do better at auto racing.

Foreign language instruction can reduce chauvinism and increase patriotism by showing that Europeans are more interested in learning English than we are in learning a foreign tongue, and that day-by-day living in urban America can be constricting if we do not keep in touch with conditions thousands of miles, and only a few hours, away.

Finally, just as *Epoca* and *Paris Match* can be put with the same week's issues of *Life* and *Look* to compare stories, photography, feature articles, and advertising, so the language teacher's local newspaper can be compared with *Il Messagero* or *Le Monde* for headline values, editorial reaction, movie news and reviews, and sports events. The *Corriere della Sera, Figaro, Frankfurter Zeitung,* and *Excelsior* are only overnight away from Chicago,

Houston, and New York! What is more actual than reading the Rome newspaper that came in this morning by jet flight!

The Teaching of the Minor Subjects

The "minor" subjects will become less minor as automation moves in and as more leisure time becomes available. These subjects—art, music, physical education, driver education, home economics—are leisure time subjects and must therefore become more demanding a part of the curriculum and more involved with the community. Of all the subjects, only physical education has established close community ties. A winning basketball team swings public relations, but art and music departments can also organize a community for art education and music education, because we must learn competence with the time we will have on our hands, lest it be on our backs.

Must people be trained to sprawl before a *cabaña,* or to play pinochle on a hotel lawn? Ask any hotel owner, camp social director, or athletic director. Whether the Hotel Excelsior at the Lido plays host for international film festivals, or the Venice Biennale fills the nearby *pensioni* with art lovers, or hotels and motels around Stockbridge are booked solid for the Berkshire Music Festival, or the fishing and snorkeling brings paying guests to Caneel Bay, or the skiing requires reservations in advance at Mont Tremblant, any hotel man knows that idleness must be given a program of activities lest it degenerate to boredom. These programs can be purely physical—which encompasses quite a range!—or purely cerebral. When scientists meet in convention, their behavior is hardly distinguishable from a convention of salesmen. Thus Grossinger's will one week play host to a meeting of Eastman Kodak executives, the next to a meeting of psychologists, and throughout art classes, calisthenic classes, golf lessons, and canasta will be humming along, with Broadway night club acts taking over after nightfall, which, incidentally, is why homogeneous grouping is needed in physical education classes. The school varsity, for example, is there to win, not to be a democratic sampling of the school's population. Similarly, physical education classes need homogeneous grouping by grade or competence, because the poor player slows down everybody else. Indeed, the physical education program needs a self-image change because of the unexplored possibilities in training for a leisure that may become more oppressive as it becomes more prevalent.

Too many spectators and not enough participants need not worry us because we have more professionals today than audiences for them. Our pianists are superb, our athletes break records, our painters are pioneering in new ways of vision, our composers in new modes of sound. We need more consumers to buy the efforts of our instrumentalists and our athletes, not only to allow professional ball players, chamber music quartets, and non-representational painters to earn a living, but also to sharpen appreciation in the audience so that its members, too, become amateur participants and activists.

We are deliberately mixing the artist and the athlete in the same brew because athleticism is a considerable part of art, as art is of athleticism, especially true of instrumentalists like Horowitz and Stern. Yet billiard players, golfers, and boxers like Sugar Ray Robinson have as much relationship to the artistry of motion as Nureyev and Margot Fonteyn do.

Finally, art, music, and physical education require instruction and application. So the coach, the *atelier,* and the practice studio play inevitable roles in education for leisure, both for the professional producer and the amateur consumer, bringing us to education for adult living, which may be the same as adult education, and then again may not. See p. 301 for more on this.

The Teaching of Science

Science, as Huizinga says, is play. Because the government spends billions on science, rivals contend for government money. Texas competes with Massachusetts for space funds, (31) the University of Wisconsin with Caltech for linear accelerators, and molecular biologists with nuclear physicists for the prior importance of their research. Can government officials judge the justness of each claim?

Linear accelerators generate data, but this accumulation guarantees no scientific breakthroughs, no new insights, no practical outcomes. We cannot predict the next major threshold. If so, no accounting procedures can assist us in assigning funds to one university versus another, one region versus another, or one discipline versus another.

But the play aspects of science enable us to liquidate this difficulty, provided that we acknowledge that scientists are as involved in the play aspects of science as congressmen in the play aspects of politics. Politics is a game played for profit and fun. Similarly, science is a game played for status and the fun in the pursuit of knowledge. (32) Should taxpayers' money allow congressmen and scientists to have fun? The answer, for any civilization, is an unhesitating affirmative, because that is what civilization is for, and why congressmen travel on public funds.

This approach sets our accounting procedures in order, allowing us practical judgments on university versus university, region versus region, or discipline versus discipline. How do we compare the level of excitement in molecular biology with that of nuclear physics? What are the bases of excitement? Is the excitement feeding on legitimate fuel?

Furthermore, this puts the science curriculum accurately in perspective. The play aspects of science should dominate the science curriculum, because that is how we get students to work at science. (33)

Next, the stuff of science is not always visualizable, despite the excellent illustrations and diagrams in each issue of *Scientific American* and the wonderful photography of the weekly covers of *Science*. Very often, the materials of nuclear physics, mathematics, and genetics approach dream-life in the way scientists conceptualize them; the caduceus of myth resembles the double-helix of DNA, Eastern philosophy is frankly reflected in Gell-Mann's "eightfold way" in nuclear physics, and the cosmology of a dream is more Einsteinian than Newtonian. (34) Perhaps, for the improved training of science Ph.D.'s, a seminar in dream analysis is appropriate, since franker reliance on the intuitive might improve performance on more cognitive levels.

Here, indeed, the intuitions of the artist are more delusory than the hunches of the scientist, whose training allows him to develop better techniques of intuition than that of the artist. Both Shakespeare and Galileo were born in the same year, but when Shakespeare wrote ". . . the thing that's heavy in itself, upon enforcement flies with greatest speed" (*Henry IV*, I:1), he was disproved by his contemporary, and by all the experimentation on gravitational acceleration that followed. One does better with Galileo on bodies in motion than with Shakespeare. Poets may dream but scientists dream just as much, and in addition, fractionate their dreams, sometimes by instrumentation and sometimes by trained intuition, because science is analysis applied to dream and play. Measurement is a result, and not the most important one, but it is for far too many teachers of science. Much more important is the *repeatability* of measurement, because here we approach the esthetics of science, a matter discussed earlier in the teaching of mathematics.

But repeatability and regularity can be distressing, especially to a culturally impoverished slum child who wants to escape bonds, not to face them or study them. Science has two aspects to present to him, science as dream or science as regularity, with one as legitimately science as the other. But science-as-dream is more likely to captivate and science-as-regularity more likely to distress—only at the outset, however, because one leads ultimately to the other, provided they are allowed to invade the student. Materials like the Adelbert Ames trapezoidal window, the telescope, time-lapse microscopy, and other instrumentation will organize science-as-dream into science-as-regularity. (35)

The Teaching of the Classics

As R. R. Bolgar warns, in *The Classical Heritage and Its Beneficiaries,* (36) the classics can be dead or alive, depending on the teacher. The teacher can make Latin so timely and contemporary that it adds 2,000 years to our lives, gives us the answer to many of our problems, makes us more popular and sought after, reduces the foolishness in us, improves our decisions and our incomes, and helps us understand ourselves by understanding Latin syntax. But this depends on the Latin teacher teaching us an appropriate Latin, putting his hand in the net to come up with different kinds of Latin, having different kinds of value and excitement. Latin is all these things, plus beauty, wit, and tears; it even has business applications for apprentice scientists, engineers, accountants, and executives who are technically competent but lack ability in being people. With technological advance heaped upon technological advance, humanity has more need of the humanities for judgment in policy, passion, humor, and inquiry. Furthermore, we speak Latin, whether we know it or not, with half the English we use every day. Raphael Demos and Peter Drucker tell us (37) that businessmen know from experience what the classics have been saying right along, that Cicero in *De Senectute* is applicable to pension plans as well as to sageness, that Herodotus on Persia and Greece is applicable to Turkey and Cyprus, and that the war to the death in Thucydides between Athens and Sparta can be applied to cut-throat business rivalries, and how careful you must always be when the enemy you thought dead is back fighting you the next spring because he wasn't so easily killed off.

But if the classics tell us what is up-to-the-minute, why read the classics? Partially because the up-to-the-minute is not so u-t-t-m after all, but also because the classics help us get a better perspective on the u-t-t-m. Where judgment and wisdom matter in terms of policy and the probability of events—as they do vitally in business—the classics bring as much to bear on human behavior patterns as quality control, fiduciary limits, confidence bands, game theory, and other mathematical models, where we again create gods in man's image. Andrew Undershot, Shaw's tycoon in *Major Barbara,* made a Latinist his industrial heir.

If esthetic judgments can be sharpened by the teacher of art and music, so can executive judgments, in and out of commerce, be similarly trained by the teacher of classics. The evidence goes back thousands of years.

12

The Training of Teachers

Leaders in the professions, in defense of status and standards, historically tend to punitiveness, like savages inducting their tribe's adolescents into maturity. Thus the American Medical Association historically opposed enlargement of medical school facilities to maintain quality by restriction of access to medical practice, but never thereby argued for curtailment of nurses, technicians, biochemists, bacteriologists, or hospital attendants, because they weren't in on the fee system, nor the ways the pie was cut. Medicare assures us more doctors than we have ever had, as our new educational programs assure us many more educational personnel and teachers; but Medicare also wants more intensively prepared diplomates, trained specialists, and medical leaders, and an improvement in quality as well as an increase in quantity. So, also, given an extended school day, week, and year, the payment-for-learning program, and our new curricular psychology, we cannot make do with the teachers we have, nor with the ways they have been recruited and trained. Just as Medicare envisages new medical relationships, so "Educare" envisages new classrooms—perhaps containing hundreds of students and a dozen teachers, with one teacher teaching and the others watching, a classroom that resembles the school assembly rather than the schoolrooms we know. The school assembly is usually an inspirational affair, concerned with the pledge of allegiance to the flag, marching in, marching out, the national anthem, school songs, and pep talks. Teachers police the audience, but discipline is better in school assemblies than in classrooms. Can learning improve when a large audience, rather than a large classroom, faces a fine teacher? Only if our fine teacher is allowed to function with full scope, thus:

He meets with his dozen colleagues, tells them why he is teaching the lesson, how he will develop it, the values he expects to derive from it, and how the assortment of ability in the auditorium is expected to respond differentially. He then instructs the dozen on how he wants the materials further developed after the lecture when the students return to their dozen classrooms, how he wants the dozen classes tested, and the assignments that these classes will have to complete before they return to the next auditorium meeting. He also sets up visiting schedules for the dozen teachers, telling them when he will visit their classes and giving them a preview of what he will discuss on these visits. He will listen to divergent approaches, almost certain to arise from some of the dozen, and see how these divergences can be fitted into his auditorium and class discussions.

Such a teacher *teaches*. He does nothing else. He corrects no papers, marks no attendance records, enters no grades, and is not responsible for discipline. His salary is one-third higher, at least, than the dozen others. His post is so desirable that the dozen others mutter about his privileges, his position, and his salary, and maneuver to replace him.

His extensive preparation, virtually up to the doctoral thesis, will not protect him; some of the others may have equivalent preparation. Nor will he be protected because he is an outstanding teacher; some of the others may feel themselves of equal merit as teachers. Even his experience will not defend him from muttering and maneuvering; some of the others will also be experienced.

On the other hand, he will obviously be working harder than the others, be getting students to work harder too, achieving performance levels that the others cannot. Next, his work schedule carries over to the extended school day, week, and year, and he does not quit at the end of the last period of the day, on Friday, or in June. He gets his results by a combination of faith and good works. He knows that these two are not divisible but mutually reinforcing. Thus he prepares his lessons knowing:

1. *Why* every single item he is teaching deserves to be taught and learned

2. *Whom* he is teaching with respect to needs, characteristics, background, and inner yearnings

3. *How* to develop the materials he is teaching by questions, illustrations, and logical sequence

To do these things without resort to shibboleth requires superior intelligence and an inner assurance that results will be forthcoming.

With just one such teacher-diplomate for English, social studies, science, mathematics, foreign language, art, and music in each junior and senior high school, we would need fewer additional teachers of the usual type. As the physician recognizes the special training of the medical diplomate, without rancor, so the special talents of the teacher-diplomate may cause shudders in the usual teacher at the work necessary to get there, rather than muttering-maneuvering at his special position.

Note also that this practice is common in large elementary courses in college, such as freshman surveys of English literature and lecture classes in psychology, with the professors handling the lectures and instructors and graduate assistants handling small-class sessions and quiz groups. This proposal for high school and junior high school instructional categories recommends quasi-professorial levels for the lower schools too.

What has been done to assure that this bridegroom cometh? Not much.

The Improvement of In-service Training

American education encourages the weak and docile. Whether in setting school architecture over teaching, or the school board over the school superintendent, educational policy stimulates the capable to go elsewhere, sucking in the second-best who aren't too sure where they want to go nor of their ability to get there. Colleges and universities contribute to this educational timidity, through teachers reconciled to teaching forever, and administrators to bureaucracy. The primacy of architecture over teaching, and school board over superintendent, is reflected in the academic priority of trustee over faculty. He who pays the piper calls the tune, even if tone-deaf; and the educationally tone-deaf in America determine the repertoire wherever universities and colleges default on educational leadership, which they do by a gentlemanly reluctance to upset applecarts, a restraint which encourages scholarship possibly and stagnation and status quo certainly.

The college not only provides new (or pre-service) teaching candidates, but also, by in-service courses, provides professional growth for those currently teaching. Ideally, a college department of education should learn what problems the nearby school system faces and who on the school staff, after training, could help solve these problems, and thereafter tailor full programs—not merely courses for in-service salary increment or promotion—to the background and professional needs of the designees and to the standards of graduate study. This would include experiences in deprived and privileged communities, in experimental and conservative programs, in secular and parochial education, in administration, in curriculum development, in guidance, in educational psychology, and in library and research facilities. These experiences would logically emerge from prescribed course work *set within the program,* and from organized contacts with college faculty, where such programs are regularly reviewed and supervised, in a framework determined by the in-service student's professional needs. Thus the college faculty would simultaneously get immediate, firing-line knowledge of what is going on in the school and the administrator's office and be kept up-to-date on school and community problems.

The ideal becomes the actual in a surprising number of instances, but more typically departments of education recruit in-service personnel by course appeal intended to keep college enrollment up and college faculty employed rather than by program appeal. Most often missionary materials are sent to the schools, publicizing courses available for increment and promotion credit. But occasionally missionary men, chosen for their persuasiveness in recruiting, finagle a place on the agenda of monthly faculty meetings, which are dull because they reflect the boredom of the supervisors, principals, or administrators who must prepare them and who will eagerly snatch at any feeler sent out by the department of education for a speaking platform. So topics like "Team

Teaching," "Utilizing the Student Teacher," "Utilizing Mother Aides," "Recent Curricular Developments," and similar discussions which will rub the least fur are led by the college representatives, who then move into what is being done at the college, thereafter to recruitment, and ultimately to sprightly statistics on "alertness" courses, while the stony-faced teachers listen inflexibly, trapped by the legislation for salary increments.

In another approach, which may be called the recruiting officer, or camp-follower, technique, college personnel are passive while school personnel are enterprising.

Here highly appetizing bait is dangled before school personnel—a principal, a supervisor, or an administrator—by way of adjunct status on the college faculty. Word is passed around the school, printed announcements from the college are tacked on the bulletin board, and school personnel get the hint and register for the course given by the adjunct professor, in order to keep more in touch with what he can do for them.

Should colleges refuse to shelter such an offering merely because someone comes equipped with a built-in following? If the offering contributes to the student's needs and the instructor is qualified, the college may legitimately house such a course, provided that everybody observes the ground rules. One is that a course offering is not a program. Another is that an adjunct faculty member with superior on-the-job experiences may need an academic oasis for his in-service personnel desiring increments and promotional opportunities, but having no interest in other professional development. If the adjunct wants an academic nesting place in order to nurture his favorites while they nourish him, the college education department cannot be less hard-boiled. Snap-pap courses lead to the forming of large circles in which everybody scratches the adjacent back. The college education department must differentiate between in-service course training with purely on-the-job outcomes and graduate level work organized around programs. The shortcoming of the adjunct college faculty member is the very experience that he brings to bear, which reduces the subject matter to a course in techniques, procedures, and day-to-day routines that paradoxically lose the virtue of practicality in a description of the job's bookkeeping operations from where he sits.

In New York, because of the half-heartedness of the colleges, the Board of Education offered free in-service courses which led to salary increments and promotions. But, although the courses were supposed to be on the graduate level, the instructors usually had no work beyond the M.A., and the courses were viewed cynically by those who offered them and those who took them. When in 1964 the Board of Education curtailed these courses, the local colleges—Columbia, New York University, City University, Fordham, Yeshiva—offered replacements with stiffer requirements, and at a fee, causing dismay among teachers who now had to work where formerly only inattentive attendance had sufficed.

Despite teacher distress, in-service courses should be offered by colleges, not local boards of education. Neither in-service courses nor in-service programs can promise better teachers, but they can furnish more respectable training to whatever reservoir of competence exists. Hence in-service work—whether by course or by program—is limited by level of teacher competence, but a worse limitation is the assumption that the course trains you to perform (what a word!) better in your current job. Perhaps it does, but any teacher with five, eight, or ten years of successful teaching should *depart* from the classroom, prepare to train his successors, and somehow radiate his influence, else classroom teaching is a dead end. The experience gained from years in the classroom should be fed into career intentions in administration, supervision, research, guidance, school psychology, curriculum construction, and the other specializations in education. Classroom teaching is but one of them, though it too has numerous specialized aspects, such as teaching on the elementary, junior high school, and senior high school levels—all very different and with little overlap. Or there are subject matter specialties—English, social studies, mathematics, science, foreign language, and so on.

Nevertheless, a major function of in-service training should be rooting you out of your present job and into a more responsible one, not sharpening you up for your current rut, even though ruts are no longer ruts if their occupants are sharp, if responsibility is no longer defined as obedience, but as leadership. Crackle, zoom, and personal fulfillment should characterize in-service training, whether by course or by program. When East Harlem offers as many exciting opportunities as East Africa, education in Bedford-Stuyvesant as much electricity as Upper Volta, educational budgets as much size as A. T. & T., and educational problems more subtleties than moon-shots or physics, we lack the people to meet the excitement, the size, and the subtleties, in both classroom and administrative posts. Some teachers are more than classroomers and some administrators are educational leaders, but too many have a spot, occupy it, and take in-service work for promotional opportunities rather than for professional possibilities.

The takeover of in-service courses by colleges was expedited by the National Defense Education Act, which pays teachers to attend summer institutes at college campuses. (Notice that it is called the National Defense Education Act, not the National Education Defense Act, meaning that defense grants funds to education, but education does not grant funds to defense. Clearly, defense is more important than education, as in any savage society.) The consequence of the act is added leverage for colleges in in-service work for teachers and a healthier direction for such in-service work, especially in transference opportunities, meaning this:

Tensions and strains accumulate in the classroom. Anybody who has taught a graduate course to teachers will remember their barely repressed violence, their thinly covered accusations that the instructor has no experience in what he is talking about—at one extreme the apoplectic teacher almost physically upset about the need for taking the course, and at the other the teacher-in-a-trance using the course as a means of getting away from it all.

Because the school-sponsored in-service course, in contrast to the college-sponsored one, is taught by somebody on the same level of bureaucratic pecking-order, the class has no transference opportunities. But where the course has college auspices and the instructor has college faculty status, members of the class can transfer as their private needs, whether violent or dreamy, dictate. However, transference needs for the goose are counter-transference needs for the gander, and college instructors themselves react to the combative or placid teachers in their courses. The best instructors deliberately rupture the teacher's ego organization, whether gently, as the late William Kilpatrick did it, or aggressively, first to gain discipline and then to repair the ego on their own terms. These instructors feel that the rupture must be attempted, else the in-service course can just as well be given under school auspices. The best college courses for teachers therefore attack their bureaucratic attachments, not in order to sever that umbilicus, but to put it in better perspective.

Education courses are unfortunately limited by vocational intentions and are slanted and conformable to teachers and classroom, thereby defining education very narrowly. Only teachers take education courses. But many people in education are not teachers. The education course that trains these classroomers has the most tenuous connection with the remainder of education, yet a teacher can be either a classroomer or an "instructional engineer," a term that some may find pretentious and presumptuous. We like it. We hurl the term in their teeth.

The instructional engineer will have had three, five, or more years of classrooming, but then, like the heroine of *Guys and Dolls,* will have said "Enough!" and turned to administration, curriculum, supervision, educational psychology, educational television, tests and measurements, guidance, personnel training, psychopharmacology, psychotherapy, international and comparative education, foreign aid, area studies, school architecture and design, communications research, or even to team teaching and team learning—like our teacher-diplomate mentioned earlier, surrounded by his dozen muttering colleagues. The instructional engineer is interested in a career, financial rewards, status, and decision-making opportunities.

Above all, the instructional engineer, unlike the classroomer, is not afraid of getting his advanced training in the disadvantaged community, where the need is greatest, the challenge sharpest, and life is in perpetual crisis. (A current example is the National Teacher Corps, a federal program to train effective teachers for slum schools.) He goes into the disadvantaged area because the crisis community is the best training ground we know of, and not only because he is well-intentioned, since communities like Harlem offer laboratory facilities superior to Scarsdale or Manhasset and far greater scope for professional growth. So the Peace Corps goes into Africa and South America—rather than into France, Italy, or Sweden—to improve Africa and South America, but to improve Americans too. We become more civilized as we improve backwardness. As challenges from Africa arise more frequently in the future, African experiences will become more important in the training of Americans. Progress in Harlem will set the pace and policy for Negro and white life in the United States. Harlem is the most challenging environment we have today, and is therefore the best training ground for teachers and educators of whatever specialist persuasion. The bottleneck in American life today is education; the bottleneck in education is teaching competence; the bottleneck in teaching competence is educational leadership; the bottleneck in educational leadership is refusal to manipulate social change. We best train for social change in the circumstances that call for social change, not for social stasis. Like in Harlem.

The Teaching Candidate's Pre-service Training

We turn from in-service work to pre-service preparation. Candidates for teaching, or pre-service personnel, should not take the same courses or programs available to in-service personnel. Pre-service candidates can be: (1) undergraduates taking education courses as part of their baccalaureate preparation, or (2) liberal arts graduates who have never taught and who are involved in programs like the Master of Arts in Teaching (M.A.T.) offered at Harvard, Oberlin, and other institutions for college graduates who have turned to teaching and are in elementary education or secondary education sequences. For example, the Ferkauf Graduate School of Education (Yeshiva University) has in Project Beacon a program for the second group that is planned around intensive field experiences and responsibilities in the deprived areas of New York City. It admitted fewer than a dozen candidates in September, 1963, perhaps because its field experiences bring the pre-service candidate into contact with family disorganization, community disorganization, delinquency, unemployment, migrancy, and illiteracy in settings like police stations, courts, hospitals, case work agencies, and political and civil rights action organizations.

The Harvard M.A.T. is more genteel. Nevertheless, even Harvard has had to send out commercial travelers to plug its M.A.T. program and beat the woods for prospective customers because superior college graduates are rarely interested in becoming classroomers. Harvard's recruiters do the Lord's work by soft sell, hard sell, and a rhetoric varying from the unobtrusively intrusive Harvard cachet to the spiels of sideshow shills, fake auctioneers, East Side clothing store *shleppers,* and magazine salesmen working their way through college—anything to get classroomers into the store and buying. More power to Harvard, but again, like Project Beacon, nibbles from qualified candidates are few, though increasing. Other institutions have had the same experience. Hunter College, for all its efforts to persuade teaching candidates to accept practice teaching assignments in Harlem junior high schools, was never able to get more than a fraction of its students to believe that being a classroomist in a deprived school, with slum children, was the best training you could get. The very strength of the Project Beacon program, in offering experiences with a deprived Negro and Puerto-Rican population, was a drawback in recruiting teaching candidates who prefer to earn their livings with the intellectually gifted, or else in the suburban schools, even though these too have their delinquents, dropouts, and reluctant learners.

Although the phrase "Domestic Peace Corps" was first used in connection with Project Beacon in 1961, the question remains: why do so many young people flock into the established Peace Corps, abroad and domestic, into volunteer tutoring work for slum children, and into various aspects of civil rights, but decline a permanent, professional commitment to teaching? Let's put the question another way: How can any person with drive and purpose retain these if he sees classrooming as the one channel in which education can go? If teachers, as years go on, become ever bigger fish in the same petty, unchanging, pond, why should qualified college graduates want to fritter away their lives in guaranteed stagnation, where the only things that grow are the barnacles on you and the children away from you?

From 1945 onward the nation's need for teachers was sharpened. Classroom population increased and teachers were lost to the greater rewards elsewhere available. In the early nineteen-fifties Albert Lynd's *Atlantic* article started the subsequent attack by Bestor and Rickover, with the consequence that teachers experienced an additional reduction in status, and their preparation and effectiveness were questioned. (1) Sputnik sharpened the need for well-prepared teachers.

In 1951 the Ford Fund for the Advancement of Education granted funds to the University of Arkansas to prepare college graduates with no prior work in professional courses. Similar plans were set up throughout the country; they undoubtedly contributed to meeting the shortage but only to a limited extent. Currently, the need for teachers, though still great, is not as acute; the disparity between classroom enrollment and teaching staff has narrowed.

As more teachers become available, teacher quality and

preparation will receive closer scrutiny. Classroom coverage will be less dominating a problem than classroom competence. With conceptions of instructional effectiveness being amplified by team teaching, teacher aides, teaching machines, programed instruction, and closed-circuit television, the redefinition of classroom competence will emerge. If this redefinition awaits us, and teaching takes on wider horizons, so must the teacher, and so must institutions of teacher training, lest teaching be downgraded by those in teaching for the wrong reasons: long summer vacations, an abbreviated working day, tenure, and a time-off-with-pay value system, rather than a professional, problem-centered value system.

As Francis Keppel said:

> . . . an ever larger number of high-quality teachers will force the public and the school systems to make ever better arrangements for them in salary and working conditions. The exciting careers that now exist in the schools can be still further developed by first-rate people. Once this becomes understood, able young men can be recruited in greater numbers, and more such posts may be formed as the public comes to appreciate the quality of its personnel. The higher the ultimate rewards, the better will be the chances of recruiting still stronger candidates, until a career in teaching will be a fully competitive position with other professions. Obviously this premise requires that a start be made by persuading a substantial number of the most promising young men and women in our colleges to start the process. (2)

One warning: The process may only pile up casualties, disappointments, and frustrations at the feet of unmoving bureaucracy; the classroom can be a dead end if it is seen as the terminal point of professional preparation, and if we continue to prepare teachers rather than teacher-diplomates or instructional engineers.

This career *cul-de-sac* is less demoralizing for women than for men. Women see the classroom as a career supplementary to homemaking and motherhood, something to be abandoned when family life begins and resumed when the family is grown. As a result, the classroom takes second place, but exerts a unique revenge when a woman juggles parallel careers as wife and mother, and as teacher. The teacher who dashes home to her children and tries to be the devoted mother, forgetting her pupils and the preparations she should be making for them, is also shortchanging her family because her class is not out of her mind, but leaves her short-tempered with her children and husband. A teacher unprepared to meet her class will have a miserable time away from class.

But the woman who attends to her home responsibilities after devoting reasonable effort and time to her school preparations is relaxed at home, is more likely to enjoy her working hours, and will return home able to do a better job there. The woman who teaches well will enrich her home life. Because her home life is in order, she will teach better too.

Men have different professional expectations. The billions we spend on education may nourish bureaucracy, unless we train for educational careers where educational problems are most acute. This training, sometime later, provides for further professional development by specialization. Will the educational specialist have deserted the classroom? No more than a diplomate in some medical specialty has deserted medicine. Departure is not desertion.

Though few, aspirants for educational leadership exist and are now getting training at Harvard, The City University of New York, Oberlin, Colgate, and in Project Beacon. But clearly, these quality programs run no risk of dilution by numbers. If we concentrate on a few educational leaders rather than on many classroomists, we could make do with the lower quality of the many if the few hold to the highest performance. And if we put a finer edge on future leadership with experience *in situ* and *in vivo*, concurrent with the apparently theoretical, lest education courses bore rather than interest, ruin the aspirant for teaching rather than prepare him, and stupefy rather than impart morale, power, and ideas, we shall be taking steps in the forward direction.

If aspiring teachers are not as highly motivated as prospective scientists and if the status of the education faculty on a college campus is low, as is the status of the teacher in the community, education courses should offer motivation and a rich cuisine of subject matter. For example, here is an idea of the content of five education courses, each of a term's duration, designed for *pre-service* candidates:

1. *An introductory course that shows that behavior is caused and not accidental.* In this course the *Meno,* Quintilian, Conant, Pestalozzi, the answer of the Jesuits to the Reformation, Melanchthon's answer to the Renaissance, the Humanists' answer to both, Rousseau's answer to the Humanists, Baron vom Stein's answer to Napoleon, Aristotle's answer to Plato, John Dewey's to Thomas Arnold, and Blantock's to Dewey, are seen as continuously emerging crises and debates in educational history and philosophy. What nonsense to say that this is theoretical! Only the blind fail to see the immediate relevance of such theory to every child in every slum school.

2. *A course that shows that behavior is patterned and organized even when disorganized,* in which Freud, statistics, experimental psychology, linguistics, tests and measurements, developmental patterns in the child, reading disabilities, learning disabilities, social and attitudinal development, language development, and educational psychology combine to show that gestalts, configurations, S-R paradigms, cognitive maps, reinforcement schedules tell us that behavior can be systematically studied, even if the systems have wide gaps.

3. *A course that shows that culture is measurable, and that we can quantify much of the qualitative*–in Negro unrest, in the ability of Sicilians in Milan to handle automated processes, in the number of television sets contrasted to toilets per dwelling. Or, how social change is engineered by government investment, and how educational sociology organizes our information about crime, family structure, urbanization, and labor relations.

4. *A course that shows how the curriculum is both manipulable and manipulated by our ideological masters;* how social needs influence curriculum; how curriculum remains unchanged and petrified despite social change, political forces, and educational shifts; how school architecture and legislative corruption affect curriculum; and how the strategy and tactics of curriculum change.

5. *A course that shows that teaching is methodologically organized and that teaching outcomes can be planned.* And that lesson planning, classroom management, school and administrative routines, professional relationships, team teaching, teaching technologies (such as teaching machines and programed instruction), community relations of the school, and professional specialization give direction and focus to the teacher's day-by-day performance.

And this is merely the nucleus in preparing educational leadership!

We may not be able to make a silk purse out of a sow's ear,

but we can a nylon purse out of coal and air (much more difficult!), and even a full one, fit for an affluent society. But no known technology can prepare for teaching, or make a good teacher out of an ineffective one, though an effective one can be improved, and the ineffective one reduced in poorness. Given a promising candidate, good education courses can prepare educational leadership.

First we must snare him, as we said earlier, by making education attractive to him through programs more difficult and demanding than standard programs of preparation, which discourage all candidates of lesser merit, who can go elsewhere for their preparation. He will be broadly involved with other faculties—medicine, law, social work, and engineering—and with community agencies, politicians, and education officials.

What shall we call this program and its personnel, to distinguish it from other forms of teacher preparation?

Nomenclature like *pedagogy, education,* and *teaching,* which lead to *pedagogue, educationist,* and *teacher,* repel rather than attract. Although derogation in *sawbones, ambulance chaser, headshrinker, pillroller,* and *slide rule boy* do not cheapen surgery, the law, psychiatry, medicine, and engineering, *pedagogue* offends. It is out of style and etymologically too close for comfort with another, and unseemly, word. *Teacher* is low level. *Educator* is inflated, and *educationist* is patronizing. *Didacticist* is stiff and *instructional engineer* is pretentious. If the education of children in a metropolitan setting is *metropeducation,* we are developing a new *metropedagese.*

Terminology is one problem. Training is another. Dean Joshua Fishman of Yeshiva University's Ferkauf Graduate School of Education, in describing Project Beacon, hoped it would

. . . also improve our understanding of how educational personnel *should* be trained. The training of teachers and other educational specialists is currently based more on hunches than on conceptually integrated theory, more on conviction than on research, more on conventional wisdom than on a detailed analysis of how and why children learn or do not learn, change or do not change. It is our hope that Project Beacon will be able to collect, systematize, analyze, and publicize information that will enable us and others to leave behind this relatively primitive stage of personnel training. Our hopes are based in part on the greater severity of the learning and behavior problems with which Beacon trainees must cope. The more exaggerated the characteristics of children, parents, schools and communities, the easier it is. . . . to provide for them, and to integrate them in the training of teachers and others. On the other hand, some of our hopefulness that Project Beacon will help bring about a better understanding of teacher training is based upon the major involvement in Beacon of special education, guidance, educational psychology, therapeutic education and school psychology. To some extent each of these disciplines is more oriented toward analysis of behavior and toward guided behavioral change than has usually been the case with teacher training programs. We hope that through Project Beacon their more advanced analytical and conceptual status will be deepened and will influence training in other educational specialties as well. (3)

Therefore breadth of scope is another way of training our prospect. And here are some questions on specific areas. Why should teachers take a course in the history of education? Is the history of education an antiquarian's delight or is it pragmatically relevant to the teacher's daily tasks? Is the liberal arts value of the history of education pertinent, or is it dragged in to make palatable an otherwise dull and uninspiring area?

More, have courses in educational sociology and curriculum made teachers and teacher groups more effective, or at all effective, in politics, economics, and legislation? Or should such courses have such outcomes? If they should, have they lifted teacher status in American society so that the teacher contributes to policy making? If they should not, are they being offered for pure pedantry?

Should not courses in educational psychology and human development make the teacher more self-aware and more understanding of his own needs and drives, as much as they give the teacher greater understanding of the pupil? Do not most texts and courses on educational psychology handle teacher self-understanding with forceps—bloodlessly, politely, and superficially—lest they disturb, when self-understanding is impossible to achieve without a shove toward disequilibrium?

Such texts in adolescent psychology offer a dull, uninteresting description of growth patterns of the entrance into the teens, the differences between the fast and slow grower, the early and delayed menarche, the social outcomes of being a taller girl and a slighter boy, and the changes in physical proportion. Like a fly in amber, the adolescent is presented for objective scrutiny. Better texts attempt to put the description in a classroom setting, to indicate classroom consequences, but no text reminds the teaching candidate that it was so for him too, and is also a portrait of him. The fly-in-amber or butterfly-on-a-pin approach requires that the reader be reminded, very personally, of how it was—that he was once thus describable and once also expended efforts either to be average or outstanding, because he was heavier, slighter, taller, or shorter; and that he bears the consequences to this day and these consequences will affect his teaching.

Objectivity with respect to the evidence is fine in science and in the humanities, but is misplaced in education courses and texts— the major reason for their dullness. Hence many instructors in educational psychology and human development use *Catcher in the Rye, The Doll Maker, Lord of the Flies,* and other works of fiction and biography not only to add vitality to the course, but to make teaching candidates realize that these books mirror them and that what they see reflected in these mirrors will be in the eyes of the pupils they face. The best instructor will remind the teaching candidate that the text and the course are describing *him,* because this increase in self-awareness opens the portals to improved teaching.

Thus, one text states, "The average boy triples his strength of grip in the ten years from 7 to 17 and doubles his quickness as shown by tapping." (4) Certainly true and even important because the high school teacher should recall this period in order to teach his material more effectively. Only such *personal* recall can tell the teacher if the adolescent who does well in school is more or less likely to sense this surge of increased physical power, how to use it, how it becomes arrogance, how it means increased application to studies, how it interferes with studies, and how the teacher should deal with this new power. Unless the teacher remembers sharply and distinctly how it was in his own case, the text and course are stuffy, windy nonsense.

The teacher must remember what she thought of herself physically during adolescence. Was she aware of disfigurements of one kind or another? How did she fit into her clothing? Did her complexion make for difficulties? Because it's still the same way with the class she is facing. Tariff history, or algebraic factoring, or the conjugation of *haber* must be taught in the context of the teacher's recall of her own private past, to avoid pedantry with the boy with a pimply face or the tall girl whose rounded shoulders are her only way of hiding her breasts.

Pressey has written an excellent text. He is a distinguished psychologist, and the father of programed instruction, but any educational psychology text is half complete that doesn't enjoin, assail, force the reader to remember himself at that age.

Maybe only education courses can take place legitimately on a college campus, because their content is too insubstantial, slippery, vague, and elusive, to be reduced to a book. Others— literature, history, mathematics, science, political science, and classics—have a substantial content which is clear, straightforward, can be discussed, and can be bound into books. These can then be given to the college student, who, presumably bright enough to be in college in the first place, can thereafter be sent home with the book, while one exterminates the superfluous college professor and inters him. The student, adjured to study the book thoroughly, does so, returns to the campus when he has finished the material, and is examined on it.

Since nothing much is going on in most books on education, education must depend on discussion and interpersonal chat, the chief reason for the existence of a college.

For example, consider a course in the history and philosophy of education. Though our instructional engineer should study the socially dispossessed in urban settings, the serf, slave, peon, peasant, and city proletarian have rarely been included in the history and philosophy of education. However, a major reason for teaching history is history as relevance—an important matter to the urban dispossessed, and also to the prospective teacher. Historical and contemporary disadvantaged groups offer comparisons of past versus present, here versus there, and them versus us. In such a framework, the history of education beds down comfortably with the philosophy of education.

The educational problems of the deprived community, though not new, have never been specifically considered by the usual course in educational foundations, but this is exactly what our teacher-diplomate/instructional engineer requires. We now outline a series of such courses, by week and topic.

13

The In-service Course—
An Example

Training the Remedial Reading Teacher

We begin with an in-service course for junior high school and high school teachers of reading, as such a course might be offered in a six-week summer session. Observe that this course is for people currently teaching, and is not intended for pre-service teaching candidates, for whom specimen courses are presented later.

To begin with, materials in figurative and literal language exist, but materials will never substitute for a competent, well-trained teacher. Reading materials exist in a vast range from ancient proverbs to today's Broadway show music—and we need not mention the enormous reservoir of the orthodox. These materials are useful and appropriate far more often than we have a right to expect. In addition, tests and diagnostic procedures are as refined as in any area of psychological testing. Why, then, is poor reading the major problem in urban education? The chief reason is that teachers do not know the methodology of reading improvement, and have not been trained in it. (1)

Typically, a junior and senior high school program in reading improvement is entrusted to an English teacher without the faintest idea of what to do with a fourteen-year-old who is physically mature, energetic, able to respond to a joke, who can understand spoken instructions and can respond to them, but who is reading four or five years below grade.

The English teacher raids the school's shelves for materials, uses them, tests outcomes, and works harder with the reading class than with her regular classes, only to find that results usually are poor. Understandably, then, the teacher's sense of reality undergoes attrition, lapses into cynicism, and needing an infusion of morale-vitamins, she takes an in-service course to get some help, to become less hard-boiled, and to regain her flexibility.

But in-service instruction varies. So, depending on the course and the instructor, some reading teachers are helped and some become increasingly cynical. (2) How should such a course, designed for the competence that withstands morale-attrition, go? Let us assume a six-week summer session course attended by an imagined teacher of reading.

First Week

FIRST DAY.   After registration is completed, course outlines distributed, and assignments explained, the instructor should clarify the differences between the reading problems on the elementary, junior, and senior high school levels, indicating the issues involved in phonics, phonetics, and the whole-word controversy. He should explain their bases in psychology and philosophy, and their antecedents in the gestalt-connectionist-psychodynamic polemics.

SECOND DAY.   The instructor describes the growth of psychological inadequacy in the poor reader, pointing out that nobody feels worse about his plight than the poor reader does, not even the teacher. The instructor classifies the underlying reasons for reading disability into their physiological, sociological, conceptual, and emotional aspects, thereby telling the teacher something about the kinds of poor readers there are. Reading impairment is not a unitary thing, but presents various syndromes. These syndromes are best presented by case histories.

THIRD DAY.   Whatever his psychological inadequacies, the instructor declares, the poor reader wants to read. You might not think so, from surface appearances, because this reading-volition is masked by his behavior, deceiving you into thinking that he is not interested. On the contrary, he is intensely motivated. There's nothing he wants more, because he knows as well as you how important reading is. You don't have to motivate him, but if so we face a paradox because we have always been told that high motivation leads to high performance. Not here. Another paradox of normal rate of speech, normal rate of listening, but slow reading rate proves that the poor reader's neurology is intact and that we must look elsewhere for the causes of reading disability. However, in pre-school children we have one modification: auditory discrimination is predictive of reading level; however, auditory discrimination is environmental. Misbehavior arises from an interior environment, where high motivation requires tempering rather than intensifying.

FOURTH DAY. The elementary school pupil, the instructor continues, is complaisant with the dull. Not so the junior high school student, who demands that materials be interesting. Most materials for the poor reader in the junior high school are cursed by being boring because the junior high school pupil has more emotional experience than the materials. He knows that this is "kid stuff." New materials now in the development stage, by the Bank Street School, Project English, and others, attempt to correct this disparity between pupil experiences and materials level.

FIFTH DAY. The instructor points out that materials for the poor reader are dull because they placate; they are inspirational, sunny. The poor reader, who is tougher than that, doesn't recognize the life they describe. His reading materials should sharpen—drives, crises, and excitement—and thereafter resolve. The teacher should tear him to pieces with whatever emotional content can be found in the material. Materials that stir the emotions are exactly what the slow reader needs, but the teacher must be able to stir the materials so that emotions emerge.

Second Week

FIRST DAY. The instructor resumes: Any reading program ever devised has an enemy; the teacher must decide whether to lick it or join it. This enemy consists of youthful gregariousness, sociability, and the mass media—chiefly television. But these major threats also constitute a promise arising from the physiological and psychological earthquake known as adolescence, and the second chance inherent in the adolescent earthquake because it is a kind of rebirth. This rebirth gives the teacher a second opportunity at remaking what family and community have wrecked. To gain success for the reading program, the teacher should intensify this rebirth trauma by raising problems, questions, and dilemmas to be found in reading materials.

SECOND DAY. The adolescent rebirth has a midwife. The midwife is the curriculum, and the curriculum is divisible by subject matter areas. The instructor takes the first of the subject matter categories, in English, to see what its curricular sources or resources are in problems, questions, dilemmas, crises, crisis-resolution, and conflict. Literature deals with the family, and therefore with parental and sibling relationships; with friends, and therefore with loyalty and deceit; with strangers, and therefore with suspicion and welcome. In all these relationships, problems and their solutions, growth, destruction, and incomplete answers will appear in the reading materials.

THIRD DAY. The instructor turns to another area, or curricular source, of crisis, crisis-resolution, and conflict, in the social studies. Social studies is a record of competition, contention, and cutthroat rivalry, so the reading materials in social studies ought to be analyzed and presented thus:

(*a*) How do you win a fight?
(*b*) How do you win followers?
(*c*) How do you persuade, or deceive, people?

Virtually everything in social studies, from tariff history to local civics, can be presented under these three rubrics, meaning that social studies are less social than asocial, antisocial, unsocial, and non-social, and when so presented become vastly more interesting to the poor reader.

FOURTH DAY. Similarly the instructor finds crisis, crisis-resolution, and conflict in:

(*a*) Foreign language, where we must arrange reading materials to fit these rubrics: What can foreigners tell us about our city that we can't possibly find out by ourselves without speaking a foreign language? How can we live better and more richly in our city by knowing a foreign language? How can we eavesdrop on a foreign language conversation?

(*b*) Art and music, these: Are the composer's techniques of listening the same as ours? Does he listen to noise as we do? Does the painter have our techniques of watching or does he have other techniques? If so, what are they?

New and modern music is unquestionably related to new and modern noises, noises never known before and rhythms never heard before. So modern nonrepresentational painting reflects things never seen before, and still not visible without a prism, a microscope, or an oscilloscope, so that common-sense vision must yield to trans-sensory perceptions rather than extra-sensory ones and develop reading materials accordingly, to subject the adolescent earthquake to even deeper tremors. The shook up generation isn't shook up enough. It is spastic and vibratory, but not truly shaken. Art and music can shake.

FIFTH DAY. To some pupils, the instructor says, scientific and mathematic predictability is motivating; to others it is a source of anxiety; therefore science and mathematics can lead either to stability or to uneasiness, depending on the pupil. What in science and mathematics materials contributes to anxiety and uneasiness? On the other hand, science and mathematics are not uniformly motivating and stabilizing. For example, mathematics can be an organizer of reality, as with the engineer and the accountant, or else an organizer of fantasy processes, as with the creative mathematician or scientist. In preparing mathematics and science materials for the poor reader, we must combine reality with fantasy.

Mathematicians differentiate mathematical talent by a vague, qualitative description which they call "power." The superior mathematician has it. The mediocre one hasn't. But what does the mathematician mean by "power"? He knows that tempo, pace, and "soak-in" time are major parameters in the learning of science and mathematics, and that computation is far less important than rumination and meditation. Working end-of-chapter problems is important because it develops imagination and conceptualization, not because it imparts computational facility.

Hence the reading of scientific and mathematics materials is related to the reading of poetry—it must be done slowly, unhurriedly, so that fantasy processes are encouraged. Ask any mathematician.

Third Week

FIRST DAY. Vocabulary-acquisition, the instructor declares, is basic to reading because it ruptures previous, and limited, compartments of experience. By breaking up older concepts, vocabulary leads to new ones. To teach word analysis by etymology, affixes, and roots concomitantly requires inner exploration, as phonetics does, again bringing us to comparisons and contrasts. Does *un*cover mean the same as *dis*cover? *man*ipulate as *ped*al? *ex*tract as *ab*stract? *retro*grade as *de*grade? Less subtle are dictionary skills and the logic of alphabetical arrangement, taught by the dictionary or by the telephone Yellow Pages, also an example of alphabetical arrangement. Given names, surnames, place names, and occupation names are another source of vocabulary-acquisition. How foreign names are Americanized, and if they ought to be, reconstitutes a sense of tradition and belonging. The discussion that arises generates the emotiveness so deeply involved with reading improvement.

SECOND DAY. But, the instructor takes care to clarify, vocabulary-acquisition, unless accompanied by sensitivity to context, can lead to inappropriateness in usage. Here the thesaurus helps in cultivating sensitivity in word meaning and word shading. Though the poor reader who is distinguishing word shades is much further along than the one still distinguishing word shapes, the reader must continue to shuttle between shades and shapes in order to learn how to gain meaning from context, then from guessing, from confirmation in the dictionary, from the same word in other contexts, and how context alters meaning.

THIRD DAY. Paragraph-comprehension, the instructor explains, requires an attack on the beginning, the middle, and the end of thought development, as well as skill with transitional structures, phrases, and ideas. Both attack and skill require practice in setting aside the unimportant and the irrelevant to gather together the germane and the relevant, in an act of simultaneous acceptance and rejection. Here workbooks are especially useful in their illustrations of topic sentence, details, connections, and other aspects of paragraph development. More useful is the ability of the teacher to pick up that day's newspaper and show how the same structures operate in an editorial, a sports item, or a financial report, because the very spontaneity of the act proves to the pupil that paragraphs are all around him. Nothing will more effectively persuade him of the interaction between the composition of ideas and the comprehension of ideas.

FOURTH DAY. The instructor now asserts that comprehension of the written word is impossible without a preliminary self-awareness of inner processes. This can be taught, even if indirectly. For example, we can use contrasting sentences, obscure sentences, and ambiguous sentences to gain sensitivity and word-discrimination. Some of the sentences that follow can perform this service for good readers who know grammar. Others have the same mission for poor readers ignorant of grammar.

1. He is in his grave. (*Is* is a "being" verb—does that mean that the man is alive? How can he "be" and still not "be"?)

2. (The student is told that the adverb *where* introduces adverbial clauses, but this is not true in the following examples, in which an adverb introduces a noun clause. Why is this so?)

    (*a*) When the iron is hot is the time to strike.

    (*b*) The time to strike is when the iron is hot.

    (*c*) (And here comes an adjective clause) The place where he lives is unknown.

3. J. C. Catford, in "The Teaching of English as a Foreign Language," has shown how slight changes indicate change in ownership: (3)

    (*a*) Is that your hat? No. *Oh,* I thought it WAS.

    (*b*) Is that your hat? Yes. *Ah,* I THOUGHT it was.

4. Notice how the word *even* is most uneven in the following sentences, as it switches from adverb to adjective:

    (*a*) Even now the enemy wouldn't surrender. Now even the enemy wouldn't surrender.

    (*b*) Even now bright children aren't promoted. Now even bright children aren't promoted.

    (*c*) Even now women scold husbands. Now even women scold husbands.

5. Charles E. Osgood's "On Understanding and Creating Sentences" offers the following examples of ambiguity: (3)

    (*a*) The shooting of the hunters was terrible.

    (*b*) Equivalent or synonymous sentences:

light	lights	lightly	light	light	lights
↓	↓	↓	↓	↓	↓
pale	flames	gently	illuminate	airy	lanterns

6. (We change meaning even when we use the identical words. Is *eating* a verb or an adjective? Is it an action-word or a describer-word?) They are eating apples.

7. (Another change in meaning using the identical words. If *lies* means "prevaricate," we get the exactly opposite meaning when it means "direction.") This way the truth lies.

8. (Another illustration of the same words meaning the exact opposite. Hence this sentence can either mean that the Russians are turning peaceful, or that they are turning belligerent.) The Russians are dropping hints about bombing Berlin.

9. (Similarly *statue* can be prior to or contemporaneous with *gate*.) The archaeologist says that the statue was here before the gate.

10. (The poor reader can be asked why placement affects meaning.)

    (*a*) He didn't think much of her.
    (*b*) He didn't think of her much.

11. (And what causes shift in meaning here?)

    (*a*) She remembered to do her homework.
    (*b*) She remembered doing her homework.

These examples show that comprehension of the inner *world* is prior to comprehension of the outer *word,* just as the hand mirror offers portals to the self-awareness that leads to word awareness and as phonetics precedes phonics.

FIFTH DAY. The instructor can now discuss the symbolic and conceptual underpinning of phonetics and phonics, citing the Russian experiences in teaching reading via phonetics (*not* phonics!) and then showing outcomes in mechanical matters, as in the techniques of oral reading. The pupil who reads syllable-by-syllable is thereby testifying to his knowledge of phonics, but the teacher must substitute phrase reading for syllable reading. The teacher does so by instructing the pupil to withhold utterance until he can utter a phrase at a time. The pupil must maintain silence while he mutely reads and re-reads the phrase, or passage. When he feels he knows it, he reads it aloud, but not before. Oral reading is thereby taught by non-reading, or by reading at judicious intervals (or gulps), the interval to be determined by the student, when he feels himself ready to read phrase-by-phrase or passage-by-passage. What is the rest of the class doing meanwhile? Similarly preparing itself for phrase-by-phrase reading by reading, re-reading, and re-re-reading the same passage—and we are not stuttering, nor will the student. Is he memorizing? No. Is he rehearsing? Yes. There's a real difference.

Fourth Week

FIRST DAY.   Like the Hungarian who says, "With such a friend, who needs an enemy?" the reading teacher wants to know how to cope with her friendly reading anthology. Transforming the dull into the stimulating is a challenge most reading teachers cannot take up. The instructor asserts that the teacher should be able to delve into the pupils' underlying problems. Recognition and analysis of these make the material interesting. Dick and Jane in blackface, in an attempt to interest the Negro student, is one spurious effort to improve reading materials. More important is an ability in the teacher to point up human problems, which are the same in Shakespeare as in a *True Confession* story. Depth makes the difference, and depth is reached by treating human problems and relationships in the sleaziest item in the anthology with perception and respect and intellectual honesty. This is as important with the poor reader as with the good one because the poor reader is also degraded by uninteresting materials.

SECOND DAY.   "All news is local," say newspapers in their pursuit of advertising revenue. The instructor points out that the teacher capitalizing on this restriction of focus makes reading immediate to the slow reader. The newspaper is superior as reading material to most materials furnished in school. The sports page, the women's page, the want ads, advertising copy, the editorial page, motivate by the contemporaneous and the contiguous. Virtually every sentence in a well-edited newspaper is a resource for etymology, vocabulary, and grammar study, and offers exercise for reading skills in social studies, science, mathematics, foreign language, art, and music.

THIRD DAY.   The instructor continues: Like the newspaper, the periodical offers an extensive reading program. The magazine's recurrence requires repetition of articles, fiction, and features, which allows the reading program to anticipate special uses of *Harper's, Atlantic,* and *The Reporter* for the good reader, and of *Popular Mechanics, Reader's Digest, Ladies Home Journal,* and trade magazines for the poor reader. Specialized appeals allow reading programs based on the fan magazines, service magazines, and women's magazines for girls; the *Saturday Evening Post, Sports Illustrated,* and technical magazines on hot rods, television, and hunting for boys; and *Life, Look,* and *Time* for all groups. Magazine illustrations, from which all captions have been removed, are used in a modification of the Thematic Apperception Test technique; students guess what the story accompanying the caption-less illustration is, write short compositions, and then match their compositions with the finally revealed caption. We have here a springboard for self-expression and vocabulary building. Magazines, because of their numerous types, offer a variety of avenues for expanding reading interests of all groups.

FOURTH DAY. Magazines require collection and permanent housing. They continue to be valuable to the reading program even though the month of issue is long past. Back issues should be accumulated and housed for easy access, making the school librarian a vital adjunct to the reading teacher, especially in such undertakings as the paperback book fair, a regular institution in many school libraries. Some school libraries have paperback books on sale throughout the school year, conspicuously displayed to motivate purchase. Naturally, the usual purchaser is the good reader, but the very presence of books-on-sale allows the reading teacher to discuss them, to whet an interest in them, and thereby move the poor reader along to the meaningfulness of reading. Still other commercially sponsored reading materials are completely free, or else inexpensive, like the many educational comics prepared and distributed by General Electric, available in whatever quantities the reading teacher may require, and intended for distribution to the poor reader, to be retained as his property. Such free and inexpensive reading materials have a wide range of topics, from feminine hygiene, to travel photos, to career materials, to telephone courtesy, to automobile models—all well within the budget for the reading program.

FIFTH DAY. Radio and television, the instructor continues, extend the experiential background that is prior to the reading program. For example, many pre-school children learn to read by watching television commercials and by recognizing institutional logotypes. These words and logotypes are later recognized on roadside billboards or other advertising. The lyrics of Broadway show music are appropriate to the reading program because they use techniques that are as old as the oldest reading instruction, as

Marrou describes it, in which the alphabet and reading were accompanied by chant and cantillation. (4) To this day, indeed, students in orthodox Hebrew schools learn the ancient texts by chant, so that thousands of Jews can read Hebrew fluently without knowing one word of the language. (5) Paradoxically, then, one can read well without the slightest comprehension.

Fifth Week

FIRST DAY. Much of the reading program, the instructor declares, depends on experiences away from the printed page, so that such experiences must be built up and extended in order to enlarge the program's probabilities of success. Thus the 1964–1965 New York World's Fair offered varied material for the reading program. Although the World's Fair was a one-shot affair, analogous opportunities for year-in, year-out programs can always be found locally in visits to the public library, a nearby museum, a zoo, a botanical garden, an art gallery, a department store, the supermarket, a local demolition or building site, and at other community institutions and events. Each of these visits should be related to vocabulary, and vocabulary in turn related to concepts and symbolic structures. A simple visit to the *supermarket* can build a vocabulary of *superior, market, supremacy, merchandise, cutlet, cutlery, branded merchandise, carton, fragile, reinforce, warehouse, housewares, shipment, ample stock, cash and carry, low denomination, high denomination, choice cut, prime cut, cut price, economy size,* which not only involves words but concepts too.

SECOND DAY. Most reading programs push on too eagerly to new passages, rather than the review of old passages, in fear of boring pupils. Similarly, the instructor declares, they stress individualized, as contrasted with team, reading. Thus oration and dramatization require memorization followed by delivery to an audience. This memorization of extended passages, by individuals and by groups, encourages deutero-learning (learning-to-learn) and gives rise to active recitation techniques, to a greater aggressiveness toward materials (rather than the poor reader's defensiveness toward them), and to a neutralization of passive reading and spectatorism; passive reading is our greatest spectator sport. Memorization with subsequent recitation, as in the oration or dramatization, engenders greater power with the written word. It compels the poor reader to dwell on the material and to master it. If recitation is subsequently desired, the embarrassment in facing an audience is wholesome trauma, especially if every member of the audience will have to run that gauntlet. Boredom is reduced if individuals are given different selections, and if the selections have sequence or some other kind of relationship, as in play dialogue. Thus memorization becomes the portal to rehearsal and rehearsal the portal to performance.

THIRD DAY. The instructor asserts that the poor reader wants to be told that he is reading the same materials that the regular class is. Hence the classics—and not necessarily in simplified versions—can be used with him, though the manner of use is different. The poor reader is content to go more slowly, given the assurance that the material is not diluted, and is less likely than the regular class to be bored, provided that we shift priorities. The fatigue that arises in the slow reader must be respected and he must not be pushed too far or too fast. He can accept the difficult and live with it, and the fatigue and recover from it, because he knows he is stabbing away at the same materials as the regular class, a greater source of morale than success with the childish that he knows is childish.

FOURTH DAY. The hard word, the instructor continues, is less baffling than the hard context. Shakespeare is hard reading not because individual words are difficult, but because language structure is. "To be or not to be," all monosyllables, is nonetheless hard to understand. Furthermore, phrase meanings aren't found in dictionaries, so in an attempt to understand passages where individual words are understood but groups of words aren't, the student may ask impatiently, "Why didn't he say it easier?" The question reveals that some illumination has been gained, else it would not have been asked, and also reveals that the abstract is accessible to the slow reader. More important, the abstract contributes to adolescent needs, to personality growth, and to a sense of competence. Since the classics are rich in the abstract, nothing less can substitute for them with the poor reader. He wants them and is more ready for them than most teachers recognize.

FIFTH DAY. Poor reading programs, the instructor declares, cause discipline problems. Although his excessively high motivation is masked by embarrassment and the misbehavior caused by embarrassment, the poor reader wants to be industrious. He knows poor reading isolates him and he doesn't want to be isolated. Whenever a reading class misbehaves, the fault usually lies with the teacher, or with the materials, or with administrative arrangements—hardly ever with the class. The poor reader wants terribly, earnestly, and seriously to stop being a poor reader. He is ashamed of himself and wants to stop being ashamed. He can look and sound defiant, and he can cut up to put the best possible face on the embarrassment. Still, because he varies in ability and interest, we have the individualized reading program which frequently degenerates into the individualistic program. The individualistic program sends the poor reader off by himself, and isolates him. The individualized program keeps him together with a group for some purposes and detaches him from the group for other purposes. He reads by himself so that he can later read to the group, and at other times becomes part of an audience that is read to, with free movement between individual and group, though each individual has a different pattern of movement because his needs and abilities are different. Undue compartmentalization can become an inflexible framework, but useful classifications are desirable. Thus, in a reverse Hawthorne effect, (6) the poor reader does more poorly than we anticipate because he has been compartmentalized as a poor reader. Deprived of morale, he compares the material he reads with the material the regular class reads. Discouragement increases, as does the reading gap. Instead, we must give him classifications in reading that approximate as closely as possible the materials that the regular class is reading. We run fewer risks that way.

Sixth Week

FIRST DAY. The market, the instructor begins, offers numerous ways of testing and evaluating the reading program for comprehension, speed, and the various causes of reading disability, thereby telling us how reading gains should be measured; but we have no measures of disinclination, nor of the various patterns of disinclination. The urban deprived have the ability to read better than reading tests show and are brighter than intelligence tests show. Observation tells us this, when we see that these children listen better than they read and perform better than they cogitate, and we also see how much their listening is improved when they are given training in reading and how much their performance improves when they are taught to think. Reading tests of various kinds exist by the dozens and are useful when placed in a matrix of performance possibilities. They should be part of every reading program, and should be used to answer two questions: (1) How far has this child gone with this reading program? (2) Why hasn't he gone any further?

SECOND DAY. Every drug manufacturer knows that illness is big business. So is reading disability. Reading panaceas are manufactured and merchandised on a massive scale. Like all panaceas, they are broad-spectrum cures and are therefore dangerous, because they cause many side effects in curing the specific ailment. Thus, reading improvement may cause trouble in the home, or among friends, and the poor reader may persevere in his disability lest improvement disturb the homeostasis that has so far worked for him. Home and community can cause unanticipated complications in the reading program. Misplaced tact may permit family culpability in reading disability to remain politely unmentioned. Community pressure, not broad spectrum cures, is the decisive remedy here. Mobilizing the community for reading improvement can put more heat on the poor reader than can the school reading program, when implemented by parent volunteers, student teachers, and other adults. The Progressive Education Association (PEA) in New York has engaged the efforts of hundreds of women in New York schools and has achieved significant gains in reading. Unfortunately, not enough trained volunteers are available, but the PEA program has tremendous promise.

THIRD DAY. Ultimately, the instructor declares, much of the reading gain will depend on the professional training of the reading teacher. The in-service course, the usual source of such professional training, must put the reading teacher in touch with all the research, useful and useless, that has been published, else the reading program will not function at the maximum effectiveness that can be achieved only after one knows what to do and what to avoid. The usual in-service course has the virtue of convenience, but it is the prisoner of the immediate problem, without much feeling for the long-range problem and the directions in which its solutions lie, like balancing the motivations in pupil, home, and community. The course usually errs on the side of the practical, not realizing that the presumably theoretical is equally relevant to day-by-day reading problems. In addition, the reading consultant must be trained in high-level administrative and supervisory techniques, as well as in the theories and practice of reading improvement. The usual English teacher is not prepared to teach reading, nor does experience with poor readers substitute for professional training. Matters like administrative liaison and administrative follow-through take a special direction in the reading program, and evaluation of results becomes an integral part of operations.

FOURTH DAY. The program is tied in with public relations, community relations, and parent relations, because it is also tied in with the securing of funds from special federal sources like the Department of Health, Education and Welfare, and the National Institute of Mental Health, and with the securing of temporary personnel, as well as with training facilities. The last is a significant part of the program, which must be wide open for professional personnel like psychologists, psychometricians, student teachers, physicians, and interested parents, all of whom can be integrated within various phases. Furthermore, sources of funds must be continuously stimulated as to the need for a reading program, its performance record, and its primacy in education.

FIFTH DAY. Reading has a long history of experimentation and research, going back to Egypt, Babylonia, Palestine, Greece, Rome, the medieval period, and the Renaissance. The history of reading has relevance to modern research directions and clinical methods in gaining reading improvement.

Summary

Thus ends the thirty-session in-service course in reading improvement for junior and senior high school teachers. The course assumes that one cannot teach the phonics approach without some use of the whole word method, nor the whole word method without some use of blends, digraphs, vowel sounds, and the rest of the phonics paraphernalia. Another assumption is that tremendous motivation might perhaps impede reading improvement because it is so anxiety-begetting; motivation can create an emotional load.

In any event, we have presented a program for reading improvement. What then? What will we have the child read in

English, mathematics, science, social studies, foreign language? And for what purposes will he read in these areas?

These questions return us to our earlier discussions on curricular psychology, but they also lead us into values that emerge in the training of pre-service teaching candidates. A course in the teaching of reading, as just outlined, is best taught to in-service people currently facing the day-to-day classroom problems of the inadequate or retarded reader because such a course requires a background of experience and a sense of classroom realities.

We now proceed to specimen courses in pre-service preparation, suitable for undergraduate or post-baccalaureate candidates, in which sensitivity to values, rather than experience, is stressed.

14

The Pre-service Course— Two Examples

Now, week by week, we present two modifications of the typical education course. These modifications are suitable for pre-service candidates; they are in addition oriented toward the problems of urban education. The two examples are:

1. Educational philosophy and history
2. Human development and educational psychology

The usual pre-service program also includes courses in educational sociology (or curriculum), and in methods and student teaching. Lack of space forbids treatment of the last course, which is almost endlessly divisible by grade level and subject. Educational sociology/curriculum has been considered extensively throughout, and the reader can perhaps amuse himself by reducing what has been said so far to course-like dimensions.

Course I—Educational Philosophy and History

First Week. Traditionalism and Professionalism

Nothing contributes more to a sense of professionalism and tradition than educational history, and if professionalism improves

234)

teaching, then knowledge of educational history will also improve teaching, provided that this knowledge compares the contemporary with its antecedents.

Egypt, Rome, Palestine, and Greece illustrate a history of miseducation, meaning that education and miseducation coexist. Ancient education was also concerned with the quality of education, or "excellence." Plato suspected, as John Gardner does, that education is not merely a concept; it is a weapon in debate. (1) Furthermore, the debate is not *in vacuo,* but reflects social, economic, cultural, and national differences:

(*a*) The crucial area of conflict between America and Russia is not military strength, but scientific excellence and an expanding economy.

(*b*) How can you train the "excellent" plumber and avoid European caste education, where you break off the late bloomer from his possibilities? Especially when American society encourages its children to become late bloomers? American wealth, comfort, and education almost compel the existence of late bloomers. If so, the late bloomer must be accommodated in our educational arrangements, particularly in adult education.

(*c*) The meritocracy hidden in the Gardner concept of excellence can lead to caste differentiation, unless continuing permeability of boundaries allows the excellent plumber to become a mediocre sanitary engineer, and the excellent electrician to become an average electrical engineer. In some cases, caste replaces excellence as a criterion. Therefore we need expanded programs of adult education in which the middle-aged do not feel that life has closed in on them, so that the executive past fifty and out of a job because pension bookkeeping makes it unwise to hire him can train himself in a new direction, just as the dropout should feel that doors in education remain open for him whenever he is ready to resume his training.

But Plato's definitions of excellence were not Aristotle's, and Zeno disagreed with Epicurus. Are these relevant to Gardner? Unquestionably, and so are Roger Bacon's attack on medieval theological instruction and the lecture method, and his defense of inquiry, discussion, and proof, which undermined the deductive faith that supported the medieval Church. So student riots at the

University of California remind us of attacks on the medieval university, where education was affected by student opinion and excellence was defined by mass popularity, which allowed Abelard to use his audience to bargain with the theology of his day—see Rashdall. (2)

Educational regress has been as typical of man as has educational progress. The Renaissance medicine of Paré and Sydenham dealt with the iatrogenic consequences of physicians blindly and superstitiously following Galen for a millennium and a half, yet tradition can lead to values. Negro education tries to spotlight the traditions in Negro history that can contribute to Negro aspirations. Tradition has contemporary force.

In presenting many faces, the past presents many traditions. French traditions split into Bourbon nobility and Bonapartist nobility, American constitutionalism into Hamiltonianism and Jeffersonianism, or strict versus loose constructionism. In the same way Episcopalianism splits into High Church, Broad Church, and Low Church. Lutheranism and Calvinism split into a variety of creeds, and Judaism similarly. The medical tradition of treating the patient competes with the incompatible tradition of treating the disease, and in philosophy monism, dualism, empiricism, deduction, and induction are contending traditions. In science and mathematics, traditions of applied versus pure thought find von Neumann debating with Gauss, Soviet scientists with Western scientists, and steady-state astronomers with big bang astronomers.

Tradition, therefore, is not a unitary thing, but has effects in the plural present, echoing past contentions in the contemporary arena, and freely accessible to anybody who wants to climb aboard, provided he prepares himself and works at the business.

Thus, one educational tradition reduces the teacher to a subordinate position, but in another the teacher is respected. Socrates and the Athenian sophists occupied powerful positions because they taught the young adult, but the Athenian teacher of the child, as often as not, was held in contempt.

Is teacher morale related to teacher-rejection of courses in the history of education? Is Negro morale related to eviction from tradition? Whenever teachers did participate in the important decisions of history, like Socrates or Seneca, they were reclassified as philosophers. Similarly, whenever Negroes did, like some of the Egyptian pharaohs, they were reclassified as kings or as artists.

Our instructional engineer must put this material to use with urban children. To supply Negro hunger for a Negro tradition, the Schomburg Collection in Harlem assembles materials on Negro history and cultural contributions for Negro participation in the larger currents of American life. At the same time, the Schomburg Collection houses ammunition for Negro separatism, thus facing two ways. Which tradition predominates? The answer is in the eye of the beholder. Pragmatically, how can such divergent traditions be used in the teacher's lesson plans in social studies, in English, or in a lesson in chemistry which uses materials found in the usual Harlem kitchen?

Readings should offer a sense of the Negro participation in history, as well as of Negro history, going back to the Nubians and Negroes in Alexandria, with evidence from Alexandrian art and Nosky, (3) or encyclopedia materials on the Falasha, or the Cambridge Ancient History for earlier material on incursions into ancient Egypt by Ethiopian tribes, or, more recently, materials on post-Civil War reconstruction by writers as diverse as John Hope Franklin or C. Vann Woodward. (4)

Second Week. The Making of a Tradition

Parades on St. Patrick's Day, Baron Steuben Day, Puerto-Rican Day, Greek-American Day, or Polish-American Day illustrate how American cultural pluralism requires the minority group to develop its cultural resources, pour these into the general stream, and thereafter partake as fully as possible of the flow. (5)

Pluralism is closer to urbanism than to nationalism—the latter is a more recent historical phenomenon, emerging only a few hundred years ago. Since cities antedate nationalism, pluralism is older than nationalism. The sense of country, or nation, is a new thing, with antecedents in the sense of tribe, or kingdom, or empire. If the history of cities is in great measure the history of cultural pluralism, and if Athens, Alexandria, Jerusalem, Rome, and Istanbul show an enduring cultural pluralism, even in their ghettos, so as America has become urban, has it become more hospitable to cultural pluralism. (5) Pluralism, however, is not separatism, or Black Muslimism, but tradition tossed into interaction (rather than the stew of the melting pot) so that all may dine and profit. But does the Negro past offer such a tradition? Only if the Negro thinks so, because nobody else's agreement is required.

Documentation is not tradition, but traditionalism, another matter. The Negro requires liberating tradition, not encumbering traditionalism. The British, Italian, or Hebrew past includes pirates, murderers, embezzlers, poisoners, peculators, and misfits. This is the stuff ancestors are frequently made of. Negroes have a similar ancestry.

Tradition is transferable. Scandinavians and Japanese share and participate in the Renaissance Italian art tradition; Americans and British in Hindu tradition; and Christians and Moslems in Jewish tradition, although they had nothing to do with their origins. Thus, although Negroes are not known to have been at Runnymede in 1215 or at Plymouth Rock in 1620, their presence or absence is less relevant to Negro tradition than the Negro's studying about Magna Carta and the Pilgrims, because the ancestors of most white Americans and Englishmen were also absent from Runnymede and Plymouth Rock. The Sicilian peasant shares less in the tradition of *quattrocento* Italian art than the Japanese student haunting European museums and galleries. One gains a tradition by *working at it,* not by being born into it. So Soviet education, despite its radical break with Czarist politics and economics, maintains continuity with the Russian past and with Russian culture, from ballet to pedagogical practices, to a point almost laughable with its claims for Czarist priority in major inventions that the remainder of the world has always supposed originated elsewhere. To this untraditional state, effective connections with tradition are so vital that they are fabricated as needed.

Salient in Negro experience is economic brutality of man against man, through classical civilization, feudalism, medievalism, to modern capitalism, and as possible in modern America as in the historic past. Yet as Secretary of Labor Wirtz has said, "Capitalism means, today, economic democracy, and the essential characteristic of democracy is voluntary respect for someone else's interests." (6) Though nothing in capitalism prevents economic brutality, it has been reduced in contemporary American society, but not to the vanishing point, by the values in the hearts of men, which is where the residues of economic brutality remain, and not inevitably in capitalism. Therefore education for the deprived must remember that impalpable attitude dominates concrete economics. Experiences contribute to attitudes, true, but even more contributory is the education Americans get in their schools. These set the matrix for the Negro future, based on whatever traditions Americans have, whatever their origins.

In this Negro future, unions will battle with management and groups will jockey for economic advantage, as they always have in the past, and as they will under the threat-and-promise of automation, but with a sense of social responsibility greater than ever in history because Americans have been educated that way, especially by an education that promises mobility in job and status to those who profit by education. Like one of the national parks, American education—whatever its regionally based ideological differences—is there, available to anybody who wants his share of it. And any child in America (even in Mississippi) can get an education right through the university level, without any investment except work, willingness, and ability. Unfortunately, where these are absent, educational opportunities are not sought, just as many Americans do not visit the national parks, although available, because what is available is not always attainable.

Educational opportunities may be similarly available without being attainable, because of geographical or psychological factors —arising from inner attitude, family, and community values—or competing and more immediate rewards. Similarly, tradition gone sour and become *traditionalism*—like a father's taking his son into a union closed to everybody else—can render education unattainable, as can contempt for the educational opportunity there for the taking. Equality of educational opportunity is a common and shared phenomenon in American life—though not a common and shared experience. The only major exception to the above is the Amerian Negro, for whom educational opportunity, though theoretically equal, is not identically shared partly because of discrimination but partly also because of Negro traditionalism. Thus New York City Negroes attend free colleges in fewer numbers than we should expect, as do Irish, Polish, and Italian youth, for whom college training is available, but traditionalism causes their under-representation. Their home and community values scoff at education. (7)

Negro traditions of economic brutality must be replaced by a future of economic opportunity and educational equality, else the former will become a form of traditionalism.

P. M. S. Blackett points to a parallel condition between the "have" (tradition) and "have not" (traditionalism) nations, where the gap in wealth between the two is not only big, but getting progressively bigger. (8) Just as poor countries urgently need money, people to instruct them, and the will to get rid of bad vested interests and traditionalism, so, within the United States, poor people need money too, but they must get rid of bad vested interests and traditionalism just as urgently.

The teacher-diplomate/instructional engineer should gain some first-hand experience with the divisions into which criminology traditionally classifies crimes: crimes against persons and crimes against property. Our candidate should interview responsible personnel in the courts and at the district attorney's office to determine if these are the same in deprived as in privileged communities, and if Negroes are equally involved in civil and criminal cases. If they are more involved than whites in criminal cases and in crimes of violence, is this in keeping with *Negro* or with *southern* tradition?

The candidate should also interview responsible personnel at organizations like the Civil Liberties Union and the Anti-Defamation League to determine the extent of discrimination on unskilled and skilled levels—for secretaries, clerks, chemists, bookkeepers, sales personnel, and research personnel. (9) To what extent does a person gravitate to unskilled work because of low self-image? And to what extent is low self-image an outcome of the tradition in which you have been raised?

Third Week. The Dangers of Education

Education is not always good; it can be superstitious, stupid, and limiting. It can perpetuate the old without preparing for the new, and encourage blind adherence to frozen forms. (10)

This has always been so. A question: "Why was the Twentieth Century so late in arriving, when it could have arrived two thousand years ago? Why did the knowledge of Alexandria disappear? Why did the Dark Ages interpose themselves between the Alexandrians and the Renaissance? Couldn't we thereby have been a thousand years ahead of ourselves in mankind's development?" (11)

The Alexandrians had the precursor knowledge in mathematics and science that could easily have led to the steam engine and the Industrial Revolution, but poor education shouldered good education aside for over a millennium. Hanns Sachs, the psychoanalyst, blames the narcissism in religion, (12) for certain groups prefer perpetuating the old to inaugurating the new, and safeguarding vested interests to investigating fresh possibilities.

Miseducation also emerges when societies are under attack by rival societies, though such periods can also encourage technological advance. So McCarthyism coincided with the development of the hydrogen bomb. Education can strengthen or debilitate. Where the past is stereotyped and frozen, one kind of education emerges. Where the messages from the past are allowed to be diverse and even dissident, current education gains breadth, for, more than we admit, education today pursues channels set by the past, and what we say and think may be less novel than we suspect. Thus, listen to Aristotle on progressive education in *The Politics,* Book 8:

> Consideration must be given to what constitutes education and what is the proper way to be educated. At present there are differences of opinion as to the proper tasks to be set; for all peoples do not agree as to the things that the young ought to learn, either with a view to virtue or with a view to the best life, nor is it clear whether their studies should be regulated more with regard to intellect or with regard to character. [Aristotle is speaking, not John Dewey, Admiral Rickover, or Professor Arthur Bestor.]

Nevertheless, much in education is new, like universal compulsory education, so that history offers no guides to some problems which are unprecedented, but does to others which have historical antecedents. For example, contemporary education assumes removal of the child from home to school and takes this removal for granted, but Cato refused to entrust the education of his children to tutors, lest they be incompetent, and educated his children himself. Cato's philosophy persists today. Occasional newspaper accounts tell of parents who have assumed the full responsibility of educating their children, to the displeasure of local school boards.

In contrast, Quintilian's belief that the best place for an education was not the home but the school has antecedents in *The Republic,* Book III, where Spartan practices of child-rearing are described and approved because the school, rather than the home, becomes the dominating influence. Compare this with Harlem, where the working mother leaves the young child to whatever neighborhood or family facilities she can find, in order to go to a job. Consider the outcome in the personality structure of the child so reared, and the kind of citizen he ultimately makes.

To what extent does decay by internal urban deprivation constitute a greater threat than external communism? More Cato or more Quintilian? How can we prevent education from becoming miseducation?

In this third week, our instructional engineer has been exposed to theory, but now should be made aware of the practical outcomes of historical and philosophical education. Community day-care centers carry on activities in housing projects and remove much educational responsibility from the home, as in Operation Head Start. Our candidate should interview personnel of these centers, study their programs, and analyze the adequacy of preparation for school work.

Candidates can also study the after-school programs, like the All Day Neighborhood School we advocated earlier, comparing behavior and activities of children retained after school who are not returned home until the mother returns from work with behavior and activities of children released at the end of the normal school day. Does the candidate see any differences? And how would he relate these differences to the Cato-Quintilian debate?

Programs like New York's "Higher Horizons" and their Philadelphia, Detroit, and St. Louis analogues offer observational opportunities on community interest, student participation, and attitude and achievement outcomes. Is educational intervention in these programs dangerous to family structure, or is family structure antithetic to educational intervention? We can answer from contemporary evidence, but must supplement this evidence by historical experience. Does the Anti-Poverty Program have any historical antecedents? Does the Great Society?

Fourth Week. State versus Individual in Education

We compare the success of the Spartans and the failure of the Athenians in the Peloponnesian War, and then compare the child raised under the strict Spartan system with the child raised under the libertarian Athenian system. Spartan education was state-oriented, state-supervised, and state-centralized from the *agogé* at the top to the *eiren,* the youth at the lower levels who supervised the training—or hazing—of younger children, in a monitorial system reminiscent of Lancastrian education, or else a historical antecedent for it, just as the organized fighting among Spartan youth is a historical antecedent of the German university duelling clubs. Physical punishment and flogging characterized Spartan education, as they do British public schools.

Athenian education was different, even in instructional techniques, because Spartan youth was taught to answer, but Athenian youth was taught to question. In Sparta, and not less so in Athens, physical education prepared for war, but Athens sought additional values in grace and athletic competence. Poetry and music were extensively involved in Athenian education.

Which system had greater survival value? History offers no certain reply. Athens was defeated by internal partisan squabbling as much as by martial inferiority, because Athenian education encouraged greater partisan squabbling than Spartan education did. Maybe that's what individualism does.

In any case, both Spartan and Athenian educational values have been transmitted across geography and across history, the Spartan perpetuated in the Israeli *kibbutz* and the Russian 1961 draft program institutionalizing the child, and the Athenian in Cremin's description of progressive education. (10) Post-Sputnik America, deeply involved in science education, reflects Spartan values when science defends the state, and Athenian values when science leads to liberal education.

Liberal education then offers a new dichotomy, of the more able versus the less able, related to another dichotomy of individual versus state. If the Romans favored the state above the individual, except with the more able, and were indifferent to the ordinary child, the feedback backlashed on the instruction of the more able. Thus, where the less able are expendable, where their instruction is not important, and where the teacher is held in contempt, standards drop, as in the later stages of Athenian and Roman education. The school replaces home and family among the more able and the less able are cast educationally adrift.

Throughout history, low teacher status contributes to low-level education, since, if early education is unimportant and remediable in later education, then teachers for the early period are unimportant too.

We feel differently these days. Standards and preparation for the kindergarten and elementary school teacher have become equivalent to those for the secondary school teacher, thereby improving teacher status. Given such standards, preparation, and status, we need not worry about Spartan-type state intervention, allowing us to remove the socially disadvantaged child, of any ability level, from the deleterious home and community. Hence our best protection against the educational erosion in classical and medieval times is improved teaching in the low-income community.

Consider the instruction in the classics as preparation for vocational education, and vocational education as an aspect of liberal education. Consider the equivalence between the individual and classical education, and the state and vocational education. Robert Graves has written:

> It became fashionable to study at Athens, the centre of Greek culture. There the Roman student discovered that he could hope to graduate as a diplomat only after taking a master's degree in rhetoric; and that rhetoric, the art of persuading an opponent by flattery, threats, or fraud to accept one's own proposition, however unsound, would help him win magisterial elections and plead public causes with confidence, besides being a valuable adjunct to warfare. (13)

Discussion of this selection can take the following directions: (a) Are vocational (state-oriented) and liberal (individual-oriented) education closer together or further apart than in the days of the Romans? (b) In upper-class education are vocational education and liberal arts education closer together or further apart than in the education of a Negro boy in a large city school?

Another seminar-discussion possibility from A. N. Whitehead:

> The typical education of our public schools was devised for boys from well-to-do cultivated homes. They travelled in Italy, in Greece, and in France, and often their own homes were set amid beauty. None of these circumstances hold for modern national education in primary or secondary schools, or even for the majority of boys and girls in our enlarged system of public schools. . . . Today we deal with herded town populations, reared in a scientific age. . . . A technical education is not to be conceived as a maimed alternative to the perfect Platonic culture. . . . Of all types of men today

existing, classical scholars are the most remote from the Greeks of the Periclean times. . . . (14)

Here discussion in seminar can take the following tracks: (*a*) Can "herded town populations" gain the education available to privileged classes? Should they? (*b*) Whitehead, (14) in describing the need for schools of business and commerce, says that the first job of the university is to impart the sense of zest, excitement, and imagination in learning. How reconcile this to the opposition of liberal arts departments to education courses in college? How can colleges insure that scholars are simultaneously involved in discovery and in the past?

Still another instance from Norbert Wiener:

> The extraordinarily precise news-gathering services of the Venetian ambassadors (which form one of our chief sources of European history) accompanied a national jealousy of secrets, exaggerated to such an extent that the state ordered the private assassination of emigrant artisans, to maintain the monopoly of certain chosen arts and crafts. The modern game of cops and robbers which seems to characterize both Russia and the United States, the two principal contestants for world power of this century, suggests the old Italian cloak-and-dagger melodrama played on a much larger stage. (15)

Therefore, does dominant white society keep secrets from Negro minority society? Do the minority society's leaders keep secrets from the dominant white society, like the face-masking in Genet's *The Blacks*? How are Negro-white sex aspirations dissimulated? James Baldwin's "Letter from a Region in My Mind," in a discussion on Negro prophets, Black Muslimism, American cultural pluralism, and Negro separatism, describes the distrust underlying this dissimulation. (16)

Again we want our instructional engineer to top off class work, seminar discussions, and reading by contact with field explorations and responsibilities. He can interview those professionally occupied with youth, like police, social workers, Youth Board workers in New York, Anti-Poverty personnel. He can learn from them about qualities in the gang leader and how gang leadership emerges, what happens to the gang leader after adolescence, his intellectual interests, what Urban League personnel know of job opportunities for skilled and untrained Negroes, what training possibilities exist, and how much unemployment prevails among Negroes adequately trained as mathematicians, scientists, auto mechanics, TV repairmen, and teachers. The information gotten from these groups may not tally with information at unemployment insurance offices, so the divergence must be researched. Incidentally, the training in interviewing people with special points of view is invaluable!

Fifth Week. Play in Education (17)

By this time our candidate begins to see that virtually everything in education is disputable. Play, as a legitimate aspect of study, provides another educational dispute. In many ancient and modern curriculums play is a part of study. But children are not uniform, nor are their origins, nor, therefore, their play needs. Harlem play needs are not the same as Scarsdale's, perhaps greater, perhaps less, but certainly different. Would greater investment in play facilities in Harlem—such as swimming pools, basketball courts, and baseball fields—dilute the quality of academic education or improve it? Similarly, is the talmudist in his study, or the scientist in his laboratory, hard at work or at play? Pliny says cheer contributes to study, *studia hilaritate proveniunt,* anticipating Montaigne and Bacon, but what kind of study do they have in mind? What are the relative proportions of sobriety and play? If Quintilian, characteristically, wants interaction of play and work, and if Athenian education saw play as integrated with study, then play, work, and study are possibly three aspects of the same thing, but we must determine their interactions for different children.

Many differences between vocationalism and liberalism could thereupon be resolved and between pointless study and useful study, depending on the grace and play involved. The cloistered medieval monk studied the same materials as Abelard; we need only compare the pious fruitlessness of the one with the frenzied excitement of the other, the absence of emotiveness in one and the excess of emotionality in the other, to see how, in the search for knowledge, man confuses pursuit of his own tail with the pursuit of light.

Play is the antithesis of tragedy, but not of work. Men with the tragic sense, like Milton and Bunyan, have not been completely joyless, but instead contributed to affirmations ultimately ecstatic in vision and insight. Play leads to optimism.

The Negro child who plays hard has made the first breakthrough toward a meaningful, serious study program, especially when the play is under a supervised and directed program, and both play and work have common auspices. In addition to everything else, the Negro child has been culturally deprived from play.

As a group, Negroes are athletic and perhaps excessively so, because sports give money and social mobility in a hurry in basketball, track and field, professional boxing, football, and baseball. The Negro high school athletic star is courted, admired, and feted until graduation.

But sports are not play, nor is play the same as leisure. The instructional engineer should find clarification in the following materials for seminar discussion.

From William H. Whyte Jr.:

> Hard work? What price capitalism, the question is now so frequently asked, unless we turn our productivity into more leisure, more of the good life? To the organization man this makes abundant sense, and he is as sensitive to the bogy of overwork and ulcers as his forebears were to the bogy of slothfulness. But he is split. He believes in leisure, but so does he believe in the Puritan insistence on hard, self-denying work. (18)

From Montaigne:

> We labour but to cram our memory, and leave the understanding and the conscience empty. Even as the birds sometimes fly in search of grain, and bring it in their beaks without tasting it, to feed their young, so do our pedants go picking knowledge out of books, carrying it at the end of their lips, only to spit it out and scatter it to the winds. . . . It is remarkable how aptly I come in to exemplify this folly. Am I not doing the same thing in the most part of this composition? I go sniffing about among books, now here, now there, for the sentences which please me, not to store them, for I have no storehouse, but to transplant them to this book, where, to tell the truth, they are no more mine than they were before. (19)

Honest Montaigne! Notice how much this tells us of T. S. Eliot's poetry, but also of authors of books on urban education who select quotations for prospective instructional engineers to chew over in their seminars! Elsewhere he says:

> It is wonderful how solicitous Plato shows himself, in his Laws, about the gaiety and pastimes of the youth of his city, and how much he dwells on their races, games, songs, leaps, and dances, of which he says that antiquity has given the ordering and patronage to the gods themselves. (20)

And from Aldous Huxley:

> If you teach an individual first to be aware of his physical organism and then to use it as it was meant to be used, you can often change his entire attitude to life and cure his neurotic tendencies. But this, of course, is something which no one-sided psychologist has been taught to do, or would approve of doing, even if he knew how. He just goes on with free association and dream analysis, and hopes for the best. (21)

After whatever discussion these quotations generate, our candidate can interview sports writers at publications like *Amsterdam News, Ebony,* and the *New York Daily News.* Much sports reporting is involved with betting, and much spectatorship is less appreciative of athletic skill than of how your money is doing. Where results are easily thrown, or points shaved without too much detection, as in foot racing and in professional wrestling, interest in betting dies down. The most popular spectator sports are those where you can place a bet, with some assurance that the jockey who pulls the horse can be detected, or the player who shaves points can be apprehended.

For a more balanced picture, our candidate should also interview sports coaching personnel in deprived community schools, settlement houses, and Y's, to find out how often sports engender sportsmanship and friendly rivalry, and how often they express enmity. Are international soccer matches more productive of international understanding and amity, or of intensified national hatreds? What about high school football games between schools representing different ethnic groups?

Sixth Week. Work and Leisure

Though there is a parallel between equestrianship in Plato's time and driver education in ours, this raises a problem: Is driver education related to Latin and Greek? Or can it encourage the study of chemistry and physics, at least insofar as these are related to the internal combustion engine?

To Plato, equestrianship prepared for living. To Ascham, archery strengthened mind, body, and the qualities of a courtier, and Zen Buddhism agrees. Dancing for Castiglione's renaissance knight and the playing fields of Eton and Harrow for the Englishmen of the Regency had legitimate educational functions. Why do not bowling and golf today?

Truly, can we prepare a young man for business without teaching him that game—golf—around which so much depends in American industry? Can he truly enjoy business, or even contribute to it, unless he plays a game of golf in which he will not be ridiculed? Are not professors of classics, history, or English, who see the relevance of Plato's equestrianship, Ascham's archery, and Catiglione's dancing, but are unable to see the relevance of golf instruction or driver education today, prejudiced in their definition of work and leisure?

Furthermore, can they differentiate between the play-work of the gentleman or the scholar? The training of the gentleman tends to an excess of play, as in eighteenth-century Oxford and Cambridge, where young aristocrats were at play until they reached their majority and thereafter became louts. American Ivy League colleges followed this example until fairly recently, as did midwestern state universities. The major task of the self-respecting university is to differentiate between pedantry and scholarship by integrating play-study as we do leisure-work.

Play, separated from study, becomes irresponsibility, whether with disadvantaged communities or with Rousseau's *Emile.* When society no longer works as hard to meet its needs as societies once did, study must become play. Here the New Leisure repeats Aristotle, substituting automation for his slave class and giving us a leisure class not envisaged in his Lyceum. The professional athlete who works at his play, or the businessman who plays at his work during a three-hour lunch, or when he closes a deal on the golf course, are both in status occupations—these allow a blurring of the distinctions between work and leisure, or study and play; but in lower status occupations the differentiation remains.

Hence education for the lower classes must bring work into driver education courses, making the chemistry of gasoline and the physics of the internal combustion engine part of the play-task. Conversely, the underprivileged child must be taught to play with Latin, history, and literature.

Historically, the false antithesis between vocationalism and liberalism reflects class and caste. Plato's philosophy students participated in the affairs of state, as did the Roman student of rhetoric; monastic training was related to vocation; the training of the humanists led to a profession by which one could earn one's bread. When Harvard was founded in 1636 to prepare ministers, the training was related to vocation, making liberal education a kind of vocational education that prepares for status-related jobs, while pure vocational education prepares for non-status-related jobs, which is how fees, salaries, and retainers are different from wages.

Automation will blur the distinction as it reduces unskilled labor to extinction and upgrades vocational training to more demanding technical education—blue collar workers must become white collar workers or technicians lest they perish. Also affected is labor heretofore considered skilled, like typesetters, stevedores, locomotive engineers, and airplane navigators. Nevertheless, pressure for advanced training will become acute among Negro and other underprivileged youth, making the usual definitions of vocational training obsolete. James Conant's recommendations for vocational training become as anachronistic as the very similar program in Booker T. Washington's nineteenth-century schema. (22)

Less challenging vocational courses like beauty culture and restaurant service cannot absorb all the mentally retarded, the poor readers, or the behavior problems because you must comprehend the written word before you can read a shop manual. *The poor student does poorly in the vocational studies too.* For those deficient in language, science, and mathematics the auto course can only prepare the grease monkey, or gas station attendant, not the expert mechanic; the food trades program only busboys, not chefs. Quality vocational education requires strong cultural and liberal infusions; and, certainly, the man who services an automated device must be trained far beyond the level of the auto mechanic or chef.

Study at the vocational level becomes harder, and many students cannot work this hard, not because the economic and social possibilities opened up to them are meaningless, but because they lack the ability even for vocational school, because shop manuals require not less reading comprehension than *Silas Marner* or *Tale of Two Cities,* and because these students are as misplaced in a vocational school as in an academic high school.

As often as not, vocational schools train neo-Luddites. The Luddites, preferring their old patterns, did not see that innovations made more goods more available more cheaply, but also made occupational mobility available, given training. Our new Luddites will not wreck machinery but themselves, unless they increase their ability to tolerate the discomfort that accompanies thought. Morris Kline points out that the popularized bird's eye view of mathematics does not lead to a knowledge of mathematics, because the bird's eye view avoids work. (23) In an appositely opposite case, Wright W. Miller says that Russians, accustomed to discomfort, do not make learning comfortable, while Americans do everything and stop at nothing for more comfort in learning. (23) Just as the Luddites saw no possibilities of occupational mobility in machinery and in industrial training, so Negroes and Puerto-Ricans may not be aware of the breakthrough in occupational mobility, once they assume the responsibility of training and education, and the accompanying discomfort.

Throughout history, from the times of Tubal Cain, status has attached to the technically trained, as Singer shows: (24)

1. (In Roman mining) *"Gradual improvement was largely due to the replacement of slave-labour by skilled artificers, who were still supplemented by condemned criminals."*

[The instructional engineer can compare this with the progression from slave labor, to peonage, to the chain-gang, and finally to the Huntsville, Alabama, industrial complex. Free labor is more efficient than slave labor, and trained labor is more efficient than free labor.]

2. *"At the Athenian quarries all the processes connected with the work were grouped together in charge of a* technites, *who was not a citizen and therefore was largely ignored in contemporary litera-*

ture. A technites *was a skilled worker in almost any trade—mason, carpenter, and so forth—although a metal-worker was distinguished by a special title—*chalkeus *or* siderius."

[For discussion: How would he get his skill? By apprenticeship, or was he imported from Egypt, Ionia, or Persia? A comparison with the imported Mexican *bracero* is limited, because the *bracero* is unskilled, but more analogous is the skilled American who goes to Mexico or Puerto Rico.]

3. *"When the Romans departed, the technique of stone-cutting fell at once into decay. At the very beginning of the fifth century the Britons sent for help to Rome, and one legion was sent back. 'Even so,' says Bede (673–735), 'the islanders raised the (Antonine) Wall, not as they had been directed, of stone, having no artist capable of such work, but of sods.' Bede relates that St. Benedict of Wearmouth crossed into Gaul c. 650 and brought back masons to build a church. For it he also imported glaziers, who could not be found in England."*

[For discussion: When the Romans left Briton, and the Belgians left the Congo, what happened to native crafts? Can national aspirations ever be achieved without skills?]

4. *"The Romans took over Hellenistic mining and smelting enterprises and enlarged their scale, stimulating subdivision of labor and the rise of mining specialists."*

[Have American nickel companies in Cuba, tin companies in Bolivia, and drug companies in Brazil been following the same historical course?]

5. *"In the sixteenth and seventeenth centuries the craftsman's knowledge was still far in advance of theory, and apart from the few great treatises already mentioned, the writings of purely practical men —mintmasters, locksmiths, jewellers, gun-founders, and the like— give the best insight into the metallurgical equipment and methods of the time."*

[Can the same be said of the relationships between theory and practice today? between advanced training and apprenticeship?]

6. *"The spread of printing released a stream of metallurgical knowledge codified in carefully prepared treatises. . . . Many medieval collections of workshop recipes must have circulated among adepts or pupils in mining and metal-working, from which these first printed manuals descend."*

[Then did the *level* of knowledge or the *diffusion* of knowledge cause the emergence of science from technology?]

7. *"A fine sixteenth-century English account of assaying copper and other base-metal ores in Cumberland has been found recently in*

the notebook of Daniel Hockstetter, one of the principal German experts who were brought over to work the deposits there."

[How does a knowledge of techniques lead to both occupational and geographical mobility?]

Knowledge allows you to get around, or to summon experts from far away to you on your home ground. Where men flow, money flows too. Conversely, we want our instructional engineer in disadvantaged neighborhoods to see how men who lack skill impede the flow of money into their communities. Thus, in New York, he should:

1. Visit the real estate departments of Harlem banks to determine the risks and benefits in real estate investment in Harlem, and how these financial realities reflect family relationships, and how family instability and financial instability interact.

2. Check businessmen's associations, like Kiwanis, Rotary, and Lions, for their policies on integration.

3. Interview Harlem trade union leadership on trade union training programs. Or do trade unions depend solely on management for such programs?

Seventh Week. The Sense of Mobility

Our candidate may ask: "Can simple workers be trained for today's technology, a 90 I.Q. for automation, or people limited in endowment for complex skills?" This contemporary problem has antecedents in the history of education.

In the medieval and post-medieval period the apprentice could not remain an apprentice forever. Upward employment mobility was set in stages: the apprentice, the journeyman, then the master. The apprentice knew the direction he could go and that experience, training, and time would bring him to the master's state.

Remarkable things accompanied this awareness of the possibilities of upward mobility. From 1400 to the present, developments in art, science, commerce, and economic opportunity have been unprecedented. When a man was prepared by a sense of worth and external opportunities, he rejected meek acceptance of his appointed place. The last few centuries offer millions of examples of poor children who improved themselves and their stations in life.

This sense of availability of opportunity is only now reaching the underprivileged child. Until recently a Negro faced employment barriers no matter how well he prepared himself, and Negro college graduates worked as redcaps and Pullman porters. In the last generation these obstacles have been rapidly vanishing, even more rapidly than Negro youth realizes, and most rapidly on the superior levels of employment. Considerable barriers remain, but Negro youth need have fewer fears about job discrimination and educational quotas than ever before. The reason is simple: American society is short of trained manpower.

Now this contemporary manifestation is analogous to the situation described in Rashdall (2) on the rise of the medieval universities. The monasteries had diluted and dispersed education, but an emerging Europe, following the Crusades, required centralization of effort. The emergence of the cathedral schools, in towns and under the aegis of the local bishop, symbolized this educational centralization. Growth of the cathedral schools required that students travel to the urban center from afar. Having little in common with the local residents, the students' and masters' guilds fought for privileges that on the one hand meant brawls between town and gown, and on the other contributed to the emergence of the professions. By 1200 medical schools were on the scene in the Italian cities. Bologna, another cathedral town, pioneered in legal education. However, the law schools—to the surprise of the church—soon became agencies of the new secularization, as local nobles and princes sought to increase their powers. In time, lawyers became more and more attached to the courts—the original source of the term—of bishops and nobles, while the scope of their work grew wider and wider. Theological education, also affected by this new mobility, could not remain static in an expanding society. It was available to all with the necessary ability, so that a bright boy from the poorer classes could enter the clergy and thus find social and economic escalation.

Centuries later, in Colonial America, Benjamin Franklin's blueprint for the Philadelphia Academy reflected the needs of another expanding society, in a break from the Latin school of the day. There, for the first time, English would be taught as a subject and its literature included in the curriculum because society required people who could read and write in the vernacular. The rapidly expanding colony-nation needed strong backs, willing hands, and minds that could understand an invoice, write a business letter, and enter numbers and calculations into business accounts. From Franklin's blueprint grew, quite rapidly, the Free Academies, and thereafter the first of the high schools, so that by 1830 the high school system could be seen in its dim beginnings.

Today, social requirements provide more channels of mobility than people are interested in using, a condition true of disadvantaged groups and of advantaged also. There are more dropouts than flunkouts, and more opportunities than people trained to cope with them. Tremendous social forces compel an emergence of minority groups from disbarment, discrimination, and segregation. Unfortunately, even more tremendous an historical force is indifference to opportunity.

Any political leader knows this. Even local politicians can offer the teacher-diplomate/instructional engineer much interesting information on voting turnout, what sends people to the polls, the kinds of people who are indifferent to voting, and how organizations like church groups, trade union groups, and businessmen's associations, function in getting out the vote.

The teacher-diplomate/instructional engineer should ponder the social expressions of indifference as brought about by demoralization. Non-voting is one. Another aspect of demoralization can be seen in visiting the social service department of a hospital (like New York's Harlem Hospital). What is the proportion of unwed mothers admitted to the maternity ward? What post-partum care is available to these mothers? What case work methods are used with these mothers? What is the age at which the average mother bore her first child? What is happening as a result of birth-control information? What effect is such information having on community morale?

Eighth Week. The House of Learning

Patterns of instruction in the crafts have changed in the last century and a half. The man-to-man, point-to-point correspondence of master-to-apprentice was highly efficient if apprentices appeared for training one at a time, as in the relationship of Sir Humphry Davy and Michael Faraday, and if apprentices could be fed into the market one at a time. However, when society's need for instructed individuals became greater and financially more rewarding, the *class,* as distinguished from older methods of individual instruction, became necessary, and thus formal instruction, formal observation, the use of texts, and some kind of formal examination system, entered technical training.

Education was thus affected by changes in production and consumption. This need for trained and educated personnel allows disadvantaged Negro youth to become full, contributing citizens, in an almost inevitable outcome of the history of the last five hundred years—provided that the Negro's drive for equality of educational opportunity, for good schooling, and for good housing is compatible with sound assessments. Thus, should the limited tax dollar go for new school buildings or for more teachers and materials? Do good teachers need a new school plant to teach effectively? Do school architects and engineers have the same educational motives as teachers do? The great and prestigeful schools in America and England (Groton, Andover, Lawrenceville, Eton, and Harrow, for example) are older than New York school buildings and no one suggests that they be torn down; they are outstanding educational plants and their students are proud of their age. Old private school buildings?—preserved and used! Old public school buildings?— turned over to the wreckers! One wonders—for Harlem students to gain a sense of identity and tradition should they not be proud of their old school buildings? The relationship between effective learning and teaching is crucial, but not between school plant and learning. No educational quarters were more ramshackle than the European *yeshivoth* where Jewish instruction took place. The great European universities are older than any school in Harlem. (25)

Education depends more on well-trained teachers, on texts in ample number, and on instructional materials of good quality, than on shining new school buildings.

The educationally acceptable school plant must make provision for:

THE LECTURE METHOD OF TEACHING.   In medieval education the single-teacher lecture contrasted with the alternative multi-teacher *disputation,* in which the professors recited while debating with each other, with the students as audience, like the discussion panels or discussion forums of today. Both lecture and disputation (or forum) involve the architecture of space, audibility, and availability of writing surfaces for each student, so that none in the audience need stand.

THE RECITATION METHOD.   This assumes available materials, storage facilities for materials, and quick accessibility of materials. Tests and examinations require that architecture provide for group and individual testing. The latter is usually oral and therefore requires provision for privacy for both teacher and student.

THE SEMINAR METHOD. Here the group participates in oral discussion. Again, provision for privacy is a prime consideration.

THE METHOD OF THE CADAVER, THE CASE, AND THE LABORATORY. Here the learner tests reality in the closest approximation, requiring that architecture provide for illumination, equipment, and ready movement around the site of educational activity.

INTRAPROFESSIONAL AND INTERPROFESSIONAL RELATIONS. Here architecture provides for office space, handling and clearance of visitors, parents, and other persons with responsibility for educational undertakings and transactions, teachers' work rooms and rest rooms, etc.

Hence, school architecture is not the substance, but only the reflection, of educational activity. New school buildings in Harlem rapidly become targets for vandalism when they are *inactive,* and not being used. You protect school buildings by making full use of them around the clock and throughout the week and year. Building use must reflect community need, so that if a *crèche* is needed for a working mother (as in Israel and the Soviet Union), the school building has facilities for that purpose, plus nursery and early childhood educational facilities, to avoid waste of human resources and get the tasks of education under way. Every age is school age, and the school day should be twenty-four hours, meaning that dormitory facilities may be necessary simply because the school in the deprived neighborhood requires a special type of contact between institution and constituency. We preach no educational innovation. Dormitory facilities are attached to colleges and universities because students come from far away, as they did to attend the University of Athens, the medieval cathedral schools, and the Renaissance universities. In deprived communities, school buildings must similarly reflect community patterns, here meaning dormitory facilities for children, to liberate the family patterns into which they were born.

Envisioning the possibilities, the teacher-diplomate/instructional engineer will be struck on his field visits with the way some school buildings are shut down at three o'clock, sealed off from the community until the opening of business the next morning. Not all are. Some remain open for after-school activities. The instructional engineer/teacher-diplomate can compare street behavior where schools remain open with behavior where school plant is closed down. He should interview responsible personnel on after-school programs and activities, the degree of participation in these programs, and the availability of evening adult education programs and the participation in them.

Ninth Week. Educational Pluralism

Decent housing is inversely related to integrated schooling. The better the deprived neighborhood becomes, the less it remains the slum, the more remote become the possibilities for the integrated school. For example, as Harlem becomes more desirable to remain in, rather than depart from, the less likely will Negroes be to send their children to other areas, via bus, or have other children imported, also via bus, to share the misery. What happens then to Negro parents who want their children aware of other groups and familiar with them?

Negro parents with the deepest dedication to education and social responsibility are not necessarily those demanding integrated schooling. These upwardly mobile parents are caught between white middle class and Negro proletariat—the first of many complications. They know that attendance in integrated schools requires transportation time in a school bus. If group understanding is thereby enhanced, will not study time be diminished? Which takes precedence, group understanding or achievement in studies? Unless the Negro child has as many *local* study opportunities as the white child, the question is meaningless and any choice nonexistent. When the Negro child's teachers are less experienced, his texts and materials in shorter supply, and his library facilities inferior, do we compensate for these shortcomings by transporting the child, or would it be preferable to transport teachers, texts, and materials? The teacher working in a pleasanter neighborhood will certainly object; furthermore, we cut off the Negro child from the wider American scene, and cut off America from the contributions of Negro life.

On the other hand, what happens when we introduce the heretofore segregated child into the school where achievement is high? Suppose the segregated child does not catch up? Will he not thereby be segregated worse than ever, when he sees himself unable to achieve what his classmates can? Under segregated circumstances, this damaging evidence could be kept from him; under integrated ones, it is inescapably thrust upon him.

To maximize group contributions to American life, education must solve the dispute between pluralism and the melting pot, or America as variety versus America as unity. Recent thinking has melted down the melting pot, replacing it by the pluralism of retention of minority habits and customs, not flight from them. A summation of unrelated mosaics is not the same as interacting social structures, in which the minority group's culture enriches the cultural ambiance in American life. For example, Greek learning was twice imported into Italy. On the first occasion, after the defeat of the Ptolemaic and Seleucid heirs of Alexander's empire, Greek scholars came as slaves and tutors to Roman youth. On the second occasion, following the capture of Constantinople by the Turks in 1453, Greek scholars again arrived in Italy—this time greeted with admiration as refugees because they could feed the growing hunger of the Renaissance and Humanism for classical Greek learning.

Hence, however vital American Negro culture becomes, it must ultimately depend on acceptance by the American majority. Just as seventeenth-century Dutch society was more accepting of Jewish culture than seventeenth-century Russian society, so contemporary American culture is more accepting of Negro possibilities than it has ever been. This is partly from guilt and partly from its need for trained manpower. The higher the training in the Negro, the less he suffers from job discrimination; this fact is new in American life, which places responsibility for training upon the Negro more than ever before, another novelty in American life. (26)

In examining pluralism *within* the Negro group, the teacher-diplomate/instructional engineer should examine how Negro churches—Revivalist, Catholic, Episcopalian, Baptist, Presbyterian, even Jewish—are not equally committed to youth, to social action programs, to the utilization of pastoral psychology, and to education. Equal commitment would mean joint action. What causes the disparate commitment?

On the political front, NAACP, CORE, SNCC, and the Black Muslims represent competing approaches, different intensities of anti-white feeling, and differences in (*a*) school integration patterns, (b) industrial training for automation, (c) influences on public opinion, and (d) gaining new members. Other interviews should be conducted with responsible leaders of these groups for first-hand information on these differences.

Tenth Week. The Teacher and the Power Structure

As we have said, not everybody in education is a teacher. In addition, teacher status has varied, historically, by level. The college teacher has generally had (not always) greater status than the secondary school teacher. The secondary school teacher has had greater status than the elementary school teacher, on the whole. For a variety of reasons, however, this situation is changing. Thus the single salary scale for elementary and high school teachers is contributing to improved status for elementary school teachers, to the complaints of secondary school teachers that it simultaneously contributes to a reduction in *their* status. Similarly, the recent recognition, in the Head Start program, that the preschool years play a more crucial role in education than we have heretofore surmised has raised the status of nursery school and kindergarten teachers.

Nor is the growth of militancy among teachers and their new willingness to go out on strike, or impose sanctions against school districts and school boards, unrelated to changes in public attitude about the importance of education and training. Education has suddenly become a major bulwark against communism. It is essential for upward mobility in a corporation-dominated economy. It puts you astride Carlyle's cash nexus. Colleges run out of places for anxious applicants who know these places are portals to better careers or better husbands.

Education becomes centralized because that's where the money begins to come from. State government re-asserts its educational control over local government and the federal government nudges state government to move over. Meanwhile everybody avows his belief in local control, in face of the fact that local control is anachronistic. Teachers and teacher organizations achieve a national cohesiveness, national standards, and a viewpoint that transcends the local and the provincial.

Educational technology, both in hardware and software, additionally contributes to teacher status and power. "Hardware" here is the world of teaching machines, programed instruction, closed circuit television, mass testing, and educational *realia*. "Software" here is illustrated by the new evidence from psychological research on what we have always suspected about motivation, needs, and attitudes. Hence Operation Head Start draws on data from Martin Deutsch's investigations, Piaget's Swiss playrooms, and Harry Harlow's cloth monkey-mothers. (27) If this psychological research is also sometimes in disagreement, it nonetheless agrees that we are on the right trail. What is important is that we are learning how to isolate and handle experimental variables that have closer and closer relevance to our hypotheses.

This educational technology, of the hard and soft variety, puts teachers in a position to sound as if they know what they are talking about. Nothing like this ever happened before; it is only in the past half-century that teachers have been able to draw on a special body of knowledge. Formerly, their knowledge of education did not much exceed the layman's intuitions. Now they can tap statistics, sociology, psychiatry, anthropology, and economics, because all these disciplines have numerous points of contact with education.

For these reasons education has moved into the power structure, even if teachers have not yet quite done so. Teachers are still, in the main, not power-minded, which may be saying that teachers are the worst thing that ever happened to education. Saying so, however, is cruel to a large number of teachers who are devoted to the classes that come their way, do their best by their pupils, and candidly admit that it's all they have time for and all they have contracted to do.

In any case, education, like Lenin's locomotive of history, has taken a sharp turn, so sharp a turn indeed that it has created a vacuum into which teachers have not yet moved because they do not recognize the political and social power they can pick up for the taking. Large corporations like Xerox advertise for teachers to prepare educational materials that Xerox will sell to schools because schools are a major market for suppliers of all kinds, whether of furniture, fuel, or fiction. Leaders of educational associations become more militant if they are on the right, and more professional if they are on the left. Thus the state education associations, affiliated with the careful National Education Association, begin to advocate strike action, while the far less numerous

American Federation of Teachers, advocating tough trade union tactics, also sees itself responsible for a more professionally oriented stance with respect to educational policy-making than it was formerly willing to accept.

In brief, places in the power structure are beginning to open up for the teacher of the young child that always existed for the teacher of the young adult. Plato, Aristotle, Quintilian, Abelard, and Erasmus were important in the power structure of their day because they taught the young adult. Occasionally a Comenius or a Pestalozzi, more concerned with the child, and hence with pre-vocational education, found a place—usually a minor one—in educational policy-making. But they dealt for the most part with children of ruling classes, and so were close to the seats of power.

And teachers are becoming ever more numerous. The approximately one million American teachers today constitute a larger proportion of the population than ever in history; hence if they do not seek power, the sources of power will seek them. They mean votes. Their pension funds are a source of loans to industry. Insurance companies sell them group contracts for hospitalization, death, and retirement. Travel agents, airlines, and hotels solicit their vacation business.

All this has come about less because of teacher activity than because of Rickovers, Conants, Bestors, a pair of recent American Presidents, and Negro leaders fighting for simple human rights. The classroom teachers have been the beneficiaries not only of what their friends have done for them, but of what certain enemies have done too.

However, if classroom teachers have typically been laggard, educational leaders have not. The National Education Association feels the hot breath of the American Federation of Teachers on its neck and becomes more activist, while the latter envies the professional image of the former and becomes more statesmanlike. Scientists, mathematicians, professors of history and English no longer fear dirtying their hands with the curriculums of the elementary, junior, and senior high schools, and not only come forth with recommendations for curriculum change, but also chivvy foundations and government agencies for funds for educational experimentation. Ivy League colleges and preparatory schools go on the prowl for qualified Negro youth. The defense establishment, freer of discrimination than the churches or the schools, does more to supplement funds for education than to compete for them.

So educational dynamism has not had to look to teachers for inspiration. To extend the quotation that war is too important to be left to the generals, and politics too important to be left to politicians, education is getting too important to be left to teachers —or so teachers seem to agree, from their reluctance to participate in plays for educational power.

This is regrettable, because it may leave teachers holding more bags than they suspect. For example, the usual Los Angeles teacher does not welcome being assigned to Watts, nor the usual New York teacher to Harlem. Teacher organizations will support the teacher against the Negro community because their primary loyalty is to their dues-paying membership, not to the educationally deprived Negro child. But our leading physicians go on rounds in charity wards (until Medicare finished off charity wards in the main) and distinguished members of the bar take cases to ascertain the law, rather than for fees. When teachers are more concerned about their compatibility with the children they teach than with the education problems brought into the school by incompatible children, their competence to teach may not necessarily be called into question, but their personal power—and their readiness to enter the power structure—becomes legitimately debatable.

Therefore the teachers who assert, "I am here to teach, not to correct a bad home and neighborhood situation," have some justification because they want to be *here* and only *here* and they don't want any enlargement of their horizons by being ordered *there*. Fair enough, but playing it safe is a guaranteed way of forfeiting the place in the power structure that is crying for all the alertness, all the drive, and all the dynamism that only the professionally oriented classroom teacher can give.

Course II—Human Development and Educational Psychology

We turn from the historical and philosophical foundations of education to the psychology of education and human development.

Learning involves the presentation of alternatives, the rejection and acceptance of things. This presentation of alternatives is built into maze-learning, approach-avoidance, punishment-reward, figure-ground, ego-id, and most recently into the design of computers which, based on a simple binary yes-no, proceeds to the vast complexities of information theory, so that we wonder if computers can learn.

Similarly, the teacher is involved in those abstractions which psychologists call learning theories. We learn by assessing alternatives—by seeing that some things are pleasant and others unpleasant, by trial-and-error, trial-and-success, bullheaded rote, native neural endowment and unstriped muscle configurations. But some learn well and some poorly, meaning that some can address more energy to learning than others. Is the individual's innate energy level for learning fixed and immutable? Or can it be increased? Answers vary, but the teacher wants this energy, whatever its level, made more available, because not everything that's there comes out. The process of bringing it out is called anxiety-reduction, closure, reinforcement, and a variety of other nomenclatures.

Although educational experimentation includes much of psychological research, it can only be carried on with people, not with monkeys, rats, or pigeons. Similarly, medical research deals with people, although it makes preliminary explorations with animals. As educational research is not coterminous with psychological research, neither is medical research coterminous with biological research, because they must prove their points with human beings, meaning that they must take risks with men and women. Medical research surreptitiously works with volunteers, prisoners, and chiefly the indigent, who therefore receive the best of care in exchange for being, knowingly or not, guinea pigs, as the Kefauver reports on the drug industry showed. (28)

Where educational matters involve physical matters, research is supervised by physicians, as with the psychomimetic drugs. Thus shock therapy and recent work with beamed ultrasonic frequencies in mental retardation is a matter for the medical man and nobody else, even if, as Professor Louis Rosenzweig has said, "the number of mentally retarded with no organic signs and no pathology far outnumber the former group (having specific syndromes) in the ratio of four or five to one." (29)

We present some aspects of a course in which the teacher-diplomate/instructional engineer faces these and other matters.

First Week. *Psychological Substrates in the Classroom*

Behavior, neither haphazard nor accidental, emerges from hidden but nonetheless regular circumstances, and is patterned either in configurations or in sequences. Therefore behavior in the classroom is also caused and patterned. In saying so, psychology talks as science does, never guaranteeing that the ultimate causes and patterns are discoverable. The basic theme of all science is that we live in a rationally ordered universe—without this assumption science would stop. Psychology also says that behavior is ordered and rationally explicable, even when irrational, without assuming that the ultimate bases of behavior are determinable. (30)

Were classroom teachers to accept this and teach accordingly, their difficulties would in great measure disappear. Their inability to do so interests educational psychology, which studies why teachers forget the educational psychology they have been taught when they reach the cauldron of the classroom. Some teachers will say that educational psychology is irrelevant. Is it? Or do stresses in the teacher drive out any awareness of the relevance?

Should the high school teacher study the development of the foetus, the neonate, and the infant, when he teaches adolescents? The educational psychologist answers that we are not only our current age but every preceding year, month, week, day, minute, and second we have lived through. The tantrum of an adolescent is "regressive" because some earlier age pattern is reactivated in the behavior of the moment. The teacher who knows this and who knows the earlier age pattern is far along in handling the child, particularly if the teacher knows of and is careful about similarly regressive tendencies in himself. Foetal, neonatal, infantile, and toddler behavior patterns are directly relevant to the high school teacher attempting to motivate stubborn seniors aimed at graduation and the job or college entrance that follow, and the relevance is even clearer with the teacher of junior high school or elementary school classes.

Teachers, because of regressive stress in them, fail to see this relevance, unmistakable though it is to psychologists, psychoanalysts, physicians, and kindergarten teachers. If physicians in general practice report that over 40 per cent of the symptoms they see are psychosomatic and psychogenic, where the external symptom is, like the visible tip of an iceberg, much smaller than the substrate, then educational psychology must also deal with behavior substrates in the classroom. Remember that they are operative in the teacher as well as in the student, and hence cannot be divorced from human development, beginning with the foetus.

On the other hand, growth is not only *away from,* but also *toward,* and has teleological qualities, so that educational psychology must deal with goals as well as with causes.

We want our instructional engineer/teacher-diplomate to consider questions bearing on educational psychology and human development, like these:

1. What does the *crucial experiment* mean to psychologists? How does it compel the psychologist to seek resources from other disciplines? Does the search for the crucial experiment reflect success in ordering psychological data, or failure?

2. Does the non-existence of the crucial experiment weaken the position of the educational psychologist in a school setting (or the clinical psychologist in the hospital team)? Or does it make him the more effective watchdog? Does this in turn open the boundaries of psychology to other disciplines? Or does it close the door to other disciplines?

3. If behavior is not fully explicable, must we nevertheless assume the presence of underlying causes? Can we study human development without postulating a basic reasonableness and process? Can we study the individual without doing so?

4. What problems in psychology are insoluble? What are the parallels in psychology to the indeterminacy principle in physics? Conversely, what does the psychologist do when answers *are* available, as in the causes of juvenile delinquency and with the gifted who do not fulfill their educational possibilities? How should the psychologist seek implementation of policy formulations when the findings are in and seem conclusive?

Second Week. Psychological Growth and Specialization

Educational psychology and human development must be relevant to the classroom, not remote. If obsessive regressiveness in the teacher will inevitably have classroom consequences, then teacher self-study is not separable from educational psychology.

The seemingly remote may have considerable pertinence to classroom matters. Consider:

1. Is the foetus a self-contained entity, impervious and impermeable to external physical stimuli, or is it accessible to these stimuli? Is the emotional state of the mother reflected in the unborn child? Does the unborn child experience emotional states? If so, would the foetal environment of an anxious, deprived Negro mother offer the same nutriment as that of an unharried, middle-class white mother?

2. The biologist transplants a cell from that region in the frog embryo where the eye will develop and places it where the leg will develop, then transplants a cell where the leg will develop to the region where the eye will develop. Up to a certain point the transplant is successful and the former eye cell conforms to its new context, rather than to its inner specificity, and becomes a leg, just as the original leg cell becomes an eye. Hence, successful transplant implies interchangeability of parts and the priority of environment over heredity. However, after a certain developmental point, transplant is no longer successful, thereby implying other considerations about maturation and irreversibility in biological process. But maturation and irreversibility also occur in educational processes, as Rene Spitz, John Bowlby, (31) Anna Freud, and Dorothy Burlingham (31) show, and Samuel Pinneau's disagreement (31) with their findings only proves the relevance of these concepts in the workaday classroom. Pinneau believes that early experiences are reversible. The others disagree. The teacher knows that both are right, depending. Depending on what?

3. In the human foetus, patterned specificity of body movement supplants random, diffuse movements, analogous to stereotyping of response, the growth of response modalities, and to frequent confusion in classroom learning when switching to new responses for old stimuli. The old response gets in the way.

4. Differentiation in the embryo illustrates the transactions between the inner environment and the outer one, by way of ionic equilibria and interchange, biochemical give-and-take of stimulus and response, isomorphic reflections, and how function relates to specialization.

5. "Granted," the teacher says, "that these things are important to the biologist and the developmental psychologist, but what's the connection to teaching multiplication, spelling, the

causes of the Civil War, and Shelley's *Ozymandias?* What has this got to do with *me?*"

6. The pupil has had many complicated experiences long before entering the classroom, or hearing of multiplication, the Civil War, or *Ozymandias.* His inner growth needs, from the earliest split-second of individuality, are prior and dominating. Maintaining intactness of his physical and psychological self may conflict with the teacher's purposes and with the syllabus.

7. Furthermore, these growth needs determine how the pupil learns. Embryology tells us that the undifferentiated frog cell can remain where it is and develop into an eye, or undergo transplant and become a limb. So then the Negro child from the South, coming into a northern urban school with an I.Q. of 80, can either sit there unchanged or move up to higher levels of intelligence, depending on how the transplant takes, or on how old the child is at the time of transplant. Klineberg's studies on the increase in I.Q. of Negro children migrating to the North deal with this.

8. For the Negro child, the success of migration North depends on the age of the child, but also on his development in hate, hopelessness, and defiance. Bowlby's studies (31) on adopted children and the irreversibility in emotive development after the eighth or ninth month, like Harlow's studies on the cloth monkey-mother, (27) tell the classroom teacher concerned with communication about children in whom communication channels never developed.

For discussion and consideration by the instructional engineer/teacher-diplomate:

If a multitude of causes operate in behavior, so that we do not always know the manner of their contrapuntal interaction, how can the investigator avoid paralysis? Instead, how can he gain breadth from the multiplication of causes that leads to confused effects?

Third Week. Reversibility and Irreversibility in Psychological Processes

The birth cry is a striking physiological example of irreversibility—and a signal that the child, on the prowl for its own oxygen supply, cannot be put off even for a quarter-minute because irreversible damage is caused to brain cells if oxygen is not supplied at once.

Almost always, oxygen arrives opportunely and irreversible damage is avoided. But some years later social, family, and community irreversibility walk into the classroom, disguised as a pupil who breathes normally, but whose other behavior shows growth opportunities stunted, delayed, or forever lost—because society, family, or community have withheld another kind of oxygen.

Oxygen deprivation offers analogues in language development, since a foreign language is learned best before puberty and is much less efficiently learned thereafter. On the other hand, college students make better progress in language learning than high school students, meaning that other kinds of language learning are best deferred. How is foreign language best learned at a given age?

Just as the pre-school child picks up the accent and intonation of a foreign language far more effectively than the college student, the college student learns far more vocabulary, grammar, and literature of the foreign language than the young child. The college student of a foreign language is past the time when he can learn the accent and intonations, but he is now at an age when he can grasp the concepts and symbols of the language, its patterns, its syntax, and its private semantics.

Timing is vital. In the dramatic imprinting experiments on barn fowl, the newly hatched chick follows the first moving object it sees—man, woman, child, experimenter—and thereafter ignores the mother hen that gave it life, illustrating irreversibility and timing in fowl both domestic and wild. (32)

So *marasmus,* or apathy, in the children of wartime England under the blitz (described by Spitz, Anna Freud, Burlingham, Bowlby, and disputed by Dr. Samuel Pinneau) relates to children raised in foster homes, institutional settings, and the lifelong consequences in irreversible emotional defect. The teacher who encounters apathy in the classroom had better not be apathetic about such research or how theory reaches into the practical pressures of the classroom, or she will fight an uphill fight about the behavior brought from home, family, and neighborhood. By determining which behavior is irreversible and doing nothing about it, restricting efforts to reversible behavior patterns, the teacher will be effective or ineffective according to the reversibility of the behavior. The teacher should be realistic about beating back the irreversible and neutralizing its noxious effects as far as possible.

Fourth Week. Readiness and Maturation

Education assumes reversibility of most behavior. Learning would be impossible were behavior neither reversible nor modifiable. The teacher must operate on the assumption that learning *can* take place that day and that the child *will* have been changed, and *will* have undergone behavioral modifications. This assumption is often sorely tried, not only because prior environmental conditions set up impediments to learning, but because certain inner mechanisms are resistant to change, and hence to learning. They operate subtly and are not too easy to discern.

These inner mechanisms are illustrated by the Rankian birth trauma (33) and the Freudian latency period. (33) But if true, the teacher's day-to-day work is affected. Rank says that a deep residuum within us would rather not be motivated into new directions, that we prefer remaining as we are to learning new things. Growth and change conflict with this Nirvana-like antecedent state as explained by Rank's theories of the shock of being born.

In Freud's Eros-Thanatos struggle, the immobilization of energy or libido, attributable to the death wish, reduces the energy available for learning. However, the Freudian latency period is a time of new motivations in reading readiness, school readiness, and a general chronologic synchrony with symbolic understanding. The end of this period coincides with the onset of puberty and the rash of educational difficulties in the junior high school. These affect not only latency, puberty, and curriculum, but also school organization, because the junior high school reflects human development, not the need for job slots for school administrators, who may find this a shock.

These stages of development are uniform for all children. Though we may reject Freud's inflexible orality, anality, genitality, Oedipal stage, and so on, the *stages* are uniform; but the *rates* at which they are reached and traversed are not, nor are the experiences accompanying each stage. These vary. Readiness for walking, speaking, reading, school, and bisexual interest is not achieved at the same chronological age, because the tempo of readiness rate varies by individual.

Furthermore, growth can destroy as well as create. Perceptions originally valuable and true may be replaced by error, and some learning can be bad. What Wordsworth said in his *Ode on Intimations of Immortality* and what Piaget's children further prove are that growth may destroy capacities. So a child's original vision, in some areas truer than the adult's, may become progressively more blunted by social bias. Therefore what the pupil brings into the classroom may require restoring to a former unspoiled state, which affects teaching. An awakening of reminiscence—e.g., Herbart's "apperceptive mass"—and of appropriate memories becomes essential in presenting the new and fresh. To help this process the teacher must learn to ask questions, rather than to make statements.

Fifth Week. The Teacher as Learner

You (the teacher candidate) are this moment your present age, obviously, but also simultaneously every age you have ever been, else "regression" would be inexplicable. In it you return to a prior level of age-related behavior, identified in Gesell's schedules. It's easy to identify regression in others, but harder in yourself.

As an example, you walk into the classroom. Two boys in back of the room look at you and start laughing and whispering to each other. Your reaction, as often as not, assumes that the boys are laughing at you. But is your assumption justified? Aren't they with equal likelihood laughing at something that happened the last period? Why your regressive backward leap that you are the target of their laughter?

We expect the six-year-old to behave at a six-year-old level, but when a sixteen-year-old does so regression becomes visible. The teacher is also mirrored in the Gesell developmental schedule, because, some layers down, he too is a six-year-old and therefore not differentiable from students.

The infant who cries at a strange face one day becomes a teacher dealing with an unfamiliar racial or ethnic group, and the crying, though submerged, may still be there. The teacher apprehensive about the class was once a child apprehensive about the teacher. The tears and the apprehension are, in part, regressive.

Educational psychology and child development should study the child still within the teacher to achieve self-understanding by that teacher. The medical interne's hypochondria as he studies the patient's symptoms and then detects these in himself testifies to successful and persuasive teaching and clinical experiences. But the training of teachers fails to move the prospective teacher from assessment of the pupil to self-inspection, so that he is assessing himself at the same time as he textbook-learns latency, birth trauma, reversibility-irreversibility, and biological and sociological transplant. One understands oneself first and thereafter one's classes. Otherwise educational psychology can become a pedantic obstruction to understanding instead of a means to it, as learning can become degraded to sciolism, or a neurotic blinds himself to his neurosis by reading books about his symptoms. Intellectualizing is not the same as experiencing.

Because recitation requires action and thereby transcends internalization, all psychological systems—whether the Freudian libido, (33) Gardner Murphy's canalization, (34) gestalt's closure, (35) Hull's habit strength, (36) or Skinner's schedules of reinforcement (37)—deal with goals and overt outcomes. In studying these systems, the teacher-diplomate/instructional engineer should put not only the student under a microscope, but himself too. He can also discuss and consider these:

1. The psychologist is often mistrusted. Physicians object to him as psychotherapist, though not as psychometrician, because lines of responsibility are involved, and fees. Similarly, businessmen and those opposed to testing call the psychometrician a psychomeretrician because he affects policy. For the same reason, school principals resist school psychologists. Can you analyze the professional and pecking-order relationships in each case? (Naturally, psychologists can say stupid things and be as corruptible as fee-splitting physicians or ambulance-chasing attorneys.) What precautions should psychologists exert in policy formulation and educational decision making? What can professional groups in psychology do about their "misguided" or venal members? Or the stupidities of psychologists? (38)

2. The clinical psychologist, social psychologist, and educational psychologist study the deprived community—not so the experimental psychologist. Is he missing a bet in its research possibilities? For example, would Benton Underwood's extensive

verbal learning experiments on a Midwest population be the same if replicated in Harlem? Would the semantic differential studies of Osgood (39) yield similar results in a Harlem school population? Would administration of LSD and other hallucinogenic or psychedelic drugs show the same consequences in Harlem Hospital patients as in Harlem student volunteers? Would Estes' probability learning statistics show similar means and variances with a Bedford-Stuyvesant group? Does Critical Flicker Fusion work with Negroes as with whites?

3. Your educational psychology text gives you an understanding of the child and the adolescent. Does it give you an understanding of yourself? Is this legitimate in a text on educational psychology?

Sixth Week. Stimulus Ingestion and Exploration

As man ingests food for physiological survival, so he requires the ingestion of stimuli for psychological survival. Man-in-space astronautics reveals how the absence of sights and sounds has deleterious effects on behavior and the psyche. Similarly, marasmus studies on deprivation of stimulation reveal adverse infant development.

Man explores and stretches out his receptors to the stimuli about him, and the baby in the crib stretches, twists, flexes muscles, and is continuously restless, so that the swaddled infant is more composed and quiet than the naked infant, indicating a relationship between stimulation and activity. Language development is especially illustrative of this.

Speech begins in stretching and probing the possibilities of the vocal organs. The child lallates, babbles, gurgles, irrespective of the presence or absence of others, in an inner exploration of sound and noise that is parallel to the child's irrepressible exploration and assessment of the outer world. Even as it examines its fingers and toes, the child simultaneously examines and listens to the sounds it makes.

The repertoire of sounds is wider in infancy than in maturity —from the Hottentot click to the Scotsman's burr—to which the infant listens and from which, in the next stage of speech, it will select those with socialized meaning, for the child learns that sounds may have desirable social consequences. These are in turn contingent upon the child's ability to repeat its repertoire. Its parents talk and coo to it, in imitation of the child's sounds. But the child not only listens; it responds with sounds and gurgles of its own.

Then, one historic day, it utters a sound with some similarity to the language of its parents and jubilation shakes the house. The mother telephones the grandparents that the baby has with perfect clarity said, "Mama," or "Dada," or "Smithsonian Institute"; meanwhile, back at the crib, the baby realizes that its sounds can gain social approval, so these are thereby reinforced and become part of its permanent repertoire. Time passes and additional sounds are reinforced; but others, like the Hottentot click, are not, and are permanently lost, for lack of reinforcement.

The same child cannot learn a second language as readily as the first because of interference among response-modalities, but if this is reduced second language learning becomes a possibility. For example, if the father addresses the child in English and the mother does so in French, and this pattern is consistently maintained, interference is decreased and second language learning occurs quite comfortably, as in bilingual households.

Some years pass, and the same child is sitting in a geometry class of a teacher taking an in-service course dealing with these matters. The teacher is disgruntled about the in-service course because she cannot see how infant language development will help her teach Euclid. The child who once learned speech and thereafter went on to the less-involved complexities of reading and writing is sent to the board by the disgruntled teacher and fouls up the demonstration. The teacher punishes the child with a "Wrong!" and the child skulks back to his seat. No reward. No reinforcement. No hits. No runs. All errors. Teacher included.

For discussion:

1. Does a reading program depend on a sense of need or a sense of concept? Does excessive need retard the emergence of concept? How is curriculum planning affected by our answers here?

2. Do Negro students have more or fewer language experiences than do non-Negro students? Is it therefore necessary to use many varied experiential approaches or few in presenting language and reading material to them?

Seventh Week. Rewards and Punishment

Why should a child who has mastered language, speech, listening, and writing, do poorly in geometry, even though Euclid is less complicated than learning to speak, write, and read? Why do most human beings learn the vastly more complex, and balk at the simple? Are there rewards and punishments in language learning that elude us in Euclid-learning?

Also, what constitutes a reward to one pupil but not to another, and a punishment to one pupil but not to another? Antecedents and backgrounds, from one pupil to another, are not the same. One pupil may skulk back to his seat at the teacher's "Wrong!" but another may smirk and clown and feel that he has gained a victory where it counts most—in the eyes of his classmates. The "Wrong!" to him is a reward, not a punishment. Why?

Our answer brings us seemingly far afield, to the rats in a maze at some psychological laboratory, the rats that throw some unexpected light on our pupils, because learning theory and animal experimentation are significantly related to educational practice. The connection between Sultan, Köhler's genius ape, (41) gestalt psychology, whole-word reading, and phonics, means that trained apes have dictated educational practices, just as Thorndike's cats (41) and numerous rats have done. Skinner's bar-pressing rodents and button-pecking pigeons are the lineal—not branched —ancestors of teaching machines and programed instruction. (37) However, Miller-rats, (23) Hull-rats, (36) or Skinner-rats (37) are not uniformly interpreted by psychologists, even when the rat's behavior is unarguable. But they illuminate certain classroom matters, whether they are harnessed in Miller's approach-avoidance, free-running in Hull's goal gradients, or lever-pressing in Skinner's prison house:

1. Miller's conflicted rats inform the classroom teacher that immobility is an end result, a consequence, an outcome of rewards and punishments in opposition. The lazy child may be conflicted, rather than unwilling to invest energy in education. His uninterest is more probably paralysis, a consequence of unresolved inner strife. Our disgruntled teacher who retorts, "He doesn't show any signs of strife—or life. He seems completely placid and satisfied and just unwilling to try," should look at Miller's rat. He rests

frozen in the middle of a maze between reward and punishment, between food and shock, giving a rat's version of immobility, while hunger and fear, attraction and repulsion, wage war, unseen, below the pelt.

2. Or note Hull's rats at the entrance to a maze, food-deprived, water-deprived, knowing every inch of the way to the goal where food is, first ambling as they begin to traverse the maze, then proceeding more rapidly, accelerating as they go, picking up greater and greater speed as they approach the goal. The closer the goal, the greater the expenditure of energy. The teacher-diplomate/instructional engineer can learn from rat psychologists that you must have numerous intervening sub-goals within sight of one another, rather than one large goal far off. Rewards must be built into each section of the lesson, rather than at the remote terminal-point of a goal box at the end of the month or term. To promise a Negro child his equal opportunity to become President of the United States will stimulate him less than his equal opportunity to go on to college. Even the latter goal is usually too remote, and needs sub-dividing into component way-stations, like weekly payments for learning.

3. Skinner's lever-pressing rats inform the disgruntled teacher, as do Skinner's pigeons, that without reward no learning is possible. Somehow, somewhere, the classroom, the teacher, or the pupil's own world must permit satisfactions, else no learning will take place. Given the assurance that the pellet of reinforcement will drop, all kinds of reward schedules are available to the teacher.

4. Herbert Birch has unabashedly preached the relevance of rat research to human learning, as have Krech and Rosenzweig (40) in their demonstration of cortical growth as a result of enriched experience.

5. The multiplication and complication of reward patterns lead to monkeys that manipulate one-arm-bandit slot machines, to Harlow rats that learn-to-learn, (27) so similar to Bateson's deutero-learning (42) and to the involvements of the Pavlovian second signal system in Soviet educational theory. These are instructive of classroom patterns in learning, even if not identical.

For discussion by our instructional engineer/teacher-diplomates:

Populations in disadvantaged communities offer unexplored possibilities for repetition of experiments carried on with groups of college students (the usual subjects). If data gathered by educational psychologists can be repeated on a Negro and Puerto-Rican population (for example, on classroom climate, composition, spelling, reading, and handwriting), would such experimentation be helpful or harmful to the new population? Would the Hawthorne effect be in a constructive or destructive direction? Would the new population resent being treated as experimental subjects? Would you suggest this resentment be handled by imparting a sense of uniqueness and special attention to the new population? Would this convert the feeling of resentment to a feeling of reward?

Eighth Week. *Reinforcement and Symbolism*

Despite rat behavior with rewards and punishments, we do not know how these are defined by human beings, because symbolic values (like art, religion, friendship, and status) govern us and generate rewards and punishments unknown in animal experimentation.

Meaningfulness and symbolic structure are basic to human learning, as shown by the 1885 Ebbinghaus nonsense-syllable experiments and the recent isolation studies of Hebb, (43) where symbolism, or emotionalism, infuses even the most abstract and intellectualized tasks. We cannot learn without imposing symbol, meaning, or emotion upon the material to be learned. Hebb, indeed, indicates that these pour out of us even when there is no objective task to be learned, as constantly as we perspire.

So symbol systems contribute heavily to reward and punishment, but social values, in turn, contribute heavily to our symbol systems. If, in some schools, teachers are targets, and in others are icon-figures, what are the social networks between student and student and between student and teacher in each case? What are the rewards in annoying the teacher? In pleasing the teacher? The student's social network, the community social network, result in symbol systems that determine what constitutes a reward and what a punishment.

The school cannot adequately deal with the child without knowing the child's history. With middle-class children the teacher knows almost automatically, because his history is not too dissimilar, as Havighurst has shown. (44)

Not so with the disadvantaged child, who experiences a sense of difference the very first day he walks into school. At how early an age does the white child know that Negroes are servants and white people not? At how early an age does the Negro child learn to prefer white dolls to dark ones? At what age can the child of either race associate superordination-subordination with skin color? All the evidence indicates an age *not later than the beginnings of organized speech.*

For discussion:

Assume a branch facility of your university set up in a nearby disadvantaged community, working in conjunction with local agencies in individual and group therapy, and augmented by the facilities of the faculty in experimental psychology and psychiatry. The facility anticipates substantial assistance and funds from governmental and foundation sources. How would you plan for effective liaison between experimentalists and clinicians? between clinicians and psychiatrists? between psychology and sociology? between clinic and school? between clinic and community? What aspects of the program would be programmatic and action-oriented? What aspects would be problem-oriented and research-oriented? Are the symbol structures of clinician and experimentalist the same? Are those of clinic and school the same? of research laboratory and school? Are the symbol structures of action-oriented programs the same as research-oriented programs?

Ninth Week. Tests and Measurements

The Negro child has an emotional and symbolic deficit by the time it learns to talk, certainly before it enters its first classroom. A spiritual expropriation has long been active and white faces express it. When, further, so much home talk deals with whites in terms of superordination-subordination, the Negro child's school expectations are different from the white child's. In brief, a long and significant pre-school biography of inner symbolism relates to school performance.

However, the early school years show fewer conflicts, overtly at least, than do the junior high school years. I.Q. scores in Negro and white children become disparate as children grow older, as educational and environmental deprivations become progressively manifest. White children in backward areas in Appalachia show a similar progressive deterioration in I.Q. scores.

Since testing is less discriminating in younger children and becomes more differentiating as the child grows older, tests are perhaps too unreliable to reflect innate differences at early ages. Given higher test reliability at later ages, one can more definitely say that environment and experience have penalized the Negro child, as they have the Appalachia whites.

In other words, scores tell us something but circumstances and context surrounding the testing situation tell us even more. As Thorndike and Hagen (41) point out, a 90 I.Q. in a Negro child in Mississippi and the same score in the son of a wealthy banker in a cultured Massachusetts suburb, require interpretation in terms of background. Are both children equally intelligent? The Negro child's score reflects a deprived educational background, bad schooling, and an unhealthy, unstable social background. He is operating at the very floor of his potential—which, under other circumstances, would be more fully realized—and is bright. Conversely, the Massachusetts child—operating at or near the ceiling of his innate ability because of his environmental advantages—is an extraordinarily well-trained, well-nurtured, and effectively coached moron who has greatly benefited by the opportunities thrown his way.

Hence statistics must be accompanied by interpretation, and testing by logic. Like Fraunhofer's diffraction grating, which takes undifferentiated white light and breaks it down to its constituent wave length and colors, a good test takes undifferentiated populations and groups and breaks them down according to the qualities being tested. The better the test, the better it diffracts the distribution, *provided the trait measured has a random distribution.*

For discussion:

1. Observe that the normal curve describes the distribution of height, weight, and intelligence. This implies that people are different. On the other hand, Floyd Allport's J-curve of conforming behavior (45) implies that people are the same. How does the J-curve involve clearly understood and policed standards? How do standards skew the normal curve to the J-curve?

2. An instructor will say that he "marks on the curve." Does he refer to the normal curve or to the J-curve? When can you infer that he has had no effect on his students? Is it the teacher's job to skew the normal curve so that it approaches the J-curve?

Tenth Week. Educational Statistics

Randomness is pictured in the curve known variously as the bell-shaped curve, the normal curve, the Gaussian curve, or the probability curve, whether we measure the height, weight, and intelligence in a large unselected population or the proportion of heads and tails when we toss ten coins a thousand times.

Note, however, that when we tighten or introduce standards, requirements, training, education, advantages, or other special circumstances for Negro children, the curve takes on a skewed appearance because we are tampering with randomness, *which is precisely the teacher's job.*

The normal curve is Calvinistic, specifying the proportion of the elect and of the damned, as given by areas under the curve. The teacher must reduce this randomness, refusing to accept it, any more than engineers passively accept the data of science. Manipulating these data, engineers design atomic reactors, water desalination plants, and automobiles. Given the randomness of the normal curve, the teacher must plan; must direct energies, curriculums, and outcomes; must design techniques that the spectrum of intelligence may shift and skew toward the upper end.

Now some people will say that the teacher can do nothing to change intelligence, or skew the curve. For example, Garrett, Weyl and others (46) claim that since the spectra of Negro and white intelligence overlap only to a slight degree, that nothing can be done about it, and that Negroes are born less intelligent, not that conditions have made them that way. Most social scientists disagree, believing that *racial* intelligence is primarily a matter of the environment in which the race finds itself, while *individual* intelligence is more a function of heredity than of environment. What does this imply for the teacher in the disadvantaged community? If limitations on human alterability restrict teacher effectiveness, we have no evidence that this alterability in white and Negro is different.

For discussion:

If intelligence *is* alterable, do you interpose your efforts at alteration with an upper-status white child as with a lower-status white child? with an eager learner as with a reluctant learner? with a defiant child as with a compliant one?

15

The Administration of the Urban School

Many urban schools are located in communities that are in crisis. The administrators of such schools can handle the crisis by setting up relationships with the community's churches, social agencies, political leaders, parent groups, financial and banking circles, and real estate owners. Observe that this goes beyond the administrator's relationships with teachers and other school personnel and may be construed as excessive meddling in matters beyond the administrator's concern.

Nevertheless the effective administrator expands the range of his responsibility, just as the avid bureaucrat does, but also goes forth to the dragons that incubate and grow, and does not huddle in his appointed rut. (1) Indeed, we can differentiate administrator from bureaucrat by the groups he communicates with face-to-face, how often they enter his office, and his relationships with them. Furthermore, he encourages other school personnel to latch on to committees in housing, real estate, free lunches, neighborhood improvement, or otherwise activate themselves; the administrator leads and does not fall conveniently into line. (2)

He also knows when to lie low. In the usual crisis school, parent meetings are usually poorly attended because Negro fathers don't come. The administrator knows he cannot persuade Negro fathers to come no matter what he does, nor how winningly. Yet he must increase parent participation, which is not the same as parent attendance at meetings, nor does the wise administrator confuse the two. Negro fathers should be seen individually because (not always, but often enough) meetings are the wrong auspices under which they can be gotten to involvement and activism. Negro fathers are willing and frequent visitors to the school, but their participation in decisions and plans is better assured when these are presented to them as individuals, rather than as members of a group. The group can inhibit.

Whatever his mode of intervention, a universe of jobs awaits doing.

The Administrator and Parent Relations

Only in communities of superior wealth, power, education, and socioeconomic class are fathers as active as mothers in parent organizations. Such fathers are not worried about being feminized because the evidence is so great that they are not. This means that in upper-status communities administrators will deal with fathers as much as with mothers, and increasingly with mothers as the school's social-class composition slides. In this slide, furthermore, *total* activity drops too, so that in schools where mothers are increasingly Negro, uneducated, and unmarried to their succession of consorts, parent organization is weak, members are few, and those few are chiefly mothers. Because many fathers feel that children—their school, emotional, and intellectual growth—are the wife's job, getting them to parent meetings is like pulling teeth. They don't intend to be poor fathers—typically, Pop needles, scolds, spanks, and generally points out that he wants the child to become the things he was never able to become. It is too late for him but not for the child, because Daddy is too busy earning a living and too tired after a day's work to practice what he preaches, the piano for instance, or the culture that he shoves over to the child's side of the table.

But too much parental involvement in school activity can interfere with school operations. This, however, depends on the level of administrative activity. Parents are not trained to operate schools and some administrators, for all their training, can't either.

But the sound administrator wants as much parent activity as he can muster because he can thereafter channel it appropriately, knowing how to protect his staff, how to use the parents in the community, how to use the interplay to strengthen the school, and how to keep the reins of responsibility untangled.

He also knows that lawyers, dentists, doctors, and accountants strengthen themselves in the community by conspicuous activity, so that parents gain economic and social advantages from being parents. They shine brightly at meetings, accept posts with alacrity, and more power to this hunger in them because the shrewd administrator can improve his school as these eager beavers improve themselves.

The bureaucrat, on the contrary, will fuss about the possibilities of meddling; and here he is childish. When a child wants its friends, it doesn't want its parents to be companions and pals, so scoutmastering, den mothering, and being a teacher's aide may invade the child's privacy, but that is because he is a child. Adult administrators should be able to protect themselves against such encroachments. If adult, they can distinguish meddling interference from good intentions that need directing. The administrator knows that where parent organization is weak, parent interference tends to increase; where parent organization is strong, meddlesomeness is less, even though parents relish involvement in school activity. Strong parent organization respects the professionalism of the administrator. (3)

In the far too numerous cases where you have stupid administration, organization doesn't necessarily collapse. The parents will pay dues, a paper membership will exist, and the administrator will have become a bureaucrat.

The Administrator and Staff Relations

An editorial in *The Nation's Schools* for August, 1957, said:

This idea will be denounced and denied, because it is not derived from a scientific sampling. But we think you will get the same answers if you will visit quietly and confidentially with teachers that you know, as we have during the past several weeks. We have been told time and again by teachers that they are discouraged. . . . "We want a superintendent who will not sit on both sides of the fence, who will not tell the board and P.T.A. one thing and give us teachers a different song and dance. We want administrators and supervisors that will become acquainted with our problems firsthand in the classroom and will help us meet those problems."

Please don't take our word for it. Don't expect, either, that teachers will tell the superintendent or his representative exactly how they feel or think. If you really want to discover the morale of your school system, provide some means whereby teachers can express themselves anonymously, without fear of identification or recrimination. . . .

This means that administrators can anticipate being distrusted by their staff members on the matter of academic freedom. (4)

Teacher organizations like the National Education Association and the United Federation of Teachers reflect increasing aggressiveness. In unprecedented militancy, teachers have gone out on strike or on work stoppages, though, considering the teacher shortage of the past decade and the seller's market in which teachers find themselves, their aggressiveness has been on the mild side. Nevertheless, they now require judicious and sensitive consultation if school morale and staff relations are to be maintained.

We mentioned earlier that the teacher who is organizationally involved either right or left of center (there are no extremist groups significantly involved in American teacher organizations) is more likely to be involved with lesson planning, professional improvement, parents, pupils, and work. Conversely, the lassitude that makes many teachers slough off these aspects of career involvement makes them also slough off organizational involvement. The administrator who wants a highly motivated, work-oriented staff will have to risk an organizationally directed staff too.

The administrator's only protection is to be sympathetic to teacher organization, without prescribing what the organization should be. Teacher groups, as education becomes more urban, become more sophisticated and tough, because that's what city living does to you. They exert pressure on administrators who, in turn, must transmit this pressure to their superiors. This pressure is generally in terms of budget, or, if not, is ultimately convertible to budgetary considerations. Hence money is always coming into the picture.

This is not true in administrator-teacher relationships on the individual level, as in the evaluation of teachers and the determination of teacher effectiveness. On some given day, the administrator walks unobtrusively into the back of the classroom and observes the teacher's performance, for such things as tenure, salary increment, or promotion. How does he evaluate this performance?

First, he looks around him and assesses the physical state of the room, the degree of litter on the floor, the ventilation, and if the blackboards are messy or in order. He can be amazingly prissy about this. A neat and orderly room can mean nothing if it is simply hygiene for hygiene's sake, but can mean much if it sets the stage for action. Similarly, a sloppy room can mean a sloppy teacher, but it can also mean a teacher who is moving fast and who is pulling the class along too rapidly to be concerned about classroom appearance. Which is it?

Next, the administrator will watch for student participation. How many students volunteer? Does the teacher call on non-volunteers also, to pull them into the mainstream of the lesson? Does the teacher succeed in getting to most of the class? Is she sarcastic, or sympathetic? Do the questions succeed in eliciting thought, or are they chiefly fact questions?

Ultimately, tests of teacher effectiveness are not better than the supervisor administering the test, because testing instruments tell the supervisor what to look for but do not test the supervisor's vision as he looks; it is peculiarly far-sighted. Every observation form the administrator signs is filed. *His* superiors review these forms not to evaluate the teacher, but to evaluate him when he comes up for promotion.

But, unfortunately, the beginning teacher is not aware that a major function of the evaluation is to provide materials for administrator evaluation, rather than teacher evaluation, and is therefore uneasy. This does no lasting harm, because even experienced teachers are uneasy, whether the observation is by administrators or by harmless student teachers, wide-eyed, intimidated, and unable to harm a fly. Hence, just as competition for college admissions is destructive of a liberal approach to education, so administration and supervision inevitably lead to an obsessive need for discipline and classroom restraint. A low decibel count is not equivalent to attentiveness, though some surviving administrators think so. Only the teacher who is at ease with administration and supervision gets controls which are not obsessive. Such teachers are infrequent.

Discipline begins with the elders, not with the children. A healthy relationship between administration and teacher is the first necessity in effective classroom management. The teaching staff that is free of minatory administrative admonition, that is relaxed when a school principal strolls down the corridors, that has immediate, nurturing administrative and supervisory help when needed, is not a "tough" school, even though it is located in a solidly Negro neighborhood. Other schools in the same neighborhood can be weak: If a teacher sends a student to the office with a note describing some classroom misbehavior and requesting suitable punishment, and if some minutes later the child returns with another note, signed by the principal, which says, "Can't you handle this matter yourself?" is the teacher weak or is the principal? Harlem schools vary not because pupils do, but in the firmness, purposefulness, and sense of direction of the administrator and how he transmits these to teachers and then to pupils. There is no "tough" school except poor administration and poor supervision make it so; the nature of the pupil population has much less to do with it.

If close and sympathetic supervision is important to school morale, so is the *esprit de corps* that ignores the administrator and confines itself to teacher-teacher compatibility, as when an experienced older teacher enters a "buddy" relationship with a beginning teacher. The administrator can help foster such relationships, remembering that experience can encrust with barnacles or lead to rich understandings; and the experienced teacher can preach two divergent philosophies of classroom discipline. In one, experience will counsel, "Be firm and rigid and show them you are the boss," and in the other, "Be kind and gentle for you can get more with praise." These philosophies describe extreme situations; like all expressions of the extreme, they are wrong.

So the administrator must be prepared in guidance techniques, both in and out of the classroom. Many old-line administrators resent the school's guidance function and the new responsibilities of guidance personnel. Relationships here are not always cordial, but the administrator's best course is not to lick 'em but to join 'em because, ultimately, the administrator must distribute the guidance function among teachers, supervisors, psychologists, and counselors. This will not diminish his administrative powers, as he sometimes fears.

The Administrator and Group Relations

Group feeling, group-mindeness, and team-mindedness sound highly desirable, but racialism is an undesirable direction that group-mindedness can take, with the administrator in the middle of the muddle. In our cities, schools house various traditions, religions, races, and nationalities. Lines of stratification are blurred in the classroom, where racialism rarely appears openly, but lurks sensitively, sub-surface, while educational democracy purrs prettily on the face of things. The stratification becomes obvious, and immediately so, outside the classroom. Thus in the school cafeteria the pack draws together and runs together. The Negro athlete is accepted on the team, but less readily at the school dances.

If passions are powerful in racialism, the school administrator must educate people out of passion—this kind, anyway. Administrative techniques exist for generating the soft answer that gives you control of the situation, not the soft answers that invite aggressiveness, but those that invite the self-acceptance precedent to social acceptance. It's tricky. People who have hungered for status sometimes gorge excessively at it, at first. Simply to be treated with respect can be soul-shaking, so the soft answer may encounter distrust when all your life you have never experienced it.

No biology teacher exploding the race myth, no social studies teacher paying special attention to Negro History Week, no English teacher showing the George Washington Carver films and discussing Countee Cullen and Langston Hughes can substitute for face-to-face, day-by-day, across-the-board and around-the-clock courtesy and good manners, expressed physically and visibly. When one bows in corridors, says "Thank you," "Please," and "If you don't mind" to students even if they don't say it to you, when orders and commands approach the vanishing point, and are replaced by requests, smiles, salutations, and farewells, initial derision soon disappears because good manners exert irresistible, avalanche-like force. Warmth sets the ice to melting.

Nor need courtesy be a mask. Teachers are human, they can lose tempers, flare up, be short-tempered. Nevertheless, students will understand and excuse such human failings when most of the time the teacher is considerate, thoughtful, and acts so outwardly in action, gesture, and speech.

A Brooklyn junior high school principal has told the author:

> From my office I can watch the Negro kids returning from lunch. Their energy, bounce, and dash can be terrifying to somebody as physically incompetent as I am. They gather in groups, boys and girls, and the language is incredible; but teachers come along, teachers they like and teachers they don't like, and you can see how the physical shape of the group changes, depending on the teacher. With a teacher they like, the group becomes less compact, with more space between individuals, as they string out. With a teacher they dislike, the group bunches together, becoming more of a group. I've heard teachers say that there's just so much you can do for these kids, considering the homes they come from; but there's just so much you can do for teachers too, considering the variety of teacher backgrounds there are.

So, just as the teacher can go a limited distance in handling racialism in the classroom because the classroom is less decisive than home and neighborhood, so the administrator can go a limited distance in improving staff levels because his staff has in large measure been pre-formed before he ever sees it. But though the distance he traverses is limited, he must negotiate it.

The Administrator
and Educational Innovation

The administrator is caught in a variety of innovative cross-fires, a sampling of which includes school integration, heterogeneous versus homogeneous grouping (sometimes preferably called groping), block promotions, age grading versus ability grading, educational technology, teacher aides, and whatever educational fads come along.

Caught in the first crossfire—integration—administrators realize that overcrowded schools in Negro neighborhoods are a legitimate administrative concern. Negro parents insist on access to schools in white neighborhoods, where educational facilities and teachers are better. So Princeton plans, 5–3–4 plans, and other substitutes for honest schooling emerge and thereupon degrade the white school without improving the Negro school. Honest administrators must yield to these deceptions that booby-trap the unsuspecting. The Negro child will in the white school face a more painful segregation than before, because it is immediate, and he will be socially segregated as he was geographically segregated before, in a contiguity that magnifies the sense of difference and separateness and every handicap of home and community that the Negro child brings to school with him.

Does democracy require the bitterness and remoteness that the Negro child will come to feel as this iron is driven into his soul? Yes, because votes are involved. The urban politician wants to get elected; to get elected, he requires the Negro vote; the Negro vote wants the integrated school.

To deflect injury to the Negro child, the administrator must broaden the *social* base of the school. Thus teachers must get to understand the special situation of the Negro child, for the child to relate to teacher, school, and learning. The teacher must be asked to make home visits a regular part of teaching and must bring the Negro child into contact with community businessmen, community labor groups, and community political organizations. Teaching schedules must become flexible to permit this, else school integration will intensify antagonisms, rather than reduce them.

After-school programs must be enlarged, and teachers must be paid additional stipends for these extra responsibilities on after-school time, because children do not get to know one another in school, but after school.

A second innovative crossfire is in heterogeneous versus homogeneous grouping (or groping), and the vested interests that such grouping represents. Local social arbiters will favor homogeneous grouping because it has the virtues of a social blue book, Jockey Club, or stud book, with important values to the social leadership. When educational authorities speak of "tracks," the educational administrator is the chief handicapper. The entries who place in the money and are in the first track are happy, but those out of the win-place-show category have strong objections to running on other tracks and want these distinctions removed, and their stigmata of inferior educational capacity. Thus we don't have inter-class struggle, as in the integrated school, but an intra-class struggle, within the privileged class, usually upper-middle, engaged in internecine strife about exclusion from the community's intellectual elite.

Current educational fashion here forces the administrator's hand. When educational democracy is modish, heterogeneous grouping flourishes. When the war-cry of "excellence" is sounded, homogeneous grouping emerges. Whichever way the administrator goes, he will be enfiladed by the bell-shaped curve of nature's making or the man-made curse of home differences since the upper-middle class is itself not homogeneous and torn a dozen different ways by creed, source of income, intellectual aspirations, and social intentions.

To protect the *superior student,* lest he be degraded by the others in his class, and the *ordinary student,* to bring him up to his fullest capacity, the administrator must in all cases demonstrate a flow in and out of the superior group, that nothing is fixed except the classification, no diminution in the achievements of the superior group nor in the gains of the ordinary group.

This second crossfire takes another form, when it reflects tempo, acceleration, sputniks, an inability to leave children alone, and a need to force-feed them and then get them off and running on their poor stuffed stomachs. Of course, administrators are justifiably troubled by the achievement lag in our children, compared with European children of the same age and intelligence. Our children are not worked as hard as children in European schools, but why should they be? (5) What's the hurry? Unlike other countries, we make provision for education through college years, and our children have a longer vista of educational perspectives facing them, so that graduates of our several dozen better colleges have done a major portion of catching up with the graduates of Oxford, Cambridge, the Sorbonne, or Uppsala. In graduate school they have at least drawn abreast, so that our Ph.D.'s—again speaking only of our several dozen better institutions—are as well trained as any in Europe. A Columbia, Harvard, Caltech, Princeton, or Chicago Ph.D. need not defer to any other doctorate anywhere in the Western world.

Europeans know this and often deplore European hurry-up and hyperthyroidism, with all its punitiveness of the young. We are rich enough not to hurry. If we succeeded in catching up with sputnik, a curriculum built upon rumination, contemplation, and meditation was responsible, which granted pupils time to explore, but not gaze off into space—it was pre-1957 American education that gave us our contemporary scientists and astronauts.

Exploration of space, ideas, and concepts requires a terrain heretofore unknown, an absence of rigid schedules, materials in effective quantity and effective relationship to the problem, and somebody who knows the neighborhood—meaning a teacher who is defended by an administrator. Exploration by thinking is the hardest work we know, but it can't be done against a stop-watch, or a syllabus, or a midterm, or a final exam, which are appropriate in determining budgets but not in defining educational tasks.

This brings the administrator into the crossfire of age-versus-ability grading and block promotions. The administrator is painfully aware that the urban community is split several ways on these and very vehemently too. Age grading, which is another aspect of homogeneous grouping, keeps children of the same age—irrespective of their ability—in the same class, which is highly acceptable to parents of mediocre children, but anathema to parents of children who perform well. The latter parents want no encumbrance on the progress of their children. For this reason the latter parents are also opposed to block promotions in which everybody is promoted to the next grade regardless of his ability, because they believe this makes promotion meaningless.

Communities are arrayed on one or another side of these issues, with the administrator in the middle because one or another policy is his responsibility. So the administrator resorts to juggling. He may, for instance, use block promotions, sending all the children ahead uniformly, only to have the children and their parents find, upon their arrival at the next grade, that classes are homogeneously grouped, with the brighter children assigned to the faster tracks and the slower ones to the slower tracks. He may thereupon be picketed (as happened recently in Englewood, New Jersey) by Negro parents who want to know why a proportionate number of Negro children are not included in the faster tracks.

The administrator knows that his community is usually impressed by technological innovation because it promises to make learning easy (wrong answer), or because it promises to make school operations less expensive (wrong answer again), or because it reduces the number of teachers (ditto). Educational technology, like all technology, requires more strategy rather than less, a greater financial investment in education rather than less, and a more competent teaching staff rather than less.

Hence a technological crossfire, in programed teaching and educational television, among other things, where parents ask the administrator if teaching machines teach. And, if they do, why isn't he buying them? The administrator's best answer is, "Only if the learning machine, the pupil, learns, and he can't if technology places a funnel in his mouth and pours down content. Let's save the money." On the other hand, communities like Freeport (Long Island) have recently rejected teaching machines, even though federal funds lightened the load on local taxpayers.

Educational technology is not necessarily new. Audio-visual materials have been with us a long time now, longer than most people realize, and go back to pictographic writing, which is about as far back as you can go. The caves at Altamira and Lascaux were audio-visual materials, so the wise administrator budgets for audio-visual materials because they are thoroughly traditional and make sense. Similarly, linear and branched teaching machine programs are not radically different from the techniques of the Socratic dialogue. O. K. Moore's typewriter is a mechanized analogue of the mother who reads to her child, but is more expensive on an hourly rate, and takes longer to amortize. (6)

Technology is legitimately budgeted if it has quality. Some teaching films are excellent, but most are a waste of funds. The same is true of teaching machine programs and closed circuit TV. Some are fine, but most are puerile, which is equally true of textbooks, teachers, administrators, and people.

Genuine innovations in educational technology are scarce. Perhaps a half-dozen worthwhile ideas emerge in a decade, hardly any more, while we strain after "new" ideas, "new" curricula, and "new" (not to speak of "revolutionary") educational practices. The National Defense Education Act urges contractors to sponsor "original" proposals, but how many such ideas are ever around, or welcomed and recognized by federal bureaucracy? Instead, when a venture is bankrolled by the government, the administrator releases some staff and plays host to nearby university researchers to foster public agreement that new directions are being explored, while his private and sometimes despairing belief is that blind alleys are being reentered and the child is but a springboard for expending funds and liberating staff from pressing responsibilities, which completes the education not of the child but of a graduate student edging toward a Ph.D. We need a research study comparing the number of Ph.D.'s granted per government dollar with the number of Negro children favorably affected.

American automobile manufacturers are successful in designing for early obsolescence only because Americans cannot repair their own cars. But when educational institutions like Teachers College put out annual educational technology that supersedes last year's obsolescent model, the "experimentation" reflects fewer revolutionary insights than the latest re-patching job on parental inadequacy—because Harlem schools, administrators and teachers do a better job than Harlem parents, as a rule. Because teachers refuse to teach in Harlem schools for the same reason that Negroes strive to leave Harlem, new educational panaceas emerge. (7)

However, even the skilled automobile mechanic cannot stretch out the life of an automobile, and planned obsolescence ultimately triumphs. But educational fads, not as deliberately planned for obsolescence, emerge from irresponsibility rather than conspiracy. Things haven't changed because Negro family structure hasn't. Daniel Moynihan's Labor Department report said nothing that school administrators haven't known for decades.

We turn briefly to another crossfire in which the administrator is caught—teacher aides—where the assault is from teachers rather than from community. A teacher aide is an adult, lacking any special training, but hired by the school to help the teacher in clerical work, record-keeping, and message running—jobs which take up at least 25 per cent of the average teacher's time and are the most abrading parts of teaching—and, presumably, a person the teacher should find highly desirable to have around.

Not so. Teachers are suspicious. Teacher aides have lower salaries. Teachers suspect that this will depress their salaries. Teacher aides are in the classroom with the teacher. Teachers suspect that they may displace them in the classroom, like the camel that finally dislodged the Arab from the tent. Teacher aides, say teacher organizations, are only a bargain counter way of avoiding hiring additional teachers.

So the administrator who has been given a budget for hiring teacher aides avoids trouble by simply not doing so.

Can you blame him?

The Administrator as Explorer and Risk-taker

The negation of distrust in students, teachers, and parents is promised through management philosophies of "feedback" or "bottoms-up management," where the administrator keeps his eyes and ears on community and staff needs, which is not eavesdropping. He seeks out teachers, parents, and pupils, because they will never come to him, and explores with them what the school can do. He must even visit classrooms, despite the demoralization in teachers who see him looming over the horizon, because he wants teachers to get the feel of him, to gain the knack of being at ease with him, as should students and those student leaders who set style and opinion. Beyond the school walls, he must know the important community jobs needing doing on which staff and students can collaborate or take responsibility. In all this, he should be prepared for Potemkin villages set up for him but should accept these and keep coming back, letting principal, supervisor, teacher, and student know he is coming back; Potemkin villages are only effective with once-over-lightly inspections and cannot withstand long-term study, because they crumble. When staff and students sense the administrator as an accustomed part of the school scenery who listens and looks more than he talks, information of value will start coming his way, and he will be backed up by a staff not composed of toadies or bootlickers but one willing to take risks.

Operating under conditions of risk and speculative investment of energy is the mental hygiene teachers need most. Virtually everybody accepts risk as a part of day-to-day living. In business risks are taken on the possibility of gain, but the teacher is not in business. He is on tenure and the administrator must teach him to do what is unusual for teachers to do, to operate "on spec" in the hope of eventually desirable outcomes. Investments contracted beyond the call of duty and beyond tenure requirements would not be putting money on the line, as people in business do, but hope, faith, imagination, and spare time, precisely as professionals and artists do.

What else is tenure for? Tenure can mean a soul-deadening rut, or it can mean that your flanks are protected against nagging financial cares, allowing you to act professionally.

Thus very few educational programs come at bargain rates, and the administrator should show that though education comes high, it inevitably brings a high return on the investment. He must not skimp on his budgeting when he scales the redoubts where money lies hidden, putting his hands on all he can, else he fails in his executive responsibilities.

The Education of the Administrator

If the education of administrators must be practical about local and state school legislation and other aspects of the status quo, it should also break new ground and prepare the aspiring administrator for pioneering work, else the program will be preparing bureaucrats. In opening new educational directions, the administrator will be inviting debate, defense, attack, combat, and will be leading with his chin; so the chin must be up and fortified with knowledge.

His education should include curriculum development, educational experimentation, and evaluation. It must differentiate between elementary and secondary school levels, giving attention to the organization of subject matter over grades, time allotments per grade, and modifications in time allotments for gifted children, slow children, and children with special cultural and sociological backgrounds. His course should cover as well such theoretical concepts as "broad fields," the "strands" principle of articulation, and the cyclical organization of content materials. Furthermore, training in secondary school organization will deal with the comprehensive high school, the vocational and technical high school, the specialty school, with prescribed and elective subjects, and relationships with junior college and college.

Preparation will also include critical studies of current practices, as in the inauguration of foreign language study on the elementary school level, or the forced expulsion of the classics from the secondary school level. This will introduce the candidate to evaluation and statistical analysis for the making of adequate policy decisions. The relationship of supervision to scholarship is tenuous on the elementary school level, but becomes important on the secondary school level, requiring separation by subject area for greater depth.

Executive training programs in industry have shown how useful the resources of clinical psychology are in harmonious business relationships, so the training of administrators cannot slight these techniques. Whether in industry or in education the proper accommodation of person-to-task and person-to-person is the essence of able administrative practice, but the variety of such accommodations is almost infinite, thereby requiring an openness of mind and flexibility that precludes going by the book. However, the very techniques that the administrator cannot slight are treated in the books that the flexible administrator cannot go by. Is this a paradox? Only insofar as the education of the administrator omits the cultivation of judgment. Once included, the paradox vanishes.

Thus, to use a specific reference, the administrator should ultimately come to see that most educational programs of merit will work—provided that the teacher has merit. A small class in the hands of an inferior teacher is an improved opportunity for the teacher to loaf. Conversely, large classes with good teachers can become chaos but less probably so than small classes with inferior teachers. Thus inferior teachers are more expensive than small class size; the biggest economy in the administrator's budget is the good teacher, not the large class.

The Philosophy of Administration

A philosopher may sneer at the "philosophy" of administration, but we need a word for the theoretical and ideological that make implementation more than hit-or-miss, and to avoid executive ukase in the study of human relations, the improvement of teaching-learning situations, pupil classification, administrative routines, the providing of books and supplies, the management of the school office, the handling of school funds, the caring of the school plant, and executive operations. Why should we want a "philosophy" about such mundane matters? How can philosophy reconcile itself with the clerical and the routine? Our sneering philosopher may reject the sanctification of administrative privilege under the guise of a "philosophy of administration," but he will quickly grant that philosophy must deal with the mundane and the routine, and hence with administrative relationships.

Furthermore, a sense of the philosophic underpinning of things is helpful to a scientist, a clergyman, an artist, or a school teacher. An example occurs in an old French film on education, *Passion For Life,* in which a school-made communication reaches the community. Should this be permitted? Should the faculty advisor of school publications actively place these in local stores, beauty parlors, doctors' waiting rooms, the public library, laundromats, and saloons? Is this a philosophic question? In part no, because the publication's advertising revenue is involved, a business matter chiefly. But should the non-advertising public also receive copies of the publication? Here values begin to seep in to the discussion, dealing with the solipsistic versus the exocentric in education, individual versus the community, and philosophy enters, as it should.

Philosophy encourages us to ask questions, a technique that the administrator must learn if he is not to become the bureaucrat. For example, the administrator is told that *de facto* segregation is bad for Negroes. Comes the question: Is it so? Northern *de facto* segregation is precisely what has given the Negro his political power, his morale, and his gains. Negro Harlem must learn that *de facto* segregation can become Negro community integration, the necessary precursor to tradition, privilege, and equality on all levels. We sing no hymns to disbarment or exclusion, but we may well question if *de facto* segregation, provided that it encourages an integrated community, prevents Negro improvement. Harlem has parks, is close to water, has convenient transportation, and handsome *fin de siècle* architecture, but must become more concerned with bringing the outside in than with breaking out. That's how barriers crumble. (8)

Philosophy not only questions but also appraises:

When educational reporters, parents, teacher organizations, state administrators, and imported consultants agree on what is wrong with education but also on the remedies, one can safely bet that their reports and recommendations will be extensively repeated by subsequent reports, recommendations, and committees, before they are implemented. One should suspect reports that report on matters that have been extensively reported on, like the New York Schinnerer and Crewsom reports, now lost under dust. (9) We repeat reports and the reports repeat, when we know enough, know exactly what we need, and how to get where we want to go. When for half a decade we have known that college students have been eager and available for tutorial duties in Negro areas, we have failed to use this resource for summer and after-school coaching, because teacher salary levels and status were involved. (10)

If philosophy is a guide to judgment and value, it is also a guide to decision and actions. The administrator must be a practicing philosopher.

Part Three

Prospects

16

Adult Education, Automation, and Leisure

The Danger of Knowing Too Much

We arrive at adult education, automation, and retraining, inescapable considerations in urban education. Industrial relations, the dropout, and the adult pushout are related to leisure time and self-image, to urban-and-adult education, to the vocational aspirations of minorities, and to the retirement plans of the aged. (1)

Man does not take kindly to his own discoveries. Fire burns him, tools mash his fingers, and wheels run him down. So he distrusts technology and men who urge it on him except for those historical intervals when education sets in and he accepts the intentions of other men and the possibilities in technology, which, neither in its attainment nor its retention, has been easy for men.

This pattern may be repeating itself in the age of automation when man begins to learn more about himself as he learns more of the world around him, where a technology of psychology develops parallel to the technology of objects, and where we find man more resistant to manipulation than the objects and forces that he so readily manipulates. Thereby automation becomes a source of heat, resistance, charge, and counter-charge.

Automation and Adult Education

Automation is not only involved with engineering problems, but with sociological, philosophical, linguistic, psychological, and esthetic considerations. A statistical correlation exists between language ability and the ability to solve problems using a data processor. If so, the student of English and literature is as likely a candidate for the automated office as is the engineer. It is not news that the special type of philosopher called a symbolic logician is on the I.B.M. payroll. Computers have already involved the musician and the classics student. They are the portal to a cross-disciplinary approach in human relations, psychology, history, ancient and modern languages.

When society embraces communication theory as applied to technology, but neglects to do so when it is applied to people—and it applies just as much to people—it puts its head in a noose and kicks the barrel. Thus automation has too often been envisaged as a means of displacing, or replacing, labor. On the contrary, labor is *emplaced* in a new dignity, elevated as men, as workers, as consumers, and as citizens. Prior to this emplacement is education. Subsequent to it are new horizons for the human use of leisure. (2)

This leads us to adult education: Men contribute to society by the work they do but also by the men they are, by the way they raise their families, appreciate art, improve their bodies, participate in citizenship and community activities, practice the piano, play bridge, read books, and profit both themselves and society by their leisure time activities. We must train our citizens, whether city workers or redundant farmers, beyond modern technological productivity to the non-productive leisure that prevents a man from going crazy or slightly silly, which happens without training in what to do with your time when it's all yours.

Hence programs for adult education must be as involved in new directions of taste as in the maintenance of old patterns of taste. More than half the products now on supermarket shelves were not there a decade ago, because manufacturers change taste in their very efforts to maintain their share in the taste market. The academic variant is publish-or-perish, or up-or-out.

Therefore programs of adult education must not only give

people what they want *now,* but must also encourage taste change so that they seek the new and untried. (3) To gain meaningful employment when the work week is going down and work requires more training than ever before, and to establish a driving, purposeful, constructive leisure as the capstone of civilized endeavors, we must train for discontent. Else we achieve a castrated society where Negroes will not vote despite their new civil rights, will not educate themselves as much as they might, and will acquiesce in the government's buying their comfort through poverty programs or special privileges.

Whether manifested as lowered college admissions standards, diluted job requirements, or eased production loads, a new servitude arises which is as deadening as the old was deadly. The Negro who wants special privileges will get them because he is entitled to them, if he insists. But as many Negroes will continue to be worthless as Italians, Jews, Irish, or WASPs, so the Negro's main job is to keep the number of worthless Negroes at that irreducible human minimum by resolutely rejecting any special privileges either for the top rank of Negroes or for the bottom. The top can take care of itself, which is why it is on top; the bottom must be explored, encouraged, and taught to move.

Let us therefore be grateful to our enemies. If we listen closely to them, they will tell us where we are vulnerable. We could manage for a long time, perhaps forever, were our enemies not promising our deprived populations advantages that we are withholding. Thus international affairs set the stage for domestic civil rights. Much of our education is a response to external pressure from our enemies, as are our travel regulations; and governments prescribe education, as they do travel regulations, because individuals are undependable. How can we strengthen the individual and thereby strengthen society? How can our programs in adult education take as their major responsibility not loyalty to government or party, but integrity of self, because no society can be stronger than its best members?

Please Pass the Bucks

We need no longer ask where the money will come from, because it has arrived, after having been appropriated. We need not be concerned about the bureaucracy (otherwise known as "experts") that will disburse the money. It is ready, willing, and able to do so, and get its own cut in the process. Of course, different bureaucracies will be trampling one another to be at the bottleneck of disbursements. But that need not concern us as long as bookkeeping procedures keep a fair percentage allocated to bureaucratic operations and the remainder funneled toward the appropriate recipients.

Things have reversed themselves. If we no longer need ask where the money for adult and urban education will come from, nor have concern about the bureaucracy with the expertise to spend the money because various bureaucracies are zeroing in on it, we must wonder about the good sense of the programs we are developing, like Head Start, Job Corps, Anti-Poverty, and various tutoring programs. Education does not come easily. Labor may not necessarily take advantage of the opportunities for upgrading and professionalization that will be available. Retraining can be laborious and the labor force may not feel itself equal to the task since this is accompanied by the need to study, to assume new responsibilities, and to undergo the discipline of mastering new skills. Who needs it, especially when the Guaranteed Annual Wage may soon be legislated?

Fortunately, we have all the evidence we require that men don't want handouts. The evidence has been accumulating ever since the thirties. Instead, we can be more constructively concerned about programs that promise human improvement; for example, with the maximum contribution that Negroes can make, not with comparisons between Negro and White maximums. Our major question is: Can Negroes be improved? The answer is an unmistakable affirmative, even with the Garrett statistics on the genetic inferiority of Negroes. A second question is: Can this improvement be significant? Again the evidence is affirmative. A third question is: Is the improvement, significant as it is, worth the financial investment? The affirmative is more resounding than before, here affecting not only Negro life but the life of non-Negroes too.

It has taken us a long time to get the money. Now let's be sagacious about the programs on which we spend it.

In their two major directions, retraining and education for leisure, adult education programs are organizing a curriculum for maturity that not only encourages growth but staves off death, or attrition certainly. Despite these promises, candidates will not enroll in this curriculum unless they are hopeful and have morale. Nobody in a state of despair or self-mistrust will be likely to be found in programs of adult education. Hence, if we are to be sagacious, we must take prior steps in our programs to encourage hopefulness and morale.

Even if our programs extend equal opportunity to all, are our candidates equally able to handle the programs? To answer, we must first be assured that we have a far larger reservoir of able candidates than we have heretofore assumed.

Looking the Gifted Horse in the Mouth

Who are the gifted?

How many people should attend college or other post-secondary institutions? The answer to this question is, ideally, all who have the capacity and the desire to benefit from postsecondary instruction of any kind. Otherwise human resources are wasted and consequences develop for both the individual and the society which are costly beyond measure. . . . The proportion of a population that has the ability and desire to benefit from postsecondary education cannot be determined precisely. . . . One widely acknowledged meas-ure is the conclusion reached by the President's Commission on Higher Education in 1947 . . . that . . . at least 49 percent of our population had the ability to complete two years of post high school general and vocational studies and 32 percent were capable of completing an advanced liberal or specialized professional education. (4)

The Regents Scholarship Examinations . . . establish an even higher potentiality. . . . (5)

Hence approximately one-third of the population is gifted enough to complete college work and about 10 per cent can do so with distinction, given suitable conditions. From this latter popula-tion come our best lawyers and our ambulance chasers, our best physicians and our fee-splitters, as well as those judges who pay for their seats on the bench, and college presidents who jockey and lobby with legislators. Which means that intellectual endowment is not always associated with probity.

Nor is classroom intellectuality associated with good behavior. Our usual assumption is that the slow student is the major source of misbehavior and that the bright are not a disciplinary problem. Beware the bright student when he is displeased! The bright can plan infractions better than the slow. The riots of college students in Havana, Mexico City, and Paris have been as violent as any in Watts. In brief, the number of those bright enough to complete college work may be greater than we suppose, and the capacity for mischief in them may also be. Inability to recognize this is a major cause of revolutions.

Hence, the first thing in educating everybody as if everybody were gifted is to keep the gifted and the ungifted in school as long as we can. Indeed, a strong case can be made for keeping the ungifted in school longer, because the gifted are presumed able to learn by themselves, not needing formal educational auspices. However, we will avoid that issue in order to avoid an argument and only maintain that a greater degree of social awareness in our citizens that guarantees social stability is gained by extending the years in school for the ungifted.

The gifted are required to work hard, to study for examinations, and to pass examinations. Working hard should also be required of the ungifted, even if the areas of work are different. The non-gifted are as capable of working hard at learning as the gifted, even if they cannot learn hard work, because working hard is not the same as hard work. By the latter we mean difficulty in material, like the abstruse in mathematics, science, poetry, or art. By the former we mean assiduity, effort, and application. We tend to confuse working hard with hard work. Indeed, by seeing that working hard is equally possible for the gifted and the ungifted we go far in opening up further areas of hard work for the non-gifted.

Santayana says somewhere that the proportion of the gifted among us has steadily decreased because they have killed off one another, like the Roman patrician class and its intra-mural murderousness. But we have more scientists alive today than ever existed in the total of recorded history and the last 200 years have offered more *visible* examples of giftedness than the entire history of man before that. Western European and American civilization have set the stage for giftedness to emerge. The gifted were there all the time, but social arrangements did not permit them to appear. American education allows more gifted to get a college education than ever before, and more boobs too, but in getting an education the boobs become less of a social drag and the gifted become more of a social stimulus. Social stability requires that the boobs and the gifted become educated up to their capacity. However, greater government involvement in education may be followed by control of the individual; it can be used either to enmesh the individual or to liberate him. The responsible citizen must become increasingly expert in bending social pressures to his individual intention. Indeed, the more he does so, the more we assure social stability, by teaching the individual the ways of slipping, sliding, and ducking organized governmental intentions (as in the ways of *legally* reducing income tax, postponing or avoiding army induction, arranging corporate policy, or slick lobbying), and the more we posit our behavior on recognized institutional ground rules, thereby not only sanctioning them but also sanctifying them. Thus, we live more by rules but, in addition, are aware of the loopholes in them. Do we then become pharisaical, in outward piety and inner duplicity? Only if we hold others to an interpretation of the rules, from which we exempt ourselves. However, a society where everybody knows the rules, knows the loopholes, and is equally adept in dealing with both is an aware society and a stable one.

Educational and policy consequences follow. First, we must make individuals aware. Second, we must organize education on the assumption that every member of society is gifted, not in the same way or direction, but in some *individual* manner. In short, we want all our citizens to do as politicians do in seeking office, as educational administrators do in seeking promotions, as scientists do in seeking grants to the advantage of their own institutions and to the disadvantage of rival institutions, or as the Strategic Air Command does to NASA in trying to remain in business. This, note, is a partial roster of our gifted, and demonstrates the training we must extend to Negroes, Indians, Puerto-Ricans, Appalachian whites, and Mexican-Americans, wherein we strengthen the rules by behaving elastically with them and strengthen the social system by our own flexibility. Naturally, this makes for some additional competition for the heretofore restricted gifted from those now being prepared to move into the jockeying. But the more jockeys, the better human society. In struggling for such equality, minorities are stating that they too are gifted and must be given the education the gifted get.

This is not cynicism. Anybody so construing it lacks a sense of reality. Instead, it is a sober assessment of the patterns of aspiration in people.

The Dimensions of Adult Education

If, therefore, people are improvable, both to a significant degree and at reasonable economic investment, and if, furthermore, we are surrounded by a greater reservoir of the gifted than we have ever suspected, the consequences to adult education are extensive and require that we revise our expectations of people. We can demand more of domestics and of executives, of clerks and of truck drivers, and insist on responsibilities they may have been reluctant to assume before. They, in turn, can justifiably insist on more status, salary, and privileges.

Our revised expectations must be accompanied by educational programs on all levels. We cannot merely offer adult education courses, but must accompany these with rewards and penalties, so that a busboy who takes a course in French cooking, or a bookkeeper who takes a course in input-output economics, or an executive who takes a college-sponsored exemption examination in political science is fulfilling a requirement that is reflected in more money and improved position. This, in turn, implies a prior agreement and closeness of liaison between adult education programs and local employers. Implied also is the responsibility on adult education programs to set appropriate standards of performance in these courses, so that the status, salary, and privileges that accrue are legitimately earned.

Such programs state that the door of educational opportunity will never close on you, no matter how old you are, or how many chances you have wasted. Every commencement period offers stories of a grandparent who returned to school and gained a baccalaureate, but these exceptional academic late-bloomers have an internalized reward system that must be externally institutionalized and regularized for the vastly greater number of adults who may be too shy, or wonder what's in it for them.

Adult education programs exist for one simple reason—adults reach maturity without being educated. Curiously, education is compulsory for the young, who cannot judge its importance, but is optional for the adult, who can better admit its significance and thereby submit to it. Note that we make education compulsory for some adults, like teachers who cannot get tenure or salary increments without courses, or college faculty, who cannot get promoted without a Ph.D. Similarly, physicians interested in a diplomate pursue post-doctoral study, bar associations present lectures to interested attorneys, and engineering societies offer facilities for further professional work to their members. In the same way, General Motors offers special courses for auto mechanics, many large corporations pay tuition costs for their employes who seek additional training, and trade unions sponsor educational programs for dropouts.

We therefore have precedents for regularizing the promotional channels for busboys, truck drivers, bookkeepers, and executives. What hampers the extension of these precedents is not merely ignorance or indifference but the absence of systematized reward-penalty arrangements which inform men of possibilities, how they can be planned for, and the price they pay for not planning. If a planning—though perhaps not planned—society like ours faces an ever-increasing shortage of skilled hands, then we need not worry about a shortage of opportunity for the men who have improved their skills in one or another program of adult education. We can deliver on our reward-penalty promise. We can hold out the alternative of opportunity or self-stultification. We are, of course, in the first stage of making adult education compulsory too.

But adult education goes beyond the vocational dimension: It also involves the leisure time dimension. Unlike other kinds of time, leisure time runs backward, or at least stands still. That's what leisure is intended to do, to keep us in the moment. Do we need training in this—in learning to play duplicate bridge, or tie a fishing fly, or appreciate art—not to be the better amateurs, but the better to be amateurs?

Next, leisure time must be an integral aspect of work time, else we forfeit civilization and become a producing society, not a productive society. A productive society, concerned with the morale of its citizens and their properly used leisure (not idle) time, contributes powerfully to morale. If self-image interacts with morale, then self-image is less an individual matter than we have supposed, but reflects the people around us, their lives, the work they do, and the way they play, so that self-image involves the social. When society arranges for leisure, leisure, like self-image, also becomes a social matter. Indeed, it is society's major organized attempt at psychotherapy, though it goes by other names.

However, training for properly used leisure cannot be accompanied by the systematized reward-penalty pattern of occupational re-training; society's interventions have no place in it, except when invited. Leisure means personal time, time the individual has for himself, time he decides about privately without society's advice. At the same time society must surreptitiously provide for any decision he may chance to make by furnishing golf courses, national parks, dancing classes, classes in home maintenance and interior decoration, or lessons in oil painting or folk guitar, in settings as varied as Yellowstone or the local high school.

A difficulty arises here. If society must be surreptitious about the leisure facilities it provides to avoid any appearance of compulsion, and if the leisure time of the individual is his personal concern, how do we effect a marriage when the parties of the first and second part are so remote? We now turn to the appropriate marriage broker between the public and the private.

The Special Functions
of the Adult Education Teacher

Unlike other teachers, the adult education teacher, whether involved in occupational re-training or in education for leisure time, must be a salesman, a demonstrator, and a practitioner, all in order to solicit and retain registration in the classes he teaches:

1. He must enthusiastically sell the value of his skill. If he doesn't, he will see his registration vanish. He must persuade the adults he faces that the material he is teaching is meaningful to their lives *now,* not at some future date. Their acquisition of his skill has immediate outcomes.

2. Unlike the elementary, secondary, or college faculty member, he can demonstrate what he teaches, whether a golf stroke,

the wiring of a house, or the preparation of *canard à l'orange*. He can show you not merely how to do it, but how *he* does it.

3. He must know the areas of applicability of the skill he is teaching, in the job market or in new showings at art galleries, and what is going on that calls the skill into play, to show that like-minded adults somewhere are also pursuing the skill, perhaps in groups, perhaps individually, perhaps many, perhaps few.

The adult education teacher faces a tougher situation than any other teacher. His preparation builds upon his accumulation of experience, unlike other kinds of teaching, where the candidate is prepared to encounter experience as yet unknown. The danger is that the adult education teacher will believe that his experience suffices. It will not. He too must undergo preparation.

Not only must he review the ways in which he accumulated experience, the difficulties he found in attaining his present mastery, and the comparative ease that accompanied other aspects of skill-attainment, but he must also tailor such a process of review to the variety of students he has. His students will have one thing only in common—they are of mature years. But if he, for example, is teaching auto mechanics, he will find job-changers, amateur hot-rodders, grease monkeys, and wealthy vintage car fanciers in his classes. Some will know physics, chemistry, and the principles of gasoline combustion. Others will be barely literate. Some will be able to read the shop manual on their own. For others it will have to be translated word by word. Audio-visual aids will make some impatient because they are too elementary, but they will be indispensable for others.

The adult education teacher will also find himself involved in public relations, which in the case of re-training is hard sell and in education for leisure is soft sell. Programs for re-training can threaten, while programs for leisure can be gentle and persuasive, but both must come forward, present themselves conspicuously in the community, and mostly so in the community that is urban and depressed. Adult education, because it is not compulsory, needs press agentry for that vast population that has yet to hear of it.

And the adult education teacher is its best press agent. He, however, must not only be convinced that extensive publics exist for the skills he sells, but he must also know where these publics are. Urban life makes them readily visible, through, for example, membership lists in groups and associations or mailing lists.

Whatever the program, teachers and administrators involved in adult education must be responsible for reaching these target audiences—through store-front placards, radio announcements, direct mailing, or word of mouth.

Having reached them, adult education must dissociate itself from the more formal educational programs which promote, expel, test, and demand a minimum level of performance within a term or year. Adult education has no timetable. No one ever flunks out. A "student" can repeat a course, or take it in one semester, or two, or three, or try a course for which he lacks certain requirements, and otherwise adjust his performance to his needs. The building porter and the clubwoman may spend varying times in a course on parliamentary procedures. The porter may seek an official's post in his union local, and the clubwoman may be studying how to oust a rival faction, so that the vocational and avocational may be encountered in the same setting, leading us to believe that two classes may be simultaneously under way, having separate curriculums, though meeting at the same time and place.

In an America more characterized by optimism than by the tragic sense, adult education tells us that the curtain never goes down short of death, and that mental vision, values, and even income are more improvable the older one gets. It flatters us that we are more steady and purposeful than we were when young and foolish, that we still can keep ahead of the young whippersnappers who were in diapers when we were already grown up, and that we not only know a thing or two but can also learn a thing or two. That adult education course has withdrawn the one foot in the grave.

17

Toward Educare—Total Education for Urban Minorities

Everybody is a member of at least one minority group—whether gifted, aged, wealthy, Jewish, Negro, Italian, Catholic, Mayflower descendant, Daughter of the American Revolution, or Mississippian—so that a majority of us are in the minority at some time or other. But if, according to George Orwell, some people are more equal than others, so some minorities are more minority than other minorities, meaning that they are more deprived than others. American society has in the last generation agreed to do something about it.

One of the great benefits of Medicare was not that it made the old young again, but that it freed them from psychological cares as well as financial ones. Educare will not make Americans Periclean Greeks—because not even the Periclean Greeks were Periclean Greeks—but will allow them to participate in society and in themselves, especially those minority Americans who need to learn how.

America has an unsavory record of vicious dealings with deprived minorities, like the Cherokee Indians, the Irish of 1846–1848, Jews, Nisei Japanese, Chinese, and Mexican-Americans, but one of the central intentions in American thinking today is to end this Balkanization and to do so through education.

Education can proceed in two ways, with accompanying awareness that one is being educated, or with accompanying unawareness, like a chicken on one of our mammoth poultry ranches that is consuming less feed and producing more eggs without knowing how it does so. Many members of our deprived minorities are not too certain about the advisability of getting an education, and we had better not frighten them off. They want their children out of school at the earliest possible age, earning a living, because they need the money now; deprived minorities must make the very best of things as they find them. And they have done so.

If we don't believe it, we need only go to the places where Americans of Italian, Greek, Polish, or Mexican-American ancestry reside. They reside together and reward one another by a common idiom. There is enough money these days for most of them to be able to eat and drink. Things on the whole aren't bad, nor have they been bad for almost a generation now. Even if they overpay on financing, they drive cars. Though deprived, they are not depressed. Discontent with economics, without being at the vanishing point, is at an all-time low. The significance for education is that we had better begin with the deprived minority where we find it and not let it suspect that we are trying to improve it. If we want to do something about the minority son, we must start where his daddy is.

But neither daddy nor the minority is homogeneous. We must therefore split up our plans for educational aspiration, remembering that the son of an Italian storekeeper is more readily inclined toward the law or accounting, the son of an Italian plumber toward civil engineering or architecture, and the daughter of a Negro domestic toward nursing, and if the sons or daughters cross us up and instead select medicine or teaching, we'll settle. Similarly, Mexican-American daddies are varied and may be farmhands, store clerks, or restaurant workers, which tells us that the probabilities are that we can more convincingly talk about schools of agriculture in the first example, a school of business in the second, and food chemistry in the third, always remembering that we must be prepared to back away from the probabilities when the educational horizons of the child broaden beyond the limits set by the work daddy does.

Nevertheless, we must be specific and work within specific

traditions. Thus, though he speaks Spanish, and has Latin-American antecedents, the Cuban refugee does not have the same background as the Puerto-Rican, and both have backgrounds that are different from the Mexican-American's. Simultaneously, the children of all three groups are torn between older family values and newer American ones. And the newer American values are not homogeneous either, as we will be told by the Mexican-American living in Albuquerque, the Cuban in Miami, or the Puerto-Rican in New York.

Furthermore, we shall have to be specific about educational aspirations associated with sex. With some minority groups, a girl attaining a college degree or professional status is endangering her marriage prospects within the minority group because she has been educated beyond the level of most young men in the group; such a girl is risking spinsterhood or else must seek marriage outside the community. Thus many Italian parents are proud that a daughter is a teacher and are simultaneously troubled that this status automatically reduces her viability for matrimony.

However, the picture is rapidly changing. The rate at which our urban minorities are accepting the importance of education reflects an impressive public relations job done by the schools, government officials, and industry. We cannot say as much for trade unions which, as Abraham Raskin has pointed out, (1) have done little for worker education in the last decade.

If willingness for education is increasing among all deprived minority groups, is minority group aptitude equal to attitude? Significantly, the minority begins to believe so. It has spokesmen from its own stock in Congress and in state legislatures, it has radio programs beamed at it, it has a press. Unfortunately, education has not used these resources as effectively as it might.

Clear examples are Hamtramck Poles, Boston Irish, or the Scotch-Irish whites throughout Appalachia, groups with leaders of the same ethnic stock who have often opposed the schools but within the last decade have seen that the position of a leader is limited by the attainments of his followers. In consequence, these leaders have now become strong supporters of federal programs of education.

This education must occur across a broad base, if the leader is to have broad power. As it does so, other issues arise, like providing textbooks for parochial schools or road-building for the purposes of attracting industry, versus school-building. On the whole, however, leakage of educational funds will not be to enemies of education, or to contenders for government moneys (like defense or industry), but to the sources of seepage within education itself, like educational officials on the make.

Here lies the greatest danger to the education of urban minorities—the tendency in educational leadership to see total education as homogenized education, and curriculum as a uniform regimen to be dosed out as prescribed in some educational pharmacopeia. Total education means a differentiated curriculum, varied by region, by family perspectives, by social class, by aspirations, and by ethnic derivation. The Appalachian whites described by James Agee (2) cannot be educated with the same materials that are given to a San Antonio Mexican-American. The weather is different, as are landscapes, race relations, patterns of prayer, notions of honor, and the availability of supermarkets and filling stations. All these affect curriculum. Even within the same city, curriculum must be varied by neighborhood. Thus Negroes in Harlem, with a higher proportion of New York-born, send more children to college than do Negroes in Brooklyn's Bedford-Stuyvesant, where a greater proportion have more recently come from the South. Negroes in Harlem are more likely to be middle-class than are Negroes in Bedford-Stuyvesant.

If total education means a differentiated curriculum, then the tasks of urban administrators and teachers become increasingly complex, because these divergences must have approximately similar goals lest the curriculum become a new instrument for discrimination. Simultaneously, then, the school must keep an eye on where the child has come from and where it intends the child to go. The school must be able to determine its own curriculum and at the same time satisfy educational authorities that learning is not being sacrificed or diluted.

Few—very few—school administrators and teachers are capable of this task, which is why homogenized education substitutes for total education. Indeed, the alternative of turning the job of curriculum development over to community and neighborhood leaders will land us in no less frustrating a *cul de sac* because their guidelines are even fewer and more likely to be affected by personal predilection.

Our only feasible approach is to have administrators and

teachers who are as much at home in the community as they are in the school. But this means that community leaders do not dominate or browbeat school personnel. As a beginning, total education requires a total acceptance by community leaders of the professional competence of administrators and teachers, provided that they have been competently trained at college and have been appropriately licensed or certified by the state or city. Given this beginning, community and diversified curriculum can make a start at such specialized interaction where particularized educational programs resonate to particularized characteristics of the pupils.

We shall then find that origins, whatever they are, can lead to the outcomes we wish. We can teach arithmetic by supermarket prices, reading by the Sears Roebuck catalog, geography by auto maps, spelling and multiplication by sing-song, foreign language by folk music. We can lead the child inexorably to the emotional liberation that comes with learning gains, where the child discovers that algebra, French, American history, and Shakespeare are not alien to his life—that's where we want our heretofore particularized San Antonio Mexican-American and Appalachian white. We have a variety of routes to get children there, all untraveled and with stand-pattism too often astride the routes.

When a Calvin Gross, a Benjamin Willis, and a Francis Keppel assume and leave office, the arrival and departure reflect politics more than education and the politics are usually dirty. Some community, local or national, has substituted for a total acceptance of educational personnel a hit-or-miss allegiance to other educational personnel. This isn't total rejection any more than it is totalitarian rejection. It is merely unprincipled educational behavior, though it may be customary political behavior. It is certainly inconsistent with a total educational commitment.

At the moment, neither our schools nor our communities seem ready for anything else.

Diversification via Data

This doleful dead end has had witnesses studying it for years now. The behavior of teachers, administrators, and community leaders has been evaluated by political scientists, historians, sociologists, psychologists, social workers, reading experts, economists, curriculum specialists, anthropologists, and statisticians. Research has accumulated on the subjects of this scrutiny, with findings that come as close to science as investigation dealing with human beings ever can. Bluntly, we have evidence, as much as we need, to nullify the inability of teachers, the caution of administrators, and the self-seeking of politicians.

In the first place, virtually every minority has been described and numbered. We know the minority's places of concentration, its average level of education, its religious inclinations, its newspapers, and its values.

Second, teachers and administrators have similarly been put under the microscope and we know, in many instances, more about them than they know about themselves. We know the salaries they earn, how they spend their vacations, how often they marry, what their children do, and how they behave in their classrooms.

Last, community leadership is no enigma to those who have extensively studied and published on it, so that evidence is ample on community power structure and community lines of command.

In nullifying such inability, caution, and self-seeking, we must bring the results of research to bear on our urban minorities, but, even more, we must bring the researchers into the urban classroom and community. If the level of teacher ability stops at instruction and cannot rise to the use of the tools of inquiry, we must compensate for this inadequacy by bringing in the experts in inquiry and their talents. We cannot undertake the total education of the urban community only by teachers, administrators, and community leaders because they lack sometimes the power and sometimes the good sense.

Not that the results of behavioral and social research are in agreement and offer unerring road markers. But the conclusions are less contradictory than complementary. When behavioral and social research comes out various ways, the most frequent reason is that more variables, not accounted for before, have been revealed. Our understanding in these areas has become more subtle, not more baffled, by the differences in answers; they warn us that unsuspected distinctions are appearing, that our knowledge is becoming more sophisticated.

No program of urban education can work if it is not accompanied by teams of researchers, partly in order to assess but even more to expose teacher, administrator, and community leader to the results they get when they too see the area of their activities as an opportunity to find out. Thereby teaching is not merely instruction but also inquiry; administration not only formulates policy but also assesses the ways it is arrived at; and community leadership becomes more knowledgeable about paths of control.

Desirable as these are, they must be policed by those especially trained in searching out the community's patterns of marriage, burial, birth, earning a living, settling disputes, as well as the number of television sets and indoor toilets, the source and level of income, its sense of social distance from other communities, its health and psychological problems, its modes of savings and insurance.

We cannot do a community a greater favor than to let it know it is being studied. Whether reaction to them is favorable or unfavorable, whether construed as busybodies meddling where they are not wanted or as scholars bringing in welcome light, the researchers help a community become more self-aware, more mindful of causes affecting situations that are accidental rather than pre-ordained, or necessarily so simply because they are so. Research allows a community to become more flexible and more objective about itself.

Research diversifies according to discipline, giving us the specialization that tells the community that more goes on in it than it ever knew. Inescapably, the teacher, the administrator, and the community leader find themselves in a stronger position, because only this kind of outsider can do the job they can never possibly do for themselves. Luckily and in most cases the outsider is not that much an outsider. He comes from not-too-distant college campuses. His funds frequently come from the same source that is supporting the community's Head Start, Anti-Poverty, JOIN, or other program, and he often accompanies these funds as watchdog or as beneficiary.

Most of all, he brings with him the values of the experimental as contrasted with the tried-and-true. The experimental in human affairs has numerous enemies, like Goldwater Republicans, John Birchers, and southern Democrats, who are sincerely and honestly devoted to the tried-and-true even with all the face-lifting necessary to keep it tried-and-working. Always, into the tried comes a time finally when it is far riskier than the experimental and hence without any truth at all, when social experimentation offers fewer perils than social stasis. The experimental is more aware of social stability because it must also provide for controls, else it cannot prove its case, which should be reassuring to anybody who doesn't mistake change for revolution.

Experimentation is our civilization's greatest contribution to craftsmanship. Its methods have worked for us on the moon, in the laboratory, in the marketplace, in health and in disease. We cannot educate without it. The nuts on the left who confuse it with the fashionable are like the nuts on the right who confuse the past with the tested and the true with the tried.

Appendix

CHAPTER **1.** **Urban Education and Rural Reclamation**

1. In a comparison of eight American municipalities, Richard E. Engle Jr.'s *The Challenge of Diversity* (N.Y.: Harper and Row, 1964) considers how cities can be simultaneously diverse and similar. Some further sources on comparisons are these: An outstanding psychologist, Edward Thorndike, turned student of urban affairs in *Your City* (N.Y.: Harcourt, Brace, 1939). See, too, John L. Fava, *The Feasibility of Inter-City Comparisons* (N.Y.: Citizens' Budget Commission, 1963); and Howard G. Schaller, ed., *Public Expenditure Decisions in the Urban Community* (Washington, D.C.: Resources For the Future, 1963), especially pp. 180–198. The two major sources for all such comparisons are *Statistical Abstracts of The United States* and the *County and City Data Book,* both available from the U.S. Government Printing Office, Washington, D.C.

Notice how inter-city variations affect education: "Expenditures for public education vary greatly within city-size groups and within the same region. In general, however, it appears that expenditures per pupil are highest in the larger cities and in the North Atlantic region, and that they are lowest in the smaller cities and in the Southeast." So says the U.S. Department of Health, Education and Welfare in *Statistical Summary of Education,* 1957–1958 (Washington, D.C.: Government Printing Office, 1958), chap. 1, p. 27. For a reflection of this in teacher income, see Research Division, National Education

Association, *Classroom Teacher Salary Schedules, 1963–64 Systems Having 3,000 or More Pupils* (Washington, D.C., November, 1963). This is a regularly issued report.

Also, in the remainder of this chapter, we shall consider the relationships of agriculture and the city. Most of the material in Chapter 1 dealing with these relationships finds its origins in Theodore W. Schultz, *Transforming Traditional Agriculture* (New Haven, Conn.: Yale University Press, 1964).

2. Cities are simultaneously loved and loathed in such books as Lewis Mumford, *The City in History* (N.Y.: Harcourt, Brace & World, 1961). For photo-editorials on cities, see V.S. Pritchett, *London Perceived*, 1962, and *New York Proclaimed*, 1965 (N.Y.: Harcourt, Brace & World). The same publisher has done Mary McCarthy, *The Stones of Florence*, 1959, from which we are quoting.

In greater depth, Dallas is put into the scales in Warren Leslie, *Dallas Public and Private* (N.Y.: Avon Books, 1964), to show how it is differentiable from Houston. This particularly notable—and to some, notorious—American city is also dealt with in Coral Estes Thometz, *The Decision Makers: The Power Structure of Dallas* (University Park, Tex.: Southern Methodist University Press, 1963).

The James Bond approach to cities is offered in the late Ian Fleming's *Thrilling Cities* (N.Y.: New American Library, 1964), a development of the knock-on-the-door-and-say-Jake-sent-me approach in the Lee Mortimer catalogs of the underworld in city living.

However, though inter-city differences exist, so do intra-city differences, which is precisely what we mean by neighborhoods. Some of these neighborhood differences are dealt with by Dorothea C. Leighton, John S. Harding, David B. Machlin, Allister M. Macmillan, and Alexander H. Leighton in *The Character of Danger* (N.Y.: Basic Books, 1963). These are reflected in psychiatric symptoms and differences in different communities.

3. For the attractions of cities, see Robert E. Dickinson, *The West European City* (London: Routledge and Kegan Paul, 1963), and other excellent and relevant titles in this publisher's International Library of Sociology and Social Reconstruction. Discussing cities as a modern care and concern are Blake McKelvey, *The Urbanization of America, 1860–1915* (New Brunswick, N.J.: Rutgers University Press, 1962); Leonard J. Duhl, ed., *The Urban Condition* (N.Y.: Basic Books, 1963); Lewis Mumford, *The Highway and The City* (N.Y.: Harcourt, Brace & World, 1963); Mitchell Gordon, *Sick Cities: Psychology and Pathology of American Urban Life* (N.Y.: Macmillan, 1963). As an example, Wolf Schneider in *Babylon Is Everywhere* (N.Y.: McGraw-Hill, 1963) discusses the history of cities, how they

developed, the ways they are culture-bound, and how technology has affected them.

4. On self-stereotyping by ethnic groups: "Although the Irish have produced men of letters and learning since the Dark Ages, and innumerable good teachers, neither the American Irish in their picture of themselves nor the popular folklore about the Irish gives much place to them as people who are important for what they do with their minds," says William Vincent Shannon in *The American Irish* (N.Y.: Macmillan, 1963), p. 397. Similar to the Irish self-stereotyping reported by Shannon is the pioneer and classical work by W. I. Thomas and Florian Znaniecki, *The Polish Peasant in Europe and America* (Boston: Badger, 1960). Like the Irish in America, the Pole in America has also limited himself by his self-stereotyping.

On the laggards in old urban populations:

(*a*) Small storekeepers impede housing improvement for one excellent reason: housing improvement impedes small storekeepers. In 1961, for example, a total of 1,528 commercial tenants in New York City had to be "relocated," which in many cases was a euphemism for putting them out of business. See Martin Arnold, "Relocation Plagues Merchants Forced Out by Urban Renewal," *The New York Times*, March 5, 1962, p. 1.

(*b*) Banks also cause lag. Charles Abrams, the well-known housing expert, describes how interest rates for low-income neighborhoods reflect caution rather than a true sense of enterprise in "Minorities, Homogeneity, and 'Values'," in *The City Is the Frontier* (N.Y.: Harper and Row, 1965). This despite what Dr. Paul S. Nadler points out—that this lack of initiative becomes an aggressive search for customer-borrowers in other areas: "The banks have ample funds available. The Federal Reserve has not tightened credit the way it did in the boom of the late 1950's, while the inflow of time deposit money continues strong. Thus the banks have had good reason to intensify their efforts at expanding loan volume . . . it has been aggressive bank efforts rather than strong demand for credit that has helped bank loan volume to rise. . . . the cause of increased holdings of home loans has been bank aggressiveness in interesting home builders and potential home buyers in taking out loans rather than a strong demand for the money the banks have available." This quotation is from his "High Loans-to-Deposit Ratios No Key to Higher Loan Rates," *American Banker*, August 12, 1964, p. 4.

(*c*) Professor Malcolm P. McNair of Harvard points out how businessmen contribute to lag in *Dynamic Retailing in the Modern Economy* (N.Y.: National Dry Goods Association, 1960). This is an excerpt from a talk to department store owners: " . . . a downtown association does not require an expensive organizational set-up. It will require aggressive leadership on the part of businessmen themselves who will face downtown problems realistically and spearhead any campaigns which may be necessary for raising funds. It must be remembered that improvements do cost money, even though they may be considered investments in the prosperity of the downtown area. . . . The biggest problem of all is getting action on the things most cities already know should be done. . . . But it must be done if we are to retain the character and prestige of our cities. Let us remember that no city can be better than its downtown area."

(*d*) Nor is labor innocent. How new building materials which are available for use in urban renewal are impeded by the building trades unions is described by John Lear in "Bricks Without Straw Bosses," *Saturday Review*, February 1, 1964, p. 45. Also A. H. Raskin in "The Obsolescent Unions," *Commentary*, July 1963, p. 18, states: "Labor has no more urgent job in the 60's than the focusing of its political energies on the conquest of want, illiteracy, intolerance; the building up of both health and decent housing; the realization of the limitless promise of the scientific age. And apart from their general social necessity, these undertakings would be vastly more inspiriting to union membership and leadership alike, than the present . . . policing of day-to-day plant grievances and the writing of mechanized contracts. Labor thus far has only one basic answer for joblessness, a shorter work week—and this at a time when two-fifths of our own people are classed as living below minimum standards of decency and want is endemic in most parts of the world. This is a policy of despair. Until we at least make a stab at abundance, we should not settle for a policy of sharing the misery. What is needed from labor is a degree of independent leadership that will give vitality to the concept of direct political action for jobs and an expanding economy."

(*e*) What our urban laggards ought to be told: "The major statistical finding . . . is that . . . the entry of nonwhites into previously all-white neighborhoods was much more often associated with price improvement or stability than with price weakening." Luigi Laurenti, *Property Values and Race* (Berkeley, Calif.: University of California Press, 1960).

5. *Rocco and His Brothers* is an Italian film about family breakup in the urbanization process, with some members responding positively to urban living while others are destroyed. Another Italian film, *The Sound of Trumpets*, offers a deglamorized and dehumanized picture of an industrial training program. A third, *Mafioso*, illuminates some relationships between the Sicilian Church, American gangster murders, and North Italian industrialism, and how international crime rings imitate the methods of legitimate international cartels.

A highly readable account of Italian education in the fifties is Joseph Justman's *The Italian People and Their Schools*, International Education Monographs, No. 1 (Tiffin, Ohio: Kappa Delta Pi, 1958).

6. For material in English on the Italian social and economic scene, see Irving R. Levine, *Main Street, Italy*, (N.Y.: Doubleday, 1963); Luigi Barzini, *The Italians* (N.Y.: Bantam Books, 1965); Carlo Bazan, "Sicily's Industrial Development—Today and Tomorrow," Address to the Italian Chamber of Commerce in Sweden, November 25, 1963, Mimeographed. See also Commercial Office of the Italian Embassy, *Italy: An Economic Profile* (Washington, D.C., 1962), which points out that in 1954, 32.4% of all Italian workers were in industry, while in 1962 over 40.3% were; that in 1954, 39.3% were employed in agriculture, but in 1962 only 27.8% were; that in 1954, 28.3% of Italian workers were in services, while in 1962, 31.9% were—proving that Italy is taking its place in the industrial revolution of the twentieth century.

7. Professor Stefano Somogyi of Florence points out ("Variations in the Italian Population in the Decade 1951–1961," *Economic Conditions in Italy*, Banco di Roma, p. 291) that the flow of capital has not staunched the outward flow of labor: "We do not wish to enter upon a controversy concerning the non-materialization of the results that a large-scale policy of intervention should have achieved, but it seems strange, to say the least, that huge investments like those of an extraordinary nature made by the *Cassa per il Mezzogiorno* (which in no way reduced normal Government expenditures in this area), instead of promoting a large-scale employment of manpower, should have allowed steady streams of workers (and their families) to flow to other parts of Italy and—what is more definitely a negative factor— also across the frontiers and above all to overseas countries where emigration nearly always leads to permanent demographic loss." However, Professor Somogyi reflects northern skepticism about investment in the South, like Harvard scientists who are dubious about the installation of linear accelerators at the University of Texas. One might speculate that although human beings continued to flow out of the *mezzogiorno* when capital flowed in, more might have departed without that inflow.

8. For the reader of Italian, a journalist's account of the population shifts in Italy is given in Mino Monicelli's "I Profughi Del Miracolo," *Il Progresso Italo-Americano*, New York, July 19, 1964, p. 3.

9. For a quick view of the cityward push in Latin America, see "Cities: The Migrating Masses," *Time*, February 7, 1964, p. 41.

10. A comparison of British slum children and public school children is offered in B. M. Spinley, *The Deprived and The Privileged:*

Personality Development in English Society (London: Routledge and Kegan Paul, 1953). The tremendous differences in working-class and upper-class values are documented in British films like *Saturday Night and Sunday Morning, Sapphire, The L-Shaped Room,* and *Room at the Top.* But these go back to the plays of Galsworthy, like *Strife* and *Loyalties,* and to the plays of Shaw; class differences are not a new thing to the British stage.

When the Sir Milner Howard report on housing was presented, James Feron, in a dispatch captioned "Report Assails London Housing: Terms Citywide Planning Vital," wrote in *The New York Times* of March 12, 1965, ". . . More than half a million households, one out of every five in the Greater London area, were still without baths. Fewer than half the households had the private use of hot and cold water, bath, toilet, sink, and stove."

Class distinctions also affect language and thought processes throughout British society. The quotation from Alex Campbell occurs in a *New Republic* review, May 2, 1964, p. 21, in a discussion of these books dealing with England: Arthur Koestler, ed., *Suicide of a Nation?* (N.Y. Macmillan, 1964); John Mander, *Great Britain or Little England* (Boston: Houghton Mifflin, 1964); Randolph S. Churchill, *The Fight for the Tory Leadership* (Boston: Houghton Mifflin, 1964); Ronald Blythe, *The Age of Illusion* (Boston: Houghton Mifflin, 1964); Rupert Wilkinson, *Gentlemanly Power: British Leadership and the Public School Tradition* (London: Oxford University Press, 1964).

Basil Bernstein offers some psychological confirmation of the language outcomes of social class differences in "Linguistic Codes, Hesitation Phenomena, and Intelligence," *Language and Speech,* 5 (1962), 31–46.

11. As to the conversion of ugly ducklings to swans, see W. D. Furneaux, *The Chosen Few: An Examination of Some Aspects of University Selection in Britain* (London: Oxford University Press, 1961). Also Harry A. Ree, "New Universities in England: Seven in the Sixties," *Saturday Review,* August 17, 1963, p. 35, discusses the new student body at the red-brick universities that have emerged in the last generation.

12. Of course, the brain drain is additional evidence of the better time made by ducks when airborne. Sidney Gruson, in "Loss of British Scientists to U.S. Brings Laborite Call for a Study," *The New York Times,* February 11, 1964, describes the departure of Dr. Ian Bush from England for an American post. A nasty comparison emerges: after having received schooling and training in his native land, is the departing scientist similar to the bank teller who embezzles bank funds entrusted to him and decamps with a blonde and a Cadillac?

13. The comparison of Russian and Minnesotan winters comes from Wright W. Miller, *Russians Are People* (N.Y.: Dutton, 1961).

14. Decentralization is not necessarily democratic. When Paul Goodman in *People or Personnel* (N.Y.: Random House, 1965) recommends decentralized schooling, he forgets how the local school board has barbarized American education. Educational control at the local level sounds fine, but also means control at the lowest levels too, and at the most provincial. On the other hand, French standards, centralized as they are and stringent, can be so selective as to be cruel.

For a good clear look at the French farmer, see Edward Higbee's "The French Paysan Is Angry," *The New York Times Magazine*, October 27, 1963. Also see Higbee's *Farms and Farmers in an Urban Age* (N.Y.: Twentieth Century Fund, 1963). P. Lamartine Yates in his *Food, Land, and Manpower in Western Europe* (N.Y.: Macmillan, 1960), p. 115, suggests that the cure for French farming is more industry: "If ways could be found for establishing some industry in parts of the country hitherto unindustrialized, and without loss of economic efficiency, this would be, after regrouping of plots, the biggest contribution possible to the progress of French farming." It might well pay British, German, Belgian, and Dutch industry to subsidize this recommendation, so that the Common Market might survive!

Henry Giniger assesses the absorption, education, and urbanization of almost 1 million *pieds noirs* into French life and employment in "Algerian Aftermath," *The New York Times Magazine*, March 22, 1964, p. 32. But Giniger took the other educational extreme in "French College Students Begin Drive for Salary," in an earlier article in *The New York Times*, February 20, 1965, p. 7. Also on the *présalaire* and French university reform, see P. E. Schneider "300,000 French Students Can't Be Wrong," *The New York Times Magazine*, February 9, 1964, p. 16.

The French may be smug about many things but they are as disenchanted with their educational system as we are told we should be, says Jean Farrar in "Onze million de mal-traités: Nos Enfants," *Paris Match*, September 23, 1963. Similarly, Victor K. McElheny discusses the monolithic structure and academic dictatorship in French faculties of science in "Jacques Monod: Further Comments on French Universities," *Science*, 150 (December 24, 1965), 1701. Covering another aspect of the same story, McElheny describes French assertiveness in science and technology in "Is French Scientific Policy Chauvinist?" *Science*, 149 (September 10, 1965), 1216.

More optimistically, James Brian Quinn says: "France has the most formalized structure for national planning in the Western world, and many countries expect her to lead in developing useful new concepts and techniques for integrating science and technology into national plans. . . . The French planning process provides a formal mechanism for presenting and weighing the views of all competing interests. Hence it militates against unwise decisions which might draw unwarranted technical support or investment into certain politically popular fields despite overwhelming costs to other more important sectors." James Brian Quinn, "National Planning of Science and Technology in France," *Science,* 150 (November 19, 1965), 993. Quinn adds: "The universities are extremely proud of their emphasis on research which lacks pragmatic orientation and long resisted even establishing departments of applied science. . . . Professors are discouraged from acting as consultants to industry. . . . Publication, not application, has been the goal of university research." See the remainder of the article (too long for extensive quotation here) on how French science and technology are coming to grips with these problems by bridging the gaps between science and technology.

15. Classrooms in the country for the entire family and the pathways by which the urban family can return to nature are described by the United States Forest Service in *Back Packing in the National Wilderness* (Washington, D.C.: Publications Service, U.S. Department of Agriculture, 1965).

William G. Weart, in *The New York Times* for September 1, 1963, "New Harvest for Farmers: Conversion of Property into Recreation Sites Proving Profitable," writes: "Motorists on the move through rural America this summer have discovered a hinterland renaissance. Something different is going on down on the farm, and it has nothing to do with milking the cows, planting the corn or pruning the orchard.

"Under the stress of agricultural overproduction, and with a big boost from Uncle Sam many farmers are finding it more profitable to cater to the city slicker's need for leisure-time recreation than to his stomach. They have, in short, converted all or part of their farm acreage into golf courses, hunting preserves, tennis courts, modern swimming pools or parkland. . . .

"The farmer's entry into the field of recreation was sparked by simple mathematics and some common sense. Under the Food and Agricultural Act of 1962, farmers can borrow up to $60,000 for the conversion of all or part of their land into recreational facilities. Many farmers have taken advantage of this opportunity.

"A study made by the Agriculture Department shows that at least one income-producing enterprise was established by 9,918 landowners during the 1963 fiscal year ended June 30. This was done in cooperation with the regional offices of the department's Soil Conservation Service. An additional 9,075 landowners said they intended to establish recreation facilities.

"The Agriculture Department found also that 945 landowners switched from livestock, dairy, crop, fruit and similar activities to recreational enterprises as a primary source of income. This involved 237,691 acres. . . ."

16. The Czarist-Leninist tradition in Russian science has always limited individual initiative, says Alexander Korol in *Soviet Research and Development* (Cambridge, Mass.: M.I.T. Press, 1965). Of course, Russian science has not been hobbled as much as Soviet agriculture, which is why Soviet science is so advanced and Soviet agriculture is backward.

Even worse than their *idées fixes*, compulsive gamblers are unable to profit by experience, says Ronald A. Roston in *American Psychologist*, 20 (July 1965), 548. Thus David Joravsky describes how "scientific" agricultural technology has stymied Soviet farm production in "The Lysenko Affair," *Scientific American*, 207 (November 1962), 41: "It remains to be seen whether or not a government preaching communism and the collective spirit can manage farmers and scientists as efficiently as governments preaching free enterprise and individualism."

17. The quotation from Gilbert Highet is in his *Poets in a Landscape* (N.Y.: Pelican Books, 1959), p. 208.

18. Of the three references on Appalachia below, two are over a generation old. How slowly we move! The most recent is Harry M. Caudill, *Night Comes to the Cumberlands* (Boston: Little, Brown, 1963). He was preceded by E. J. Asher in "The Inadequacy of Current Intelligence Tests for Testing Kentucky Mountain Children," *Ped. Sem. and Journal of Genetic Psychology*, 46 (1935), 480–86; and Claudia Lewis, *Children of the Cumberland* (N.Y.: Columbia University Press, 1946).

For a very recent discussion on the sliding I.Q. of the children of Appalachia, see Robert Coles, "What Migrant Farm Children Learn," *Saturday Review*, May 15, 1965, p. 73.

19. How the schoolhouse gang puts its fingers in the public till is considered in an editorial, "Is South Carolina ETV a Worthy Model?" *Phi Delta Kappa*, October, 1963, where the political nepotism and the political gravy train in educational television are analyzed, in another instance of how educational budgets can be raided, or milked, for political payoffs.

20. We have several items on Appalachia that deal with geographical-social-psychological mobility:

(*a*) John Walsh in *Science*, 141 (September 6, 1963), 889.

"Development of the Appalachian area, however, is now getting more serious attention than it ever has before.

"John F. Kennedy seems to have been lastingly disturbed by what he saw in 1960 as he campaigned in the hills of West Virginia, a state which gave him a crucial primary victory.

"In Congress, Representative Carl D. Perkins (D.-Ky.), whose district includes the northeastern tier of the coal counties of the plateau, has been working with what he feels is increasing effectiveness for a major resource and economic development program for the Appalachian Highlands area.

"Perkins's bill provides for the formation of an Appalachian Highlands Commission composed of federal agencies and representatives appointed by the governors of the 11 states in the region. This commission would formulate plans for the development of the area, and Perkins hopes that an interstate compact would be eventually formed by the Appalachian states to facilitate development. The development plan would include flood-prevention and flood-control measures and a whole range of industrial and community development, conservation, and public health programs."

(*b*) Homer Bigart in *The New York Times,* November 19, 1963.

"Harry M. Caudill, Whitesburg lawyer, and author of 'Night Comes to the Cumberlands,' warned that the resentment of the people might explode in another winter of violence.

" 'When miners sit around on cold winter nights with nothing to do but meditate on their futility, trouble develops,' he said. 'Last winter this region was brought to the verge of anarchy. . . . The same legislators who have for fifteen years voted untold billions of dollars for the relief of oil and banana dictators around the world suffer qualms of caution when called upon to assist fellow citizens who have been reduced to poverty and whose land for more than a century has been systematically looted for the enrichment of the rest of America.' "

(*c*) Jack E. Weller describes family-stasis and how family feeling can paralyze in "Is There a Future for Yesterday's People?" *Saturday Review,* October 16, 1965, p. 33. Of course, natives of Appalachia who leave for the big city may do worse, when they lack training or experience in big city living, than if they had stayed home. Willingness to be mobile is not enough; it must be accompanied by skills that allow you to earn a living. See Richard Martin's "City 'Hillbillies': Appalachian Migrants in Slums Fail to Benefit from Antipoverty Drive," *Wall Street Journal,* September 30, 1965, p. 1. For the sociology of this problem, in which security on the job means more than better possibilities elsewhere, and job equity is valued above opportunity, see

Gladys L. Palmer, Herbert S. Parnes, Richard C. Wilcock, Mary W. Herman, and Carol P. Brainerd, *The Reluctant Job Changer: Studies in Work Attachments and Aspirations* (Philadelphia: University of Pennsylvania Press, 1962).

These other materials deal generally with the exodus from the farms and the consequences to the migrants: D. E. Hathaway, "Migration from Farms and Its Meaning," *Monthly Labor Review*, 83 (February 1960), 136; M. F. Baer, "America on the Move," *Personnel and Guidance Journal*, 37 (February 1959), 408–9; G. W. Johnson, "Denizens of Rural Slums," *New Republic*, May 23, 1960, p. 14; C. Karraker, "Task for a Peace Corps," *Christian Century*, February 20, 1963, p. 237; see also "When Whites Migrate from the South," *U.S. News and World Report*, October 14, 1963, p. 70.

(*d*) For additional aspects of the roadbuilding porkbarrel in Appalachia, see Harry M. Caudill, "Misdeal in Appalachia," *Atlantic*, June 1965, p. 43, which shows how the rich get richer by means of anti-poverty programs.

21. The text reference is to this dispatch in *The New York Times*, from Lagos, Nigeria, September 2, 1962, "Gulf Unit Helping To Train Nigerians." The text:

"The Nigerian Gulf Oil Company, a subsidiary of the Gulf Oil Corporation of the United States, presented today a check for £64,371 ($180,238.89) to the Federal Minister of Mines and Power, Alhaji Yusuff Maitama Sulf.

"The check was the first installment of the £321,855 ($901,184) that the company was making available to the Nigerian Government over the next five years for the training of Nigerian nationals.

"Accepting the check, the Minister disclosed that the Government would use the money to establish an institute for petroleum studies at the University of Lagos and to award scholarships for scientific and geological studies.

"Gulf is one of the foreign companies prospecting for oil in Nigeria. The fund was set up by the company last year to help the Government expand and improve the rapid availability of skilled Nigerians in the engineering, scientific, medical, and administrative fields."

Why Gulf Oil and other American corporations should reevaluate their grants programs is indicated by Luther J. Carter in "Education: U.S. Institutions Prepare African Students for Development Tasks at Home," *Science*, 149 (September 10, 1965), 1213. The qualitative improvement, over the years, of African students studying abroad is indisputable. American corporations in Africa that offer promotional opportunities for African students returning home after study abroad are finding that these students are getting better all the time. This, naturally, means that the courses of study should get more demanding.

22. The symbolic relations between money-flow, power-flow, and authority-flow are treated by Hugh Dalziel Duncan in *Communication and Social Order* (Totowa, N.J.: Bedminster Press, 1961).

23. Let's distinguish between adult education and urban education. Urban education is not big city education only. If urban populations are defined (as in the 1960 census) as those living in places of 2,500 or more, then Manhasset, Grosse Pointe, Shaker Heights, etc., also offer urban education and are involved in it, though their adult education programs may vary from those offered in the metropolis.

24. Michael Harrington in *The Other America* has brought home to us that we have greater reservoirs of poverty and subsistence living than we suspect. See also Bernard D. Nossiter's *The Mythmakers* (Boston: Houghton Mifflin, 1964) for an effective answer to the dog-in-the-manger economics of those who interpret expansion as inflation, especially his chapter 6, "The Split-Level Society."

What is a city? Is it the metropolis? Is it the metropolis plus suburbs? Is it the politically defined unit or the economically interdependent unit?

The Bureau of the Census has attempted to clarify definitions here. Thus the Standard Consolidated Area of New York and northeastern New Jersey (or the New York contribution to megalopolis) has a population of almost 15 million, or twice as many as the political unit called New York City (which decreased 1.4% for the 1950–1960 period, dropping from 7,891,957 to 7,781,984). In contrast, the population of the Standard Consolidated Area increased 14.3% for 1950–1960; its non-white population is 11.0%. Similarly, the megalopolis of Chicago-Northwestern Indiana has a population of 6,800,-000, an increase of 21.6% for 1950–1960; its non-white population is 14.8%.

See *The Municipal Year Book* (Chicago: International City Manager's Association, issued annually), for other indications that the suburban white population has grown at a faster rate than the inner-city non-white population has. The flight to the suburbs is at a greater flood than the move to the inner city.

CHAPTER 2. **Family Structure and Education**

1. Family relations are complex beyond parent-child relationships and include sibling relationships, father–mother relationships, in–law relationships, and numerous others, all of which color and con-

tribute to emotion and behavior. For a review of the research on these relationships see Gerald Handel, "Psychological Study of Whole Families," *Psychological Bulletin* (January 1965). On the other hand, George H. Frank doubts that family structure contributes significantly to behavioral problems and disorders, or to psychopathology, in "The Role of the Family in the Development of Psychopathology," *Psychological Bulletin* (September 1965).

2. Urban education unavoidably deals with minorities. If one can speak of a major minority, then our major minority problem is not with Miami Cubans, El Paso Mexicans, Detroit Poles, San Francisco Orientals, or New York Jews, Irish, and Italians, but with native-born, presumably English-speaking Negroes, who by now comprise over 25 per cent of the population in Chicago, Philadelphia, Cleveland, Detroit, Newark and elsewhere. For a highly readable sociological analysis of New York's minorities, see Nathan Glazer and Daniel Patrick Moynihan, *Beyond the Melting Pot* (Cambridge, Mass.: M.I.T. Press and Harvard University Press, 1963). A beautifully handled job.

3. David Riesman, "Observation on Changes in Leisure Attitudes," in *Selected Essays from Individualism Reconsidered* (Garden City, N.Y.: Doubleday Anchor Books, 1954), p. 138.

4. The accusation that white liberals are sunshine patriots is considered by Christopher Jencks in "The Great New York Boycott: What Will Happen If the Cry for Better Schools Fails?" *New Republic*, February 15, 1964, p. 12. Also, in this connection see I. N. Berlin, "Desegregation Creates Problems Too," *Saturday Review*, June 15, 1963, p. 66.

5. The difficulties in getting the poor to lift themselves by the bootstraps you lend them are described by Murray Kempton's article on New York's Mobilization For Youth, "When You Mobilize the Poor," *New Republic*, December 5, 1964, p. 11.

6. R. J. Havighurst and H. Taba, *Adolescent Character and Development* (N.Y.: Wiley, 1949).

7. In "How *Not* to Integrate the Schools," *Harper's*, November 1963, p. 57, Inge Lederer Gibel says that Negro parents want improvement in their own neighborhood schools *before* any premature integration. They want integrated schools, but not at the price of a failure to improve the neighborhood school.

8. Three discussions on the dropout: Thelma Veness, *School Leavers* (N.Y.: Humanities Press, 1962); Daniel Schreiber, Bernard A. Kaplan, and Robert D. Strom, *Dropout Studies: Design and Conduct* (Washington, D.C.: National Education Association, 1963); Daniel Schreiber, "The Dropout and the Delinquent: Promising Practices Gleaned from a Year of Study," *Phi Delta Kappan*, 44 (February

1963), 215. The last item stresses the importance of beginning at kindergarten, or even before, if we are ever to solve this problem.

One of the earliest works on the dropout-delinquent (not that these are the same) was Paul L. Crawford, Daniel I. Malamud, and James R. Dumpson, *Working with Teen Age Gangs* (N.Y.: Welfare Council of New York City, 1950), preceded in turn by Frederic Thrasher's *The Gang* (Chicago: University of Chicago Press, 1963) and William F. Whyte's *Street-Corner Society* (Chicago: University of Chicago Press, 1955).

9. For a curriculum developed for our most difficult adult population, see *Training the Hard-Core Unemployed* (OE–13027, Cooperative Research Monograph 13), Office of Education, U.S. Department of Health, Education, and Welfare (Washington, D.C.: Government Printing Office, 1964).

Considering that this is the *first* report of a *first* effort, we can be more than modestly optimistic about future training possibilities for those adults, sometimes illiterate, who have never had any training at all. Also, such adults with family responsibilities *must be paid for being educated,* unpalatable though some may find the idea.

The home stability that sets the stage for adult retraining is considered by Nathan Glazer's "The Puerto-Ricans," *Commentary,* July 1963, p. 1, in an optimistic picture of the *future* possibilities of Puerto-Ricans in an urban setting. Clear-eyed about the transitional difficulties, it gives evidence of cultural improvement as time goes on. See particularly the reference to the Puerto-Rican self-help organization, *Aspira.* See also Julius Horwitz, *The Inhabitants* (N.Y.: New American Library, 1961), a novel that describes relief and welfare life and the culture that subsists on public assistance.

10. Governmental intervention is continuous on behalf of the privileged but sporadic on behalf of the underprivileged. Philip M. Stern shows how tax laws make the rich richer and the poor taxable in *The Great Treasury Raid* (N.Y.: Random House, 1964).

Such governmental intervention begins to reach across the entire spectrum of intellectuality, from scholarship to mental deficiency: "Mental illness and mental retardation are among our most critical health problems. . . . The time has come for a bold new approach. New medical, scientific, and social tools and insights are now available. . . . This approach relies primarily upon the new knowledge and new drugs acquired and developed in recent years which make it possible for most of the mentally ill to be successfully and quickly treated in their own communities and returned to a useful place in society. These breakthroughs have rendered obsolete the traditional methods of treatment which imposed upon the mentally ill a social quarantine. . . . It will be possible within a decade or two to reduce the number of patients under custodial care by about 50 percent or more. . . ." John F. Kennedy, "A Message from the President of the United States Relative to Mental Illness and Mental Retardation," *American Psychologist*, 18 (June 1963), 280.

11. Ralph Ellison, *Invisible Man* (N.Y.: Random House, 1952).

12. E. Franklin Frazier, *Black Bourgeoisie* (N.Y.: Collier Books, 1962).

13. Important reading: Kenneth B. Clark, *Dark Ghetto* (N.Y.: Harper & Row, 1965). The author originated the basis of HARYOU. Comment on HARYOU's proposal to city, state, and federal government for funds for Harlem education is found in Joseph Michaluk, "Harlem's Social Dynamite—$80 Million to Defuse It," *Sunday Herald Tribune*, February 16, 1964.

There's money in having others be poor, according to *The New York Times* for February 28, 1965, in a dispatch from Paterson, New Jersey: "Kenneth E. Marshall, former program planning director of Haryou in New York, was named director of this city's antipoverty program yesterday. The annual salary will be $18,500, which is $1,800 less than the city's Mayor, Frank X. Graves Jr., is paid. The Mayor has warned officials of the Community Action antipoverty program that he will ask the city's Board of Finance to withhold city funds from the program if the director's salary exceeds his own. . . . Mr. Marshall is completing credits towards his doctorate. . . . He holds a Masters degree . . . from Columbia University's School of Social Work, where he has been an assistant professor for the last three years."

14. Relevant to Negro soft-pedaling talk of Negro family structure is E. P. Thompson's notion of an "opaque society," which furtively hides its plans and feelings from other groups in society. According to Thompson, this was characteristic of the British working class in the Napoleonic period. Until the Chartist movement this conspiratorial incommunicativeness was a reaction to the repressiveness of the British ruling class, which also was an "opaque society," as are the CIA, the Mafia, and the Negro society today. See his *The Making of the English Working Class* (N.Y.: Pantheon Books, 1964).

But this incommunicativeness coexists with attempts to penetrate. Thus on March 13, 1965, an editorial in *The New York Times* commented: "Haryou-Act is the weapon through which the Federal and city governments are trying to change the whole character of Harlem. From its beginning Haryou-Act has operated under the shadow of Representative Adam Clayton Powell, the most powerful man in Harlem. Its organization was long delayed by a battle between supporters of Mr. Powell and those who charged he was seeking to dominate it for his own political purposes." How else do editorial writers expect politicians to behave when they see money coming their way? Let's not be sanctimonious.

15. Robert Graves, *Hercules, My Shipmate* (N.Y.: Grosset and Dunlap, 1945).

16. Abram Kardiner and Lionel Ovesey, *The Mark of Oppression* (Cleveland: Meridian Books, 1962).

17. After the Moynihan Report discussed the Negro father imago, William Ryan retorted sharply in "Savage Discovery: The Moynihan Report," *The Nation*, November 22, 1965, p. 380: ". . . it is important to make public the serious shortcomings of the report that a careful analysis uncovers. Briefly, it draws dangerously inexact conclusions from weak and insufficient data; encourages (no doubt unintentionally) a new form of subtle racism that might be termed 'Savage Discovery,' and seduces the reader into believing that it is not racism and discrimination but the weaknesses and defects of the Negro himself that account for the present status of inequality between Negro and white."

18. In addition to Professor C. Vann Woodward, *The Strange Career of Jim Crow* (Oxford, Eng.: Oxford University Press, 1958), see also John Hope Franklin, *Reconstruction* (Chicago: University of Chicago Press, 1961). Kenneth M. Stampp's "The Tragic Legend of Reconstruction," *Commentary*, January 1965, and his *The Era of Reconstruction, 1863–1877* (N.Y.: Knopf, 1965), discuss how Negro passivity contributed to the sellout of the Reconstruction.

19. For a quick fill-in on the apathy of the American voter, see Richard M. Scammon's "Why One-Third of Us Don't Vote," *The New York Times Magazine*, February 17, 1963.

20. Charles Vanderburgh, a young draftee with the Army of Occupation during the Meredith affair in Mississippi, writes: "A Negro college man told me, 'The NAACP must be out of their minds.' None of the white troops would deny Meredith's right to an education but 'If he has any smarts why doesn't he go to a real school?'" See Mr. Vanderburgh's "A Draftee's Diary from the Mississippi Front," *Harper's*, February 1964, p. 42.

However, let's not give up prematurely on the wandering Negro father, the sluttish Negro mother, or the Negro adult apparently irredeemable and irremediable. David C. McLelland has a bold program of redemption that makes enormous good sense, in which he presents twelve propositions, or steps, that are not only optimistic about the prospects for retraining the Negro adult, but are altogether realistic. See his "Toward a Theory of Motive Acquisition," *American*

Psychologist, 20 (May 1965), 321, for psychological theory at its most pragmatically workable.

Mr. Vanderburgh's piece in *Harper's* can be contrasted with the viewpoint of a University of Mississippi faculty member. See James W. Silver's *Mississippi: The Closed Society* (N.Y.: Harcourt, Brace, 1964); and Russell H. Barrett, *Integration at Ole Miss.* (Chicago: Quadrangle Books, 1965). Professor McLelland's *American Psychologist* article can be seen in the background of the Moynihan Report as given in "New Crisis: The Negro Family," *Newsweek,* August 9, 1965, p. 32.

21. The official name for the Moynihan Report is *The Negro Family—The Case for National Action,* United States Department of Labor, Bureau of Labor Statistics (Washington, D.C.: Government Printing Office, 1965).

22. For two additional statements on the dropout, see Lucius F. Cervantes, *The Dropout: Causes and Cures* (Ann Arbor: University of Michigan Press, 1965); and Burton A. Weisbrod, "Preventing High School Dropouts," in Robert Dorfman, ed., *Measuring Benefits of Government Investments* (Washington, D.C.: Brookings Institution, 1965). Note that Cervantes points out that the dropout comes from the family in which father image is weak, not strong, and where family values are attenuated, not binding. This opinion does not seem borne out by the descriptions in Glazer and Moynihan (note 2) of the Italian family, or by Thomas and Znaniecki of the Polish family (note 4, Chapter 1).

In this connection William R. Morrow and Robert C. Wilson declare that bright high-achievers' parents engage in more sharing of activities, ideas and confidences, and are more approving, affectionate, and encouraging with respect to achievement. See "Family Relations of Bright High-Achieving and Under-Achieving High School Boys," *Child Development,* 32 (September 1961), 501–10.

23. For some further statements on the acquisition of knowledge, carnal and otherwise, in American women, see Margaret Mead and Frances B. Kaplan, *American Women* (N.Y.: Scribner's, 1965).

Of course, there are various types of working mothers, and one cannot too casually generalize about the effects of maternal employment on family structure. See F. Ivay Nye and Lois Wladis Hoffman, *The Employed Mother in America* (N.Y.: Rand McNally, 1963), for a discussion of the various consequences of maternal employment, sometimes bad, sometimes good.

For anthropological background, see Beatrice B. Whiting, *Six Cultures: Studies in Child Rearing* (N.Y.: Wiley, 1963).

24. *Time,* January 24, 1964, p. 54, deals with "Sex in the U.S.:

Mores and Morality," but neglects to say how *Time* itself has contributed to the change in American standards. *Time* doesn't forget what it said the week before; it merely ignores it.

For example, shortly after Sputnik I, a *Life* editorial ("Euphoria and the Scythians," *Life*, December 16, 1957, p. 39), pilloried Americans for their softness, self-indulgence, and love of luxury, but conveniently omitted the contribution *Life* had made to these all-American traits. After reading a call to Spartan belt-tightening and rigor for the greater glory of America and in order to catch up with the Russians, the reader had only to turn the page and find advertising for heavily-chromed automobiles, perfumes, make-up, and all the luxuries and gimcracks of which Americans are fond. If you are harsh, you call it hypocrisy; if gentle, you call it inconsistency; if you enjoy playing fast-and-Luce with language, as *Time-Life* reviewers do, you merely accept it as an attempt to be fashionable and modish, as one must be to bring out a magazine every week. In any case, because it is a leading example of American journalism, *Time-Life* should be in every school library, and by that token pupils must be taught the ways of reading it and assessing what it says, and not accepting what it says.

On family management, birth control, and contraception:

(*a*) In a ringing call for birth control as a preliminary for a better world order, where the Lysistrata theme is heavily played on, see John Fischer's "What Women Can Do for Peace," *Harper's,* April 1963, p. 14. The author states that birth control has been dropped into the laps (or lapse?) of women, and that they can thereby improve the odds for a peaceful world.

(*b*) Because of the increased availability of birth control techniques, world population will soon stop its cataclysmic rise. Even in India birth control is beginning to make inroads into popular opinion and to be favorably received. See J. Mayone Stycos, "The Outlook for World Population," *Science,* 146 (December 11, 1964), 1435. But the drop in birth rate means an increase in extra-marital copulation. Birth control will become available to high school students too, and married folk can also have a succession of sex experiences without worry about engendering successors. What will this do to the stability of the marriage relationship?

(*c*) For a discussion on the differences between "coitus-connected" and "coitus-independent" techniques of contraception and why the latter shows great promise of success in family planning, see Steven Polgar and Alan F. Guttmacher, "A New Chapter in Family Planning," *Columbia University Forum,* Fall 1965, p. 34.

25. Says Sidney H. Schanberg in "Florida Worried by Cuban Influx," *The New York Times,* October 17, 1965: "Since 1960, when

the United States and Cuba severed diplomatic ties, about 180,000 emigres have poured through the Federally operated Cuban Refugee Center in Miami. More than 100,000 are still in Florida, almost all of them in the Miami area. . . . A view generally shared by Florida's government officials is that Cubans displace Negroes when they get here by taking unskilled jobs at pittance wages but that they are an industrious people and often leave these jobs for better ones once they adjust to the new country and the new language. . . . In Tallahassee, the Governor's office, though expressing 'complete support' of the United States open-door policy, is pressing Washington for even firmer assurances on the handling of the new Cubans, including a guarantee of strict Federal controls 'to compel and require their resettlement in cities throughout the United States.' "

26. On the mutual antipathy of minorities:

(*a*) Ruth Glass, *London's Newcomers: The West Indian Migrants* (Cambridge, Mass.: Harvard University Press, 1961), especially in the chapter "Misunderstandings," p. 103, deals with the ways ethnic and racial frictions arise unnecessarily, and through ignorance and indifference, rather than through intention.

(*b*) Elena Padilla's *Up from Puerto Rico* (N.Y.: Columbia University Press, 1958), described the first Puerto Rican postwar impact on New York and how it increased strife among the Harlem minorities and how the incoming Puerto Ricans stratified themselves as they had never been stratified back home.

(*c*) "The stepped-up public and private aid being channeled into the Negro community as a result of the Watts riots has stirred sharp resentment among a much larger minority group in Los Angeles—the Mexican-Americans. . . . Anti-Negro feeling is running so strong among Mexican Americans that some residents and community leaders express fear of renewed rioting. . . . Officials estimate that there are as many as 2.5 million Mexican-Americans in California, or nearly twice the number of Negroes. About half live in the Los Angeles area." Peter Bart, "Negro Gains Vex Coast Mexicans," *The New York Times*, October 17, 1965.

(*d*) In describing the first peril to encounter the immigrant, Robert Ernst says in *Immigrant Life in New York City, 1825–1863* (N.Y.: King's Crown Press, Columbia University, 1949), p. 176: "Irish runners preyed on the Irish, Germans upon the Germans, English upon the English, and Americans upon them all." He continues: ". . . another element of disunity among the immigrants was the surviving provincialism which set natives of the same country against one another. The Irish Corkonians, who rivaled the Leinstermen and the Far Downs, had their counterparts in Germany, where the southern

Germans hated the *Plattdeutschen* from the lowlands of northern Germany" (p. 177).

27. David Rosenhan, of the Educational Testing Service, has found that lower class children (both Negro and white) will respond more to reward than to punishment, while middle class children respond more to disapproval than to approval. See *American Psychologist,* 20 (July 1965), 592.

Education for the disadvantaged has now achieved the desirable stage of its own nomenclature, and is coming to be known as Compensatory Education. For example, see Benjamin Bloom, Allison Davis, and Robert Hess, *Compensatory Education for Cultural Deprivation* (N.Y.: Holt, Rinehart and Winston, 1965), which also includes an excellent annotated bibliography prepared by Susan B. Silverman. A good survey of what is being done in Compensatory Education throughout the country is offered by the American Association of School Administrators and Research Division, National Education Association, 1201 Sixteenth Street N.W., Washington, D.C. 20036. But notice how each city fishes for its own nomenclature, so that in Detroit and Philadelphia we have the Great Cities School Improvement Project, a Madison Area Project in Syracuse, a Banneker Project in St. Louis, a Cardozo Project in Washington, D.C., a Safford Exploratory Program in Tucson, a HOPE program in Pasadena, an Early School Admissions Project in Baltimore, an Operation Counterpoise in Boston, a Lincoln Project in Albuquerque, a Project Springboard in Newburgh, and in New York City a Higher Horizons Project, a More Effective Schools Program, and a College Discovery Program. Such are the strange noises that public relations programs make when education and politics meet.

CHAPTER 3. **Stupidity and Ignorance**

1. The quotation is from C. D. Darlington, "Psychology, Genetics and the Process of History," *British Journal of Psychology* (November 1963), 293.

2. The early age at which Negro children begin to be traumatized by race differences and antagonisms, with the consequences in learning and growth, are presented in Robert Coles, "A Child's Questions," *New Republic,* April 11, 1964, p. 10.

3. The quotation is from Nicholas Hobbs, "Sources of Gain in Psychotherapy," *American Psychologist,* 17 (November 1962), 741.

4. For declarations that Negro children can be traumatized before birth see Phyllis Greenacre, "Pregenital Patterning," *Inter-*

national Journal of Psycho-Analysis, 33 (1952), 410. Also, L. Sonntag, "Difference in Modifiability of Fetal Behavior and Physiology," *Psychosomatic Medicine,* 6 (1944), 151.

5. R. C. Tryon, "Genetic Differences in Maze Learning in Rats," The National Society for the Study of Education, *The Thirty-Ninth Yearbook* (Bloomington, Ill.: Public School Publishing Co., 1940).

Calvin S. Hall, "The Genetics of Behavior," in S. S. Stevens, ed., *Handbook of Experimental Psychology* (N.Y.: Wiley, 1951). Related to this source is R. C. Tryon, "Individual Differences," in F. A. Moss, ed., *Comparative Psychology* (Englewood Cliffs, N.J.: Prentice-Hall, 1942).

6. Jacob W. Getzels and Philip W. Jackson, *Creativity and Intelligence* (New York: Wiley, 1962).

7. Bayard Rustin, "From Protest to Politics," *Commentary,* February 1965, p. 25.

John Holt, on the basis of classroom observations, describes how stupidity aids survival in *How Children Fail* (N.Y.: Pitman, 1964).

8. Frederick S. Hulse, *The Human Species* (N.Y.: Random House, 1963), p. 382.

9. Vilhjalmur Stefansson, *Great Adventures and Explorations* (N.Y.: Dial Press, 1952).

10. Jerry Hirsch has discussed the modifiability of inherited behavior and the interaction between heredity and environment in his "Behavior Genetics and Individuality Understood," in *Science,* 142 (December 13, 1963), 1436, where he considers how heredity is also modifiable, given the right environment. The question then arises: How do you define "environment"?

11. Jurgen Ruesch and Gregory Bateson, *Communication: The Social Matrix of Psychiatry* (N.Y.: W. W. Norton, 1951).

12. The dissipation of school learning in after-school forgetting is treated under various aspects in:

(*a*) Seymour B. Sarason, Kenneth S. Davidson, Frederick K. Lighthall, Richard R. Waite, and Britton K. Ruebush, *Anxiety in Elementary School Children* (N.Y.: Wiley, 1960), who consider how anxiety interferes with performance and the ways of re-routing anxiety for improvement in learning.

(*b*) H. J. Eysenck in "The Measurement of Motivation," *Scientific American,* 208 (May 1963), 130, declares: ". . . under suitable conditions reminiscence can be used as a measure of drive," a statement of some importance if we are to see why students fail to recall what they have learned, why poor readers persevere in poor reading even after having been given reading instruction, so that even longer rest periods between instruction may be required.

(*c*) Benton J. Underwood, "Forgetting," *Scientific American,* 210 (March 1964), 91, for further substantiation of Ebbinghaus on the role of interference in forgetting, and how competing experiences cause loss of retention.

(*d*) Robert B. Zajonc, "Social Facilitation," *Science,* 149 (July 16, 1965), 269 for a discussion on crowded slum living, learning, performance, and behavior.

13. Lawrence P. Shehan, "Reaching Slow Learners," *The English Journal,* 51 (January 1962), 44.

14. The merits and drawbacks of intelligence testing, the public's concern with mass testing, and the status of mass testing are discussed in a series of articles in *American Psychologist,* 20 (February 1965).

More important, evidence that the poor can be engineered into social change, and that McClelland's motivational patterns for incentive development (David C. McClelland, *The Achieving Society* [Princeton, N.J.: Van Nostrand, 1961]) are applicable even to a *lumpenproletariat,* is offered in Alexander H. Leighton's "Poverty and Social Change," *Scientific American,* 212 (May 1965), 21. People, no matter how demoralized, can be improved and can learn to sustain improvement in their living conditions.

15. For a statement from a psychologist who thinks that Negroes are genetically inferior see Henry Garrett, "The SPSSI and Racial Differences," *American Psychologist,* 17 (1962), 260–63.

16. N. Weyl and S. Possony in their racist *The Geography of Intellect* (Chicago: Regney, 1963), also claim that Negroes are genetically inferior.

That we inherit cultural genes just as we inherit biologic ones, that we are just as affected by the one as the other, and that neither type of gene is manipulable is stated by John Greenway in *The Inevitable Americans* (N.Y.: Knopf, 1964). The cultural gene concept is an important one, but whoever said that biologic genes were beyond manipulation? They aren't, and neither are cultural genes. Both are responsive to experimentation.

The discussion on the genetic constitution of Negroes will shortly become outdated and a historical curiosity because if Negro genetic constitution is inferior, it can, like inferior Caucasian genetic constitution, be repaired and improved. Very soon, biochemistry will be able to control human evolution, just as sperm banks can *right now.* See discussion on this in the following:

H. J. Muller, *Studies in Genetics: The Selected Papers of H. J. Muller* (Bloomington: Indiana University Press, 1962).

T. M. Sonneborn, ed., *The Control of Human Heredity* (N.Y.: Macmillan, 1965).

P. H. Abelson, editorial, *Science,* 149 (July 16, 1965), 251.

"Letters" section, *Science,* 149 (September 10, 1965), 1171, particularly that signed by Hermann J. Muller.

James F. Crow's book review, "Modifying Man: Muller's Eugenics and Lederberg's Euphrenics," *Science,* 148 (June 18, 1965), 1579.

Gordon Wolstenholme, ed., *Man and His Future* (Boston: Little, Brown, 1963).

Samuel Eiduson, Edward Geller, Arthur Yuwiler, and Bernice T. Eiduson, *Biochemistry and Behavior* (Princeton, N.J.: Van Nostrand, 1964).

17. The quotation is from the Board of Education of the City of New York, *Curriculum and Materials,* XVIII (Spring 1964), 3.

18. Additional evidence that "biochemistry is coming within target range" is Francis O. Schmitt's "The Physical Basis of Life and Learning," *Science,* 149 (August 27, 1965), 931, in which the concept of protein-protein molecular recognition is presented as the elementary basis of learning and behavior. Can man, by taking thought, add to his knowledge of thought? Inevitably, yes. Schmitt says that the ultimate weapon is not rocketry or the bomb, but the human brain.

One indication of how close biochemistry is coming to solving the problem of intellectual function is seen in Wesley Dingman and Michael B. Sporn, "Molecular Theories of Memory," *Science,* 144 (April 3, 1964), 26, which discusses the alterations in RNA during learning, as the adenine-to-uracil ratio changes, and how yeast RNA seems to improve learning.

See these discoveries against the background described in G. A. Harrison, J. S. Weiner, J. M. Tanner, and N. A. Barnicot, *Human Biology* (London: Oxford University Press, 1964); and Stanley M. Garn, *Human Races* (Springfield, Ill., Thomas, 1965).

19. For the humanist's—not the humanitarian's—revolt against scientific manipulation of human biology, see Joseph Wood Krutch, "Calipers on the Human Mind," *Saturday Review,* June 19, 1965, p. 22. Also Joseph Wood Krutch, "Men, Apes, and Termites," *Saturday Review,* September 21, 1963, p. 22, is another instance of the author's refusal to subject man to measurement in any measure of man, and a re-statement of his anti-Skinnerism. For additional light on the Skinner-Krutch duel refer to David Bakan's "The Mystery-Mastery Complex in Contemporary Psychology," *American Psychologist,* 20 (March 1965), 186.

The Trilling-Barzun-Leavis-Krutch attack against science and its life of reason is logically concluded in Genet's *Thieves Journal* (N.Y.: Grove, 1964) and *Our Lady of the Flowers* (N.Y.: Grove, 1963). What a termination!

20. See, for example, Banesh Hoffman, *The Tyranny of Testing*

(N.Y.: Collier, 1962); Joel Hildebrand, *Is Intelligence Important?* (N.Y.: Macmillan, 1964); Martin Gross, *The Brain Watchers* (N.Y.: Random House, 1962).

21. Joseph Michaluk, "Schools To Drop Group I.Q. Tests," *New York Herald Tribune*, February 7, 1964, says: "Yesterday Dr. Loretan called the existing I.Q. tests 'diabolical instruments. The intelligence test is a status symbol,' he said, in an interview, 'that has no relation to the facts. It does not measure innate abilities, as the community thinks it does.' . . . Dr. Loretan said the new tests would be supplemented by an elaborate program of achievement tests." And he would wind up with the same results!

22. John P. Zubek, G. Welch, M. G. Saunders, "Electroencephalographic Changes During and After 14 Days of Perceptual Deprivation," *Science*, 139 (February 8, 1963), 490.

Benton J. Underwood, "Forgetting," *Scientific American*, 210 (March 1964), 91.

23. Lee J. Cronbach, *Educational Psychology* (N.Y.: Harcourt, Brace and World, 1963).

24. Immanuel Kant, *Critique of Pure Reason*, trans. J. M. D. Meiklejohn (N.Y.: Willey Book Company, 1900), p. 98.

25. Cyril Burt, "Factor Analysis and Its Neurological Basis," *British Journal of Statistical Psychology*, 14 (1961), 53–71.

In the same connection: "As both everyday observation and more precise psychological studies demonstrate, college grades and the measures that best predict them are relatively poor predictors of other kinds of achievement and of later success in most professional fields. Stories of the class dunce who turns out to be the most successful alumnus are at best atypical, but the correlations between intelligence or class standing and later success in science, medicine, law, military life, or any other profession are usually discouragingly close to zero. . . . good predictors of professional accomplishment are stubbornly elusive. . . . It is useful to know how to select students who can earn good grades. It would be more useful to know better how to select those who will be real achievers in a variety of fields." Dael Wolfle, editorial, "The Freshman Class," *Science*, 149 (September 24, 1965), 1453.

Hence, aptitude tests predict aptitude, but do not predict imaginativeness or creative power. Thus high scholastic aptitude may predict who gets a Ph.D., but not who will make an important scientific, intellectual, or artistic contribution. See Henry Chauncey and Thomas L. Hilton, "Are Aptitude Tests Valid for the Highly Able?" *Science*, 148 (June 4, 1965), 1297.

26. Jacob W. Getzels and Philip W. Jackson, *Creativity and Intelligence* (N.Y.: Wiley, 1962).

27. Arthur Bestor, *The Restoration of Learning* (N.Y.: Knopf, 1955).

28. Frank Riessman, *The Culturally Deprived Child* (N.Y.: Harper & Row, 1962).

29. L. Susan Stebbing, *Thinking to Some Purpose* (N.Y.: Penguin Books, 1948).

30. William M. McCord and Nicholas J. Demerath III, "Negro Versus White Intelligence: A Continuing Controversy," *Harvard Educational Review,* 28 (Spring 1958), 120.

31. The quotation is from Margaret Mead, *New Lives for Old* (N.Y.: William Morrow, 1956), p. 443.

32. Kenneth B. Clark and Mamie P. Clark, "Racial Identification and Preference in Negro Children," Eleanor E. Maccoby, Theodore M. Newcomb, Eugene L. Hartley, eds., in *Readings in Social Psychology* (N.Y.: Holt, Rinehart & Winston, 1958), p. 602.

33. Bernard W. Harleston, "Higher Education for the Negro," *Atlantic,* November 1965, p. 139, for similar programs at Tufts, Oberlin, Princeton, and Dartmouth.

CHAPTER 4. **Militancy and Intelligence**

1. Interesting background for man's aggressiveness is to be found in J. D. Carthy and F. J. Ebling, eds., *The Natural History of Aggression* (N.Y.: Academic Press, 1964), especially in Derek Freeman's chapter dealing with psychoanalytic explanations.

2. In Thorsten Sellin and Marvin E. Wolfgang, *The Measurement of Delinquency* (N.Y.: Wiley, 1964), crimes against persons and things are scaled, equated, measured, added, and matched for degrees of severity, to see on what basis we can determine that some crimes are worse than others, and thereby to determine the appropriate punishment.

3. When a heretofore depressed population is granted civil and political rights, the conflicts that emerge are described by Harold R. Isaacs in "A Reporter at Large: The Ex-Untouchables," *The New Yorker,* December 12, 1964, p. 60 and December 19, 1964, p. 75. Most striking is the decisive importance of education and the level of purposefulness in the heretofore depressed group (in this case the Untouchable caste of India). Educational intentions in the heretofore subordinate society become more decisive than any friendliness or enmity in the superordinate society.

4. Martin Deutsch, "Courage as a Concept in Social Psychology," *Journal of Social Psychology,* 55 (1961), 49–58.

5. The Protestant Ethic, as Max Weber described it, was incon-

sistent with the Principle of Least Effort, as George Zipf described it. Is it more rewarding to work hard or to work little? For an answer, see Michael Lewis, "Psychological Effect of Effort," *Psychological Bulletin*, 64 (September 1965), 183.

6. Fred Powledge, "Who Leads the Negro?" *The New York Times*, January 13, 1964, p. 18, discusses the proliferation of Negro groups, civil rights as a means for gaining upward mobility in leadership, and the jockeying among Negro organizations.

That violence may be the only way out for the Negro is suggested by Lewis Killian and Charles Grigg in *Racial Crisis in America: Leadership in Conflict* (Englewood Cliffs, N.J.: Prentice-Hall, 1964).

7. Black Muslimism's intellectual poverty and intellectual aspiration are described by Clemmont E. Vontress, "The Black Muslim Schools," *Phi Delta Kappan*, 47 (October 1965), 86.

8. Lewis Feuer, *The Scientific Intellectual: The Psychological and Sociological Origins of Modern Science* (N.Y.: Basic Books, 1963).

9. Max I. Dimont, *Jews, God and History* (N.Y.: Simon and Schuster, 1962).

10. Milton Himmelfarb discusses the reasons for the disproportionately large number of Jews in all the left-of-center movements in "How We Are," *Commentary*, January 1965, p 69.

The quote is from Oscar Handlin, *Adventure in Freedom* (N.Y.: McGraw-Hill, 1954), p. 253.

11. Hannah Arendt, *Eichmann in Jerusalem* (N.Y.: Viking, 1963).

12. H. R. Trevor-Roper, "Nazi Bureaucrats and Jewish Leaders," *Commentary*, April 1962, p. 351.

13. Theodore Draper, *The Roots of American Communism* (N.Y.: Viking, 1963).

14. Charles E. Silberman, "The Businessman and the Negro," *Fortune*, September 1963, p. 97.

15. For the pro-Negro and pro-Puerto-Rican *numerus clausus*, see "Hunter College Demonstration School," *The New York Times*, February 5, 1965.

16. On shared childhood experiences: "Our observations sustain the significance of the maternal relation, particularly in facilitating the interaction of the infant with other infants. But at the same time we have found compelling evidence that opportunity for infant-infant interaction under optimal conditions may fully compensate for lack of mothering, at least in so far as infant-infant social and heterosexual relations are concerned. It seems possible—even likely—that the infant-mother affectional system is dispensable, whereas the infant-infant system is the *sine qua non* for later adjustment in all spheres of

monkey life." Harry F. and Margaret Kuenne Harlow, "Social Deprivation in Monkeys," *Scientific American,* 207 (November 1962), 137.

And, as an extension, the relationship between preadolescent white and Negro boys in the South is sensitively described by Erskine Caldwell in *In Search of Bisco* (N.Y.: Farrar, Straus and Giroux, 1965).

17. For non-mathematical considerations in the learning of mathematics:

(*a*) G. Hendrix, "Learning by Discovery," *The Mathematics Teacher,* 54 (May 1961), 290–99.

(*b*) G. Hendrix, "Non-verbal Awareness in the Learning of Mathematics," *Research Problems in Mathematics Education,* Cooperative Research Monograph #3, U.S. Department of Health, Education and Welfare (Washington, D.C.: Government Printing Office, 1960), pp. 57–61.

Also see the article by Hendrix in Thomas A. Sebeok, Alfred S. Hayes, Mary Catherine Bateson, eds., *Approaches to Semiotics* (The Hague: Mouton and Company, 1964).

CHAPTER 5. **The Teacher**

1. Myron Lieberman, "Who Speaks for Teachers?" *Saturday Review,* June 19, 1965, p. 64. Trenchant, punchy, and calculated to further the uneasiness in bureaucrats.

2. The disinclination and apprehension of middle-class teachers to teach lower-class youngsters was the reason for Vernon Haubrick's "The Culturally Different: New Contexts for Teacher Education," *Journal of Teacher Education,* XIV (June 1963), 163.

3. The period of educational revolution now upon us, paced by and based upon the technological, social, and cultural revolution, creates tremendous opportunities for cracking teacher conservatism, administrative bureaucracy, and curricular reaction, says James D. Finn's "A Revolutionary Season," *Phi Delta Kappan,* XLV (April 1964), 348.

4. The possible historical antecedents of programed instruction and teaching machines are discussed by Ira S. Cohen in "Programed Instruction and Socratic Dialogue," *American Psychologist,* 17 (November 1962), 772. Also see Harry S. Broudy, "Socrates and the Teaching Machine," *Phi Delta Kappan,* XLIV (March 1963), 243. This issue of *Phi Delta Kappan* (March 1963) is almost completely devoted to programed instruction.

In another indication of how teachers are missing a bet in classroom exploration of the last frontier of all, the inner one, Arthur Brayfield refers to the school and education as *terra incognita* in which problems dealing with goals and values can be psychologically investigated and researched, in his article "Human Effectiveness," *American Psychologist*, 20 (August 1965), 645.

5. Bruno Bettelheim, *Love Is Not Enough* (N.Y.: Free Press, 1950).

6. For information on fifth-year and M.A.T. programs:

(*a*) Frances Keppel "Master of Arts in Teaching," *Saturday Review*, June 17, 1961, p. 63.

(*b*) William H. Cartwright, "Fifth-year Programs in Teacher Education," *Journal of Higher Education*, XXXII (June 1961), 297–311.

7. Nothing more excoriating on teacher education has been written than James D. Koerner's "How Not To Teach Teachers," *Atlantic*, February 1963, p. 59.

8. Gilbert Highet, *The Art of Teaching* (N.Y.: Knopf, 1950).

9. G. Hendrix, in Thomas A. Sebeok, Alfred S. Hayes, and Mary Catherine Bateson, eds., *Approaches to Semiotics* (The Hague: Mouton and Company, 1964), p. 190.

10. Oscar Lewis, *Children of Sanchez* (N.Y.: Random House, 1961).

11. For discussion on the roots of classroom behavior, see J. L. Hymes, "Something Is Wrong Someplace," *NEA Journal*, 45 (September 1956), 343.

12. How the language of education obscures more than it enlightens is presented in James S. Le Sure's *Guide to Pedaguese—A Handbook for Puzzled Parents* (N.Y.: Harper & Row, 1965). Unfortunately, the author's humor is heavy, heavy, heavy.

More sober-sided—humorless, indeed—is Admiral H. G. Rickover's *American Education: A National Failure* (N.Y.: Dutton, 1963).

As a counter-balance, put in prose that Barzun would not despair of, is an excellent description of the scope of psychology and the other behavioral sciences in Carl Pfaffman's "Behavioral Sciences," *American Psychologist*, 20 (August 1965), 667.

13. Richard H. Shyrock, *The Status of University Teachers* (Ghent, Belgium: International Association of University Professors and Lecturers, 1961). This publication is available through UNESCO.

The brain drain of clinical psychologists and experimental psychologists away from the academic world into the professionalism of psychotherapy and human factors engineering places the first psychologist under the psychiatrist and the second under the engineer, who assumes dominance because the psychologist has relinquished his research function. The process is described by Robert C. Tryon in "Psychology in Flux: The Academic Professional Bipolarity," *American Psychologist*, 18 (March 1963), 134.

14. The well-known James Conant was in fact preceded in his praise of all-institution involvement in teacher preparation by Lindley J. Stiles, "The All-institution Approach to Teacher Education at the University of Wisconsin," *The Education of Teachers: New Perspectives* (Washington, D.C.: National Commission on Teacher Education and Professional Standards, National Education Association, 1958), p. 153.

15. For background see Clark Kerr, *The Uses of the University* (Cambridge, Mass: Harvard University Press, 1963).

16. The innocuous, meaningless, and offending inoffensiveness of education professors is discussed in Myron Lieberman's "Professors of Education as Critics of Education," *Phi Delta Kappan*, LXIV (January 1963), 164.

17. The qualities of returning Peace Corps veterans that fit them superbly for teaching and education are described by Frank G. Jennings in "Are They Asking Too Much?" *Saturday Review*, May 15, 1965, p. 65. However, young volunteers and tutors without Peace Corps experience are doing splendid work in educating Negro youth, says Arthur I. Waskow in "Young America's Newest Vocation," *Saturday Review*, June 5, 1965, p. 12.

18. One of the early examples of the new militancy among teachers was described by Lavor K. Chaffin, "Utah Teachers Prod Legislature with Threat of Boycott," *Phi Delta Kappan*, XLIV (May 1963), 358. Since then teachers have gone on strike and the NEA has extended the practice of sanctions against school systems.

19. Simultaneously, teachers have moved into more dominating positions in international education. See, for example:

(a) Frank Bowles, *Access to Higher Education* (Paris: Unesco and The International Association of Universities, 1963), Vol. 1.

(b) R. Freeman Butts, *American Education in International Development* (N.Y.: Harper & Row, 1963).

Hence, both at home and abroad, teachers are lifting their heads, looking about them, and beginning to recognize that there is more dynamism in being a teacher than they have heretofore known.

CHAPTER 6. **The Curriculum**

1. For an interesting comparison: David P. Ausubel, *Maori Youth* (Wellington, New Zealand: Price Milburn, 1961), and Sylvia Ashton-Warner's *Teacher* (N.Y.: Simon and Schuster, 1963).

Observe the journalism: "Unlike the bland readers in which Dick and Jane never say an angry word or present unwashed faces . . . current educational thought calls for pupils to be introduced to . . . the slang or informal level as well as the standard or conventionally correct level. . . . This year most major publishing companies have published texts with realistic settings portraying life in an integrated society." Gerald Grant in the *Washington Post* and *Los Angeles Times* for July 11, 1965.

But an integrated society is *not* a realistic setting! It's a fake setting. We are decades away from having an integrated society being identical with a real one.

Similarly, note the optimism-pessimism dichotomy in drug addiction. Compare Nat Hentoff's optimistic approach to Dr. Marie Nyswander's work in drug addiction in "Profiles: The Treatment of Patients," *The New Yorker*, July 3, 1965, p. 32, with Robert Rice's more pessimistic picture in "A Reporter at Large—Junk," *The New Yorker*, March 27, 1965, p. 50. The latter article is a convincing picture of recidivism back to drug addiction, even after the addict has presumably "dried out," once he returns to his family, neighborhood, and former routines.

Edward J. Sachar pleads for more behavioral science to substitute for the punishment that so often fails to be a deterrent, in order to overcome the recidivism in criminals. Accordingly, he recommends "milieu therapy," of the kind that has been successful with the mentally ill. See his "Behavioral Science and Criminal Law," *Scientific American*, 209 (November 1963), 39.

2. For the relationship between man and machine:

(*a*) Note the concept of "software" (man and his flesh) as compared with "hardware" in space exploration, as indication that man is less dependable and durable than his inventions.

(*b*) "Instead of asking which came first, the chicken or the egg . . . a chicken was an egg's idea for getting more eggs," says Marshall McLuhan in *Understanding Media* (N.Y.: McGraw-Hill, 1964). McLuhan stresses that the machine, by simply being, commands us. In his fantasy, man is the genital organ of the machine, and merely a means to the reproduction of new generations of machines!

(*c*) "With the onset of automation the Negro is moving out of his historical state of oppression into uselessness. Increasingly, he is not so much economically exploited as he is irrelevant. . . . The Negro . . . is not so much oppressed as unwanted; not so much unwanted as unnecessary; not so much abused as ignored. The dominant whites no longer need to exploit him. If he disappeared tomorrow he would hardly be missed. As automation proceeds, it is easier and easier to disregard him. . . . The Negro is merely a weathervane for the future. . . . *His* experience will be a common one. . . . As more of us become unnecessary—as human energy and thought themselves become increasingly unnecessary—the greater will be our social anxiety." Sidney M. Wilhelm and Edwin H. Powell, "Who Needs the Negro?" *trans-action* (September–October 1964).

(*d*) For a collection of readings on the above matters, with extensive accompanying annotation by the author-editor, see Charles R. Walker, *Modern Technology and Civilization* (N.Y.: McGraw-Hill, 1962).

3. B. J. Chandler, Lindley J. Stiles, and John I. Kitsuse, *Education in Urban Society* (N.Y.: Dodd, Mead, 1962).

4. Strongly favoring the affirmative in the debate on programed instruction is The Fund for the Advancement of Education, *Four Case Studies of Programed Instruction* (N.Y.: Ford Foundation, June 1964).

5. The need for especially conscientious preparation in team teaching is discussed in *Elementary School Principal,* January 1965.

6. Note this pitch for enlarged classes: "In a setting with teacher aides, specialist teachers, and a team arrangement, class size can and should break away from a fixed mould." Yes, provided that the all-important introductory prepositional phrase is not detachable from the remainder of the sentence. The quotation is from *Time, Talent, and Teachers* (N.Y.: Ford Foundation, June 1960).

A more objective approach to team teaching is available in the extensive bibliography on the subject assembled by Dr. Harold S. Davis of the Staff Utilization Project, Educational Research Council of Greater Cleveland, Rockefeller Building, Cleveland 13, Ohio.

How team teaching will affect school design and school architecture is discussed in *Schools for Team Teaching,* prepared by Evans Clinchy for the Educational Facilities Laboratories (N.Y.: Ford Foundation, 1960).

7. Jacques Barzun, *Science: The Glorious Entertainment* (N.Y.: Harper and Row, 1964).

Jeremy Bernstein's review of the Barzun book (*The New Yorker,* November 21, 1964) states: "Some programs are posed merely because they can be programed for a computer and not because they are in themselves interesting. (I have been asked, when I was working in a research establishment, whether I could think up a problem for the local computer, because it seemed a pity to keep it idle. In fact, inasmuch as machines are getting faster and more numerous, one wonders whether there can possibly continue to be enough sensible problems for them to go around.)"

8. For teacher howlers, see J. Weston Walsh, *Successful School Discipline* (Portland, Me.: J. Weston Walsh, 1958).

8a. See Frost's explanation in Cleanth Brooks and Robert Penn Warren, *Understanding Poetry* (N.Y.: Holt, Rinehart & Winston, 1960), p. 524.

9. Arthur T. Jersild, *In Search of Self* (N.Y.: Bureau of Publications, Teachers College, 1952).

10. Robert Lindner, *The Fifty-minute Hour* (N.Y.: Holt, Rinehart and Winston, 1955).

11. Melanie Klein, *Contributions to Psychoanalysis* (London: Hogarth Press, 1948).

12. The original announcement of the Citizenship Education Project's "Hours on Freedom" appeared in *The New York Times,* article, "Armed Forces Get Citizenship Course," April 24, 1951, p. 19.

13. Alistair Horne, *The Price of Glory: Verdun 1916* (N.Y.: St. Martin's Press, 1962), presents evidence on the stupidity of the professional military and why they cannot avoid being stupid. A discipline based on the complete worthlessness and expendability of human life necessarily makes stupidity a built-in feature of military life.

14. G. H. Blantock states his opposition to John Dewey and everything Dewey is purported (here at any rate) to represent in his *Education in an Industrial Society* (London: Faber and Faber, 1963). An unnecessarily unpleasant book by a Tory who arrived at educational conservatism only to find that the nobility had renounced its titles and was assuming the names and habits of the commoner—how non-aristocratic! Blantock's philosophy, more than American financial temptations, lies behind the British brain drain.

15. Teaching the practical need not be separated from teaching the symbolic, provided we remember that classification is not definition; classification (the concrete) can lead to definition (the symbolic). For a discussion on how this is done, see Donald M. Johnson and Charlene A. O'Reilly, "Concept Attainment in Children," *Journal of Educational Psychology,* 55 (April 1964), 71–74.

16. A letter written by T. E. Blackburn, of Marquette University, in *Harper's* for July, 1963, offers the more narrow view of what a curriculum should offer in a good public high school:

"Why *should* top academic high schools like New Trier (Illinois) and Whitefish Bay (Wisconsin) have to siphon off money for an auto workshop? Why *must* carpentry, plumbing, and auto mechanics be taught in schools? Whatever happened to on-the-job training? . . . Whoever said schools should teach people to earn a living, in the first place? Schools originally taught history, language, philosophy—the arts and sciences that, in theory anyway, enable people to cope with changes in the big picture, not necessarily changes in ways to earn money for groceries.

"I pity the poor schools. Every time someone finds a new national need, understaffed, underfinanced schools are pressured to add new courses. It matters not whether the courses are academic. We need plumbers? Schools must provide them. We need pianists? Schools must provide them. . . . The school is not the only place people can learn to drive a car or fix a sink. But it is the only place large numbers of people can learn to read, write, and think.

"Let's leave the jobs that can be done by other agencies after school or on Saturdays to the other agencies. . . ."

And watch how fast these other agencies become schools too! The error in the above is that all education is vocational and always has been, something Barzun forgets too.

17. Jerome S. Bruner points out: "A generation ago, the progressive movement urged that knowledge be related to the child's own experience and brought out of the realm of empty abstractions. A good idea was translated into banalities about the home, then the friendly postman and trashman, then the community, and so on. It is a poor way to compete with the child's own dramas and mysteries. . . . to personalize knowledge one does not simply link it to the familiar. Rather one makes the familiar an instance of a more general case and thereby produces awareness of it. . . . The cultivation of reflectiveness, or whatever you choose to call it, is one of the great problems one faces in devising curriculum." This excerpt from "The Growth of Mind," in *American Psychologist*, 20 (December 1965), 1014–15, describes the pedant who substitutes experience for wisdom, and the Blantockian who teaches the "practical"; it says what we have been saying about rumination, meditation and "soak-in" time for the slow child as well as the bright child.

18. Johan Huizinga, *Homo Ludens* (Boston: Beacon, 1955).

19. *The Republic*, Book VII, translated by W. H. D. Rouse (N.Y.: New American Library, 1957), p. 336.

CHAPTER 7. The Bureaucracies in Urban Education

1. The quotation is from Harrison Salisbury, *The Shook-Up Generation* (N.Y.: Harper & Row, 1958), and *The New York Times*, November 18, 1961, p. 26.

2. How the Kefauver Committee ploughed into the drug industry and drug pricing is described in Richard Harris, *The Real Voice* (N.Y.: Macmillan, 1964).

D. P. Barr reports, "One out of every 20 patients admitted to a large hospital in New York City was there because of adverse reaction to treatment," in *Journal of the American Medical Association*, 159 (1955), 1452. Illnesses caused by physicians and arising from medical care are called *iatrogenic*. Similarly, should we call the learning and educational difficulties originating with the teacher (not with the pupil) as *ludigenic* (from the Latin for school, *ludus*)?

3. Saul Friedman, "The Rand Corporation and Our Policy Makers," *Atlantic*, September 1963, p. 61. Also see D. S. Greenberg, "Mohole: The Project That Went Awry," *Science*, 143 (January 10, 1964), 115, and (January 17, 1964), 223, for a description of scientific juggling that affects politics and political juggling that affects science, and how science has now become embroiled with political log-rolling. See "Letters" section in *Science*, 149 (August 6, 1965), 584, as to jockeying for funds among various branches of science. Data on the NASA wheeling-dealing and on the scientific and political trafficking of the "gapsmen" are presented by Edwin Diamond in *The Rise and Fall of the Space Age* (N.Y.: Doubleday, 1964). The government-educational-industrial complex around Harvard and M.I.T. and the influence of science in government is treated by Christopher Rand's "Profiles—Center of a New World," *The New Yorker*, April 11, 1964, p. 43. The second installment, April 18, 1964, p. 57, deals with Harvard's contribution to the Indus River Project.

In short, the large scientific institutes and laboratories adjacent to college campuses give universities a spurious sense of control of their scientific staffs, when the reverse is true. Universities are losing control. As scientists become less the professors of science and more the practitioners of it, laboratories divest themselves of college control. Indeed, all scientific institutes need do, right now, to tear apart the fabric of college science faculties, is to offer the same tenure and pension privileges that colleges do, and they would wreck every college department of science in the land.

4. In the face of Dr. Conant's recommendations and Paul Goodman's praise of local school autonomy, the number of school districts seems to be decreasing as educational opportunity increases. Notice the difference between 1942, when there were 108,579 school districts, and 1962, when there were 34,678

5. The quotation is from John Walsh, *Science*, 140 (June 21, 1963), 1293.

6. Lawrence Cremin, *The Transformation of the School* (N.Y.: Vintage Books, 1964).

7. Arthur S. Trace, Jr., *Reading Without Dick and Jane* (Chicago: Regnery, 1965).

8. Exploratory drives in learning, in contrast to hunger, thirst, and punishment-avoidance drives, are reviewed by R. H. O'Connell in "Trials with Tedium and Titillation," *Psychological Bulletin* (March 1965). The curiosity that kills cats more frequently educates them.

9. The day-by-day impact of art is treated by McNeil Lowry and Gertrude Hooker, "The Role of the Arts and the Humanities," and by Philip Coombs, "The Past and the Future in Perspective," in Robert Blum, ed., *Cultural Affairs and Modern Relations* (Englewood Cliffs, N.J.: Prentice-Hall, 1963).

Harlem has had many excellent poets, but none as excellent and as little known as the late M. B. Tolson, who wrote *Harlem Gallery: Book I, The Curtain* (N.Y.: Twayne, 1964).

10. Jane Jacobs, *The Death and Life of Great American Cities* (N.Y.: Random House, 1961); Lewis Mumford, *The City in History* (N.Y.: Harcourt, Brace & World, 1961); V. S. Pritchett, *London Perceived* (N.Y.: Harcourt, Brace & World, 1962) are good examples.

11. Warren Weaver, Jr., "An Antipoverty Test in Harlem," *The New York Times*, February 3, 1965, p. 1.

Consider how mortgage-lending banks profit from rent strike agitators of the Jesse Gray type: "Philadelphia provides a good example of what can happen in the private market when a housing code is widely enforced in a community. When values began to decline under the impact of enforcement, the small holders sold out to large investors . . . [who] . . . were able to schedule enough improvement to comply with the requirements of the code. . . ." Martin Meyerson, Barbara Terrett, and William L. C. Wheaton, "Low-income Rehabilitation," in *Housing, People, and Cities* (N.Y.: McGraw-Hill, 1962).

12. For the rivalry between Leonardo da Vinci and Michelangelo, see Kenneth Clark, *Leonardo da Vinci* (London: Pelican, 1961), p. 13. For the Rouault-Chagall rivalry, see Carlton Lake, "Artist at Work," *Atlantic*, July 1963, p. 85.

13. The Weston La Barre quotation is from his *The Human Animal* (Chicago: University of Chicago Press, 1954), p. 149.

14. Theodosius G. Dobzhansky, *Heredity and the Nature of Man* (N.Y.: Harcourt, Brace & World, 1964).

15. E. M. Forster, *Howard's End* (N.Y.: Vintage Books, 1954).

16. Margaret Mead makes precisely this point in "Recapturing the Future," *Saturday Review*, June 1, 1963, p. 10.

17. Staughton Lynd tells how slavery was related to constitutional origins and the Two Constitutions in "A Constitution Divided," *Columbia University Forum* (Spring 1965).

18. The quotation is from Dwight J. Ingle, "Racial Differences and the Future," *Science*, 146 (October 16, 1964), 375. For some strong replies to Ingle, see "Letters: Race, Science, and Social Policy," *Science*, 146 (December 11 and 18, 1964), 1415, 1526.

For the abatement of demoralization and the incursion of self-respect, see Mobilization For Youth, *A Proposal for the Prevention and Control of Delinquency by Expanding Opportunities* (N.Y.: MFY, 1961).

19. John Kenneth Galbraith agrees with Gunnar Myrdal that the affluent society has large pockets of poverty on which we must move with a program, in "Let Us Begin: An Invitation to Action on Poverty," *Harper's,* March 1964, p. 16.

20. This tongue-in-cheek quotation is from T. R. B., "From Washington," *New Republic,* December 21, 1963, p. 2.

But the same comes from the right of center, when one of the country's most successful advertising men calls for *special* incentives for the poor, like providing money for health, literacy, and "exposure to communication," by which he means accessibility to radio, newspapers, television advertising messages, and "incentives to move up in the world of options, into the market place where so many Americans are." A new, and almost unbelievable, stage in American life! Even though the advertising man may be interested in urban education because it helps him move goods and products! See Marion Harper Jr., "Marketing the Poverty Program," *Saturday Review,* May 9, 1964, p. 65.

21. For the interrelations of sex relations and race relations, see Nat Hentoff, *The New Equality* (N.Y.: Viking, 1964).

22. Marshal Sklare, "Intermarriage and the Jewish Future," *Commentary,* April 1964, p. 46.

CHAPTER 8. **The Budget and the Program**

1. On educational budgeting and financing, see John Vaizey, *The Economics of Education* (N.Y.: Free Press, 1962).

On education as a capital investment, see Fritz Machlup, *The Production and Distribution of Knowledge in the United States* (Princeton, N.J.: Princeton University Press, 1962). Also Frederick Harbison and Charles A. Myers, *Education, Manpower, and Economic Growth: Strategies of Human Resource Development* (N.Y.: McGraw-Hill, 1964). Also T. W. Schultz, "Capital Formation by Education," *Journal of Political Economy,* 68 (1960), 571–83. A somewhat different point of view is stated in Robert L. Heilbroner, *The Great Ascent* (N.Y.: Harper & Row, 1963).

However, these economists will generally agree that ". . . if we let our minds be bold, then the taxes and the balanced budgets and fiscal resources, and ultimately the man-and-womanpower will take care of themselves." From Harry Gideonse, "Democracy in Education: A Forward Look," *Chicago Union Teacher* (April 1960).

2. Julius Duscha deals with the country's largest financial drain, the largest impediment to society's progress, in "Arms and the Big Money Men: Congressmen, Contractors, and the 'Defense' Pork Barrel," *Harper's*, March 1964, p. 39. However, the same author says that the defense establishment is not the only drain on the economy, in his *Taxpayer's Hayride* (Boston: Little, Brown, 1964); so is the American farmer. But, predicting an enormously expanded role for education in the next generation, Peter Drucker claims that the educational budget will soon exceed the defense budget and points out that it is now two-thirds of the defense budget, in "American Directions: A Forecast," *Harper's*, February 1965, p. 39.

3. For the involvement of the defense establishment with education, see Harold F. Clark and Harold S. Sloan, *Classrooms in the Military* (N.Y.: Teachers College, Columbia University, 1964).

4. Edgar L. Dale, Jr., feels that economic prosperity will do more for the Negro than anti-poverty legislation will, and that the Gross National Product is a more important statistic for Negro improvement than the number of integrated schools. In his "The Big Gun on Poverty," *New Republic*, August 7, 1965, p. 13, he says, "The [Walt] Hellers and [Gardner] Ackleys with their manipulation of the Gross National Product have improved far more human individual situations, if almost unwittingly, than the [Willard] Wirtzes and the [Sargent] Shrivers with their effort to reach individuals."

If Mr. Dale is in favor of overall planning, rather than pinpointed planning, then the overall picture can sometimes be adversely distorted by pinpointed impediments. An excellent example of how economic change and planning depend, very specifically, on an educated populace and of how the small matter of political dissension impedes the larger picture of economic growth is offered in Gilbert F. White's "The Mekong River Plan," *Scientific American*, 208 (April 1963), 49, which shows that we know what must be done for men as a whole, if only particular men would get out of our way and let us do it. The article can also be interpreted as a statement on behalf of the New Colonialism.

5. The contrasting quotations are from Philip H. Coombs, "Education's Role in the Developing Nations," *Saturday Review*, August 17, 1963, p. 29, and Arthur Krock, "New Definition of 'Work and Sacrifice,' " *The New York Times*, February 23, 1965, p. 32.

As to the emerging nations:

(*a*) Written with a light hand on a heavy topic, including a discussion on Negritude, and fast reading for its 171 pages is Melvin J. Lasky, *Africa for Beginners: A Traveller's Notebook* (N.Y.: Lippincott, 1964).

(*b*) To change the culturally backward, we can be "problem-oriented" or "program-oriented," says George M. Foster in *Traditional Cultures and the Impact of Technological Change* (N.Y.: Harper & Row, 1962). Orientation by "program" gets in the way of progressive, forward-looking change, but orientation by "problem" is salutary.

(*c*) Margery Perham's *The Colonial Reckoning* (N.Y.: Knopf, 1962) deals objectively with African "liberation" and nationhood and the fuzziness of much native and colonial thinking. She refers to the "supreme racial compensation of sexual intercourse with a white woman," and how a sense of personal outrage affects political thinking.

(*d*) An argument for not educating native populations above their accustomed station is offered in James Duffy, *Portuguese Africa* (Cambridge, Mass.: Harvard University Press, 1959).

(*e*) Pierre Moussa, *The Underdeveloped Nations* (Boston: Beacon Press, 1962).

6. One example of American government solicitude for its citizens is in education. See Frank Bowles, *Access to Higher Education* (Paris: UNESCO, and N.Y.: Columbia University Press, 1964), which compares college admissions policies in various lands, and contrasts high selectivity in the United Kingdom, France, and Germany, with low selectivity in the United States and the U.S.S.R.

Also see Harold Orlans, *The Effects of Federal Programs on Higher Education* (Washington D.C.: Brookings Institution, 1962), and Homer D. Babbidge Jr. and Robert M. Rosenzweig, *The Federal Interest in Higher Education* (N.Y.: McGraw-Hill, 1962).

What the anthropologist feels about such institutional intervention is offered in Jules Henry, *Culture Against Man* (N.Y.: Random House, 1963). Similarly, differences among economists emerge in Gunnar Myrdal, *Challenge to Affluence* (N.Y.: Pantheon Books, 1963), which opposes J. K. Galbraith's *Affluent Society* (Boston: Houghton Mifflin, 1958). Myrdal calls for consumption-and-use orientations in dealing with poverty, rather than an investment orientation. One would begin at the bottom, and the other at the top, in a dribble-down approach.

7. Architects are tough people, much tougher than teachers. "Their attitude in college appears to have been one of profound skepticism. They were unwilling to accept anything on the mere say-so of their instructors. Nothing was to be accepted on faith or because it had behind it the voice of authority." How can the usual educator compete with such a person for the educational buck? The quotation is from Donald W. MacKinnon's article on architects, "The Nature and Nurture of Creative Talent," *American Psychologist,* 17 (July 1962), 484, in which the primacy of intelligence in creativity (specifically in the case of architects) is played down. The author feels that I.Q. does

not predict creativity, but only sets a lower limit for it, in agreement with Getzels and Jackson.

CHAPTER **9.** **Educational Extenders, Fore and Aft**

1. "News and Comments," *Science*, 140 (April 5, 1963), 35, reports that preparation and orientation for graduate education begins in kindergarten. College chairmen and deans are quoted thus: "[the] problem of reducing loss of good people is not a purely academic one. It involves disinterest, cultural alienation, and lack of motivation in the high schools, and particularly in the big city high schools. Most graduates of the suburban 'quality' schools now go on to college, and from there to graduate school. Our losses occur at the lower level, where brighter students never acquire an interest in intellectual problems." This statement is by Robert I. Walter, of Haverford College.

In contrast, "News and Comments," *Science*, 141 (July 26, 1963), 339: ". . . it is not inconceivable that Congress will continue to bloat the graduate levels with fellowships and other forms of support while the lower levels of education continue to suffer." See in this same issue A. W. Astin's "Undergraduate Institutions and the Production of Scientists," p. 334, which says that the decision to enter science is made and firmly fixed at college *entrance* and is not changed by subsequent college experience. In other words, you've got to get the aspiring scientist *before* he enters college, if you are to fix his science career plans firmly.

The Russians have had a Head Start Program since 1961. It was announced in the 1961 Draft Program of the Communist Party. See Urie Bronfenbrenner, "Challenge of the 'New Soviet Man'," *The New York Times Magazine*, August 27, 1961, p. 21, and Abram Kardiner, *Saturday Review*, August 26, 1961, p. 9. Despite the Russian head start on Head Start, our program was foreshadowed by Martin Deutsch in "The Disadvantaged Child and the Learning Process: Some Social Psychological and Developmental Considerations," *The Ford Foundation Work Conference in Curriculum and Teaching in Depressed Urban Areas* (N.Y.: Columbia University Press, 1962).

For a report on the first summer's achievements of the Anti-Poverty, Operation Head Start, and Job Corps programs, see "Shriver and the War on Poverty," *Newsweek*, September 13, 1965, p. 22. More penetrating as to the political realities is William Haddad, "Mr. Shriver and the Savage Politics of Poverty," *Harper's*, December 1965, p. 43.

2. Early social experience is crucial to later behavioral adjustment, so kindergarten training may prevent adolescent school dropout.

Pre-school Head Start programs are thereby related to post-school Job Corps programs. See Victor H. Denenberg, "Early Experience and Emotional Development," *Scientific American,* 208 (June 1963), 138.

A *Science* editorial (Vol. 139, March 22, 1963, p. 1173) suggests that colleges be graded for quality. The late bloomer, admitted to a lower level institution (a junior college would be ranked below a state college, which would be ranked below a higher level college) could, as he blossomed, transfer to better institutions as he proved his merit. There are antecedents here. We differentiate vocational high schools from academic high schools, and differentiate high school certificates from high school diplomas. It is one answer to the pressure to admit all high school graduates to the colleges.

3. Dr. Adele Franklin, founder, describes the origins and subsequent development of "The All-Day Neighborhood Schools," *Crime and Delinquency* (July 1961), 255.

3a. *The New York Times,* January 3, 1962, p. 1.

4. For a description of a school that never closes down, the Dunbar School of Chicago, see Benjamin C. Willis (who almost *was* closed down), "Education the Year Round," *Atlantic,* January 1965, p. 83.

5. Charles G. Bennett, "Brooklyn Antipoverty Program Is Set," *The New York Times,* July 26, 1964, p. 42, and, same date, same newspaper, see "Youth Advisers Going to School," p. 43.

Even in ancient Greece, the value of the right environment was recognized: "All above ten years of age in the city. . . . must be sent out into the country; and all the children among them must be taken charge of and kept outside their present surroundings and the ways of life led by their parents; and the reformers must bring them up in their own ways and customs. . . ." Plato, *The Republic,* Book VII, in *Great Dialogues of Plato,* W. H. D. Rouse, trans. (N.Y.: New American Library, 1956), p. 341.

6. William B. Stapp, *Integrating Outdoor and Conservation Education into the Curriculum* (Minneapolis: Burgess Publishing Company, 1965).

William E. Cole and Charles S. Montgomery, *High School Sociology* (Boston: Allyn & Bacon, 1959).

7. Sidney L. Pressey feels that education ought to be accelerated and that students ought to do more independent study on their own. See "Two Basic Neglected Psychoeducational Problems," *American Psychologist,* 20 (June 1965), 391.

8. Editorial, *Wall Street Journal,* June 27, 1963.

9. Melvin Spiro, *Children of the Kibbutz* (N.Y.: Schocken, 1965). A. I. Rabin, *Growing Up in the Kibbutz* (N.Y.: Springer, 1965).

CHAPTER 10.   **Money Incentives for the Learner**

1. B. F. Skinner and C. B. Ferster, *Schedules of Reinforcement* (N.Y.: Appleton-Century-Crofts, 1957).

2. Irving Lorge, "Psychological Bases for Adult Learning," *Teachers College Record,* 41 (October 1939), 4–12.

3. Earl Ubell reports in the *New York Herald-Tribune* for December 31, 1965: "If you want a non-reading child to learn to read, just pay him nickels. If you want an unruly child to behave, just pay him quarters. It works even with retarded or severely disturbed children." He thereafter describes the success of Dr. Arthur W. Staats, of the University of Wisconsin, in improving the learning of culturally deprived children when paid in money, *not* in praise or approbation.

Another spokesman on behalf of payment for learning is Michael Harrington, in *The Accidental Century* (N.Y.: Macmillan, 1965).

4. Raymond G. McCarthy edits a source book, *Alcohol Education for Classroom and Community* (N.Y.: McGraw-Hill, 1964).

5. Sheldon and Eleanor Glueck, *Family Environment and Delinquency* (Boston: Houghton-Mifflin, n.d.).

6. William McGehee and P. W. Thayer, *Training in Business and Industry* (N.Y.: Wiley, 1961).

CHAPTER 11.   **Curricular Psychology**

1. John Walsh states that the "behemoth of American public education, with its decentralization, its conservatism, and its formidable difficulties with such practical matters as finance, school size, staffing, and scheduling," has baffled scientists and mathematicians trying to improve the high school curriculum, accounting for the meager results to date. See his "Curriculum Reform," *Science,* 144 (May 8, 1964), 642. Education is more refractory than outer space or the inner atom!

2. On reading:

(*a*) Though weak in classroom suggestions, Ralph D. Rabinovitch covers the diagnostic and psychiatric background in reading impediments in his "Reading and Learning Disabilities," in Silvano Arieti, ed., *American Handbook of Psychiatry,* Vol. 1 (N.Y.: Basic Books, 1959).

(*b*) Professor Louis Heil has told the author, "You may develop skill in reading and at the same time reduce interest in it."

(*c*) A. D. Miller, J. B. Margolin, and S. F. Yolles, "Epidemiology of Reading Disabilities: Some Methodologic Considerations and Early Findings," *American Journal of Public Health,* 47 (1957), 1250–56.

(*d*) Dr. Wilma T. Donahue has pointed out that illiterates are quite comfortable in their illiteracy. For them, the pleasures of reading are as remote as the moon and not more inviting. See her "Adult Learning Limits and Potentialities," in *Automation and the Challenge to Education* (Washington, D.C.: The Project on the Educational Implications of Automation, National Education Association, 1962), p. 32.

The contrary is true of the poor reader, who is very highly motivated. Herbert E. Krugman says in the same volume, p. 67: "We may distinguish between two types of employee morale, one which more properly deserves the term and is characterized by enthusiastic striving and ambition, and another type more properly labeled contentment (or mere satisfaction) which is characterized by an apathetic absence of complaint or grievance."

3. How Omar Khayyam Moore's typewriters exemplify the differences between teaching machines and learning machines is described in Maya Pines, "How Three-year-olds Teach Themselves to Read—and Love It," *Harper's,* May 1963, p. 58.

A skeptical appraisal of the ITA alphabet in teaching reading appears in an editorial, "They're Trying To Put a Man on the Moon Too," *Phi Delta Kappan,* XLV (April 1964), 321: "Perhaps the most compelling reason why the Downing-Pitman experiments with a simplified teaching alphabet will spread and grow is commercial, and hence in the Yankee tradition. Sir James Pitman happens to own a publishing house and it is churning out 'the douning readers' by the thousand. American dissatisfaction with the reading achievements of its younger generation can be counted upon to combine with the profit motive like gasoline on a brush fire." But, in the same issue, John Downing, "Teaching Reading with i.t.a. in Britain," p. 322, offers a preliminary study on the results gotten with the initial teaching alphabet in English schools. From results reported, gains seem amazing.

The Russians have a related approach. See D. B. Elkonin, "The Psychology of Mastering the Elements of Reading," in B. Simon and J. Simon, eds., *Educational Psychology in the USSR* (London: Routledge and Kegan Paul, 1963). The Russians depend on the motor activity involved in speech training for reading improvement. Their elementary school children have had experience in analysis of their own speech sounds (or phonetics) before they go on to phonics.

Also dealing with the importance of speech training as prior to reading readiness is D. D. Durrell and H. A. Murphy, "The Auditory

Discrimination Factor in Reading Readiness and Reading Disability," *Education*, 73 (1953), 556–61.

4. Techniques that influence public opinion, many of which can be used by the English teacher to motivate reading, are found in Carl I. Hovland, "Effects of the Mass Media of Communication," in Gardner Lindzey, ed., *Handbook of Social Psychology*, Vol. 2 (Cambridge, Mass.: Addison Wesley, 1954).

5. Abel Green, *Variety*, February 23, 1955, p. 2.

6. The description of Mishna chant is from Peter Gradnewitz, *The Music of Israel* (N.Y.: W. W. Norton, 1949), p. 82.

7. Language growth and development are discussed by Joseph Church in *Language and the Discovery of Reality* (N.Y.: Random House, 1961).

8. H. L. Mencken, ed., *New Dictionary of Quotations* (N.Y.: Knopf, 1948).

9. Verbal learning is prior to all other learning. Hence the great importance of native-language instruction, says Jerome S. Bruner in "The Course of Cognitive Growth," *American Psychologist*, 19 (January 1964), 1.

10. Geraldine Murphy, review of Abraham Bernstein, *Teaching English in High School* (N.Y.: Random House, 1961) in *Harvard Educational Review*, 33 (Winter 1963), 135–39. For similar icon-worship, see Selma Fraiberg, "The American Reading Problem," *Commentary*, June 1965, p. 56. The Fraiberg article makes sense when it speaks of reading difficulties and reading pathology, but not when it deals with reading materials of superior literary value. A work of superior value is valueless as an icon, except to icon-preservers. For an example of the slaughter of literary values, see Edgar Z. Friedenberg's free-wheeling editorializing of teenage poetry preferences in *Coming of Age in America* (N.Y.: Random House, 1965), especially the complaint that "erect and strong" are not construed by his adolescent subjects as they are by him (p. 120). Note also Professor Friedenberg's derisive "cognitive skills . . . that attract schoolteachers much as feminine musk attracted Don Giovanni, leading them to keep, as he did, extensive numerical records" (p. 193). But it wasn't the sexually potent Don Giovanni that kept records. It was the sexually deprived Leporello. Furthermore, see the extensive numerical records that Professor Friedenberg himself employs in his book. A case of the pot calling the kettle black: especially when most teachers are reluctant to keep extensive numerical records and are forced to do so by the Leporellos in administrative posts. For the musk Professor Friedenberg is sympathetic to, see his *The Vanishing Adolescent* (N.Y.: Dell, 1962), chap. 6.

11. The prospective English teacher who wants an excellent, readable introduction to the psycholinguistics he will never be called on to teach, and the grammar he will, should read John Carroll's *Thought and Language* (Englewood Cliffs, N.J.: Prentice-Hall, 1964). One of the earlier efforts here is George A. Miller, "Psycholinguistics," in Gardner Lindzey, ed., *Handbook of Social Psychology,* Vol. 2 (Cambridge, Mass.: Addison-Wesley, 1954).

12. Noam Chomsky, *Aspects of the Theory of Syntax* (Cambridge, Mass.: The M.I.T. Press, 1965).

13. Myron H. Vent, in *The Linguistic Reporter,* VI (December 1964). Also Tom Bryan, "Teachers of English Explore Techniques at Reading Institute," *El Paso Times,* July 4, 1965, p. 4.

14. Among recent authors who want time for rumination, meditation, and "soak-in" is Z. P. Dienes in *An Experimental Study of Mathematics Learning* (N.Y.: Humanities, 1962).

Also pointing out the inadequate preparation of teachers in these areas, the unsatisfactory teaching conditions under which they work, and the program assignments that remove them from their proper areas of work is "NSF: New Study on Science, Math Teachers in High School Focuses on Their Education, Assignment," *Science,* 140 (May 24, 1963), 878. This article quotes from a government document, *Secondary School Science and Mathematics Teachers, Characteristics and Service Loads* (Washington, D.C.: Government Printing Office, 1963).

15. Eugen Herrigel, *Zen in the Art of Archery* (N.Y.: Pantheon, 1953).

16. Cambridge Conference on School Mathematics, *Goals For School Mathematics* (Boston: Houghton Mifflin, 1963), pp. 9, 26, 17, 80.

17. The problem of "teaching for the test" is discussed in relationship to national testing programs by Harold C. Hand's "National Assessment Viewed as the Camel's Nose," *Phi Delta Kappan,* 47 (September 1965). Ralph W. Tyler's answer appears in the same issue: "Assessing the Programs of Education."

The March, 1965, issue of *Phi Delta Kappan* is almost completely devoted to the problems and issues in college admission, from which it becomes clear that entrance examinations reflect new curriculums. But it remains less clear that new curriculums reflect examination practices. However, we can be sure that new curriculums are hastening to do so.

18. The quotation is from Robert J. Schaefer, "Anti-intellectualism in the Pursuit of the Intellectual," *Teachers College Record,* 65 (November 1963), 132–38.

19. Max Beberman, *The Emerging Program of Secondary School Mathematics* (Cambridge, Mass.: Harvard University Press, 1958).

20. Recent efforts to re-formulate the social studies from grades 1–12 are described by Richard E. Gross and Dwight W. Allen in "Time for a National Effort to Develop the Social Studies Curriculum," *Phi Delta Kappan*, 44 (May 1963), 360. The curriculum described makes good sense, but seems neither revolutionary nor particularly new. It leaves unanswered this question: How will you get students to work at it more than they have worked in the past? The programs recommended are not antithetic to orthodox social studies, nor to quasi-experimental citizenship education courses.

21. The numerosity of gods and the relationship to infinite regress are considered by Martin Gardner in "Mathematical Games," *Scientific American*, 212 (April 1965), 128.

22. Some of the mechanisms affected when civilized man has dreadful nightmares are discussed by Charles R. Tart in "Toward The Experimental Control of Dreaming," *Psychological Bulletin* (August 1965). See also Calvin Trillin's "Reporter At Large: A Third State of Existence," *The New Yorker*, September 18, 1965, p. 58.

23. How Negroes and Jews divide over an educational and economic *numerus clausus* (why Jews oppose it and Negroes favor it) gets considered in Nathan Glazer's "Negroes and Jews: The New Challenge to Pluralism," *Commentary*, 38 (December 1964), 29.

24. A *New York Times* editorial for April 25, 1962, especially boxed for emphasis, said: "As the miracle that might have averted new nuclear tests has failed to materialize, President Kennedy has now issued the fateful order to go ahead with the scheduled tests in the Pacific as soon as operationally feasible. . . . With deep reluctance and regret, which we share, he decided that our own and free world preservation demands the tests. . . . We have pursued peace in accordance with our principles and to the very limits of our own and free world security, and of our financial resources. At this unhappy moment when we are about to proceed with new atmospheric testing—in the long-range interests of peace—let the record speak for us against those who would malign us."

On the next day, April 26, 1962, the United States resumed nuclear testing, and later came the partial ban, but stopping and starting reflected awareness of mutual fear rather than awareness of possibilities.

See Arthur Koestler, *Arrival and Departure* (N.Y.: Macmillan, 1943).

25. On sex and espionage, both international and industrial:

(*a*) "Joshua sent out two men to 'spy secretly' (Joshua, II) and they were received in Jericho in the house of Rahab, the harlot. It was, I believe, the first published instance of what one now calls in the intelligence trade a 'safe house.' " This quotation, from Allan Dulles, "The Craft of Intelligence," *Harper's*, April, 1963, pp. 128–74, points out the ancient and not-so-honorable relationship of sex and military espionage. See also Richard Wilmer Rowan, *The Story of Secret Service* (N.Y.: Doubleday, 1937), for a more sanitized version. On Allan Dulles, see Andrew Tully, *CIA: The Inside Story* (N.Y.: William Morrow, 1962). For a recent British instance in Profumo-Christine Keeler, see Bernard Hollowood's *"What* Would Queen Victoria Say?" *The New York Times Magazine,* June 30, 1963, p. 7.

(*b*) An employee with confidential information is limited in his ability to seek work elsewhere, because occupational mobility is difficult when your boss has entrusted you with information useful to a rival. See John Brooks, "Annals of Business: One Free Bite," *The New Yorker,* January 11, 1964, p. 37.

On the electronic invasion of privacy:

(*a*) Samuel Dash, Richard F. Schwartz, Robert E. Knowlton, *The Eavesdroppers* (New Brunswick, N.J.: Rutgers University Press, 1959). Also dealing with the wire-tapped world is Vance Packard, *The Naked Society* (N.Y.: David McKay, 1964).

(*b*) Should not all officials submit to truth detection so that their statements can be verified? Should politicians take lie-detector tests when they run for office? And cabinet members appearing before Senate committees? See Ralph W. Gerard, "To Prevent Another World War: Truth Detection," Journal of Conflict Resolution, 5 (1961), 212–18.

(*c*) If a concierge can be a spy (Marie Ridder, "Madrid: An Outspoken New Generation," *Show,* December 1963, p. 24), how do you defend yourself against miniature transmitters hidden in your telephone or wall? How can you speak freely, no matter what the political system? You communicate differently and circumspectly and you suspect the partisan of free speech as a fool or an agent-provocateur. You no longer speak freely about free speech but develop new ambiguities to circumvent the wire tappers, thereby maintaining your freedom of speech. It requires additional alertness, which is an inconvenience and a strain, but it can be done.

26. Montaigne, *Selected Essays* (N.Y.: The Modern Library, 1949).

27. The laboratory simulation of international conflict, which can be taught *in vitro,* is described in Joseph De Rivera, "Teach a Course in the Psychology of International Relations," *American Psychologist,* 17 (October 1962), 695.

"Camelot is . . . a plain warning to social scientists, who seem to do a lot of talking about infra-structure, that they had better do something constructive about their own," declares John Walsh in "Social Sciences: Cancellation of Camelot after Row in Chile Brings Research Under Scrutiny," *Science,* 149 (September 10, 1965), 1211.

For a discussion on the killers—the Sullas, the Stalins, the Hitlers—to whom life is meaningless in comparison with doctrine or pleasure, see Erich Fromm, "Creators and Destroyers," *Saturday Review,* January 4, 1964, p. 22.

28. That big business may soon cast an appraising eye on ESP (extra-sensory perception) and PK (psycho-kinesis) and is already on the verge of taking them seriously as possible sources of profit is revealed in "Beyond the Senses: Once Termed Fakery by Many, ESP Study Wins More Tolerance," *Wall Street Journal,* November 17, 1965, p. 1.

29. On the audio-lingual method in modern language instruction:

(*a*) For a defense and explication see Nelson Brooks, *Language and Language Learning* (N.Y.: Harcourt, Brace and World, 1960).

(*b*) Less favorable are George A. C. Scherer and Michael Wertheimer, *A Psycholinguistic Experiment in Foreign Language Teaching* (N.Y.: McGraw-Hill, 1964).

30. Aubrey Menen, *Speaking the Language like a Native* (N.Y.: McGraw-Hill, 1962).

31. Johan Huizinga, *Homo Ludens* (Boston: Beacon, 1955).

32. Philip Morrison notes the usual authoritarianism that prevails in the science class, and recommends that the fresh air of thought be brought in, in "Experimenters in the Schoolroom," *Science,* 138 (December 21, 1962), 1307.

33. On improving the level of science instruction:

(*a*) The recommendations of the Jerrold Zaccharias committee are presented by The Panel on Educational Research and Development in *Innovation and Experiment in Education* (Washington, D.C.: Government Printing Office, n.d.).

(*b*) P. G. Ashmore, "Book Reviews: On Teaching High School Chemistry," *Science,* 148 (June 4, 1965), 1312, discusses recent textbooks that use the new approach to secondary school science teaching.

34. The natural unity between science and the arts is dealt with in Harold Gomes Cassidy, *The Sciences and the Arts* (N.Y.: Harper & Row, 1962).

35. Scientists may not always be the best judges of instructional material in the sciences, states J. K. Brierly: ". . . the level of the texts seems to be pitched too high for the 15-year-old. It is a little surprising that the school teachers on the various committees let some of the texts through, but so often a schoolmaster is humbled into

silence by a scientist, intellectually quick on the draw, yet the schoolmaster's experience with boys and girls is the touchstone of the ideas being debated." See his article, "The Biological Sciences Curriculum Study Publications, *Science,* 143 (February 14, 1964), 668.

See Wallace R. Brode, "Approaching Ceilings in the Supply of Scientific Manpower," *Science,* 143 (January 24, 1964), 313, on the limited supply of possible scientists. This supply cannot be raised by relaxing college admissions standards. Hence, scientific education should stress quality of training rather than the encouragement of numbers.

36. R. R. Bolger, *The Classical Heritage and Its Beneficiaries* (Cambridge, Eng.: Cambridge University Press, 1954).

37. Peter F. Drucker, *Landmarks of Tomorrow* (N.Y.: Harper & Row, 1965).

CHAPTER 12.　**The Training of Teachers**

1. Albert Lynd, "Quackery in the Public Schools," *Atlantic,* March 1950, p. 33.

2. Francis Keppel, *Saturday Review,* June 17, 1961, p. 64.

3. Dean Joshua Fishman's description is from his *Training Programs in Project Beacon* (N.Y.: Ferkauf Graduate School of Education, Yeshiva University, 1963).

4. Sidney L. Pressey, Francis P. Robinson, and John E. Horrocks, *Psychology in Education* (N.Y.: Harper & Row, 1959). The same text says, p. 26: ". . . late-maturing boys appeared handicapped as regards relations with associates of their own and the other sex in the same age group, and on the whole were appraised less favorably by adults who knew them well. . . . In strange contrast, girls seemed to have an advantage by maturing late, and to be handicapped by maturing early—at least, in our culture. The girl who matures late does so at about the average age of the boys with whom she associates, and she tends to have the slim build they consider most attractive. But the early-maturing girl is first embarrassingly bigger and stronger than the boys of the same age, is embarrassingly early in development of heterosexual interest, and tends to become stocky and overly plump." Should not the teacher remember her own history here?

CHAPTER 13.　**The In-service Course—An Example**

1. For an extensive, though somewhat outdated, bibliography on reading, see Sidney L. Pressey, Francis P. Robinson, and

John E. Horrocks, "Psychology of a School Subject," in *Psychology in Education* (N.Y.: Harper & Row, 1959).

2. The professional barnacles that grow, multiply, and slow you down and what the professions try to do about barnacle-removal are discussed in an editorial, "Continuing Education," *Science*, 150 (November 12, 1965), 831, and responding letters, "Preventing Obsolescence," *Science*, 151 (January 7, 1966), 27. The older you get, the more you need to go back to the educational well for refreshment!

3. J. C. Catford, "The Teaching of English as a Foreign Language," in Randolph Quinn and A. H. Smith, eds., *The Teaching of English* (London: Secker and Warburg, 1959).

Charles E. Osgood, "On Understanding and Creating Sentences," *American Psychologist*, 18 (December 1963), 735.

4. H. J. Marrou, *History of Education in Antiquity* (N.Y.: Mentor, 1964).

5. "The complexity of the [reading] task was made evident to me . . . when I participated with friends in a Seder, the Jewish passover ceremony. The *Haggadah* was in Hebrew; others at the table could read it; I could not. They symbols all looked alike to me. In my attempt to follow, I was constantly losing the place, starting on the wrong page and on the wrong side of the page," says Anne McKillop, "Why Many Children and Youth Are Retarded in Reading," in M. Jerry Weiss, ed., *Reading in the Secondary Schools* (N.Y.: Odyssey Press, 1961).

But how did Dr. McKillop know that her hosts comprehended what they read? Many Jews can read Hebrew but do not understand a single syllable of what they read. Thus readers of Yiddish can read Hebrew and Aramaic (*Targum*) but do not need a knowledge of Hebrew to do so. Reading fluently need *not* involve comprehension.

6. For an explanation of the Hawthorn effect, see F. Roethlisberger and W. J. Dickson, *Management and the Worker* (Cambridge, Mass.: Harvard University Press, 1939).

CHAPTER 14.   The Pre-service Course

1. John Gardner, *Excellence: Can We Be Equal and Excellent Too?* (N.Y.: Harper & Row, 1961).

2. Hastings Rashdall, in Frederick M. Powicke and A. B. Emden, eds., *Universities of Europe in the Middle Ages*, 3 vols. (Oxford, Eng.: Oxford University Press, 1936).

3. William Foxwell Albright, *History, Archaeology, and Christian Humanism* (N.Y.: McGraw-Hill, 1964).

4. John Hope Franklin, *Reconstruction* (Chicago: University of Chicago Press, 1961); C. Vann Woodward, *The Strange Career of Jim Crow* (Oxford, Eng.: Oxford University Press, 1958).

5. For a discussion on cultural pluralism in the urban complex, see Lewis Mumford, *The City in History* (N.Y.: Harcourt, Brace & World, 1961).

6. The Secretary Wirtz quotation is from *The New York Times,* August 31, 1962.

7. Roscoe Griffin defines a "minority group" as a category of people aware of prejudices against them. As Griffin describes the influx of the white mountaineer into Cincinnati, the resemblance to the Negro influx into northern cities is close, even if not identical. The white mountaineer coming to the city is hampered by his own limitations, not by racial ones. See his "The Southern Mountaineer in Cincinnati," The Mayor's Friendly Relations Committee and the Social Service Association of Greater Cincinnati, March 1960.

Similarly, Negro segregation is not the same as segregation experienced by white immigrant groups like Italians or Poles: ". . . Negroes and immigrant groups have moved in opposite directions, i.e., declining segregation for immigrants and increasing segregation for Negroes. . . . Negro residential patterns are not to be viewed as simply being more highly segregated than immigrant residential patterns." Stanley Lieberson, *Ethnic Patterns in American Cities* (N.Y.: Free Press, 1963).

8. P. M. S. Blackett, quoted by John Hillaby, " 'Have Not' Lands Becoming Poorer," *The New York Times,* August 31, 1962, p. 4.

9. The teacher-diplomate/instructional engineer should do his interviewing after doing some reading in the following, for perspective:

(*a*) James Baldwin, *Notes of a Native Son* (Boston: Beacon Press, 1957).

(*b*) Stewart G. Cole and Mildred Wiese Cole, *Minorities and the American Promise* (N.Y.: Harper & Row, 1954).

(*c*) Everett C. Hughes, "Ethnic Relations in Industry and Society," in Sigmund Nosow and William H. Form, eds., *Man, Work and Society* (N.Y.: Basic Books, 1962).

10. Lawrence A. Cremin, *The Transformation of the School* (N.Y.: Vintage Books, 1964).

11. E. M. Forster, *Alexandria: A History and a Guide* (N.Y.: Doubleday, 1961), p .146.

How European universities have impeded science and technology is described in Alexander Robertus Todd's "Scientific Policy in Britain," *Science,* 149 (July 9, 1965), 156, with particular reference to the injurious effects of British educational tradition.

12. Hanns Sachs, *The Creative Unconscious* (Cambridge, Mass.: Sci-Art, 1951).

13. The quotation is from Robert Graves' Introduction to *Lucan's Pharsalia* (London: Penguin, 1957), p. 10.

14. The quotations are from A. N. Whitehead, *The Aims of Education* (N.Y.: Mentor, 1958), pp. 51, 64, 66, 95.

15. Norbert Wiener, *The Human Use of Human Beings* (N.Y.: Doubleday, 1954), p. 112.

16. James Baldwin, "Letter from a Region in My Mind," *The New Yorker*, November 17, 1962, p. 59.

17. The following, from varying tangents, concern the relationship of vocationalism and liberalism in education:

(*a*) *Phi Delta Kappan* for April, 1965, covers the new directions and redefinitions required for vocational and technical education in an automated America.

(*b*) From Robert Graves, *op. cit.*, p. 15: ". . . the Fathers of the Christian Church had experienced much of the same difficulty in consolidating their empire as had the Fathers of the Republican Senate. How were they to combat the clever arguments of the pagan sophists? Faith in timely intervention by the Holy Ghost was not reckoned enough; and Paul's tactical success when he caused a division between Sadducees and Pharisees in the Sanhedrin offered so hopeful a precedent that they allowed their deacons to study under professors of rhetoric. The Classical curriculum, with certain necessary changes, became the basis of clerkly education throughout Christendom— though Virgil and Cicero ousted Homer and Demosthenes—and Virgil was actually credited with divine inspiration."

(*c*) In discussing the limitations of vocational education and the need for re-vamping it, Edward T. Chase, in "Learning To Be Unemployable," *Harper's*, April 1963, p. 33, says: "This menacing situation is a direct consequence of the gross imbalance in our educational system. Its attention has been overwhelmingly concentrated on the 20 per cent of students who go through college. The vocational future of the other 80 per cent has been either ignored or sabotaged by an archaic system of job training. It is a system that produces unneeded farmers, cabinet-makers, and weavers, while the demand is rising for business-machine repairmen, chefs, auto mechanics, and electrical servicemen—to mention only a few of the skills in short supply."

18. The William H. Whyte, Jr., quotation is from *The Organization Man* (N.Y.: Doubleday, 1956), p. 20.

19. The Montaigne quotation is from his "Of Pedantry," in *Selected Essays* (N.Y.: Modern Library, 1949), p. 116.

20. Also see there "Of the Education of Boys," p. 142.

21. The Aldous Huxley quotation is from "The Oddest Science," *Collected Essays* (N.Y.: Bantam Books, 1960), p. 322.

Here also see Montaigne, *op. cit.*, "Of Custom, and That An Established Law Is Not Lightly To Be Changed," p. 99.

22. James B. Conant, *Slums and Suburbs* (N.Y.: New American Library, 1964). Also Booker T. Washington, *Up from Slavery* (N.Y.: Dell, n.d.).

23. Morris Kline, *Scientific American*, 206 (January 1962), 157. Wright W. Miller, *Russians Are People* (N.Y.: Dutton, 1961).

24. On the history of industrial training:

(*a*) See chiefly Singer, et al., *A History of Technology* (N.Y.: Oxford University Press, 1954), especially Vol. 3, chap 5, on tradesmen's tools. However, all four volumes have germane material, in addition to excellent bibliographies, like these recommendations: O. Davies, *Roman Mines in Europe* (Oxford, Eng.: Clarendon Press, 1935); and L. F. Salzman, *English Industries of the Middle Ages* (Oxford, Eng.: Clarendon Press, 1923).

(*b*) On the training of apprentices in Colonial America, see Esther Forbes, *Paul Revere and His Times*, and her novel on the same period, *Johnny Tremain* (Boston: Houghton Mifflin, 1942 and 1943).

25. For materials on school architecture:

(*a*) U.S. Department of Health, Education and Welfare, *School Sites: Selection, Development, and Utilization*, Special Publication 7 (Washington, D.C.: Government Printing Office, 1958).

(*b*) *Planning America's School Buildings* (Washington, D.C.: American Association of School Administrators, 1960).

(*c*) John H. Herrick, Ralph D. McLeary, Wilfred F. Clapp, and Walter F. Bogner, *From School Program to School Plant* (N.Y.: Holt, Rinehart & Winston, 1956).

26. Two of the references below are standard. The third is typical of left-of-center thinking. In order:

(*a*) Gunnar Myrdal, *An American Dilemma* (N.Y.: Harper & Row, 1962). A classic that caused a major social change in American life. It states the economic reasons for the loss of masculinity in Negro men.

(*b*) E. Franklin Frazier, *Black Bourgeoisie* (N.Y.: Free Press, 1965), angers many Negroes. The Negro man who has retained his masculinity by entering the middle class does not want to be the halfman that so many Negroes around him seem to be.

[Author editorializing on these two books: The masculine Negro must extend a sense of paternity to the father-deprived child and must be the first to exercise a feeling of extended family. Thereby he makes a major contribution to the masculinity of other Negro men.]

(c) Harold R. Isaacs, "Integration and the Negro Mood," *Commentary,* December 1962, p. 487, discusses Negro divisiveness and unity.

27. Jean Piaget, *Language and Thought of the Child* (Cleveland, O.: Meridian Books, 1955). Martin Deutsch, "Courage as a Concept in Social Psychology," *Journal of Social Psychology,* 55 (1961), 49–58. Harry F. and Margaret Kuenne Harlow, "Social Deprivation in Monkeys," *Scientific American,* 207 (November 1962), 137.

28. For a description of the Kefauver Committee work on the drug industry, see Richard Harris, *The Real Voice* (N.Y.: Macmillan, 1964).

29. Louis Rosenzweig, *Report to Task Force on Education,* The Mental Health Planning Committee of New York State, n.d.

30. For the underlying simplicity in nature and the related purposes in education, see Albert Szent-Györgi, "Teaching and Expanding Knowledge," *Science,* 146 (December 4, 1964), 1278.

31. Samuel Pinneau, "The Infantile Disorders of Hospitalism and Anaclitic Depression," *Psychological Bulletin,* 52 (September 1955), 429; René H. Spitz's reply, p. 453; Pinneau's reply, p 459. John Bowlby, *Child Care and the Growth of Love* (London: Penguin, n.d.). Anna Freud and Dorothy T. Burlingham, *Infants Without Families: The Case For and Against Residential Nurseries* (N.Y.: International Universities Press, 1962).

32. Eckhard H. Hess, "Imprinting in Birds," *Science,* 146 (November 27, 1964), 1128–39.

33. Otto Rank, *Trauma of Birth* (N.Y.: Basic Books, 1953); Sigmund Freud, *The Basic Writings of Sigmund Freud* (N.Y.: Modern Library, 1938).

34. Gardner Murphy, *Personality: A Biosocial Approach to Origins and Structure* (N.Y.: Harper & Row, 1947).

35. Karl Koffka, *Principles of Gestalt Psychology* (N.Y.: Harcourt, Brace & World, 1935).

36. Clark Hull, R. T. Ross, M. Hall, D. T. Perkins, and F. B. Fitch, *Mathematico-Deductive Theory of Rote Learning* (New Haven, Conn.: Yale University Press, 1940).

37. B. F. Skinner's rats and pigeons have outcomes in school and educational technology. Professor Skinner discusses these practical, day-by-day outcomes in "Why Teachers Fail," *Saturday Review,* October 16, 1965, p. 80.

38. The weak reed that psychology sometimes is gets a going over in the editorial, "Wonderful World of Psychology," *Advertising Age,* September 18, 1961.

Ray Jeffrey points out that cross-examination in court trials demonstrates the foolishness of psychologists in "The Psychologist as an Expert Witness on the Issue of Insanity," *American Psychologist,* 19 (November 1964), 838.

39. Charles Osgood, "On Understanding and Creating Sentences," *American Psychologist,* 18 (December 1963), 735.

40. Mark R. Rosenzweig, "Environmental Complexity, Social Change, and Behavior," *American Psychologist,* 21 (April 1966), 321.

41. Wolfgang Köhler, *The Mentality of Apes* (N.Y.: Harcourt, Brace, 1931). Robert L. Thorndike and Elizabeth Hagen, *Measurement and Evaluation in Psychology and Education* (N.Y.: Wiley, 1964).

42. Jurgen Ruesch and Gregory Bateson, *Communication: The Social Matrix of Psychiatry* (N.Y.: W. W. Norton, 1951).

43. Peter Suldfeld, Robert J. Grisson, and Jack Vernon, "The Effects of Sensory Deprivation and Social Isolation on the Performance of an Unstructured Task," *American Journal of Psychology,* 77 (March 1964), 111–15.

44. Robert J. Havighurst and Hilda Taba, *Adolescent Character and Personality* (N.Y.: Wiley, 1963).

45. Floyd H. Allport, "The J-Curve Hypothesis of Conforming Behavior," *Journal of Social Psychology,* V (1934), 141–83.

46. Nathaniel Weyl and Stefan Possony, *Geography of Intellect* (Chicago:Regnery, 1963); Henry Garrett, "The SPSSI and Racial Differences," *American Psychologist,* 17 (1962), 260–63.

CHAPTER 15. **The Administration of the Urban School**

1. H. A. Otto, "The School Administrator's Mental Health," *Mental Hygiene,* 45 (October 1961), 603–12.

2. If you want to climb to power without showing how hard the climb is, read Edward E. Jones, "Conformity as a Tactic of Ingratiation," *Science,* 149 (July 9, 1965), 144.

3. Lay determination of public school policies occurs only because educational procedures are indefinite and imbedded in private, armchair philosophy. Were they grounded in research, lay interference would disappear. Because the educational research that does exist is low-level and full of contradictory findings, any number, even if uninformed, can play in setting educational policy.

4. The administrator must defend his staff against extremists. Academic freedom is a major trust of the administrator, and this means freedom to teach and freedom to learn, says Frederic Heim-

berger in "The Grass Roots of Campus Freedom," *Saturday Review,* July 17, 1965, p. 60.

Administrators sometimes use the school's intercom system to eavesdrop on teachers. Robert F. Carbone comments on how this undercuts morale. The administrator with his ear to the ground, or the underground, via the two-way intercom, may always reply that he has a right to know what's going on; but the teacher will have a concomitant right to demand that the administrator participate in what's going on. If the administrator eavesdrops on a noisy class, let him leave his private office and help the teacher control the noisiness, not reprimand the teacher for loose management. If he eavesdrops on a parent-teacher dispute, let him substitute his active presence for his absent ear. The two-way intercom can also invade *his* privacy; and let teacher organizations not be indifferent to that side of the two-edged, two-way intercom. Any administrator who, on the basis of two-way intercom snooping, tells a teacher, "You're supposed to be able to handle that," should be told, "And you're supposed to be here with me if I can't, not sitting with your ear glued to the monitor." The intercom can also pry the administrator from his privileged sanctuary. See Robert F. Carbone, "Big Brother Is in the Office: Invasion of Privacy in the Schools," *Phi Delta Kappan,* 47 (September 1965), 34–37; and J. Lloyd Trump's rejoinder, "Somebody Better Be Watching—Here Is Who!" in the same issue.

5. A UNESCO study shows that the American school year of 180 days runs shorter than the 234 days annually in the Soviet Union, 233 days in West Germany, and 210 days in Japan. The American school day is also shorter. These statistics contribute significantly to Johnny's not learning to read as soon as Ivan does.

6. O. K. Moore's typewriter is described in Maya Pines, "How Three-year-olds Teach Themselves To Read—and Love It," *Harper's,* May 1963, p. 58.

7. On this touchy matter, see Barry Gottehrer and Claude Lewis, "Harlem Dread: Leaders' Flight, Growing Decay," *New York Herald-Tribune,* January 28, 1965, p. 1.

8. See "Mrs. Motley Seeks Plan for Harlem," *The New York Times,* September 7, 1965, p. 36.

9. For the Schinnerer and Crewsom reports, see *The New York Times,* November 8, 1962, pp. 1 and 44.

10. For an early article on college students as tutors in Negro Harlem, see *The New York Times,* November 23, 1962. Since that date, volunteer tutoring activities have expanded enormously on a planned basis.

CHAPTER 16.   **Adult Education, Automation, and Leisure**

1. For some aspects of automation:

(*a*) Luther H. Evans, *Automation and the Challenge to Education* (Washington, D.C.: National Education Association, 1962) compares Venezuela and Denmark. Denmark is devoid of natural resources but rich in education. Venezuela is rich in natural resources but devoid of education. Similarly, you can compare Switzerland and Mexico, Israel and Iraq—in all cases, education makes the difference.

(*b*) Geriatric living in Del Webb's "Sun City" for the retired is described in Calvin Trilling's "A Reporter At Large—Wake Up and Live," *The New Yorker,* April 4, 1964, p. 120, in a preview of the aged under automation.

(*c*) D. Dempsey, "Myth of the New Leisure Class," *The New York Times Magazine,* January 26, 1958. Written almost a decade ago, indicating how we mark time in this whole area.

(*d*) For background, Blake McKelvey, *The Urbanization of America, 1860–1915* (New Brunswick, N.J.: Rutgers University Press, 1962).

2. *Fortune* has been concerned with the New Leisure for almost a generation now, so maybe the New Leisure is no longer so new. Here are some examples from the last fifteen years: Dero Saunders and Sanford Parker wrote "Thirty Billion Dollars for Fun" in the June 1954 issue, p. 115; Charles Silberman's "Money Left Over for the Good Life" appeared in the November 1959 issue, p. 134; Gilbert Cross wrote "The Costly Crush to Get Outdoors" in the July 1962 issue, p. 157.

Elsewhere, P. F. Douglass edited the issue entitled "Recreation in the Age of Automation," *Annals of the American Academy of Political and Social Science,* 313 (September 1957). Also see Robert Bendiner's "Could You Stand a Four-day Week?" in *The Reporter,* August 8, 1957, p. 10; and Georges Friedman, "Leisure in an Automated World," *The Nation,* September 1, 1962, p. 89, and the reply to Friedman in *The Nation,* September 15, 1962, p. 120.

As to the effects of automation on education: "Nothing is more obsolete than the notion that education is something that takes place in a solid block of years between, roughly, ages 6 and 22. From now on, the individual is going to have to seek formal instruction at many points throughout his career. Under such a system, much of the present anxiety over young people who quit school prematurely will disappear. The anxiety stems from the fact that today leaving school signifies the end of education. Under the new system there will be no end to education." John W. Gardner, "Education as a Way of Life," *Science,* 148 (May 7, 1965), 759.

3. Numerous articles have appeared in *Printer's Ink* and *Advertising Age* on traffic clocking and test market research. See also George Katona, *The Mass Consumption Society* (N.Y.: McGraw-Hill, 1964).

4. The President's Commission on Higher Education, *Higher Education for American Democracy* (N.Y.: Harper & Row, 1948), pp. 39–41.

5. The University of the State of New York, *The Regents Statewide Plan for the Expansion and Development of Higher Education* (Albany: State Education Department, 1965), p. 12.

CHAPTER **17.** **Toward Educare—Total Education for Urban Minorities**

1. A. H. Raskin, "The Obsolescent Unions," *Commentary,* July 1963, p. 18.

2. James Agee and Walker Evans, *Let Us Now Praise Famous Men* (Boston: Houghton Mifflin, 1960).

Bibliography

CHAPTER 1. Urban Education and Rural Reclamation

Abrams, Charles, *The City Is The Frontier*, New York: Harper and Row, 1965.

Barzini, Luigi, *The Italians*, New York: Bantam, 1965.

Caudill, Harry M., *Night Comes to the Cumberlands*, Boston: Little, Brown, 1963.

Duhl, Leonard J., ed., *The Urban Condition*, New York: Basic Books, 1963.

Engle, Richard E., Jr., *The Challenge of Diversity*, New York: Harper and Row, 1964.

Higbee, Edward, *Farms and Farmers in an Urban Age*, New York: Twentieth Century Fund, 1963.

Justman, Joseph, *The Italian People and Their Schools*, International Education Monographs, No. 1, Tiffin, Ohio: Kappa Delta Pi, 1958.

Laurenti, Luigi, *Property Values and Race*, Berkeley: University of California Press, 1960.

Levine, Irving R., *Main Street, Italy*, New York: Doubleday, 1963.

McKelvey, Blake, *The Urbanization of America, 1860–1915*, New Brunswick, N.J.: Rutgers University Press, 1962.

Miller, Wright W., *Russians Are People*, New York: Dutton, 1961.

Mumford, Lewis, *The City in History*, New York: Harcourt, Brace and World, 1961.

Schultz, Theodore W., *Transforming Traditional Agriculture*, New Haven, Conn.: Yale University Press, 1964.

Shannon, William Vincent, *The American Irish*, New York: Macmillan, 1963.

Wilkinson, Rupert, *Gentlemanly Power: British Leadership and the Public School Tradition*, London: Oxford University Press, 1964.

CHAPTER 2. **Family Structure and Education**

Bloom, Benjamin, Allison Davis, and Robert Hess, *Compensatory Education for Cultural Deprivation*, New York: Holt, Rinehart and Winston, 1965.

Clark, Kenneth B., *Dark Ghetto*, New York: Harper and Row, 1965.

Ellison, Ralph, *Invisible Man*, New York: Random House, 1952.

Franklin, John Hope, *Reconstruction*, Chicago: University of Chicago Press, 1961.

Frazier, E. Franklin, *Black Bourgeoisie*, New York: Collier Books, 1962.

Glazer, Nathan, and Daniel Patrick Moynihan, *Beyond the Melting Pot*, Cambridge, Mass.: M.I.T. Press and Harvard University Press, 1963.

Havighurst, R. J., and Hilda Taba, *Adolescent Character and Development*, New York: Wiley, 1949.

Schreiber, Daniel, Bernard A. Kaplan, and Robert D. Strom, *Dropout Studies: Design and Conduct*, Washington, D.C.: National Education Association, 1963.

Stampp, Kenneth M., *The Era of Reconstruction, 1863–1877*, New York: Knopf, 1965.

Stern, Philip M., *The Great Treasury Raid*, New York: Random House, 1964.

Thompson, E. P., *The Making of the English Working Class*, New York: Pantheon, 1964.

Thrasher, Frederic, *Gang: A Study of 1,313 Gangs in Chicago*, Chicago: University of Chicago Press, 1963.

Vann Woodward, C., *The Strange Career of Jim Crow*, Oxford, England: Oxford University Press, 1958.

Whyte, William F., *Street-Corner Society*, Chicago: University of Chicago Press, 1955.

United States Department of Labor, Bureau of Labor Statistics, *The Negro Family—The Case for National Action*, Washington, D.C.: Government Printing Office, 1965.

CHAPTER 3. **Stupidity and Ignorance**

Bestor, Arthur, *The Restoration of Learning*, New York: Knopf, 1955.

Cronbach, Lee J., *Educational Psychology*, New York: Harcourt, Brace and World, 1963.

Eiduson, Samuel, Edward Geller, Arthur Yurwiler, and Bernice T. Eiduson, *Biochemistry and Behavior,* Princeton, N.J.: Van Nostrand, 1964.

Garn, Stanley M., *Human Races,* Springfield, Ill.: Thomas, 1965.

Getzels, Jacob W., and Philip W. Jackson, *Creativity and Intelligence,* New York: Wiley, 1962.

Greenway, John, *The Inevitable Americans,* New York: Knopf, 1964.

Gross, Martin, *The Brain Watchers,* New York: Random House, 1962, and Signet, 1963.

Hoffman, Banesh, *The Tyranny of Testing,* New York: Collier Books, 1962.

Holt, John, *How Children Fail,* New York: Pitman, 1964.

Riessman, Frank, *The Culturally Deprived Child,* New York: Harper and Row, 1962.

Ruesch, Jurgen, and Gregory Bateson, *Communication: The Social Matrix of Psychiatry,* New York: W. W. Norton, 1951.

Sarason, Seymour B., Kenneth S. Davidson, Frederick K. Lighthall, Richard R. Waite, and Britton K. Ruebush, *Anxiety in Elementary School Children,* New York: Wiley, 1960.

Weyl, N., and S. Possony, *The Geography of Intellect,* Chicago: Regnery, 1963.

CHAPTER 4. Militancy and Intelligence

Ardley, Robert, *The Territorial Imperative,* New York: Atheneum, 1966.

Carthy, J. D., and F. J. Ebling, eds., *The Natural History of Aggression,* New York: Academic Press, 1964.

Dimont, Max I., *Jews, God and History,* New York: Simon and Schuster, 1962.

Draper, Theodore, *The Roots of American Communism,* New York: Viking, 1963.

Feuer, Lewis, *The Scientific Intellectual: The Psychological and Sociological Origins of Modern Science,* New York: Basic Books, 1963.

Lipset, Seymour Martin, and Sheldon S. Walin, *The Berkeley Student Revolt,* Garden City, N.Y.: Doubleday, 1965.

Lorenz, Konrad, *On Aggression,* New York: Harcourt, Brace and World, 1966.

Miller, Michael V., and Susan Gilmore, eds., *Revolution at Berkeley,* New York: Dell, 1965.

Osofsky, Gilbert, *Harlem: The Making of a Ghetto,* New York: Harper and Row, 1964.

Pettigrew, Thomas F., *A Profile of the Negro American,* Princeton, N.J.: Van Nostrand, 1964.

Sellin, Thorsten, and Marvin E. Wolfgang, *The Measurement of Delinquency,* New York: Wiley, 1964.

Weaver, Robert C., *The Urban Complex,* New York: Doubleday Anchor 1964.

CHAPTER 5. The Teacher

Bettelheim, Bruno, *Love Is Not Enough*, New York: Free Press, 1950.

Butts, R. Freeman, *American Education in International Development*, New York: Harper and Row, 1963.

Crow, Lester D., Walter I. Murray, and Hugh H. Smyth, *Educating the Culturally Disadvantaged Child*, New York: David McKay, 1966.

Highet, Gilbert, *The Art of Teaching*, New York: Knopf, 1950.

Kerr, Clark, *The Uses of the University*, Cambridge, Mass.: Harvard University Press, 1963.

Koerner, James D., "How Not To Teach Teachers," *Atlantic*, February 1963.

Le Sure, James S., *Guide to Pedaguese—A Handbook for Puzzled Parents*, New York: Harper and Row, 1965.

Lieberman, Myron, *The Future of Public Education*, Chicago: University of Chicago Press, 1960.

National Commission on Teacher Education and Professional Standards, *The Education of Teachers: New Perspectives*, Washington, D.C.: National Educational Association, 1958.

Passow, A. Harry, ed., *Education in Depressed Areas*, New York: Teachers College Press, 1963.

Rickover, H. G., *American Education: A National Failure*, New York: Dutton, 1963.

Strom, Robert D., *Teaching in the Slum School*, Columbus, O.: Charles E. Merrill, 1965.

CHAPTER 6. The Curriculum

Ashton-Warner, Sylvia, *Teacher*, New York: Simon and Schuster, 1963.

Ausubel, David P., *Maori Youth*, Wellington, New Zealand: Price Milburn, 1961.

Barzun, Jacques, *Science: The Glorious Entertainment*, New York: Harper and Row, 1964.

Blantock, G. H., *Education in an Industrial Society*, London: Faber and Faber, 1963.

Chandler, B. J., Lindley J. Stiles, and John I. Kutsuse, *Education in Urban Society*, New York: Dodd, Mead, 1962.

Huizinga, Johan, *Homo Ludens*, Boston: Beacon, 1955.

Klein, Melanie, *Contributions to Psychoanalysis*, London: Hogarth Press, 1948, and New York: McGraw-Hill, 1964.

Lindner, Robert, *The Fifty-minute Hour*, New York: Holt, Rinehart and Winston, 1955.

McLuhan, Marshall, *Understanding Media*, New York: McGraw-Hill, 1964.
Walker, Charles R., *Modern Technology and Civilization*, New York: McGraw-Hill, 1962.

CHAPTER 7. The Bureaucracies in Urban Education

Blum, Robert, ed., *Cultural Affairs and Modern Relations*, Englewood Cliffs, N.J., Prentice-Hall, 1963.
Diamond, Edwin, *The Rise and Fall of the Space Age*, New York: Doubleday, 1964.
Harris, Richard, *The Real Voice*, New York: Macmillan, 1964.
Hentoff, Nat, *The New Equality*, New York: Viking, 1964.
Jacobs, Jane, *The Death and Life of Great American Cities*, New York: Random House, 1961.
Riesman, David, *Constraint and Variety in American Education*, Garden City, N.Y.: Doubleday, 1958.
Salisbury, Harrison, *The Shook-up Generation*, New York: Harper and Row, 1958.
Trace, Arthur S., Jr., *Reading Without Dick and Jane*, Chicago: Regnery, 1965.
Weaver, Robert C., *Dilemmas of Urban America*, Cambridge, Mass.: Harvard University Press, 1965.

CHAPTER 8. The Budget and the Program

Bowles, Frank, *Access to Higher Education*, Paris: UNESCO and New York: Columbia University Press, 1964.
Clark, Harold F., and Harold S. Sloan, *Classrooms in the Military*, New York: Teachers College, Columbia University, 1964.
Foster, George M., *Traditional Cultures and the Impact of Technological Change*, New York: Harper and Row, 1962.
Harbison, Frederick, and Charles A. Myers, *Education, Manpower, and Economic Growth: Strategies of Human Resource Development*, New York: McGraw-Hill, 1964.
Lasky, Melvin J., *Africa for Beginners: A Traveller's Notebook*, New York: Lippincott, 1964.
Machlup, Fritz, *The Production and Distribution of Knowledge in the United States*, Princeton, N.J.: Princeton University Press, 1962.
Millis, Walter, *Arms and Men*, New York: Mentor, 1956.
Moussa, Pierre, *The Underdeveloped Nations*, Boston: Beacon Press, 1962.
Orlans, Harold, *The Effects of Federal Programs on Higher Education*, Washington, D.C.: Brookings Institution, 1962.
Vaizey, John, *The Economics of Education*, New York: Free Press, 1962.

CHAPTER 9.   Educational Extenders, Fore and Aft

Proceedings of the Fourth Annual Invitational Conference on Urban Education, *Environmental Deprivation and Enrichment,* New York: Ferkauf Graduate School of Education, Yeshiva University, 1965.

Spiro, Melvin, *Children of the Kibbutz,* New York: Schocken, 1965.

Stapp, William B., *Integrating Outdoor and Conservation Education into the Curriculum,* Minneapolis: Burgess Publishing Company, 1965.

CHAPTER 10.   Money Incentives for the Learner

Glueck, Sheldon, and Eleanor Glueck, *Family Environment and Delinquency,* Boston: Houghton-Mifflin, n.d.

Harrington, Michael, *The Accidental Century,* New York: Macmillan, 1965.

McGehee, William, and P. W. Thayer, *Training in Business and Industry,* New York: Wiley, 1961.

Skinner, B. F., and C. B. Ferster, *Schedules of Reinforcement,* New York: Appleton-Century-Crofts, 1957.

Wellens, John, *The Training Revolution,* London: Evans, 1963.

CHAPTER 11.   Curricular Psychology

Beberman, Max, *The Emerging Program of Secondary School Mathematics,* Cambridge, Mass.: Harvard University Press, 1958.

Bolger, R. R., *The Classical Heritage and Its Beneficiaries,* Cambridge, Eng.: Cambridge University Press, 1954.

Brooks, Nelson, *Language and Language Learning,* New York: Harcourt, Brace and World, 1960.

Cambridge Conference on School Mathematics, *Goals for School Mathematics,* Boston: Houghton Mifflin, 1963.

Chomsky, Noam, *Aspects of the Theory of Syntax,* Cambridge, Mass.: M.I.T. Press, 1965.

Church, Joseph, *Language and the Discovery of Reality,* New York: Random House, 1961.

Dienes, Z. P., *An Experimental Study of Mathematics Learning,* New York: Humanities, 1962.

Panel on Educational Research and Development, *Innovation and Experiment in Education,* Washington, D.C.: Government Printing Office, n.d.

Project on the Educational Implications of Automation, *Automation and the Challenge to Education,* Washington, D.C.: National Education Association, 1962.

Scherer, George B., and Michael Wertheimer, *A Psycholinguistic Experiment in Foreign Language Teaching,* New York: McGraw-Hill, 1964.

Simon, B., and J. Simon, eds., *Educational Psychology in the USSR*, London: Routledge and Kegan Paul, 1963.

CHAPTER 12. The Training of Teachers

Fishman, Joshua, *Training Programs in Project Beacon*, New York: Ferkauf Graduate School of Education, Yeshiva University, 1963.
Pressey, Sidney L., Francis P. Robinson, and John E. Horrocks, *Psychology in Education*, New York: Harper and Row, 1959.

CHAPTER 13. The In-service Course—An Example

Henry, Nelson B., ed., *Development In and Through Reading: The Sixtieth Yearbook of the National Society for the Study of Education*, Chicago: University of Chicago Press, 1961.
Marrou, H. J., *History of Education in Antiquity*, New York: Mentor, 1964.
Quinn, Randolph, and A. H. Smith, eds., *The Teaching of English*, London: Secker and Warburg, 1959.
Weiss, M. Jerry, ed., *Reading in the Secondary Schools*, New York: Odyssey Press, 1961.

CHAPTER 14. The Pre-service Course—Two Examples

Bowlby, John, *Child Care and the Growth of Love*, London: Penguin, n.d.
Conant, James B., *Slums and Suburbs*, New York: New American Library, 1964.
Cremin, Lawrence A., *The Transformation of the School*, New York: Vintage Books, 1964.
Freud, Anna, and Dorothy T. Burlingham, *Infants Without Families: The Case For and Against Residential Nurseries*, New York: International Universities Press, 1962.
Freud, Sigmund, *The Basic Writings of Sigmund Freud*, New York: Modern Library, 1938.
Gardner, John, *Excellence: Can We Be Equal and Excellent Too?* New York: Harper and Row, 1961.
Hashens, Charles Homer, *The Rise of Universities*, Ithaca, N.Y.: Cornell University Press, 1965.
Nosow, Sigmund, and William H. Form, eds., *Man, Work and Society*, New York: Basic Books, 1962.
Piaget, Jean, *Language and Thought of the Child*, Cleveland, O.: Meridian Books, 1955.
Rank, Otto, *Trauma of Birth*, New York: Basic Books, 1953.
Singer, Charles, E. J. Holmyard, and A. R. Hall, *A History of Technology*, New York: Oxford University Press, 1954.

Stevenson, Harold W., ed., *Child Psychology: The Sixty-Second Yearbook of the National Society for the Study of Education,* Chicago: University of Chicago Press, 1963.

Thorndike, Robert L., and Elizabeth Hagen, *Measurement and Evaluation in Psychology and Education,* New York: Wiley, 1964.

Whitehead, A. H., *The Aims of Education,* New York: Mentor, 1958.

Wiener, Norbert, *The Human Use of Human Beings,* New York: Doubleday, 1954.

CHAPTER **15.** **The Administration of the Urban School**

Drucker, Peter F., *The Practice of Management,* New York: Harper and Row, 1954.

Grimshaw, Austin, and John W. Hennessy, Jr., *Organizational Behavior,* New York: McGraw-Hill, 1960.

Lewis, L. J., and A. J. Loveridge, *The Management of Education,* New York: Frederick A. Praeger, 1965.

Smith, George Albert, Jr., and C. Roland Christensen, *Policy Formulation and Administration,* Homewood, Ill.: Richard D. Irwin, 1959.

CHAPTER **16.** **Adult Education, Automation, and Leisure**

Clarke, John Henrik, ed., *Harlem: A Community in Transition,* New York: The Citadel Press, 1964.

Evans, Luther H., *Automation and the Challenge to Education,* Washington, D.C.: National Education Association, 1962.

Mangum, Garth L., *The Manpower Revolution: Its Policy Consequences,* Garden City, N.Y.: Doubleday, 1965.

CHAPTER **17.** **Toward Educare—Total Education for Urban Minorities**

Adams, Velma, *The Peace Corps in Action,* Chicago: Follett, 1960.

Agee, James, and Walker Evans, *Let Us Now Praise Famous Men,* Boston: Houghton Mifflin, 1960.

Clark, Burton R., *Educating the Expert Society,* San Francisco: Chandler, 1962.

Gottmann, Jean, *Megalopolis,* New York: The Twentieth Century Fund, 1961.

Harbison, Frederick, and Charles A. Myers, *Manpower and Education,* New York: McGraw-Hill, 1965.

Kimball, Solon T., and James E. McClellan, *Education and the New America,* New York: Random House, 1962.

Lynn, Kenneth S., and the editors of *Daedalus,* eds., *The Professions in America,* Boston: Houghton Mifflin, 1965.

Shriver, Sargent, *Point of the Laws,* New York: Harper and Row, 1964.

Index